B
Leahy
    Twombly, Wells
    Shake Down the Thunder!

Center Frank Leahy, of the 1928 Notre Dame team at practice. (*Notre Dame photos*)

Coach Leahy and Captain Ernie
Schowtzer of the Boston College
team talking things over at opening sessions of the final practice
before the 1939 season. (*Wide
World Photo*)

First year as Notre Dame Head
Coach. (*Notre Dame photo*)

Head Coach and Athletic Director Frank Leahy posing for movie reels at the opening of practice March 12, 1941. (*Notre Dame photo*)

The Coach at the blackboard, 1941. (*Notre Dame photo*)

Leahy's coaching debut at South Bend on September 29, 1941. Halfback Jack Warner gets a chewing out (top) while Quarterback William Early (No. 1) is admonished as he is sent into the game. (bottom) *(Wide World Photos)*

The Coach at war. (*Notre Dame photo*)

(*Notre Dame photo*)

Edward (Moose) Krause and Coach Leahy. (*Notre Dame photos*)

Coach Leahy and some of the 81 football players who reported for practice on August 26, 1946. (*Wide World Photos*)

Their prayers answered, this is the scene in front of the Notre Dame bench on December 4, 1948 as Guard Steve Oracko booted the extra point in the closing seconds of the game that gave the Irish a 14-14 tie with Southern California before 100,571 fans in Los Angeles. Coach Leahy is kneeling at left. (*Wide World Photo*)

The Coach sprinting from mass at Sacred Heart Church on game day.
(*Notre Dame photo*)

(Leahy family photo, Wally Kunkle photographer)

(Leahy family photo, Ted Lau photographer)

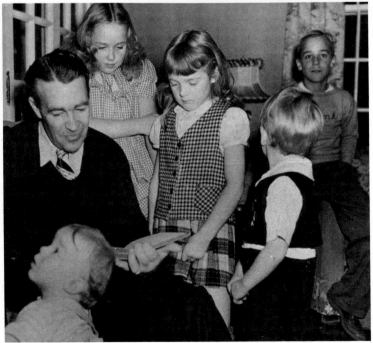

With Floss and the kids. (*Leahy family photo; Notre Dame photo*)

(Notre Dame photo)

At the end of an undefeated season, December 5, 1953, the Coach is carried by Tackle Frank Varrichione, 60; Johnny Lattner, 14; Art Hunter, 80; Guard Jack Lee, 65; and Captain Don Penza, 83. They had just defeated Southern Methodist 40-14. (*Wide World photo*)

The Crusader (*Leahy family photos, Bob Sands photographer*)
(*Notre Dame photo*)

The Crusader (*Leahy family photos, Bob Sands photographer*) (*Notre Dame photo*)

Shake Down
the Thunder!

Shake Down the Thunder!

The Official Biography of Notre Dame's
Frank Leahy

B
LEAHY
HQ

by
Wells Twombly

Chilton Book Company   Radnor, Pennsylvania

Copyright © 1974 by Wells Twombly
First Edition   *All Rights Reserved*

Published in Radnor, Pa., by Chilton Book Company
and simultaneously in Ontario, Canada,
by Thomas Nelson & Sons, Ltd.

Designed by Cypher Associates, Inc.
Manufactured in the United States of America

Library of Congress Cataloging in Publication Data

Twombly, Wells.
  Shake down the thunder!

  1. Leahy, Frank William, 1908-1973. 2. Football.
3. Football coaching. 4. Notre Dame, Ind. University
—Football. I. Title.
GV939.L35T92   796.33'2'0924 [B]   74-17348
ISBN 0-8019-5943-8

Second Printing, January 1975

Dedicated to the memory of Frank Leahy,

*Who genuinely believed in all the
old frontier verities, now dying.*

*Who chased the American Dream with
a single-minded passion.*

*Who may have been America's last
knight-errant.*

1908–1973

FOREWORD

By Billy Sullivan
Former President, The New England Patriots

The sign on the wall at the Naval Academy during World War II read: "The difficult we do immediately, the impossible just takes a little longer."

It seems to me this description fits the task the author of this book, Wells Twombly, must have had in chronicling the life of a truly extraordinary man, Francis William Leahy. Consider the difficulty of capturing the complexities of this man. Here was a person whose life had so many ups and downs, so many triumphs and so many defeats, so many moments of glory and so many periods of depression and despair. It must have been nearly impossible to sort out all the things that happened to the man, who for more than three decades, was referred to in our household as, simply, The Coach.

It was never necessary to identify which coach we were talking about. There was only one Coach, and you spelled it with a capital letter. No other man in his profession could compete with him in any way. Even with his players there was nobody else who deserved the title more than he did. He was The Coach—The Master Coach.

Conjuring up his image in my mind brings back a surge of memories. There were many sad moments in his life, ones that still bring tears to my eyes even a year after his death. Therefore, I try to think only of the happy moments, the incidents of high humor and peaks of glory. It is better that way, I think.

I remember so well the headline in the *Boston American* when The Coach left Fordham to begin his incredible success story at Boston College. The words screamed forth on the full back page of its tabloid format: "UNKNOWN LEAHY SIGNED BY BOSTON COLLEGE."

When I met him, he looked at me and said, "Aaaah, how do you do? I am Unknown Leahy." It was typical of his wit, a quality about him that was generally overlooked by writers who later insisted that he was dour and distant. He was neither of those things.

I remember, too, the frustration of the Boston College alumni who were seeking a better known coach. That disappointment vanished when he stood up at the varsity club dinner and in his penetrating, analytical, forceful tone suggested that he had not come to Boston College to "lose football games." It was a benign fate that permitted me to be with him as his secretary at BC's Sugar Bowl triumph over Tennessee and during many of his successes at Notre Dame. I can see once again the endless stream of victories, all-American players and Heisman Trophy winners.

From a personal standpoint, I am most aware of Frank Leahy's loyalty to a friend. He never forgot someone who stood at his side. It was 1959 and the American Football League had just been formed. It had granted seven franchises and the expansion committee consisted of Frank, then general manager of the Los Angeles Chargers; the late Harry Wismer of the New York Titans; and Lamar Hunt of the Dallas Texans. They were given the authority to select an eighth city to round out the league.

I knew Wismer well because he did the broadcasts of Notre Dame games when I was there working with Frank. But Lamar Hunt didn't know me whatsoever. Many cities were considered. There was sentiment for locating in San Francisco, Oakland or Philadelphia. At the last moment I got on the telephone and told The Coach that I not only wanted a franchise for Boston, I had a group put together that had enough money to make the project a success. There was one major objection to us—we had no place to play. I was quite worried about the situation. I should have known The Coach better than that.

I learned later that, out of sheer loyalty to me, he contacted each of the club presidents and persuaded them that Boston should have a team even though there was no place to play and even though the Boston Redskins, Boston Bulldogs and Boston Yanks had all failed in less than two decades. Frank Leahy was a most persuasive man. There were some owners who still wanted the Patriots shifted to another city right up until the moment we played our first game. But The Coach held firm.

Years later, when the Patriots were seeking a coach and general manager, Leahy volunteered to serve as an advisor. It was he who called from M.D. Anderson Hospital in Houston and convinced his friend Chuck Fairbanks to leave Oklahoma and join the professional league. His recommendation to us was as strong as any that he could have given. He meant it in all modesty.

"William," he said to me, "this Fairbanks is the same sort of coach I was when I was younger. I think he will do splendidly for you."

He always swore that when we finally opened our new stadium in Foxboro he would be present to watch a game. I shall never forget his courage. He weighed about 144 pounds and was doing something that he never would have done when he was in his prime. He was accepting the arms of people who wanted to help him up the steps. He had been in Chicago getting his every-eighth day blood transfusion when he called me.

"William," he said, "I suppose your stadium is all sold out for the game against Miami on Sunday and I really hate to ask this, but could you squeeze in just one more—a thin, sick, old football coach?"

"If his name is Francis William Leahy," I replied, "you can sure bet on it."

He stayed at our house for four days and even insisted on speaking before the Patriots' Veterans Club, because, he said, he wanted to pay for his ticket. He lunched with old Boston College players. His spirit was magnificent. On the morning of the game, he was excited as he had been during the days when he was head coach at Boston College and then at Notre Dame. You would have thought he was going to lead the Patriots out onto the field himself.

"Take it easy, now, Frank," I cautioned.

"I am, William," he said. "I am. Nothing makes me feel better than a football game."

Sickness never slowed him. To some extent, I think it rather irritated him. Certainly, it never stopped him. When my father died, The Coach, who had great difficulty walking, got on an airplane in Portland, Oregon, and flew all the way to Boston. It was an all night flight and he was in terrific pain. Still, he was amazed that people thought it unusual for doing what, to him, came very naturally.

Frank Leahy was the most incredible man I ever met. He added dignity and a new dimension to the expression, "Fighting Irishman." He had his faults. I make no attempt to portray him as a saint, faultless in every way. He was not. He was quite human. But he did practice what he preached, unlike so many coaches who only mouth the words. When the going got tough, Frank Leahy was tough enough to get going.

Of the many articles written about The Coach over the years, none has ever touched me deeper than the column written by the author of this book in *The San Francisco Examiner* on the death of my great friend. Wells Twombly was there and he portrayed the final hours of Frank Leahy in a dramatic manner seldom matched in American journalism. Of all the writers with whom The Coach was friendly for close to four decades, it is fascinating to me that when his life's blood was ebbing, the only person who was visiting him at his home would have been Wells Twombly and the only person, other than his family, who was present when death came was this same gifted writer.

It is not necessarily a cliche to say that that was the way Frank Leahy would have wanted it. It is with the understanding of the Leahy family, who have seen writers come and go, that this book is dedicated to perpetuating the legend that was Frank Leahy. It is comforting to me, personally, that it should be written by an author who has the complete blessings of all the members of a truly remarkable family.

For my part, as one who personally received more favors from The Coach than any individual in America, as one who collaborated with him in King Features columns and in radio and television productions, I share the feeling that those who want to savor the ingredients which made Frank a living legend can find no better source in which to accomplish that objective than in the pages of this book.

Francis William Leahy was the greatest man I ever knew. His story should not be permitted to die.

PROLOGUE

A GREAT AMERICAN FOLK HERO IS DYING!

One evening while I was in prison, I had this awful dream. I could see the headline on a printed page. It said: "A Great American Folk Hero Is Dying!" I knew that it referred to my father. That's what he was, you know, a great American folk hero. He belonged to the frontier, in a way. He was from an age of heroes. Maybe he was the last of the great ones. He never lost his love for the moralistic America he knew when he was growing up.

—Jerry Leahy, on the morning when his father died in a Portland, Oregon, hospital.

Some men die easily, with little grace. Others die tragically and far too soon for the good of humanity. Once there was a man who acted as if he would never die. He wanted to live because he actually believed there was such a thing as The Great American Dream. Certainly, he pursued it as furiously as any man ever has.

Even when it must have become quite obvious that it was mere fantasy, a fulfillable ideal made up by hordes of immigrants anxious to believe that tyranny would not follow them across an ocean, he refused to surrender. He believed it all the more, as surely as Don Quixote believed in his tattered visions of a nonexistent chivalry. He died, firm in the knowledge that if he could last one more week, one more day, one more hour—good God!—even one more minute, he could bring it to fruition.

The man was Frank Leahy, one of the two greatest football coaches who ever lived. The other was Knute Rockne. Both of them worked for the University of Notre Dame, which must be one of the most fortunate schools planted on the North American continent. To have one and then the other is to exist in an amazing state of grace. Both were Camelot-builders. Both were men of character.

Like Rockne, whose unmerciful twisting of the rules would have made him a modern scandal, Leahy was hardly free from sin. He was largely unloved by other coaches for his aloofness during the years of his great glory. But his friends insisted it was merely a matter of jealousy because he produced four national champions, six unbeaten teams and a streak of victories that lasted through 39 games. His overwhelming dedication touched on fanaticism at times, ruining his health and causing the president of Notre Dame to ponder the question of whether or not too much success wasn't damaging to the school. And there is strong evidence that he was forced to resign.

There were frequent personal problems. His wife, despondent over his frequent absences, fought an 18 year battle with alcohol. And one son, Jerry, spent one year, of a six year sentence for smuggling hashish, in McNeil's Island prison. His business deals were often disastrous, mostly because he thoroughly believed that businessmen were actually guided by sportsmanlike instincts.

"My father could not bring himself to believe that an American businessman was any different than a football coach, which is why he was hoodwinked so often," said Frank Leahy, Jr. "Coaches were forever pulling cute little tricks on each other. Dad was considered some kind of moral leper because of the incident in 1953 when Frank Varrichione faked a faint that stopped the clock against Iowa. Years later, Dad learned that Iowa also had a designated fainter. That's about as dirty as he felt business ever got. He was wrong."

In his prime as a coach, Frank Leahy was a proud man, erect, stern, righteous, shrewd, resourceful, tough, tremendously successful. In his final years, his body literally betraying its owner, he became a moral crusader, wobbling to podium after podium to caution America about the decay he thought he saw. His speeches were filled with Babbitt-esque sophistries, warning about the dangers to God, motherhood, home and the chamber of commerce. Frank Leahy was no intellectual. There were only five books in his possession the day he died. Rather, he spoke from the honesty of his own emotions and his intrinsic sense of nobility.

Thus, this is not so much a description of the glory of his times, although they are present; rather, it is the story of how he struggled not to die until his mission was complete, a knight-errant in the truest sense.

—Wells Twombly,
Burlingame, California

ACKNOWLEDGMENTS

Special thanks for candor and cooperation go to the following members of the Leahy family: Floss, Frank, Jr., Gene, Tom, Jack, Anne, Jerry, Sue (Moustakas), Flossie (Harter), Jim, Fred, Mary and Chris. Also to Roger O. Valdiserri and Robert P. Best, the current publicity men at Notre Dame and Charlie Callahan, who used to be. To Billy Sullivan, president of the New England Patriots. To Moose Krause, athletic director at Notre Dame. To Dave Condon of *The Chicago Tribune* and to Joe Doyle of the *South Bend Tribune*. To Bill Conlin of *The Sacramento Union* and to D. C. (Chet) Grant, director of the Sports and Games Collection at the Notre Dame Library. To Bob McBride and Joe McArdle. To Rev. Frank Cavanaugh and Dr. Walter J. Lamertz. To Patrick L. O'Malley of Canteen Corp. and to Diane Tidwell, who was Frank Leahy's secretary with the organization for the last five years of his life. And to Mrs. Peggy Zera Twombly, staff Director for Research and Development of Scorpio Publications, who takes good notes and asks even better questions. And to Miguel de Cervantes, wherever he is.

A partial reference list: *The Glory of Notre Dame*, edited by Fred Katz; *A Treasury of Notre Dame Stories*, edited by Gene Shoor; *The Vince Lombardi Story*, by Dave Klein; *Bypaths of Glory* and *Great College Football Coaches of the Twenties and Thirties*, both by Tim Cohane; *Frank Leahy and The Fighting Irish*, by Arch Ward; *Notre Dame Football and The T-Formation*, by Frank Leahy; *Notre Dame—From Rockne to Parseghian* and *Dementia Pigskin* and *The Notre Dame Story*, all by Francis Wallace; and *The Coaches* by Bill Libby.

—Wells Twombly

CONTENTS

PART ONE
THE QUEST

EPISODE 1

SAN FRANCISCO

The taxi rolled cautiously through the rain glazed streets, skillfully avoiding the office secretaries from San Francisco's financial district who seemed to be blooming everywhere like wildflowers in a darkened field. The driver, no rookie, kept squinting at the address one of the passengers had handed him. He seemed vaguely apprehensive, repeatedly asking his customers if this was the place where they actually wanted to go. It was not located in a district frequented by tourists from less happier lands. Finally, he surrendered and lurched into a tedious discussion of northern California weather habits. He seemed delighted when the man in the rear of the taxi actually seemed to be enjoying it.

Eventually the gray tones of banks and insurance buildings faded into the mists. Now the taxi splashed past the ersatz pagodas and plastic dragons of Grant Ave. and turned into a long, narrow alley, just missing an old Oriental gentleman who had stepped out from behind a pile of wooden packing crates on the corner. Now the taxi came to a halt in front of a battered brick building that might have once housed a Chinese grocery store. It was the sort of place that Occidentals fantasize about when they hear stories about the sinister side of the city's sprawling Chinatown.

Struggling not to let either his pain or his striking physical decomposition show, Frank Leahy pushed open the door, dug his fingernails into the small rain gutter on the roof of the car and clawed himself into an upright position. Tottering forward on nearly useless legs, he thanked the driver for a

3

most enjoyable ride—which it had not been—and paid his fare with another courtly compliment.

"And," he said, "for your services and good cheer, you may keep a dollar for yourself." Despite the fact that the usual tip for an $11.85 ride from San Francisco Airport to the darker depths of Chinatown is customarily higher than a dollar, the driver seemed genuinely pleased.

The rain was beginning to blow down the alley in unholy gusts, but Frank Leahy had thought of a parable. While his wife and the man he had asked to collaborate with him on his life story learned against the brick building to take advantage of what little protection the overhanging roof provided, he stood there like a penitent, taking abuse from nature, while he recited a teaching story.

"Courtesy is very important," he said. "When I was coach of football at the University of Notre Dame, I taught my, ah, lads that they should always say something nice to people so that it would reflect favorably upon themselves and upon their school. Once our team was invited to a dance at an all-girls school. My tackle, Zygmont Czarobski, weighed about 230 pounds and he asked this young lady who was about his own size to dance. When it was over I strained to hear what pleasant thing he would say. He said: 'Miss, even though you are big and fat and sloppy, you sure don't sweat much when you dance.' I believe she was actually pleased."

Satisfied that he had made a suitable point about ethical conduct, he began the agony of climbing a flight of nearly vertical stairs. The first four seemed easy, but he was pretending. On the fifth step, he caught hold of the railing and waited for his wife, Flossie, to press a firm hand against his back. Slowly, they made it to the top. He sagged noticeably and Flossie placed a protective arm under his shoulders and caught him before he fell.

"It is a good thing that I had a blood transfusion before I left Portland today," he said. "Otherwise I would not have had the strength to climb the stairs. It is a strange, ah, feeling to live off the blood of others. I try not to think of it that way, only that other people have been kind enough to donate their blood for my use."

Beyond the door was a waiting room with patients sitting on chairs that may have been ancient when the earthquake

4

rattled the ground beneath the city in 1906. Flecks of faded green paint had dropped on the raw wood floor. In the corner was a partition with Chinese characters covering one side. Next to it stood a large, gray Oriental statue, one arm extended, "calling for a fair catch," Leahy explained. Faces of all races stared eyelessly as the couple literally staggered through the door. Leahy—his once handsome Irish features muted by suffering—came to a halt and waited for the nurse to motion him in.

Since this was an emergency, the doctor had promised to rush him through. Time was important. Frank Leahy's life clock had been running down for some time. Now the ticks were coming so rapidly there hardly seemed to be any pause between the minutes.

"I am trying this acupuncturist," he explained, "because he has had excellent results with people of my acquaintance. He was recommended to me by a Notre Dame graduate whose wife has been in such terrible pain from a back injury that she literally begged God to take her. I have read where these people can perform miracles. That is exactly what is required in this case—a miracle."

The nurse motioned him to sit down on a stool. The doctor, carrying a box of needles nodded. Leahy nodded back. The nurse explained that Dr. Bea Chi Kwong was from Taiwan, a rather recent arrival. There being no licensing authority for acupuncturists, he was operating more or less illegally. Silence was absolutely necessary. On the wall behind the doctor's examination table was a sign in English: "Since acupuncture is a non-licensed profession, Dr. Bea will administer only healing herbs." Leahy laughed.

"This man has a good game plan," he said. "Actually, I am told that he has an herb called 'Musk Deer' in Chinese which is supposed to be, ah, excellent for the treatment of leukemia. I certainly shall try some. I need all the help I can get and from as many sources as possible."

Leahy had returned from a string of speaking engagements more dead than alive. It was not uncommon. Once his oldest son, Frank, Jr., had to meet him with an ambulance. In order to get back out on the road again, he had gone, several days early, to St. Vincent's Hospital in Portland to get a fresh transfusion, to keep the leukemia in remission. Then the arthritis in his spine began to tighten his legs and stiffen his back. He remembered the acupuncturist.

"I called and asked one of my, ah, doctors if it would be advisable to take this kind of treatment. He told me, 'Frank, the best experts at the Mayo Clinic and M.D. Anderson Hospital in Houston have not been able to do a thing for any of your ailments. Try this. It can't hurt.' I am quite willing to, ah, pay the price for the privilege of going on this next speaking tour. It is most important."

He sat backward on the stool, took a deep breath and said something complimentary to the doctor, who spoke only Mandarin. This was a sallow image of the heroically handsome man who coached at Notre Dame when the college game was enjoying its last hurrah, just before the ascendancy of professional football. Frank Leahy was a picture-book coach, his fine Celtic face peering, with worried eyes, out from underneath a gray, George Raft fedora.

It was almost as if they composed the Notre Dame Victory March, that most tearful of football's tunes of glory, just for him. He was Knute Rockne's legal heir. Unlike Rockne, who was Norwegian and a Lutheran-turned-Catholic later in life, Francis William Leahy was a genuine Irish Catholic with a pedigree that fitted Notre Dame's image as a Gaelic-flavored institution perfectly.

Here was a descendant of people named Torpey, Kane, O'Boyle and Leahy who deserted County Mayo and County Tipperary one jump ahead of the disastrous potato famines, found the quay at Galway where the boats were sailing to Canada and drifted south across the border to the great American West. In thirteen seasons as a head coach—two at Boston College—Leahy won 107 games, lost 13 and tied 9 for an .892 percentage that still stands second only to Rockne after the passage of two decades. He literally scorched the earth of every stadium he played in. He had six unbeaten seasons, four national champions in seven years and managed to run off a 39 game unbeaten streak.

Nobody has ever recruited players so skillfully. One season, 1947, some 42 of his varsity athletes went on to play professional football. He coached four winners of the Heisman Trophy, the bronze statue that is awarded to the finest player in the nation. He was far too perfect for his own good. His theories, based almost entirely, curiously enough, on the Protestant Work Ethic, were so perfect that they embarrassed certain factions in his own school.

Frank Leahy was largely without honor in his own time. Other coaches cursed him in private and tried to wriggle off Notre Dame's schedule. He was frequently criticized, frequently with reason. His whole character became distorted in the minds of others. His shyness was mistaken for aloofness; his dignity for stuffiness; his craft for underhandedness; his brilliance for dishonesty; his discipline for persecution; his righteousness for hypocrisy; and his caution and innate respect for an opponent for blatant false modesty. He was an enigma to those who refused to understand him.

Now a Cantonese-American nurse named Edna Wong was asking him to remove his shirt and sit forward on a low stool in an acupuncturist's office. The doctor moved forward and, with insect quick jolts, began to probe for the proper nerves. The whole operation lasted only a few minutes.

Halfway through the treatment, Leahy began to smile.

"Excellent!" he said. "This gentleman, ah, knows what he is doing. Very good! It is important that I stay alive and regain my health so that I can, ah, go on making speeches. There is a terrible moral decay threatening our land. I want to combat it. If I can reach enough people, I know I can help. I want one more victory, just one more. I will get well, you will see it happen."

The illnesses began with a simple numbness in the legs back in 1966. It was fatigue, Leahy thought, something that could easily be overcome but it was not. In those days, he still thought he could make a million dollars in the business world by listening to men he trusted, men he knew wouldn't cheat him because they were a part of the American Dream themselves. The condition persisted. Finally, he went to the Mayo Clinic, a place that held such warm memories. It was there, in 1930, that he and Knute Rockne shared a room. It was there, while they were both getting over operations that his old coach told him he could have his choice of five jobs as an assistant— at other schools, of course.

It was a pre-leukemic condition, not quite chronic, but too

close to think about. That was the start of his physical decline. After that came the arthritis in the back. Then, in 1969, he had a fierce pain in his abdomen. It was shortly after his return from Houston and the discouraging news from the cancer hospital there. They drove him to St. Vincent's in Portland. An intestine had become gangrenous. Only a few people survive such news. On the operating table, his heart stopped twice and the Associated Press moved an obituary on the wires. A priest came and administered extreme unction. That might have been the third or fourth time. Leahy was losing count.

For days he lingered near death.

"I never gave up on the man," said Frank, Jr. "He taught me never to quit and I knew he wouldn't. They could rub oil on his forehead and pray over him all they wanted, but he wasn't ready to die. He believed all those things he told the players at Notre Dame. They all sound corny now, I guess. But he meant them. I knew he wouldn't die."

And Frank Leahy survived again. He came out of it with a serious heart problem and bowels that would not permit him total relief. He was a shattered man, physically, but not mentally. He was warned by every medical man he knew to retire completely, to simply sit on his porch at Lake Oswego and watch the ducks fly off toward the nearby pine trees. But he could not.

The treatment ended and the doctor rose, bowed and smiled. Leahy thanked him and his wife presented the nurse with a plant. An old Irish custom, she said. The nurse seemed to understand, even if it wasn't exactly an old Irish custom. Down the stairs they wobbled, one supporting the other. In the street, the rain had slacked. There was a wistful drizzle in the air and the streets were greasy wet. Leahy kept waiting for a taxi that had been promised from the acupuncturist's office. It never came and he waited testily. Finally, his collaborator ran down the street and found a telephone booth.

"This should have been provided for," he told his wife. Leahy was upset. Even so, the waxy look of death had temporarily departed from his face and he seemed oddly comfortable. His wife stretched out an arm and he took it, gratefully. At last the taxi arrived and he walked toward it resolutely. For the first time in days, he noticed an improvement.

8

"My feet have been like blocks of concrete," he said. "I would not, ah, say that I'm cured, but I do feel better. Let us get a cab and find an outstanding restaurant. What about the Blue Fox? They tell me that's excellent. It would not do for the former coach of the University of Notre Dame to eat in a place unworthy of Our Lady. Would it?"

The restaurant, one of the most expensive in San Francisco, was located only a block away and Leahy moved his feet forward into the cab. The driver had been told in advance that he would be paid well for moving an immobile man around the corner to the Holiday Inn in Chinatown. Instead, the man decided to be clever. He went on a grand tour, up Sacramento St. to Stockton, six blocks over to Broadway and then back down Kearney to Leahy's destination. He grinned, exposing a row of even teeth that were just starting to yellow with age.

"He thinks he's doing something clever," Frank said, digging his companion in the ribs. "He will pay the price. There are no short cuts in life, only those which we, ah, imagine. He will get his."

When the cab came hissing to a stop in front of the restaurant, Leahy pushed the door open gently and turned toward the driver. "Here is $2.25, kindly keep the extra dime and nickle for yourself. You have certainly earned it."

A couple of doormen, who couldn't possibly have been there when Notre Dame was winning all those football games, moved forward to help him. He waved them away with a small gesture. Frank Leahy loved to be recognized. He hated to be helped. While there was still life, he was able to function.

"Once you stop and let somebody do something for you, ah, that is the time when you decide you can no longer do something for yourself," he said, smiling at the waiter. "That may sound vainglorious, but it is my firm conviction."

They snickered over the way Leahy talked when he was at Notre Dame. They said it was pompous and stilted, a bit of Victorian nonsense. They mocked him, copied him and laughed at him. Hardly anyone knew that when he came to college, fresh off the train from Winner, South Dakota, he was not only shy to the point of being unable to carry on a full conversation, he had a nervous stammer. Desperate, he went to a speech professor and asked for help. When the course was

9

over, Leahy came out talking like a character in a Bert L. Standish novel. There was no difference between Frank Leahy and Frank Merriwell, when the Notre Dame coach opened his mouth.

"I feel excellent," he said. "Oh, I probably won't take a windsprint around the restaurant, but I feel excellent. That Chinese doctor, ah, is a genius. Yes, he is. My back does not hurt. It is, ah, quite numb. And that is excellent. To have no feeling of pain is certainly better than having pain. If you ever suffer from a disease—and I hope you do not—you will understand what I mean. No feeling seems like a terrible thing until you have constant pain."

The waiter, who couldn't have been more than ten when Notre Dame had its last national champion under Leahy, bowed stiffly and asked if his customer was who he thought he was. Leahy made a gracious remark. The waiter asked for an autograph. At another table, a group of younger people smiled and nodded their heads.

"So this is what it's like to be a living legend," he was told.

"There is a serious question over whether I am really living," Leahy said, chuckling at his own black humor. "You must understand that I am old and very sick. There are now two Frank Leahys. There is the Frank Leahy who has just had a transfusion of blood and an acupuncturist's treatment. He is feeling fairly fit and can give a good imitation of the man he once was, the coach who commanded respect. There is another Frank Leahy, who is overdue for blood, who is overdue for just about everything, who has found a suffering even he finds hard to bear, who goes on only because he was disciplined to go on by the heat of competition and by coaching, but who wonders sometimes, as I wonder now, why go on?"

"How much do you miss coaching, Mr. Leahy?" asked a redheaded lady at the table.

"Please, my dear," he said. "Don't call me 'Mister Leahy' anymore. We've known each other well enough to address each other on a more intimate basis. Please call me 'coach' from now on."

Leahy toyed with the wine list, asking the steward this question and that question about certain vintage years and certain labels. Then he ordered a beer, chuckling at his own ability to confuse the opposition. The steward looked at him with a severely pained expression. Leahy's phalanx of smooth, even teeth were showing and he was laughing to himself. Here he was, the first gentleman in a family of wild Celtic rogues and he could not resist the urge to be roguish. He drank the beer and ordered another. Some of the pain was returning.

"I am a man who has lived beyond his times," he said. "That is true. I will never, ah, deny it. I am a preacher of old-fashioned virtues. My children tell me this, even the ones who love me most. Those virtues I talk about are no longer popular. That is why I have to live. If I die, those virtues may die with me. That is why I struggle. Again, that sounds vainglorious, but it is the truth.

"I give my speeches and I am called a Bircher. But I don't ever recall joining that particular group. I am not heckled. I am applauded. I see lads sitting out in front of the podium listening intently. Afterwards, I am applauded with enthusiasm. My counsel is sought out. Do you honestly think these virtues are dying? Oh, I don't believe that right was any less right than it is now. I believe too many men in coaching positions have given in to pressure. I truly do. If the present times are better, then I am sorry for present times.

"No coach can permit himself to be altered by changing times. I believe that they are letting themselves be talked out of demanding discipline because they are afraid to take command. You simply must insist upon improvement from your players. That is how character is developed. I tell you this, if I were coaching today I would do no different. I would be the same man I was. I would not care if I survived as a coach as long as I could demand that my players make certain sacrifices that would make them better people. Is there anything wrong with that?

"Years have passed and I continually run into players who told me that they, ah, hated the long, demanding practices we had at Notre Dame. They tell me, too, that those same long practices hardened them."

Leahy sat back savoring the importance of his own words. They seemed good, so he took a sip of beer and continued. Frank Leahy almost always speaks for the record.

"I missed coaching more than I anticipated," he said. "I

missed working with the young, molding their character. Now some of them, such as Leon Hart, would tell you I was a, pardon the phrase, son-of-a-bitch. I suppose that I was. But I liked working with young men, turning them toward things I know to be right. I wanted my young men to be the best. I wanted them to be heroic in the truest, finest sense. I set impossible goals for myself. I got a ten year contract from Notre Dame when I returned from World War II. I was ready to coach the Cleveland Browns. I had a one million dollar contract ready to sign.

"Instead I went back to Our Lady. I vowed that I would go undefeated for ten years, right through the 1956 season. That was a foolish goal, yet I came close to it. I would get terribly nervous, terribly worked up. I neglected my friends, the alumni and my family. My health suffered terribly. What you see here is the result of what I did."

His eyes were drifting in dark pools. His body was functioning off and on. He seemed like a spirit betrayed by his own physical form.

"I would not trade one minute of my life for a different ending," he said. "So man suffers some. The only thing that matters is: To what end does that suffering come? I think it, ah, means something to devote your life to a worthy profession. A coach shapes lives. In reality I am a teacher. At least, that is the way in which I thought of myself. I believe that some of us must assume leadership. I believe young lads hunger after leadership. They want to be told what to do by somebody better than they.

"That's the whole thrust of mankind. One generation leads another until the old generation cannot lead anymore. What is happening in this country is quite simple. We are raising a generation that does not wish to be led or to lead. That is why my final mission is so important. I must tell young people that life is hard and that success is survival. In war men see their comrades fall around them, but they do not quit. Do you know that I hate war. I told this to a young man who told me he was for peace. So am I. The strife that plagues mankind could easily be settled by friendly battle, the kind that does not kill.

"There is no need to die, but only to be ready and to fight hard. Is that wrong? I raised the threshold of pain that some young men had and I taught them to work harder. That is the test."

Somewhere, deep in the bowels of the kitchen, the waiter found some food. No one will dine in haste when the bill for it is going to be $132.89, plus tip. Leahy sat back and ordered a third beer, strictly against the orders of the doctors who were treating him for diabetes.

"Do you think you talk too much, Frank?" asked Floss Leahy.

"No Leahy I ever knew thought he did," he answered, chuckling.

From another table came two young men who may or may not have known Leahy until the waiter mentioned who he was. They wanted an autograph on their menus. They slobbered for awhile and then explained how closely they followed Notre Dame when they were kids, even though one was an Episcopalian and the other was a Jew. With a slight nod, Leahy told them how wonderful they were for recognizing him. They departed as if they had been touched on the brow by Jesus.

"I was a fine salesman with the gift of, ah, language. I believed in myself and I believed that by bringing young lads to the University of Notre Dame I was providing them with the finest education possible. They wanted to play for Frank Leahy and that made me very proud. When I was a lad myself I wanted to play for Knute Rockne. He didn't have to recruit me and it reached a point where I didn't have to recruit that hard either. I took a young lad and stood him in front of Our Lady up on that Golden Dome and I didn't really have to say all that much."

It was, he said, a blessing to play for Notre Dame and there wasn't a single scholarship case who didn't find himself in a state of grace just for signing the admission form. Dinner was over and, on the way out, several more people recognized the coach and asked him to say something before he left. Leahy moved from table to table benignly, like an archbishop. Finally, he reached the door. The rain had stopped and he smiled cheerfully. A taxi came rolling out of the darkness.

"It's wonderful," he said.

"What is?" was the question.

"To be able to fully evacuate one's bowels," he explained. "Bless that Chinese."

EPISODE 2

SALT LAKE CITY

The great jetliner rumbled through the midnight skies, bearing Frank Leahy on his holy mission. Stewardesses in short skirts moved up and down the aisle, feeding people, fawning over people and putting people to sleep by slipping pillows behind their heads. They fetched booze and brought sandwiches, modern handmaidens in an airborne harem.

They managed to extinguish everybody but Leahy, a sick old man with a yellow tint to his skin and the ugly odor of death escaping from every pore. He sat there under a shallow light, indomitable, working on his next speech. He had in front of him tracts from the John Birch Society and from Common Cause, two widely divergent organizations. He had a number of articles clipped from inspirational magazines, both Protestant and Catholic. He was scribbling notes and looking deeply satisfied. There were moments when he seemed like a small boy in a dying man's skin.

"I am asked why I do not give the same speech in every town," he explained to a man who was slumped back, head against the cabin wall trying to sleep. "This is not proper. If you are to really truly reach people you have to give them an individual message. I prepare each speech differently."

Pleased that he had made a point, he went back to scribbling, pausing only to ask the young lady—who looked like no lady—if she might have a spare beer in the forward cabin. She did and Leahy patted her hand like a benign grandfather. For several long moments he stared out into the darkness, watching the necklace lights of small Western towns pass beneath the wing tips.

"May I speak about my brother Jack?" he asked.

"About who?"

"About my brother Jack? A most delightful and charming man," he explained. "I think you would have liked him. He was, ah, what you might, ah, call a free spirit. Yes, that is the best way to typify Jack Leahy. He was free. I sometimes wish that I could have been like him. But I was never free to be free, if you understand me. Jack was free. I was not. That

14

was the essential difference between us. I genuinely admired him for his ability to move beyond himself."

Some men live the lives they have to live and wish they could have been something different. It was obvious that this man of stern discipline and deep morality genuinely wished that he could have been his own brother Jack and let the world take it from there. For the first time in two days, Frank Leahy's face softened. No longer was he a leader of men and a great teacher of truth. Rather, he was a charmingly profligate brother named Jack. His entire face shifted. His hands relaxed. His jaw slackened.

"What a rogue he was!" Leahy said. "There was the time that he took a local beauty queen away from my brother Tom. They were both single at the time so this story will not be as shocking as you might suspect. Jack was running a saloon in Laramie at the time. He asked the lady if she would like to accompany him to Portland, Oregon, of all places. She said that she would and they left on the next plane.

"Alas, poor Jack! He was a drinker of great ability, which meant that he could not wait long enough to enjoy the charms of the lovely lass. He checked into a hotel with her under assumed names. Quickly, he excused himself. Several hours later he discovered that he could not remember which hotel he had checked into and he could not remember which names he had used. It was three days before he got back to Laramie. But the lady was no longer interested in him.

"On another occasion, when I had Boston College in the Sugar Bowl, I discovered that my brother was coming to New Orleans. He was mad, but beautifully mad. One evening he fell asleep in the lobby, the result of too much pre-game partying and somebody shaved off half his mustache. On yet another occasion, when I was coaching the University of Notre Dame's football team, he showed up at the Roosevelt Hotel after our lads had defeated the University of Southern California."

Frank Leahy and his wife were having dinner with Pat O'Brien who had played the coach in "Knute Rockne, All-American." He had no physical resemblance to any other actor. Jack Leahy insisted upon crashing the dinner.

"Well, Jack, this is Pat O'Brien," said Frank Leahy, trying to be civil.

15

"I will never forget the great actor who played Father Flannigan in Boys Town," Jack shouted.

"That was Spencer Tracy," said O'Brien, visibly pained.

"I'm sure," said brother Jack, "that if they had given you the part you would have done just fine."

While the pilot circled the vastness of the great Salt Lake, lowering his landing gear and dropping his flaps, Leahy sat there laughing. There never was anybody quite like brother Jack Leahy. He was, in fact, the alter ego of a stern Victorian gentleman. They shared a common bond too difficult to break. Jack was Jack and he was also part of Frank.

EPISODE 3

SALT LAKE CITY

At the gate, the attendant moved forward with a wheel chair. Most of the passengers came staggering off, their eyeballs awash with the residue of sleep. But Frank Leahy was totally alert. He had been alone with his thoughts and his memories. Both of them gave him comfort and strength.

"Aren't you Frank Leahy?" asked the flight attendant, who couldn't have been more than a first grader when Notre Dame was defeating every team that moved.

"I used to be," said Leahy, chuckling at his own mischief.

"I thought that's who you used to be," said the kid. "I was a big fan of yours. Well, actually, my father was. We're not even Catholic. We're Mormons."

"Good people, the Mormons," said Leahy. "Never apologize for not being something else. I've read a lot about the Mormons and they were very much like the Catholics. Lord knows they took the same kind of abuse the Catholics did in Ireland. Very fine group, young man, very fine group. I have been reading your Bible on the airplane."

On the way to the rent-a-car stand, Leahy was asked if indeed he had been reading the Mormon version of the Bible on the airplane. He looked bemused.

"No," he said, "but I'm sure if I had been it would have been very interesting and very uplifting. It never hurts to

16

make a man feel good. If you meet a Mormon tell him how much you respect his religion. From everything I have ever been told, it is an exceptionally moral group and I don't think many of them have three or four wives like they used to. One's enough for any man and probably one too many."

Even though it was abnormally early in the morning, Leahy insisted on stopping at the airport barber shop. The group he was speaking in front of was not receptive to long-haired types, which seemed humorous considering that Leahy's own hair was only slightly longer than a Marine drill instructor's.

"A man cannot be too careful about his appearance," he said, uttering one of those phrases that somehow would have looked better stitched to a sampler and hung over a fireplace. The barber recognized him. It was a pure matter of fact that Frank Leahy, two decades past the glory of his times, could not go anywhere in the United States undetected. He enjoyed the phenomenon.

"Young man," he said, "cut them both short."

"What do you mean, coach Leahy?"

"Cut both the hair and the conversation short," he said, fully aware that his remark had not hurt the barber's feelings. The two of them chatted amiably and Leahy began to discuss the Notre Dame football team's chances. While swearing absolute fealty to Ara Parseghian, the current coach, he proceeded to say some unkind remark about how the talent was being handled.

There were those who insisted that Terry Brennan might have had a chance at Notre Dame if Leahy hadn't written some exceedingly ugly things in a column being processed by a Chicago newspaper. The truth is that Leahy resented being replaced by a 25-year-old man. It was one thing to leave Notre Dame and quite another to be pushed aside for a mere child, a former philosophy student of the school's new president, Fr. Theodore Hesburgh. When the opportunity came, Leahy reacted, perhaps too violently. Now his deep sense of personal honor would not let him admit that he had done anything so human.

"When the time came that it became obvious Terry had committed certain blunders, I, ah, wrote what I thought," he explained, while the barber tried to find a hair long enough to cut. "Under no circumstances did I feel that I was undercutting him. They said that I did, but, ah, they were not inside my heart. I did not feel that he was doing right by Our Lady. It certainly never kept me from discussing my capabilities. I was an alumnus of the University of Notre Dame and had a perfect right to say what I wished about the head coach of football."

Frank Leahy paused for a second, getting ready to say something important.

"You know," he said, while the man clipped away, "the Good Lord has to be the complete envy of every man on the face of the earth who has ever attempted to coach a football team."

"Why is that?" asked a man who only wanted to go back to bed.

"Because the alumni can never undertake to replace him," Leahy said.

His eyes narrowed to slits.

"What should I tell those Mormons tonight?"

"Tell them how much better than Catholics they are," he was told. "They'll never forget you for it."

"A most gracious suggestion," he said. "Most gracious."

During the day, Frank Leahy suffered severe pain in his hotel room. A doctor came from the nearby hospital and hovered over him. He insisted upon a complete medical record before he could treat him. The leukemia was creating severe problems in Leahy's legs and he hated the idea that he might have to say something that sounded weak. Finally, expediency got the better of him. With massive strength, he reached for a telephone.

"Please," he said, "I know this is not in keeping with the services normally rendered by a man who is writing your biography, but I need a blood transfusion . . . ah . . . ah . . . I need it damn bad. Can you assist me? I would consider it most gracious, most gracious indeed."

"Help me," he said with a voice that was too strong for a sick man. "I can reach these people. They are most reachable. Help me, please."

Another doctor was summoned and the plasma began to trickle down through the small tubes into Leahy's arms. The transfusions were coming closer and closer and he knew it.

This was not a good sign. Still he talked about the banquet that evening and the message he was going to present. He was fighting pain, a kind of pain that should have engulfed him. It did not.

"You know there is a famous biography of Ty Cobb in his later days, written by a fellow named Al Stump. Cobb got kind of crazy down toward the end," he was told. "He had the same kind of physical troubles you've had. Have you ever read the book? It isn't a pretty piece of writing. It sort of makes you want to weep."

"They tell me that Tyrus' final days were not attractive," Leahy said. "I knew the man. I met him at a dinner. They tell me he was, ah, much disturbed. I mourn for him."

With some difficulty, he waved his arm toward the bureau top where several dozen bottles and plastic jars had been placed. When he traveled, Leahy was a walking drugstore. There was, he said, Darvon and Digoxin and Librium and other compounds he couldn't remember. He carried with him a check list and each bottle had a number on it. At a certain time of day he was to take two from bottle No. 1 and four from bottle No. 14 and so on.

"I need a game plan just to stay alive," he said as the doctor left. "I'm glad I believed in all the principles I espoused at Notre Dame. If not, I would surely, ah, have been gone some time ago. For many years, I was sustained by the possibility that I might return to coaching, although in my heart I knew that I could never be content any place but at Notre Dame.

"Still, there was that possibility. These diseases have robbed me of that one comfort—that I might coach again. It is impossible now. You know, I have not really missed the glory. I thought I would. I have been honored many times since I left. Being removed from the spotlight seemed to sap my wife's spirit, though. For many years, she was . . . ah . . . not really herself. Fortunately that is no longer the situation."

Slowly he moved from the bed and wobbled toward the bathroom. He stopped, propped his hand against the wall and sighed like a man balancing on the edge of eternity. Then he smiled at an impudent thought that was streaking across his brain.

"Would you believe I once boxed the great middleweight

19

Ace Hudkins and did quite well against him?" he asked. "You wouldn't? Well, neither would anyone else, certainly not my doctors."

The only fragment of his once imposing good looks left intact were his teeth and they glittered firm and clear from a face that seemed to be made of ancient leather. The eyes were far back in their sockets and the hair was drooping down over the brow. Frank Leahy's body seemed dead already. Only his spirit seemed unaware of the fact.

"Perhaps you'd better cancel the speech, Coach."

"No. Give me a few hours," he said. "These speeches are all I have left."

EPISODE 4

SALT LAKE CITY

The hotel lobby had been carefully constructed of brass and old wood in a more conservative era when quality had not yet been replaced by low cost plastic beams and cheap mirrors. A group of people had gathered by the elevators because someone had told them a famous old football coach was going to emerge and then proceed to the grand ballroom for a speech.

Two teenage girls, one with pert buckteeth and eyes as black as vest buttons, the other with white skin and flesh-colored hair like an underdeveloped photograph of a redhead, stood there with autograph books. It was doubtful if their parents were even married when Frank Leahy was busily destroying every college football team foolish enough to remain on the Notre Dame schedule. How much was his autograph really worth to them?

The elevator door hissed open and out stepped a reasonable facsimile of the Leahy of blessed memory. Somehow he had forced the yellow tint from his cheeks. His skin seemed smoother and he walked with only a slight shuffle. He was moving into battle, getting ready to fight for the flag and the safety of the Republic. By rights, the Notre Dame Victory March should have been playing in the background, for dramatic effect, Only a few hours earlier, this had been more corpse than man. He seemed to be thoroughly aware of the miracle he had personally created,

On the way to the ballroom he talked, almost enthusiastically, about his leukemia. He was winning this round against it and he wanted his companion on this trip to understand just how rare and dangerous it really was. It was almost as if he were meeting Army on the field of honor again.

"If you think that I was unhealthy this afternoon, you should have seen me when I checked into M.D. Anderson Hospital in Houston a few years ago," he said. "Ah, yes, that was bad indeed. Very bad. My weight had dropped from 180 to 169 pounds. I was dehydrated and paralyzed. My team of doctors searched medical records for the 20 years previous. In all that time, throughout America, they could find only nine cases similar to mine. Of those nine, five survived and got well. Four were lost. With those kind of odds in my favor, I'm going to live.

"It is a rare type of leukemia. My body manufactures four times the usual amount of red blood cells. But only two percent are reaching the blood stream due to a blockage. My body is trying to destroy itself. But with massive doses of hormones and frequent transfusions, I am able to carry on. I'm going to live. The odds are 5-4 in my favor.

"By the way did you like the story about Zigamont at the dance?"

"Yes," he was told, "although I've heard it before. I still found it funny."

"Good," he decided, "then I shall use it this evening. A spoonful of humor makes the serious message go down easier. You might, ah, ask why I am delivering this address to people who are already aware of the Communist menace to our great nation. That would be a proper question. They need to be reinforced. They need to hear somebody tell them that the old virtues this country was founded upon are still being defended. We cannot let our precious freedoms, ah, slip away. I truly believe that God is sparing me so that I can bring this message to as many people as I can.

"When I was coach of football at Notre Dame University I used to insist that everybody 'pay the price.' I believe I have mentioned that before. I am paying the price, but I will do my duty to this wonderful country which has given me so much."

Leahy was walking briskly now, although placing most of his weight on his heels. The years and the pain were leaving his face. He was off on another holy quest, not too different in his mind from bringing honor and glory to Our Lady by smashing Michigan State at football.

"Certainly!" he said, almost indignant. "People must have a code to live by. It is wonderful to say that by simply practicing love all problems will cease. But men seek discipline. That is why football builds character. It creates self-discipline. When that fades, man is lost. As a small boy, my family lived on the frontier. I was not always a perfect model of deportment, but my father taught me discipline and the value of hard work. Those things never change. We did not win football games for Our Lady by loving the opposition. Rather we sought to find respect for ourselves. I do not understand why things have changed so. What was right in 1928 is still right today. There is a danger in such thoughts as we now see on campuses. You will hear what I mean in my talk this evening."

The program chairman was waiting by the door. In recent years, Frank Leahy could count his life in the number of program chairmen he had met. He sighed and tried not to brace himself against the door.

As soon as Leahy moved into the banquet room, a four piece band began to thump away, predictably assaulting the Notre Dame Victory March. Maybe the man had heard the piece a hundred thousand times in his life. Even so, it seemed to be pumping more and more life into his aching body. Hands kept reaching out to clutch his hand. Old friends came swirling out of the crowd. The music grew louder as he moved toward the podium until it sounded like some sort of liturgical anthem. Frank Leahy could feel the warmth of attention. He was not just an ex-coach with a record growing more archaic every day, but an important person again.

Every now and then he stopped and said something gracious to the people who reached out to him. He remembered most of their names and mentioned some mutual friend. Somebody recalled the score of an old Notre Dame football game. Somebody wanted to know what Johnny Lujack was doing these days. ("Running a most successful automobile agency!") And what did Leahy think of the present Notre Dame coach Ara Parseghian. ("A splendid man with a splendid record of accomplishment! A great credit to Our Lady and he's a Presbyterian, you know.") Just short of the podium a small boy came forward and asked him to autograph his menu. Leahy said something gracious and asked the boy if he played football. He did not. Leahy looked sad.

"Let's hear a good one tonight, coach," yelled some great red beet of a man at a far table. "Give it hell!"

"A Notre Dame man among all these fine Mormons," said Leahy to no one in particular.

With only a minor assist, he managed to reach the raised platform and the head table. Some people were giving him a standing ovation. He smiled a full, toothy smile and waved. Showing no signs of pain he sat down and said something gracious to the waiter. Then opened a couple of bottles and rolled out some pills, gulping them cautiously so that nobody would see what he was actually doing.

"Do you know that I was once offered a chance to run for the United States Senate from the state of Indiana?" he asked, obviously exhilarated.

"Why didn't you take the opportunity?"

"I thought I might still have a chance of getting back into coaching. I felt I could do more good in that capacity than I could in the Senate. But if I had ran I would have won. You, ah, understand that part of me, don't you? All I ever wanted to be was a football coach. That is not a frivolous occupation. It is a profession degraded by many and one that torments many.

"It is not an easy way of life nor does it offer the security or riches of other professions. But it is the kind of calling that captures the hearts of many who follow it, those who are young at heart forever and wish to be part of youth forever—something most people would not understand."

He sat back and toyed with his salad, totally lost in thought. Something was plaguing his spirit.

"Do you consider me to be, ah, pompous?" he asked finally.

"I think you have a unique personality and you certainly have an unusual manner of speaking, but pompous is one of the last things I'd call you. Why do you ask?"

"Well, ah, lad, somebody wrote that about me once," he said.

"When?"

"It was, ah, 1939. I have never forgotten it."

The master of ceremonies was one of those dreadful drones who recognizes everybody in the audience but the busboys and then pays tribute to everyone who sold a single ticket to the dinner. Ponderously, he proceeded to the main speaker, who only five hours earlier seemed on the verge of perishing in his hotel room. Frank Leahy was writing furiously on the back of his menu. The introduction was saccharine and vainglorious to a fault, but Leahy nodded approvingly. Somewhere in that disease-shriveled body adrenalin was pumping furiously. He almost leaped for the microphone.

Leahy began by telling everybody how wonderful they were and how wonderful it was to be invited to this wonderful dinner for such a wonderful cause on such a wonderful night. Having been gracious, he moved into a few humorous stories, retelling the story of Czarobski and the fat girl as he had promised. Now it was time for a homey touch.

"Just the other day I was riding on an airplane heading for Salt Lake City and this man next to me asked how many children I had. I told him that the Good Lord had blessed my wife and I with eight children. I told him it was amazing, considering that I was only home two nights a week. (Laughter.) I told him you know we have, ah, always believed in the offensive system in our family. (Chuckles.) You know what he said to me, 'It seems to me you scored every time you had the ball.' (Overwhelming laughter.)

"It would be remiss for me not to mention two very wonderful, personal friends of mine, who represent two magnificent facets of our society. Let me go quickly to them.

"One is Ed Downey, the local branch manager of Canteen Corporation, the company for which I work. If he so desired, he could be the most honorable playboy in the western world. He could move from Palm Springs to Palm Beach to London to Paris to Cannes and no one would blame him for never working a single day in his entire life. He and his father have more money than they would be able to count in a week or ten days or even a year. But that wasn't what Ed Downey wanted out of life. No sir!! This is a true, hardy American. He wanted to work and be a productive member of our great society.

"He took a job at the lowest level of the organization. He

drove a truck for our company for a couple of years and then moved into management. He wanted to prove he could do something on his own and not sit around waiting for his father to hand him a living. He's branch manager here in Salt Lake City and I predict with his kind of winning attitude, he'll go a long way in our business. Stand up there, Ed."

The applause was shattering. These were all good fellows out there in the audience, men who were once granite-sure of their character and their righteous place in a righteous community. Until the shaggy-haired dope smokers began to drop out of the game and denounce it as a de-humanizing experience, there wasn't a football coach anywhere in the nation who didn't feel secure in the knowledge that he was doing something noble for humanity. Then players began wearing their hair long and forming committees and making outrageous demands. Who in the hell did they think they were, anyway, questioning the wisdom of their coach? Here was Frank Leahy, old, bent and noble, one of the two or three greatest coaches who ever lived, to tell them that they were right and proper in their behavior. They were proud just to be in the same building with him. He was slowly turning a ballroom into a soaring cathedral sanctified by football and blessed by the American Way. They loved him for it.

After all, there was only one other coach whom Frank Leahy was willing to accept as a close personal friend and that was Wallace Butts of Georgia. Leahy knew he'd love Wallace long before he ever met him. He had heard the story of Butts' first day on the job when the co-chairmen of the Players' Committee called on Wallace to introduce themselves and inform the new head coach at Georgia that there was a group within the team that decided who would wear what on the road, who would appear in the starting line-up and who would comprise the traveling squad. Butts leaped over his desk, thumped their heads together and told them the Players' Committee had been disbanded. This was an absolute monarchy and the coach ruled by divine right of the alumni. Leahy liked that story and sought out Butts as soon as he could.

". . . my next friend is a man who has been almost like my own brother," said Leahy, his voice becoming more nasal in tone. "I had naval duty with this wonderful gentleman years ago in World War II—that was the one we tried to win, if you'll recall. He was my commanding officer and he used to wonder where I was when I was on duty. He finally located me in my room writing notes about football in my notebook. He came back and said, coach, I know what you've been doing and I'll make a deal with you. If you'll share those notes you're putting in that book, I'll give you even more time off. Even in the midst of as terrible a conflict as World War II, this man recognized the fact that peace would come and there would be a need in our society for football and for competent, inspirational coaches.

"So my dear, dear friend went back to his coaching job at Brigham Young and the three simple things that we developed seem pretty old now, but at the time they were revolutionary in the extreme. But what Eddie Kimball and I did out there in the Pacific were: Using different blocks on the same play with tackle calling the offensive blocks, the possibility of the quarterback audibilizing plays at the line of scrimmage and the possibility of having the defense read the offense. Eddie considered all of these things not only possible, but practical. I am more sold on this gentleman than my meager vocabulary will permit me to say. Here is a man who could dream big dreams and make them work.

"Let me say something about the power of thinking positively. I think that is what these two wonderful men represent, another reason why I singled them out. As I look at them in the audience, my mind drifts back to a Notre Dame football game of many years ago. We had played five games and won them all and we were matched against an exceptionally fine Army football team. And by some strange set of circumstances, the Monday prior to that game our All-America quarterback—Angelo Bertelli—was called into the army by his draft board. Gone was the best passer I've ever seen. So we had to go with our next best, an 18-year-old boy named Johnny Lujack.

"Before the game in New York in the big dressing room, just before we went out to play this nationally important match, I called everyone together and said, 'Lads, everyone within range of my voice should fall to his knees and thank the God above that made him. The Lord has furnished us with such great leadership for this monumental, tremendously important game. Our leader today is a great, flawless caller of plays, a great forward passer and a great runner. On defense he makes tackles all over the field.'

"I said, 'Not only that, he is a defensive back of magnificent ability. If a pass is thrown in his zone he will not only knock it down, he is quite liable to run it back all the way for a touchdown. God has truly blessed Our Lady with such a talent. Oh, lads, we are so fortunate. I think you all know of whom I speak.' "

He roared the terminal words, at the same time clipping them short. This gave them the sound of a general giving a command to his troops, which could not conceivably be disobeyed. Frank Leahy was not disappointed, the audience surrendered completely. He had the situation well under control. They understood exactly who he was—The Coach, not just any coach, but the Coach of football at Notre Dame, where the echoes still whispered his name, he assumed.

"They tell me that Lujack sat there utterly amazed. He started turning around, trying to figure out which immortal we have brought back to play quarterback for Notre Dame on that day. Later on, Lujack told me, 'Coach Leahy, my teammates were doing the same thing.' I think that shows exactly what firm, positive thinking can mean, because the University of Notre Dame did splendidly.

"Gentlemen, I'm extremely happy to be here in Mormon country," he said, moving forward with the thrust and power of a fullback going up the middle. "Like all of you I'm thrilled over the fact that Joseph Smith, born in Sharon, Vermont, was the first Mormon prophet. When he entered our world, human nature and religion were deeply enriched. I've read briefly about your Mr. Joseph Smith, Brigham Young and other great Mormon leaders.

"There isn't a corporation in America better organized than the Mormon Church . . . or the Catholic Church. Your success, as ours, is based upon a sincere belief in God, good organization, self-discipline, decency, honesty, dedication, ambition, repentance, and a good family life. Where the Mormons excel is asking and exacting from their members an amazing amount of family participation at a very early age in life. I think this one of the contributing factors why your wonderful religion is spreading so rapidly and so successfully all over the world. Nothing can be more important today than a return to a pure, old-fashioned, unaltered belief in God. The life style of religious individuals is most inspirational to me now, as it always has been.

"Maybe people today are searching for that which you religious people already possess, especially the youth, who in many instances, are spiritually lost. They are unsure.

"Allow me to say this: The good youth in the United States of America is better, in my studied conviction, than it has ever been in the nation's history. The good ones are fine, they *are* the greatest, they *are* the best. Those who are not on the right track are seeking inner peace. They haven't learned to give of themselves to worthwhile, decent projects. They are thinking only of the here, not of the hereafter. My admiration for those who believe in and adhere to religion is totally unstinting. God has a game plan for everyone. Playing the game of life without God as your coach is like riding on a ship without a captain, without a crew and without a rudder in the middle of the ocean."

It was an outrageous analogy, but one that audiences had come to expect from Frank Leahy. They were present in that wonderful atmosphere, not so much to criticize the pearly rhetoric he used, rather to experience the fulfillment of a boyhood dream. Here they all were, men with beltlines starting to droop and hair starting to depart, actually listening to an inspirational halftime talk from the master coach himself. They could see themselves as they were in 1948—grammar school kids or members of the high school junior varsity. There they were in their mundane surroundings wishing they could be in the locker room at Notre Dame. Now they were. For a few days, anyway, not a single one of them would admit to ever having an irreligious thought.

"You know, I have a confession to make. I have always preached, as a coach, the value of preparedness. And I found myself today trying to get this talk prepared for this very wonderful audience. The word 'confession' leads me to an experience I had while I was at Notre Dame. On the practice field my very last year there as head football coach, the offensive line performed so ineptly that I began to use harsh language, something I had not been in the habit of doing. I lost my temper many, many times during the practice sessions. My language became so foul that our players were shocked.

"I was ashamed to the point where I hated to go to confession and have to tell the priest what I had been up to. Then we got into a big game with Southern Methodist University and I had to go to confession because I did not want to miss going to Mass and Communion with the team on the day of the game. So I waited until the sun disappeared in Indiana and I went to the big church on campus and I walked way, way back into the deepest corner and, sure enough, there was a priest still hearing confessions. I sneaked in hoping he wouldn't recognize my voice.

"When he had listened to my confession, he leaned forward and said, in a wonderful Irish accent, 'Please tell me, son, how's the line?' I said, 'Father, in answer to your question, our line is pitiful. They're no good. They're lazy. They will not block at the line of scrimmage. They won't go down field to block. They do not deserve the rare privilege of wearing the colors of the University of Notre Dame and Our Blessed Mother. And it's too bad because in the backfield we have Ralph Guglielmi, Joe Heap, Neil Worden and Johnny Lattner. If we had a line to go with them we might have a fighting chance of making a first down.'

"And so, that poor priest paused and said, 'Ach, you poor man. I don't know what it is that's gotten into you. Maybe it's the heat of the day, maybe you've been drinking too much. All I'm trying to find out is how long the line is outside the confessional box.'"

Having flattered, amused, cajoled and identified with his audience, Frank Leahy moved forward into what he privately called the sermon portion of his speech. His hands were gripping the lectern and the pain was flashing like fire up one leg and down the other. But his eyes, somewhat hooded by nature, were flared wide. He looked straight into the spotlight. He was leading lads into battle, fighting for glorious causes and impossible dreams. This time the enemy was something less tangible than the Army football team, but far more insidious. Across the field, on the opposing bench, was Communism and it was responsible for everything that had gone wrong with America. It was obvious to Frank Leahy, but so many others had been completely fooled. Now the master coach would prepare them for the struggle that most surely lay ahead.

"Let me say a few words about Vincent Lombardi. I would

be remiss to leave him out. I coached him when I was line coach at Fordham. He was an assistant with Fordham later himself. He was an assistant at West Point and an assistant with the New York Giants. He did not get his first head coaching job until he was 46 years old. He went to the Green Bay Packers and the rest is in the history books. I would like to make this point to the young gentlemen present who are just coming up in the world. Vincent personified the power of perseverance. Why did Vincent Lombardi make it so big?

"He knew that in order to reach the top rung of the ladder, nothing comes easy. Ask yourself what has to be done to get to the top. Then ask yourself, am I willing to perform all of those unpalatable chores necessary to reach the top. If you aren't willing to do that, you had better work overtime on your self-discipline.

"We all *must* learn more about the values attached to self-discipline. It is a matter of national survival. Our whole society is at stake. I'd say that 95 percent of all the young men who leave college know what to do to attain success. But they do not wish to do what is necessary to get there. They become wishful thinkers. I tell you, this is a nation based on success. It is the only reason for a person to exist—to attempt to do his very best through hard work. There is no other path. You have to know all the things that have to be done if you are going to be a big time winner. Nothing of value can be achieved without desire, self-discipline, ambition, dedication, a willingness to sacrifice and a willingness to accept authority.

"We need much more self-discipline in America than we can hope to lay claim to. In our push-button age, people have lost the ability to control themselves and do without. Sure, our brilliant scientists have conquered the oceans and outerspace. We've sent many men to the moon. We've conquered the beasts in the forest. But we will never learn true happiness until we learn to conquer ourselves and those who are striving so diligently to conquer us.

"I realize that this fine banquet of yours has been founded entirely on sports and many of you might wish that I would stick entirely to sports in this talk. That isn't my plan. I'm going to talk about something that is more important than sports. Unless we do something—all of us working together as a team—to circumvent the enormous strides being made against America by our arch-rivals, the Communists, there might not be any sports. We might be doing what we're told to do by them. We might not be going to any church at all. We might possibly become slaves.

"I favor sports banquets because sports people can become a bastion of strength by simply banding together and deciding to be the leaders moving the country forward along paths that are tried and true. We must return the United States of America to its original position of power, pride, prestige and popularity. Our position is unique because the coaches and the players are absolutely idolized. And they should be. There has been a movement afoot in recent years to discredit athletes and coaches and athletics as a whole.

"Our immediate future problems are truly awesome. The fate of our society is literally in the balance. We must not allow the well-trained, dedicated matadors of Communism to march on our campuses and create anarchy.

"America must concentrate on the moral, the mental, the religious and the physical development of its youth because the Communists are aiming their most devastating shots at the young people of our great nation. We must have the courage, leadership and concentrated effort. Therefore we should all pledge to give up certain pleasures today so that we can be sure there will be a civilized world tomorrow. Our country needs a re-birth of those great principles upon which she was founded. If we go, the word freedom will be deleted from every single dictionary in the world. Please believe what I say, gentlemen. I am not an alarmist but I have procured information from the proper sources. I know what is happening.

"In 1917 Lenin wrote out a game plan in Moscow with only 20,000 followers. After 50 some-odd years over two billion people are living—no, existing—under Communistic slave rule. In his long hand-written game plan, which I have seen copies of, Lenin said that one day the Communists would take America like plucking over-ripe fruit from a limb. The campus riots, the sex orgies, the sex books, the wedges between parents and children, the proliferation of dope, the loosening of morals are all part of what he advocated.

"You athletes and coaches are heroes. Encourage youngsters to get hooked on sports and indoctrinate them in the fine old American values. Dedicate your lives to this goal and we'll survive—with God's help. The Commies must not, cannot and *shall not* succeed. America is a nation of winners! Winners!"

There was no need to even pronounce a benediction. The audience came crashing to its feet, shouting and cheering and clapping. This was a group made up largely of people who believed exactly as Leahy did, despite the savage persecution of their ancestors for their Mormon religion. They had received a triple jolt and they were high on the effects. They had heard religion, the uplifting effects of athletics and a clanging call to arms against the foreign devils. Leahy leaned forward against the lectern, his head slightly bowed, blazing with a special power that comes only to the righteous.

When the program ended, he moved smoothly through the crowd, shaking hands and saying something gracious. He paused with a couple of old friends by the door and then walked into the hallway. Chagrined, he reached out and grabbed the arm of a man near him. Leahy winced. The pain was becoming apparent again.

"Was I too strong in my remarks?" he asked.

"I don't happen to agree with very much of what you said. I think it is a different world than you once knew. And I'm afraid I'm not what you would call a conservative. I think we need new ideas for changing times. But if you honestly believe in what you said, then you have a duty to say it as strongly as you can." The answer seemed to satisfy him. His color was nearly spent and he seemed in instant danger of collapse, although his grin was still painted across his face.

"Do you know what I really am?" he asked, puffing badly.

"No, not really."

"I'm a football coach without a team," he said. "That is what drives me on."

EPISODE 5

"I am now convinced," answered Don Quixote, *"therefore let us waive that resentment of these injuries, which*

we might otherwise justly show; for considering these en-
chanters can make themselves invisible when they please, it is
needless to think of revenge. But I pray thee, if thou canst,
Sancho, and desire the governor of the castle to send me some
oil, salt, wine and rosemary that I may make my healing bal-
sam; for truly I want it extremely, so fast does the blood flow
out of wounds which the phantasm gave me just now,"—
Cervantes, who died never knowing a retired football coach.

CHICAGO

For days a rain squall had been lashing the towers
of Zenith, charging in off that most angry of lakes and turning the downtown canyons into canals. At O'Hare Airport,
airplanes were thundering in from the distant clouds at indecent intervals, their afterburners flickering like candles in
the darkening skies. They were so frequent that one hardly
landed before another was snarling at its tail.

Despite the lateness of the hour, despite the lateness of the
previous evening in Salt Lake, despite the incredible delay at
the ticket window, Frank Leahy was absolutely ebullient. He
had scored heavily the evening before and he was going on to
further triumphs on his home turf. What's more he was going
to see the statue of Our Lady shining down from that golden
dome. Notre Dame men never died. They try not to fade away.

When they finally brought the rent-a-car around, he tried
his best to leap into the front seat. South Bend was only 90
some miles away, a mere hour and a half romp through the
slums of Hammond, the surrealistic factory smog of Gary and
the corn-stubble fields of Indiana, where the candlelight keeps
burning bright through the sycamores that surround the Notre
Dame campus. There are only a few places that are truly
home. To Francis William Leahy, home was not Winner, S.D.
or Denver or Portland or San Diego or Los Angeles or any of
the countless places the man had lived. Home was Notre
Dame; a university that, save for its mystical power to seduce
young minds, is not so impressive as Harvard or Stanford or,
God love us, even Indiana.

Leahy was going home to witness a football game, to stand
around and let alumni who had not forgotten his classic in-
ability to lose, fawn all over him and to see, once more, some

33

of the lads who had played for him. Somehow he sensed his place in history. His own immortality had occurred to him.

"Wait until you see the University of Our Lady," he said, as his driver turned off the complicated tangle of freeways surrounding O'Hare and pointed the rented Ford LTD toward Indiana. "It will thrill you, even though you are an Episcopalian. I do not mean to be rude. I think that a Scots-Welsh Episcopalian is about as close as a man can come to being an Irish Catholic and still fail. Ah-hah-ah-hah-ah."

The corners of Leahy's mouth stretched out into a satisfied smile. He permitted himself an hour of blessed sleep as the car moved down the toll road, buzzing through the smothering atmosphere of Gary where the factory smoke blots out heaven. Here was a world that looked far distant from the mother planet. Daylight died. Great orange flames belched into the sky. Birds flew on radar. It was impossible to think of children growing up and never knowing that the world had a different tone than gray.

Suddenly the coach's eyelids began to quiver. He had been thinking of politics and the thoughts had been especially sweet. There was a time, by golly, when Frank Leahy stood so close to the White House that he could almost smell vicuna fur, which has a distinctive odor. His victory in Utah had been so complete that he could only think of what might be ahead. Somehow, he would save the nation. He had this vision.

"Have I ever discussed the 1956 Republican Convention?" he asked his biographer, who was struggling with the Illinois-Indiana highway system. "It was a wonderful moment in my life. It truly was."

There was Frank Leahy, himself, out playing golf on the Cherry Hills Country Club course in Denver back in those tranquil years when nobody dropped bombs on anybody and nobody believed that the President would lie, even about his golf score. There were still a few holes to go, but Leahy was talking with some men who absolutely swore they could make him a multi-millionaire in this oil stock deal they were proposing. He believed them, every single word, because they were honest businessmen and no American businessman would think of cheating anybody else. He believed them. He did. He did.

Then this telephone call came in. It was so urgent that FBI

agents came looking for the former football coach at Notre Dame. When they found him they drove him back to the clubhouse. "The President wants to speak to you," he was told. Being a model citizen, he did what seemed to be best.

"It's the White House calling, Coach," said one of the agents. "The President wants to talk to you." There was Ike on the phone talking about games the two men had played in the past. The President simply wanted to know what Leahy would be doing in a couple of weeks."

"Anything my President wants me to do," Leahy said, acting something like a right tackle who had just heard the word from Knute Rockne.

"I would like very much to have you make one of the seconding addresses at the Cow Palace in San Francisco when the Republican convention starts," he was told.

For days afterwards, he wondered why anyone would want him to second a nomination that was already a certainty. Leahy, struggling always with the problems of honesty, wondered if he hadn't done the wrong thing. He asked his wife Floss about the situation. He went to the library to see if there had been many great seconding speeches. There were none on record. All the way to the convention, while he labored over the speech, he kept wondering why Eisenhower had asked him, of all people. This was long before presidents started calling football coaches after games or sending in pet plays.

"I suddenly realized that Ike had suffered that heart attack near the end of his first term and he had successfully overcome it. He wanted me because he knew that I had collapsed at halftime in the 1953 game with Georgia Tech with a severe intestinal attack and I had lived to lead a productive life as a businessman. He wanted me there as proof that a man could overcome physical misfortune."

When Leahy arrived at Republican headquarters, he discovered that he was about to be programmed by a computerized press agent, who handed Leahy a specially prepared speech. He shook his head and employed the frown that used to turn defensive tackles into blobs of jelly in the old days at Notre Dame.

"This doesn't register with you, does it?" said the press agent brightly.

"You are a most perceptive lad," said Leahy.

The messy business being over, Leahy marched to the podium and, in his own classic style, compared Eisenhower to a quarterback who was starting the second half of an important football game. He pointed out to a national television audience that a quarterback quite often learned things in the first half that were invaluable in the second half. The only way to ensure success was to stay with the quarterback that got you ahead on the scoreboard at the half. So it should be with the presidency. America could not afford to squander Eisenhower's first half experience. Like so many of Leahy's speeches, it was so astonishingly banal that it was good. There wasn't a delegate who didn't come to his feet screaming with pleasure. Afterwards, Ike himself pressed Leahy's hand and told him there would be a place for him close to the president at the next inauguration. He had even fired up Eisenhower, an old Army halfback who had gone into the convention somewhat pessimistic about his chances for reelection.

"After he won renomination I was passing the hotel where he was staying," said Leahy. "I decided to say hello to him. His floor was crawling with, ah, secret service people. I went in and Mamie poured me a drink. The President was napping, but when he heard my voice he came out in his robe and had a drink with me. With me was one of California's leading amateur golfers. Well, Ike had two real hobbies—golf and football. Ike was a member of the Army team that played Notre Dame the first time. He didn't see action because of a broken ankle. He explained exactly how Army copied the Notre Dame passing formations—from Gus Dorais to Knute Rockne—to beat Navy later in the season.

"What a heart-warming gentleman he was. A most gracious man, that Ike. The day I could second his nomination was a proud moment. I felt that I had done something most important for my country. I felt like a true patriot."

As the freeway disappeared and the road to South Bend turned into a narrow rural lane, snaking its way through Indiana towns of no great importance except to the people living in them, Leahy's face dissolved into a satisfied grin, almost a smirk. Nobody ever expected an Irish cowboy from the Dakotas to rise so high, did they?

Suddenly the sight of a crossroad excited him. He sat straight up and laughed like an old warrior seeing the battlefield again after so many years. He pointed joyously and turned himself half around to watch the road fade behind the car. Despite the pain he chuckled.

"Ah, lad, that is a most famous road," he said. "Most famous! I was coaching at the University of Our Lady and we had an important game coming. Oh, they were all important, I guess. But this was more important than most. Floss had not seen me for several days. I used to stay overnight on campus and go to our house in Long Beach only after the games. At any rate, she wanted me home for some desperate reason. I was thinking about a special play we had discussed using. That is the turn-off for Long Beach. I was so lost in thought I didn't even see it. Ended up in Chicago before I realized what had happened. Ah, Floss was angry. That is a most famous road; most famous, indeed."

Leahy glanced at his watch, removed a plastic bottle from inside his coat pocket and dropped two pink pills on his tongue, swallowing them without water. With only trifles to occupy his mind, he could not molify the pain. As long as he was stimulated, exhilarated or excited, he could sublimate his physical agony. He was searching through his brain, looking for something to dwell upon.

"May I tell you a story, one I think you will find most amusing," he said. "My old coach, Knute Rockne, always had an answer for anything that was said to him. When I was a senior, I played right tackle until an injury put me out of football playing forever. The man who played next to me was a guard named, of all things, John Law. When it came time for John Law to take a job, he went to coach Rockne and asked him what opportunities were available.

" 'I have five letters from institutions that want football coaches,' Rockne said. 'I suggest you take the one at Sing Sing prison.' Law was absolutely speechless. Why, he asked. 'Because,' said Rock, 'every day of the year you'll have every policeman in America recruiting for you. You'll play all your games at home and you'll have your players around longer than four years. Most important, the alumni will never come back to haunt you.' Do you know that John Law took the job. Ooooooh, he was most happy there, too."

The country road disappeared. Now the car was moving past rows of sleazy franchised food joints with their plastic roofs and outdoor stools. The Notre Dame campus was only a few miles to the left. As the landscape changed from pizza parlors and hot dog stands to tree-lined fields that partially hid institutional buildings, Leahy leaned forward, squinting.

Out of the darkness of late afternoon, with the Indiana rain threatening to turn into snow, the golden dome of Notre Dame still managed to glitter above the tree tops, reflecting not the light of the sun, but some sort of mystic inner glow. Leahy gazed at it for several long seconds. It seemed as if he might weep, but he refused to. Instead, he slumped back against the seat, took a sigh so deep and soulful that it almost rattled the car.

"Ah, lad, did you ever see anything as beautiful as Our Blessed Mother up there on top of that dome?" he asked, not really expecting an answer. "The most beautiful Lady in the entire world. They have nothing in the Vatican as pretty as she."

Then he closed his eyes, like a man at prayer. Frank Leahy was home.

EPISODE 6

SOUTH BEND

High above the St. Joe River
Hordes of Poles and Greeks,
Fresh from Gary's fragrant steel mills
Fill the football weeks.

Letts and Slovenes, Montenegrins,
Magyars join the game,
And, with Czechs and swart Sicilians,
Fight for Notre Dame.

Dzisiaj, zvicezen, nem, nem soha,
War cries fill the air;
To be echoed in purest Gaelic
With Vendetta, guerre!

In the stands, one lone, thin student,
Keens his ancient name:
Aloysius Hugh Mulcahey,
Last Irishman at Notre Dame.

—Vincent Fagan, 1948.

It is one of history's cheerful little ironies that the priest who founded the University of Notre Dame du Lac was built like a defensive tackle, the only pity being that there was no such thing as American Football in the year 1836 when he made his decision to attend college. It is also interesting to note that Rev. Edward Fredrick Sorin was described in his time as having "the zeal of a fanatic, the practical sense of a businessman and the daring of an adventurer." In other words, he could have played for Frank Leahy if he had been born a century or so later.

He was, however, recruited, but not for sports. The Bishop of Vincennes, Indiana, was traveling through France attempting to find young men willing to become priests and aid in the church's work on what was then still the American frontier. Sorin was a pious giant with no prodding urge to leave his family's comfortable country home outside of LeMans. But the Bishop offered free room, board and tuition at the Congregation of the Holy Cross' seminary. Without even asking for laundry money, Sorin accepted.

Proving his courage, to say nothing of his sense of humor, he wrote that he and six other brothers, all of them recent seminary graduates, had crossed the Atlantic Ocean in steerage with, "a company of French comedians and German Protestants." The passage took 29 days and upon his arrival in New York, he dropped to his knees and kissed the ground, even though there weren't any Subway Alumni* present. Almost immediately, he set off for Indiana where he was granted a 900 acre tract near South Bend to build his university upon. He and seven other Holy Cross brothers, four of them predictably Irish, marched the final 250 miles through the snow on the last ten days of their trip.

"When we reached our destination everything was frozen," Sorin wrote. "Yet it was so beautiful. The lake, particularly, with its mantle of snow, was to us a symbol of the stainless purity of Our Lady. We stood in the clear bright moonlight

---

* New York Catholics who did not go to college, but actively rooted for Notre Dame because it was the nation's best known Catholic school. They came pouring out of the subway, pretending to be Notre Dame alumni, just like Rockne or Leahy or the Gipper.

and sang all the hymns to Our Blessed Virgin tnat we knew. Then, like little children, we ran from one end of the lake to the other, perfectly enchanted by the beauty of our new home."

For one hundred dollars, Father Sorin promised to feed a boy, wash and mend his clothes, give him medical attention and teach him the complete English course, which included spelling, reading, grammar, history, surveying and astronomy. If money was scarce, Sorin would take articles in barter. Acceptable items were hogs, grain, produce or furniture for the school.

Electives were extra. Latin was taught at the cost of an extra hog and if a boy wanted to learn to play the piano it was two large hogs. At one point, Sorin's capital was reduced to fifty cents. His ability to raise money would genuinely amaze a modern college president. Once, in desperation, he sent a group of students to the California gold fields, looking for a strike, which brought him a letter of censure from his superiors in France.

When the great fire of 1879 leveled every building on campus except the church, it was Father Sorin who grabbed a wheelbarrow and personally started the construction of a new five-story building. It was he who began the custom of seeking the favors of the Golden Virgin on the Golden Dome. It was he, even more than Knute Rockne or George Gipp or Frank Leahy, who was responsible for the school's uncompromising spirit.

"If all men fail me," Sorin wrote, "there is one treasury that is always full, the treasury of our Most Holy Mother. I have raised her aloft, so that men will know without asking why we have succeeded here. To that Lovely Lady, raised high on a dome—a Golden Dome—men may look and find the answer."

He was not a man totally devoid of sin. He had one naggy prejudice. Father Sorin had a tendency to be uneasy around the Irish. They were, he concluded, "not inclined to obedience." And so it came to pass that no one would ever think of Notre Dame without associating the school with the Irish, and not just any Irish, but the Fighting Irish. Fortunately for Father Sorin's sensitivities, he was a long time in heaven before the name came into general use.

40

"I believe that I was on the very last all-Irish team at Notre Dame," said Leahy. "Oh, there might have been a few non-Irish on that 1929 team. I believe that it was a most fortunate thing for Our Lady when lads of other ethnic backgrounds began to find their way to South Bend. It is my, ah, firm conviction that a heavy concentration of Irish is not conducive to tranquility. There is that strange quality about us. I read somewhere that a man wrote, 'The Great Gaels of Ireland are the men the Gods made mad, all their wars are happy and all their songs are sad.' If I'm quoting correctly that is a most apt observation.

"For instance, it is never too wise to concentrate too many Leahys in the same general area. Ooooooh, lad, very bad indeed. Once when Notre Dame was playing the University of Southern California at Los Angeles, we had a family reunion at the Hollywood Roosevelt.

"There was an abundance of strong spirits and quite a good deal of arguing. Finally, the house detective came around to investigate what someone had described as a full-scale riot. It wasn't quite that. However, I took him out into the hall and explained that my brothers and sisters and nieces and nephews and children were part of an actor's group and we were actually rehearsing for a play. He chose to believe me."

The car rattled down a dirt road leading toward the campus. Sycamores lined either side and beyond them the stalks of what had been a cornfield in the golden heat of an Indiana summer still persisted. The land was chilblained, getting ready for the temporary death of winter. The rain was falling faster now, but Leahy's enthusiasm was still intense.

"Ah, over there lies South Bend," he said, pointing beyond the campus. "I fear the town never truly understood many of my motives. They considered me aloof. Notre Dame football is a very social matter here. The head coach was expected to spend much of his time socializing—up until I took the job. Elmer Layden, who preceded me as coach, told me that it was most distracting. So I took my family to Long Beach, just outside of Michigan City, some 35 miles away. It was not a popular move, but I thought a house there would be better for my family. Perhaps I did the wrong thing. I doubt it."

There is nothing luxurious about the city of South Bend which slumps in Midwestern dreariness on both sides of a crook in the St. Joseph River, itself a curious and perverse stream that rises in Michigan, wanders into Indiana, enters the city from due east, departs to the north and then empties into Lake Michigan on the far side of the line. This freakish piece of geography long ago isolated the citizens from the rest of Indiana, turning them northward to Michigan which lies only five miles away. The main street is Michigan Street. The downtown area is called Michigana and only the license plates on the cars give a foreigner any indication that he is truly in Indiana.

In the 1920s, it somehow managed to avoid the hoodlum overflow from Chicago and turned instead to another form of civic disease. Despite the presence of the nation's best known Roman Catholic University, the city of South Bend was a center for the Ku Klux Klan. Less than four decades later, it was winning awards from the National Conference of Christians and Jews for its remarkable tolerance. Nobody has ever been able to adequately analyze the place. It is a mill town with culture, a Midwestern city with books.

Nothing is quite so important as Notre Dame, although most citizens resent the fact.

"There is more to South Bend than Notre Dame and its football team," is the popular thing to say. Yet, if Notre Dame were located in Vincennes or Delphi or Valparaiso, it is doubtful if the nation would be more than mildly conscious of the town's existence. And that is festering boils on the psyches of the people who have decided to spend their entire lives in this less-than-picturesque community. It is a form of reverse-snobbery not necessarily unique.

Putting down football is almost as much fun as attending the games. "The average Notre Dame football player has an interesting face," an amateur anthropologist once said. "There is just the trace of the Cro-Magnon and Upper Paleolithic which revives itself in Ireland, coming through the later-arrived Mediterraneans and Celts."

Football in South Bend is similar to skiing in St. Moritz or sun-bathing in Miami—it is the inevitable curse or delight, and possibly both. There is no evading it. It knits the town in thousands of ways, brings hundreds of thousands of extra dollars to South Bend every fall and, socially, is an asset comparable to the Mardi Gras in New Orleans. The brief football season takes care of nearly everybody's social obligations for the entire year. The presence of the head coach in one's home or an acknowledgment that he knows your name is extremely important.

Knute Rockne walked the streets of downtown South Bend frequently, smiling from behind that gnomish face and being, well, quite gracious. He opened practices to the public and there were afternoons when Cartier Field looked like a picnic ground. There are still citizens old enough to recall him shooting pool with the boys down at Hullie and Mike's on Michigan Street. They expected Frank Leahy, his prize disciple, to be exactly the same way. After all, here was a man of warmth and charm and humor. Trouble was, Leahy was also a man of fanatical determination. When he would not attend their parties or chat with them on street corners, they were openly bitter.

They read of his humor, but they rarely witnessed it. All they knew was that he worked in a monkish cell in the basement of a freshman dormitory with a picture of his patron saint, Rockne, above his head. He labored well into the morning hours and then slept overnight in a firehouse dormitory. He lived on the shores of Lake Michigan. There were occasional parties there, but only a precious few of the South Bend super-elite were ever invited.

They would have hated him completely, except for one thing. He was a winner, a coach every bit as good as Rockne. When he fell, there were not that many tears in South Bend.

The car rolled through the slippery street beside the stadium where a huge sign advertised 1972 home games. Leahy looked at his watch and swallowed some more pills. He sighed unhappily. The great surge of excitement had passed and the dark dog of melancholy was sitting on his soul.

"Ah, yes, lad," he said. "They expected me to imitate Rockne. But it wasn't possible. If I thought I could have, I would. I mean that. But some men are flamboyant. Others are plodders. If you are a plodder you are a plodder. Rockne was a power in the town. I had no interest in that sort of avocation. I was at Notre Dame to win football games. 'Restore the glory of Rockne,' they told me when I was hired. I did just that. South Bend is a town with many, many cliques. It is difficult to please them all. Do you know that I was even criticized for pronouncing the name of the school 'Notruh Dawm' instead of 'Noter Dame.' I wonder what difference it ever made."

He sat slumped forward in the front seat for several long moments, his mind wandering backwards in time, darting in and out, totally unstuck from any logical sequence. Suddenly Leahy sat up and pointed at two Notre Dame coeds walking past in yellow slickers. His lips moved upwards in a smile. His mind was clicking furiously.

"Ah, lad. Look at that. Ooooooh, I wish that they had been here when I was football coach for Our Lady. Ooooooh, can you imagine how wonderful it would have been to tell those fine young lads I was recruiting that the University of Notre Dame had young ladies enrolled? Oooooh, that was my biggest difficulty . . . trying to explain what it would be like on a campus with nothing but boys. Ah, lad, I was born far, far too soon."

EPISODE 7

SOUTH BEND

For several hours, a bunch of the boys have been whooping it up at Randall's Inn, a nondescript but wildly popular motel located on the perimeter of the Notre Dame campus. The lobby is sparse except for a wall that is crowded with pictures of former players and ex-coaches. The restaurant is fake French provincial, which would undoubtedly distress Father Sorin. The bar is small, uncomfortable and difficult to enter on the evening before an Irish home game. There is one saving grace. On the wall are the coats-of-arms of such fine Celtic gentlemen as Frank Leahy, Dan Shannon, Terry Brennan, Terry Hanratty and George Connors.

At no other university do former players and coaches consider it such a holy mission to return at least once or twice a year to attend a home game. They gather in a fraternal group, usually at Randall's Inn, to consume numerous heroic mugs of strong drink and contribute to the legends and mythology of Notre Dame by repeating the same stories over and over until it seems that they were not actually playing football, but pursuing the Holy Grail.

In the center of this particular gathering stood the eternally imposing figure of Moose Krause, his head bent forward to catch the words of shorter human beings. Now the athletic director, Krause, as an undergraduate was something of a Notre Dame rarity, a fine football tackle who somehow was permitted to become an All-American basketball center. Standing before him was Ara Parseghian, inheritor of the shards remaining from the two football Camelots built by Rockne and Leahy. The evening had progressed to the point where it was proper to drink to the brilliance of this third great Notre Dame head coach.

"I have worked with three genius coaches," said Krause, whose face and voice are hauntingly similar to those of the late actor Paul Douglas. "First there was Rock. Then there was Leahy. And here's to the other one . . . Ara Parseghian."

The manly toasts had barely stopped echoing when Gerry Cowhig leaned over and touched Johnny Mazur's arm. "Hey, The Coach is here," he whispered. "He's in the motel and he's coming down later." One former player turned and whispered to another. There was John Lattner smiling and Johnny Lujack shaking his head and even Leon Hart, who smarted under the discipline more than anyone else, chuckling to himself.

"It's the Man," said Krause. "The Coach is here."

Parseghian's lips tightened out into thin white lines. To be the head coach at the University of Notre Dame is a wonderful thing. To be successful is to invite canonization. No coach since Leahy has done so well as Parseghian, this darkly handsome French-Armenian with the enigmatic expression. Yet, despite a brilliant record of achievement, he is regarded as only the third best coach in the school's history. It could only happen at Notre Dame, somebody once told him, and that was little comfort. Football coaches suffer from the sin of pride.

"Frank's dedication to Notre Dame rubbed off on one of his sons," said Krause, shifting the topic swiftly from great coach No. 3 to great coach No. 2. "I'll never forget that Jimmy

Leahy. Was he something? He was a great big red-headed guy with a heart you couldn't believe. He was as amiable as he was slow. But he worked his big tail off.

"I don't think there ever was a more amiable, hard-working kid on the Notre Dame football team than Jimmy Leahy. He knew damn well he was out of his league, but he wasn't going to admit it. He wanted to prove to his father that he could hang in there at Notre Dame. For four years, he never missed a practice. He was like that cliche—the first man on the field and the last man off. They gave him a suit and he waited and waited and waited. He was a senior and we closed our home schedule with Georgia Tech that year. Poor Jimmy hadn't logged a single minute of game time.

"With about three minutes to go, Ara finally sent Jimmy Leahy in to play right tackle, his father's old position. He did alright. When the gun went off, there was Jimmy grabbing the game ball. The officials tried to yank it away and he fought them off. In the dressing room, the manager tried to take it from him. He absolutely refused. That damn Jimmy took it into the shower with him. Can you imagine the dedication of a kid who waited four years just to get a Notre Dame game ball?

"Afterwards I asked him why he had been so adamant. He said, 'I'm going to show my father that I was good enough to play for Notre Dame even if it was only for three minutes. He'll respect me now.' You know we've had great players at Notre Dame and nobody could decide who was the greatest. We've had a lot of fine players and some excellent mediocre ones. But when it comes to really bad players, I'd have to say that Jimmy Leahy was one of the greatest bad players in the school's history. He never surrendered. He worked harder for those three minutes than most players do for a full season."

Even Hart grew sentimental. He recalled an afternoon at Yankee Stadium when college football was so big that hardly anybody knew the National Football League existed. The score at halftime was Notre Dame, 6, and North Carolina, 6. This was totally unsatisfactory to Leahy who came swirling into the dressing room like a Dakota sandstorm. It was a dramatic moment, one that Leahy absolutely gloried in.

"Leon Hart. Oooooh, Leon Hart. Some day you will cause the Pope himself to leave the church. Oooooh, you do not deserve to represent Our Lady. Perhaps somebody else should take your place. Do you think that might be best? And you, John Mazur. Ooooooh, John Mazur! Why don't you go back to the Pennsylvania coal mines where we found you? That's where they could use another jackass. Herb Jones! Oooooh, Herb Jones! Cancel the first class transportation back to South Bend because we are going to scrimmage all day tomorrow at Bear Mountain.

"Give Leon Hart seventy-five cents for meal money and let him start hitchhiking home right now. I see absolutely no hope for his immortal soul. Let us now bow our heads and pray to Our Lady for forgiveness, for we have disgraced her terribly."

The second half was thoroughly brutalizing. Notre Dame, on a religious crusade, scored over 40 points and North Carolina never got near the scoreboard. It was a dazzling example of Leahy's ability to mix recriminations with Catholicism and come out a winner. Where Rockne simply used naked emotionalism, stirred neatly with a soupçon of schmaltz, Leahy somehow managed to convince his players that they were defenders of the Faith, protecting Notre Dame against the Infidel hordes. The Muslims were always at the gates of Vienna. And the One True Church was in desperate danger.

"One year Frank was sick and I had to bring the team to Southern California," said Krause. "I wanted to look good. I didn't get that many chances to be head coach. The last time it had happened I got so involved in a Leahy-style pep talk that I sent the boys out onto the field without telling them the starting lineup. Frank never forgave me. This second time, I got a call from The Coach in the dressing room at the Los Angeles Memorial Coliseum. He dictated a starting lineup just in case I forgot. I committed sheer heresy. I eliminated one of his starting halfbacks and used this little greyhound from Texas named Coy McGee.

"Well, the kid was sensational. He went 80 yards with the kickoff, but the touchdown was called back. He repeated it with another touchdown run of about 80 yards and had a tremendous afternoon. Notre Dame won big. Right afterwards, I called Frank on the long distance telephone. I figured he'd be happy because we looked so good. I was actually hoping for a word of praise for myself."

Instead, Leahy's first words were: "Who in the hell is this Coy McGee you stuck in my starting lineup?"

There is no end to the Leahy stories, said former quarterback Johnny Lujack. They said he was a dull, stilted, humorless coach, but his critics didn't spend that much time around him. Oh, this was a very funny man, not only in words but in action. His sense of droll irony was incredible.

"In that damn scoreless tie with Army back in 1946, our Bob Livingston missed a tackle," said Lujack. "I was as high as anybody and I screamed at him, 'Livingston, you son-of-a-bitch.' I just let it slip. It didn't mean a damn thing. But there was The Coach and he was angry at me. I could feel the heat up my spine like a blow torch."

Leahy roared at his quarterback, cursing him for his disloyalty to a colleague. It was an unthinkable act, committed in the blazing heat of a holy war. The coach was indignant.

"Another profane outburst like that, Jonathan Lujack, and you will be asked to disassociate yourself from our fine Catholic University. You might well remember that when I recruited you, I promised your parents that you would have a splendid Catholic upbringing." Thoroughly ashamed, Lujack slumped backward and pulled the hood of his parka up over his head. On the next play, Livingston did exactly the same thing. Lujack bit his lip, but Leahy looked like a man ready to swoon. Turning toward the bench he yelled, "Gentlemen, I fear that Jonathan Lujack is right about Robert Livingston."

Now the love feast was at its height. Every injury suffered years earlier was pleasure. Every insult was now an act of affection. Frank Leahy was more than a coach, he was a stern father to be hated and resented in his time and loved and admired in retrospect. Gone was the pain, lost in the turmoil of the post graduate years. Given enough time, pain becomes pleasure. Survival does such things to the male animal. Perhaps this is what coaches mean when they claim that they actually build character.

"How about the time I fumbled five times against Michigan State?" asked Johnny Lattner. "What did the coach do to me? He went around mumbling, 'Oooooooh, Jonathan Lattner. Oooooooh, you heretic, Jonathan Lattner. What am I to do with you? Oooooooh, Jonathan Lattner you should be denied the final rites.' He had an unusual way of letting you know that he was unhappy. He was a father figure and he was threatening you with rejection."

What Frank Leahy did would be considered sadistic now. Chances are, Johnny Lattner considered it so back in the early 1950s. It simply wasn't fashionable to talk about a coach that way. The coach took a football and taped it to Lattner's hand. He made his finest running back spend an entire week that way, trying to spoon soup into his mouth with his hand wrapped to a Notre Dame ball. Lattner slept that way, walked that way, went to class that way and, if he had a lady friend at the time, had to kiss her goodnight that way. In a later era, he would have written an angry book condemning Leahy as a fiend from hell. Instead, he enjoyed it.

"So I looked stupid," he said. "I was in college. It was a time for looking stupid and I didn't care. They knew who I was and they knew what I had done and everybody took it pretty well. I wasn't resentful. At least, I know I'm not now. I didn't fumble any more and I won the Heisman Trophy because of The Coach. It hasn't hurt me since I graduated, winning the trophy."

Everyone roared with laughter. Like Gen. George S. Patton, Jr., it was best to take Frank Leahy in the context of the past. War is hell at the time. But when it ends, everyone gratefully remembers the funny things that happened back at the base. No matter how thin the humor may have seemed at the time, it helped ease the grimness of the moment. Therefore, it was the sweetest humor ever invented.

"Don't let The Coach fool you," said an elderly newspaperman from Chicago, who was sinking slowly into a vat of booze. "He was great to the press only after he left Notre Dame. There is a whole generation of writers who think he was the nicest, most kindly man who ever coached a football team. But when he was here, he could be a real rotten son-of-a-bitch. I don't think he did it on purpose exactly, he was just being Frank Leahy, head coach at Notre Dame and he wasn't ready to accommodate you. Not that many writers—at least guys who weren't Notre Dame sucks—were that fond of him."

"Oh, from all evidence I've uncovered, he could be quite candid with the press," he was told. "What makes you think he wasn't?"

"He was an uncooperative son-of-a-bitch. That's what he

was. If he had coached at any other school, he wouldn't have got away with the stuff he did at Notre Dame. There were at least two trips to USC when he stayed inside his drawing room compartment on the train and talked with his family and his big buddy Fred Miller. That's because Fred was president of Miller High Life brewery and Leahy was impressed with big shit guys with a lot of money. You know that after his team clinched the national championship in 1947, he didn't even go down to the train station to see his 'lads' off on their return trip to South Bend."

Still, there are stories of Leahy openly exposing pre-game strategy in front of the press as he did before one memorable match against Purdue. The writers had gathered for a final conference and he acted as if they were all Notre Dame alumni who wouldn't reveal a secret if somebody was shoving burning bamboo under their finger nails.

"Against Purdue we plan to use a unique defensive shift. It will be the first time we have ever employed it," he said. "When Notre Dame is on defense, Leon Hart will shift from right end to right tackle and Bill Fisher will go from left guard to left tackle. We will use the following configurations on defense which we have not used previously this season. I hope you understand this."

With a gracious smile, he excused himself and left the room, leaving writers stunned.

Someone stopped him in the hall later on and asked him what he would have said if Gordon Graham, sports editor of the Lafayette paper and a notorious Purdue partisan, had been present in the hall. Would he have revealed so much of Notre Dame's strategy? At stake was Frank Leahy's integrity and he answered as if he had just encountered someone who wished to blow up the golden dome. He lost all semblance of a smile. His hooded eyes almost disappeared. His lips faded back into a snarl. All those Celtic furies were stomping on his soul.

"I most certainly would have," he said, his voice dropping lower and lower with every word. "I consider Gordon Graham to be a most honorable person and an honest newspaperman. Perhaps I should reevaluate my estimation of some of his colleagues."

Now two decades had passed and nostalgia was heavy on

everyone's brain. The sins of the past are easily forgotten. The Coach was upstairs, swallowing pills, getting ready to join his fellow alumni. Nobody could recall any real grief, only a bit of transitory suffering that didn't seem all that important in retrospect.

"When I used to cover Notre Dame and he was the head coach, I always had a problem," said Joe Doyle, sports editor of *The South Bend Tribune*. "When I saw him coming I never knew whether to say hello or genuflect."

"What did you do?"

"I played it safe . . . I did both," he said, wobbling like a man trapped in the aspic of history. What else could an honest journalist, with a sense of timing, do?

EPISODE 8

*"Know then, Sancho, I was born in this iron age to restore the age of gold. And I am the man for whom heaven has restored the most dangerous and glorious adventures," said Don Quixote. "There rides the Knight of the Sun. That is he, they will cry, who vanquished in single combat the huge giant Brocabruno, surnamed of the invincible strength. If some notice be taken of knight-errantry and the feats of their squires, yours will surely come in for a share,"—*Cervantes, who probably would have covered Notre Dame for the *Chicago Sun-Times* except for an accident of birth.

SOUTH BEND

In his hotel room, Frank Leahy was sputtering angrily as he attempted to prop himself up and tie his bow tie at the same time. He was mindful of the fact that those were his lads downstairs waiting for him, even though most of them were around the age he was when circumstances forced him to leave Notre Dame. It would never do for them to see The Coach aged and infirm. So he primped like a coed getting ready for the first prom of the year. His pills and sundry medicines were scattered all over the bureau, the night stand and the lavatory.

"Ooooh, what a pleasure it is to see all of those familiar

faces again," he said. "That is what has made my life so worthwhile. Those lads down there are a constant source of good in their communities. They provide real leadership. That is very important to our country. Our society is changing and not, I suspect, for the better. It is up to us to restore what went before."

Leahy was preparing himself mentally and spiritually for another patriotic speech, which had become a compulsion with him. A few years earlier they had held a Frank Leahy testimonial dinner in the new field house and auditorium on campus. It had been a smashing event. Tears poured from every eyeball in the place. The warm radiance of Notre Dame was everywhere. There were so many sentimental, funny stories being told that it seemed like an Irish wake. The torrent of praise for The Coach flowed stronger and faster. Then at last came that moment of fierce emotion.

Up toward the microphone strode Frank Leahy, his teeth shimmering in the spotlight, his eyes bright as twin comets. For ten minutes, he spoke of the beauty and glory of the university they all loved. He eulogized Rockne and told wonderfully witty tales of his days as a coach. The audience was charmed, hypnotized, enthralled. Then, abruptly, Leahy turned to his sermon and the evening grew uncomfortable. Not everyone yearned for the old virtues quite as strongly as The Coach did. Afterwards, there was grumbling at the bar. Frank Leahy had never truly learned the proper way to make people love him. He would never be Rockne no matter how long he lived, just as Parseghian would never be Leahy no matter how hard he worked.

To coach football at Notre Dame is to seek perfection and whoever seeks perfection is liable to perish in the process. It is impossible to stare into the sun and not go blind, as Frank Leahy had already discovered but was too proud to admit.

"Let me tell you how intense my fidelity to Our Lady was," he said. "When I was in the Navy in 1944 I received a letter in the South Pacific from a man named Mickey McBride.

"This fine Irish gentleman had been awarded the new Cleveland franchise in the All-America Conference. He was making what, at the time, was a fabulous offer. If I would coach the Cleveland team, McBride would give me a five-year contract calling for $35,000 a year. At the time I was on leave from a Notre Dame contract that was paying me $13,000 a year for the three years after the war's end.

"McBride was also offering me 15 percent of his football corporation. If I had accepted I would have roughtly a $3 million interest in a National Football League team. In addition, he offered me so many fringe benefits that I did not believe he was serious. He said he would send Floss and my children $1,000 on the first day of every month until the war was over. All I had to do was sign the contract.

"I realized that McBride's offer had to be genuine, because I had known his son at Notre Dame and knew the lad to be a person of high character. I was also aware of the family's vast wealth. I was much impressed, so I took the letter to my commanding officer. I told him I'd like a chance to negotiate with McBride personally. He told me that I had a one week's leave to go home. He said, 'When the war is over I hope you'll have some free tickets for the old admiral.' I made a vow that I would."

Leahy begged rides on military airplanes and headed for his home in Long Beach, Indiana. Roughly an hour after his arrival, he received a telephone call from the Rev. John J. Cavanaugh, president of the University of Notre Dame. It seems there had been some insane rumor that Leahy had flown home from the South Pacific in order to sign with a team in this new professional football league everyone was talking about. Would The Coach like to come down to South Bend and talk about the situation?

They spent the entire afternoon walking from one end of the campus to the other, not unlike Father Sorin and his colleagues when they first set eyes upon the site. Finally, Father Cavanaugh pointed to the Lady on the Dome. It was a sentimental moment no 1930 Hollywood movie could even capture.

"Our Lady has blessed you and she trusts you," said the priest. "I know in her sacred heart she knows that you are here at Notre Dame to help young boys become fine Catholic gentlemen. I don't blame you, Frank, for considering this offer; $35,000 is a lot of money. It is the opportunity of a lifetime. However, if you return to Notre Dame and work as astutely as you did before the war, you will establish a reputation no pro coach could match.

"I will also discuss matters with some of our more affluent

alumni and I can guarantee you that you will have excellent financial opportunities outside football. There are many things that can be done. There is really no limit to what you can do at Notre Dame and your heart must be sure that you have the eternal blessing of Our Lady. As for the University's part, your salary will be raised to $15,000 and we will give you a ten-year contract."

With tears streaming down his cheeks, Frank Leahy placed his hands in the hands of Father Cavanaugh and took an awesome vow. "I pledge that I will go undefeated for ten years. I pledge that to Our Lady and to you, Father John. I promise you I will not take that professional offer."

The next morning, Leahy drove to Chicago and had breakfast with McBride and Arch Ward, the promotional genius who also seemed to have time to be sports editor of the *Chicago Tribune*. It was Ward who conceived the baseball All-Star game, the College All-Star game and now he was working on the foundation of a second professional football league, placing himself some 16 years ahead of Bud Adams, Lamar Hunt and Barron Hilton.

"You have been most generous, Mr. McBride, but I have decided that I shall spend the rest of my coaching career at Notre Dame," said Leahy. "I want to thank you so much for thinking so highly of me."

McBride was openly distressed. He had come looking for the best man he could find, thinking surely that he would get him. He had no idea that a golden statue on a golden dome would defeat him. "Haven't I offered you enough money?" he asked. "I'll give you $50,000 a year for ten years. Would that do it? Write down the salary you want. I'll sign the check."

"It's really not the money," said Leahy, who at the time was in his mid-30s and hardly wealthy. "We can't negotiate because I have promised Father John Cavanaugh that I would stay at Notre Dame and serve Our Lady. If I were in your place, I would now turn toward Paul Brown, who was head coach at Ohio State before the war."

"Who the hell is Paul Brown?" asked McBride. "I've never heard of him."

"If you think I am a worthy coach, then you will be pleased by Paul Brown. We are one and the same in our philosophies toward the game. If you wanted Frank Leahy, you will find yourself cheated not one bit by, ah, Paul Brown. I find him exceptional in every way."

Now Leahy was standing in his hotel room, gulping pills and taking injections. A whimsical thought passed across his mind.

"It is probably just as well that Paul took the job instead of me," he said. "I think Cleveland Browns has a very nice sound. Very euphonious. But I don't think the public would have bought the Cleveland Leahys. I often wonder why Paul let them name the team after him. Somehow it just doesn't seem right."

Leahy's eyes disappeared inside his thoughts. When the war was over, he did return to Notre Dame and he did, indeed, try to go undefeated; a fanatic approach to the game that destroyed his health and, some say, his ability to reason properly. There is no question that Leahy suffered severe emotional disturbances over losing a single ball game. By the spring of 1953, his final season at Notre Dame, there were those who were betting which would go first, his nervous system or his body. It was a photo finish and Leahy admitted it.

"When I started my ten-year contract," he said, still brushing his hair back. "Oooooh, I meant to go undefeated. I saw no reason in the world why we should not aim toward that horizon. Was not the University of Our Lady worthy of such a sacrifice? I thought so. I could have gone through those ten years without losing a single game. It could have happened."

He paused as tears began to form. The holy quest had been cut short by nonbelievers, people who didn't honestly understand what hard work, sacrifice and discipline truly meant. There was Our Lady on that sacred dome. What else could a young man find that was finer or more noble?

"If certain factions within the University had not cut our recruiting so drastically, I firmly believe that ten undefeated seasons would have been possible," he said, near to sobbing. "We put together four undefeated seasons—1946, 1947, 1948 and 1949—and we were so close to our quest, only six more years. It could have been accomplished. But they ruined our recruiting in 1950 and I could see what was ahead. I tell you this: I nearly lost my religion. I could not believe that Our

Lady wanted anything less than perfection. I could not believe that we could honor her any other way than to remain the finest example to young boys that we could be.

"This was not entirely for Catholicism. I had many Protestant and a few Jewish boys on my teams. I recall one fine morning when I saw four of my best Protestant players at Mass with the rest of the team. Only the Episcopalian genuflected, because his people were used to such things. But they were there, just the same. They loved Our Lady, too, it would seem.

"I was so despondent that I slumped over in my office after the victory in our final game of 1949 over Southern Methodist. I was trying so hard to collect my thoughts. I wanted to resign because I knew what was coming and I knew that if I continued on the path mapped out for me by certain members of the faculty, I would only bring disgrace to Our Lady. So I tried to think how my resignation would sound in the press. I planned to call Father John and then call Arch Ward and let them know how things were going to turn out. I wanted to leave. My faith was nearly ruined.

"There is no difference to me between serving Our Lady and winning a football game. That may be old-fashioned, but that is the way I am and that is the way I was. Anyway, there I was sitting there, getting ready to let somebody else do my job when our center Jerry Groom saw me and came into my room. It was a wonderful moment, one I shall always consider strongly to be among my finest."

Groom put his arm around The Coach's neck and reminded him of a promise not kept. When Leahy came around to the Groom family home, he said, "You need not worry, lad, I will coach Notre Dame until you are a senior." It sounded just great and Jerry Groom signed a letter of intent.

"Coach, you promised me, my mother and my father that if I went to Notre Dame instead of Iowa, you would be my coach until I graduated. I considered you to be an honest man. The way I figure it, you owe me at least one more year because I'm only a junior. Will I see you at spring practice?"

Leahy recalled the incident with a touch of sentiment. This was obviously one of his favorite athletes and he wasn't going to hold him at arm's length. So The Coach told him not to worry. A vow was a vow and no Notre Dame man would ever go back on his word. So Frank Leahy showed up at spring practice.

"A very wonderful man, Jerry Groom. He knew he had a problem after he left Notre Dame and he defeated it with utmost courage," Leahy said, filled with pride. "I prayed for him, do you know that? It wasn't necessary. He had the inner strength necessary to defeat what was ailing him. He is one of the finest people who ever played for me. I like to think that I somehow helped. He is an inspiration to me, even unto this day. It restores my faith.

"There is only one thing that troubles me about that time. If I *had* quit Notre Dame, I would have been 60-3-5 and nobody has ever had a record like that. I suppose my vanity is showing. That is not gracious.

"I could not quit as I had planned to. I had made a promise to Jerry Groom. More than that I had made a promise to his mother and his father. I think that because I did not waiver in the face of the problem that Jerry Groom did the same thing when he was faced with a problem that most men would have given in to. Oooooooh, I do not mean to sound sanctimonious, but I think moral strength has to start someplace, does it not? If I had quit on Jerry Groom, don't you think it would have been easy for Jerry Groom to quit on Jerry Groom. That is the question he made me face and, in the end, that is the same question he had to face himself. Oooooh, I am most proud of that one particular lad. A fine lad. Ah, yes, fine indeed, by anyone's measure."

Downstairs, the talk was still concentrated around Leahy and the Glory Years at Notre Dame. In his time he was criticized. But he had made the remarkable mistake of outliving his time. A few people could actually forgive him his one greatest sin. He came so close to a dramatic, Rockne-style death, but he evaded it.

"Every guy on that bench at the Georgia Tech game was weeping when they carried him out," said assistant coach Joe McArdle. "They thought he had suffered a heart attack. They called over the public address system for Father Edmund Joyce, now the Vice-President of Notre Dame. They asked him to give Frank the last rites. It looked that close. That was the first time they gave him the holy oils. It wasn't the last. The next morning he was as feisty as he had ever been. The evening before at St. Joseph's Hospital we were all clustered around and nobody knew whether he would live or not. But on the morning, he was his same old self.

"The oil from the final sacrament was still on his forehead when he looked up at me and said, 'Joe, you forgot the rule about allowing photographers into the dressing room after a game. And what the hell happened with Georgia Tech's belly series? The officiating was just awful and you never said a word. What about those pictures of John Lattner in the dressing room? I can't imagine you letting something like that happen. Oooooh, Joseph McArdle, we have been together so long that I cannot believe you would be so careless.'"

McArdle shook his head. There never was a person quite so demanding as Frank Leahy and there never was a person quite so correct in his demands. It was humiliating, disturbing and precise. But, dammit, Leahy was always right. He had this nasty habit of finding the only mistake an otherwise proud subordinate made and bringing the blunder to the man's attention. Details were his pride, his passion and his only grounds for serious criticism.

"Lad," he said to a man who was the same age as his 37-year-old son, "you will have to assist me because there aren't any elevators in this motel, which is a fine establishment. After I reach the bottom of the main staircase, you must permit me to move on my own strength. Is that agreed upon? Anything else would be a perversion of all that I stand for. Those lads knew me as a firm, strong man. For their sake, I can be nothing else. You will help me, won't you?" A show of valor was somehow still necessary.

Frank Leahy could barely stand. He knew that. He accepted that. His soul would not permit him to be an invalid. Another man would be home in Lake Oswego watching the Oregon sun slip into the ocean. Absolutely nothing would keep him from the fulfillment of this task.

"Ooooh, Jonathan Lattner, you have displeased our Sacred Mother by getting chubby around the jowls. Ooooooh, Leon Hart, you have disgraced all of us by not keeping your weight down. Oooooooooh, Leon Hart, you will cause the archbishop himself to toss and turn at night because you have let yourself get out of shape. Ooooooh, what a blessing it is that your fine mother and father do not have to see what has happened to you this evening. They would reject the fine Catholic education that I promised I would see that you received."

Everyone waiting in that side pocket of Randall's Inn expected that kind of treatment. They were conditioned for it. Once they loathed it and now, looking backwards, they seemed to love it, even Leon Hart. "Did you really play for Leahy at Notre Dame? Was he the son-of-a-bitch they all said he was? Did you really feel some special kind of fire? How in hell did you ever survive?" White men call it heart. Black men call it soul. Mexicans call it machismo. It is all the same thing, except that Leahy called it paying the price. Who cares?

EPISODE 9

SOUTH BEND

Most of the players were prepared for something stronger and sterner than themselves. They remembered Frank Leahy as a dark, enigmatic figure in a trench coat and a gray fedora hat, walking up and down the sidelines with his personal secretary, Francis Sullivan, transcribing every word he said, lest some great chunk of wisdom be lost to Notre Dame forever. Nobody expected that he would decompose. This was the indestructible man. He taught everybody to play beyond their endurance. He made everybody think they were ten-feet tall. He wanted everyone to believe they weighed 310 pounds and could move like small insects.

Leahy himself was a congenital pessimist. Not even during the years of trumpets and drums did he actually think that Notre Dame had a chance to win a single game. He was convinced that every other team was stronger than his.

"That was not an act," said Moose Krause. "When Frank was the head coach of football, he could take another team and mentally coach it to defeat Notre Dame. He was like a great chess master. He knew exactly how he could be beaten. It always amazed him that the other coach could not find Notre Dame's weaknesses. The writers laughed at him and the public said that he was a weepy fool. But you know, if Frank Leahy had been coaching the other teams, Notre Dame wouldn't have won that many games. That's how great a coach he was."

When Leahy turned the corner and pushed open the door there wasn't a man inside who didn't have to suppress the urge to gasp. Only in the center of his eyes did he look the same. His face had shrunken and grown yellow to match the votive candles in the great church from where they buried Rockne. Leahy moved like a man with wires leading from his fingers to some invisible hand in the sky. Where once his walk had been forceful, it was now delicate to the point of absolute artificiality.

"Oh, God," said one of the players. "He looks like death."

One by one and then, swiftly, in a mass, they moved to embrace him. One of them reached out as if to support him and then pulled his hands away for fear that The Coach would reprimand him. Leahy walked through them with grace, saying something that would please each of them. They were his lads, every damn one of them. He had made them, just as they had made him. He had taught them what it was like to chase success and they had learned better than anyone else. Down inside their brains they had all modeled themselves after Leahy. No matter what they did the rest of their lives, they would always be a part of Frank Leahy. In this special respect, he was indeed a builder of character—his own! There wasn't a man in the entire room who wasn't, to some small extent, the possessor of a fragment of Leahy's personality. They imitated, without thinking, his mannerisms, his strange and stilted mode of speech and they all talked of great goals yet unrealized.

"Jesus," said Czarobski, "whenever we get a few drinks in us, we all sound like The Coach. He's the most infectious man I've ever known."

Over in the corner stood Lou Rymkus, who left the coal mines of southern Illinois where Slavic bodies were worth $18.50 a week in a prime market. His family moved to the stockyard district of Chicago. He went to Tilden High, which is where Frank Leahy rescued him.

"That man was like a father to me when I was here at Notre Dame," he said. "I never really had a father. Whatever there is that's good about me, I owe to Frank Leahy. I mean that.

I could have become a complete bum if it weren't for him. He taught me how to act decent in public. He gave me a reason for wanting to live right. I wonder how many guys there are that owe their whole existence to him. He's a great man, the greatest I've ever known. I played tackle for him, then went on to play with the Washington Redskins when he went into the Navy, but I've never forgotten him. If I could be one person other than Lou Rymkus, I would want to be Frank Leahy. And that's a tear you see in my eye. That's how much I admire him."

Now Leahy was over in the corner, talking with Parseghian. They laughed together, knowingly. Only an ex-coach can understand the real trauma a present coach lives through, day-by-day. Afterwards, Leahy shook his hands.

"A most worthy man," he said. "Ara is a most worthy man."

"Glad you approve of him," Leahy was told.

"I do," he said. "I am also quite jealous."

"Why?"

"Because he is head football coach at Notre Dame," he said. "And I used to be."

EPISODE 10

SOUTH BEND

Shortly before game time, the rain cloud hunched off toward the horizon, leaving the Indiana landscape fresh and clean. In the front row of the press box Frank Leahy accepted the love and adoration due him as a former Notre Dame coach. Sitting in the cold sunshine, he somehow looked younger. His eyes were brighter and he talked as if he had never left. His mind was swamped with memories.

"One of the first things I did when I came here was to cut the squad from around 75 men to about 50," he said. "Oooooh, it was the correct thing to do. It is shameful to bring too many lads in and then just let them sit there. Elmer Layden had as many as 100 lads one year. I do not know why Elmer would do such a thing. Many coaches get too concerned with their own well-being. They do not consider the lad himself. When I cut the squad back it caused talk, oooooh, I want you to know that it did.

"When I arrived, I discovered that there were seniors who had been on the team for three years without ever getting into a game. They were disappointed and they made poor alumni.

"Perhaps it was more the fault of tradition. Perhaps Elmer was not to blame. It is difficult to tell. Do you know that Rockne had so many players here on scholarship that as many as 100 lads would go through Notre Dame and never see game action? I loved that man. But I consider that sinful. The idea is to, ah, keep good players from playing against you—that is squandering humanity. Do you know that Rockne would red-shirt a man for two years and get away with it? He was most incredible.

"My first year I talked to a number of my sophomores and asked them if they really wanted to play at Notre Dame. If they did not, I encouraged them to attend institutions where the competition was not so keen. In every case, the lad in question took the advice as kindly as it was intended. I was greatly criticized for this. They said that I was driving these boys away, but I wasn't. What I wanted was for them to attend a good school and play football regularly. In recent years, a number of them have told me that it was the best thing that ever happened to them."

He watched the over-bloated figure of Czarobski disappear down the aisle. He laughed at this oddly malevolent appearing creature whose real life nature is so kind. If Frank Leahy had to choose just one of his players who pleased him most, it would obviously have to be Zygmont. There could be no other.

"I genuinely loved that lad. He had a certain, ah, quality about him. He was a mean man on the football field, Zygmont was. Ooooooh, but off it he was a charmer. I am sure you have heard a number of the classic stories about Zygmont. It is usual for a coach who has witnessed an exceptionally poor performance to hold up a ball and say, 'Gentlemen, we are going back to fundamentals. This object you see is a football.' Well, I did that on one occasion and Zygmont observed it for a few moments and yelled, 'Not so fast, coach.' He was a charming individual."

There were times when Leahy waited for the opportunity to strike back. There was the afternoon when a certain Notre Dame player had been working out for hours, running so many laps that his feet were ready to bleed.

"What is the matter, James? Are you tired?" Leahy asked.

"Coach, I'm ready to drop," said the young man.

"That is probably because you are not in shape," the Coach said. "Better keep on running. It will do you good, lad."

A few feet away, Zygmont Czarobski was slaving away in the fiendish heat of early September. He had listened to the conversation carefully. There was Leahy staring him in the eyes, asking how he—Zygmont—felt.

"Oh, just fine," he said, with forced enthusiasm. "Great, coach. Never felt better." To show just how well he was, he thumped his chest a couple of times. Somehow he resisted the urge to get sick to his stomach.

"That's nice, Zygmont," said Leahy, not smirking. "You keep right on working until you get tired."

The game ended with an almost effortless Notre Dame victory. Leahy said that he would go down to the dressing room to shake Parseghian's hand, but it did not seem fitting. Instead, he thought it might be best to call in the morning. Between coaches there is a code of behavior. When one man over-shadows another, ever so slightly, he is quite careful not to stand in the light. Parseghian was Parseghian and not quite a Leahy. Not yet anyway. When he was, Leahy would let him know. At the moment, it was too close to permit offending the other man.

"How did you happen to leave Notre Dame?" Leahy was asked.

"It was illness, nothing more," said The Coach.

"There were whispers that Father Hesburgh asked you to resign? Is that true?"

Leahy's teeth crunched together. His eyes flashed. Somewhere deep in his innards old angers were stirring. He turned with a snap of his head.

"That is a damnable lie," he said, trying not to shout. "Father Hesburgh called me and begged me to stay. I told him that it was impossible. I owed it to my family to resign while I was still alive. It has been said . . . well, so many things have been said. They said that he hated me because I kept him waiting outside my office too long on one occasion. I don't ever recall that happening. They said that I asked for a one year sabbatical. That never happened. They said that Father Hesburgh had Terry Brennan in his philosophy class and decided to make him head coach then. That is also sheer nonsense. Brennan was in his class. But I doubt if Father Hesburgh knew then that he wanted him as a head coach.

"I left Our Lady because I had to in order to stay alive. There was no other reason. I was not fired. Father Hesburgh wanted me to continue. Those stories have gone on far too long. It is time they were all laid to rest. All of them."

The crowd was pouring out of the stadium. The Victory March was booming inside. Slowly, Leahy made his way out in total silence. The band noise almost rattled the pavement.

EPISODE 11

SOUTH BEND

In the late afternoon, the wind goes slicing through the skeletons of the sycamore trees that border the cemetery where all the immortals are moldering in their graves. The golden dome still glitters in the weakening sunlight of late autumn and priests still shuffle by the shores of the lake, their bodies nearly formless in black cassocks, their minds lost in meditation. On the field where legends are manufactured with a timeless precision, padded bodies collide in the season's most solemn rite.

Flesh and blood human beings produce mythology on the Notre Dame campus and then wait their turns to be absorbed into the fabric of football's folklore. This is the never-never land of college athletics and it is the Monday afternoon following a football victory. It is business as usual. This is a mighty academic institution that reached its present intellectual status because football made contributing to the University's endowment fund so attractive.

It is painful to a lot of important academic figures, but it is true. Without football to turn it into an institution of almost mystical stature, Notre Dame would have developed into a first rank school, but not necessarily a great one. It is probably as much a fault of that song as it is of anything else. Notre Dame football is very big, but the Victory March made football so dramatic and football made the Victory March so exciting. One could not possibly have done well without the other.

Around the turn of the century, the captain of the Notre Dame baseball team, Johnny Shea returned to Holyoke, Massachusetts, and discussed the matter with his brother, the Rev. Michael J. Shea, S.J., who was the organist at St. Patrick's Cathedral in New York. The brothers wrote the words and the music and, together with four friends, went to the local Catholic church to try it out. The rector was dubious and ordered everyone to leave. And so it came to pass that the Notre Dame Victory March was first played on an organ in an Episcopal church.

"Very nice," said the priest at St. James Church. "And what is it called?"

The brothers Shea were almost afraid to tell the poor man. "It's a fight song for Notre Dame," they said.

"Oh," said the Anglican. "And where is Notre Dame?"

"In South Bend," said Rev. Shea.

"That's nice," said the Episcopal priest. "Where is South Bend?"

Meanwhile, Johnny Shea was pounding away on the organ.

> Cheer, cheer for old Notre Dame
> Wake up the echoes cheering her name
> Send a volleyed cheer on high,
> Shake down the thunder from the sky.
> What though the odds be great or small
> Old Notre Dame will win over all.
> While her loyal sons are marching
> Onward to victory.

They translated the song into three dozen foreign languages. One Japanese unit on Saipan charged into battle singing it during World War II, mistakeningly thinking it was the American national anthem. Nearly half the high schools in the nation have adapted its tune and used it as the basis for an Alma Mater. It is clearly part of the Notre Dame mystique.

On the upper floor of Corby Hall, where the priests of the

Congregation of the Holy Cross spend their final prayerful years on the planet, the Rev. Frank Cavanaugh sits rocking in a comfortable chair, his rubber-soled slippers slapping against the naked floor. This is not a luxurious retirement home. It is sparse and antiquated. There are no niceties here, only a place to live. On the wall there are pictures of Robert Kennedy, Knute Rockne, Frank Leahy, Pope Paul, Pope Pious and other religious figures such as George Gipp.

Father Frank Cavanaugh is in touch with all the spirits that walk the campus, both living and dead. Consider this: Father Cavanaugh was a classmate of Gipp. He was there in the chapel when Rockne left his native Lutheranism and joined the Roman Catholic Church. He was proctor of Leahy's dorm when the latter was a sophomore tackle.

"I was also the one they called when they wanted someone to tell Terry Brennan he was fired," said Father Frank. "So I went over and I listened to them. I had a drink on them and I told them to get somebody else to do their dirty business. That wasn't my way of looking at things. My brother, Father John Cavanaugh, was president of Notre Dame. It was he who asked me to go and talk to Frank Leahy. I was the agent who actually brought him here. I was not going to be the man who would tell Terry Brennan to leave. That was up to someone else."

Once Father Cavanaugh was head of the arts and science department at Notre Dame. Even though his hands shake from Parkinson's disease, he has been keeping a book on Leahy and Rockne for some time, one he will probably never get to write.

"Every time I read a story about either one of them, I get sick to my stomach. I read someplace in one of the Chicago newspapers that they wanted to do a movie on Frank's life. I hope it's better than the one they did on Rock. Sheer garbage! That's what that one was. The stories about both of them are absolutely stuffed with mistakes. I can't understand why a newspaperman with nothing else to do but drink and go to football games can't occasionally check a fact. One man makes a mistake in print and the thing is repeated for 50 years until somebody who knows better wonders if it didn't happen just that way."

66

There are two scenes from the Rockne movie that Father Frank Cavanaugh cannot erase from his mind. They still torment him, he said, and it has been years since he last saw the film on the late, late show in his monkish cell. The Hollywood wowsers had Rockne in New York watching a bunch of chorus girls move left and move right on a stage. Somehow, they concluded that this was where Rockne got the idea for the Notre Dame shift that drove opposing coaches to the ragged edge of suicide back in the 1920s.

"What a crazy lie that was," said the old priest grumpily. "Why don't they tell the truth? There was so much more to Rockne as a human being than they ever tried to show in that movie. I suppose they'll do the same stupid thing to Leahy. I hope Ara never lets them get near him."

The reason that Rockne had his four backs switch from the single wing to the Notre Dame box formation just before the snap was that he had a bunch of ball carriers who weighed about as much as drowned puppies. By keeping them agile, he got maximum use out of them.

"Then there was the scene where they had George Gipp being discovered by Rockne while he played inter-hall football. They had him kicking a ball back toward Rock and then they had Rock begging him to come out for the team," he said. "That was fiction, too. Gipp came to Notre Dame on a baseball scholarship. If he had lived, he would have been a major league outfielder with the Chicago White Sox. But he was on the freshman football team because he wanted to. Rock knew exactly who he was."

The movie also showed Gipp as the sort of faultless, clear-visioned young man whose morals were so sound he might one day grow up to be the ultra-conservative governor of California.

That's the way the actor playing the part interpreted the role. However, Gipp was not quite as trustworthy, loyal, brave, clean and reverent as he came across on the screen. He was a cheerful creature whom everybody loved. Gipp was a gambler and a pool hustler who spent much of his time at Hullie and Mike's on Michigan Street in downtown South Bend.

There is some question whether he actually said, on his deathbed, "Sometime, Rock, when the team is up against it, when things are wrong and the breaks are beating the boys, ask them to win one for the Gipper. I don't know where I'll be then, Rock, but I'll know about it and I'll be happy."

That is the version Rockne related to the team in the locker room at Yankee Stadium at the halftime of the 1928 Army-Notre Dame game. Shortly after Gipp perished in 1920, Rockne told some intimate friends a far different version. The real Gipp deathbed scene was even described in the *South Bend Tribune.*

"It must be tough to go, George," said Rockne, who had just witnessed Gipp's conversion from Methodism to Roman Catholicism.

"No, it's not so tough," the great halfback said. "I'm content."

None of his contemporaries saw much wrong with Gipp, even though Rockne twice had to go and fetch him back from schools he had defected to, namely Michigan and the University of Detroit. Each time, he returned in utter peace with the world and with Notre Dame.

"George was not an ordinary student," said Father Cavanaugh. "He had his social lapses, but he was older than most of the students—about 21 when he entered Notre Dame. He was also brilliant and didn't have to spend much time studying. If they could have convinced him to come to class regularly, George Gipp could have been an honor student."

It didn't work out that way. Gipp was a wild wind. And if it is true, what the legend says, he caught a fatal cold during a wild drinking spree in Chicago because he forgot his overcoat when he left the Notre Dame train without permission after the final game of the season.

"You know," said Father Cavanaugh, "the truth about Leahy is that I was the man that hired him away from Boston College. They always credit it to my brother, Father John Cavanaugh. They even say that he was president of Notre Dame when we got Frank. That isn't so, either. John was president later. Father Hugh O'Donnell was president. In fact, I was at a basketball game when Elmer Layden resigned. It was 7:30 P.M. and they sent somebody over to get me.

"Father O'Donnell met me in his office and he said, 'Well, I guess you know what happened?' I told him that I did. He asked me if I thought I could get hold of Frank Leahy right away. That's how badly Notre Dame wanted him. Anyway, he told me that it had to be very secret. There couldn't be any news leaking out or anything. Boston College had just signed him to a five-year contract. But we were fairly sure that he had an 'alma mater clause' which meant he could get out of it if his alma mater offered him a job. I called Eddie Dunigan, a mutual friend of ours, and asked him if he thought he could get in touch with 'our friend in the East.' He said, 'You mean Boston College, don't you?' I told him that's exactly what I meant."

All that Father O'Donnell wanted was the answer to three questions: (1) Did Leahy have a legitimate right to a release from his contract? (2) Could Leahy be in Albany, N.Y., under an assumed name on the following Monday? (3) Did he want to return to Notre Dame with the idea that he would build Notre Dame into a national champion again? So Dunigan got on the telephone and asked if Leahy could get out of his contract and did he want the job. Neither answer was unexpected. Fine, could Leahy be in the Ten Eyck Hotel in Albany to meet with Father Frank Cavanaugh? Leahy said he could have a train ticket bought inside of half an hour.

"Frank said that he thought it would be better, under the circumstances, if I came instead of Father O'Donnell and we both agreed," said Father Cavanaugh, rocking steadily. "This was real spy stuff. When Notre Dame makes a football coaching change, it's a big deal. I didn't even take the train out of South Bend. I went through Elkhart, just to be sure. I stayed in my compartment and didn't come out until we got into Albany.

"I registered under the name of Jack McDowell. I didn't wear my collar because I didn't want anybody to think that Leahy might possibly be speaking to a priest from Notre Dame. There was a lot of talk at the time that he might be replacing Layden. Anyway, he called me from his room and said, 'This is Francis O'Leary.' That was the name he was registered under. Frank was so anxious that he came running down to my room. He took $1,500 less than he was getting at Boston College. I told him he could hold for more, but he didn't want to. He was getting $12,500 there and my first offer was $11,000. I told him inside of a couple of years his salary would only be a fraction of his income. He agreed.

"He insisted on bringing his assistants. I told him it would be $20,000 for the three of them, and we'd hire them even though we preferred alumni for coaches. I didn't want to tie his hands and neither did anyone else at Notre Dame. Not at that time.

"There was only one other candidate and that was Buck Shaw. He was out on the Coast and we contacted him just in case Leahy wasn't available. But Shaw had an iron-clad contract. There was some talk about Clipper Smith, but Frank was the only man that we really wanted. But it was all over in a half hour, that's how bad Leahy wanted to come to Notre Dame. I don't think the school has ever had an easier time getting a football coach."

For several minutes, Father Cavanaugh moved back and forth in the rocker, his eyes small points of light. His brain was churning. Finally, it struck him that something should come out. He picked at his words, trying to select the proper ones.

"I don't know if this should be told, but they pushed him out."

"Who?"

"Why, Frank Leahy," he said. "There wasn't any real reason. Not one you could explain. It's just that he was winning so easily and they thought anybody could do it. He had all those undefeated seasons and all those national champions. He wasn't well. Oh, he was all worn out, not only physically, but emotionally. They were afraid he'd have a nervous breakdown. He'd had one before and they told him the spring before the 1953 season to relax or his nerves couldn't take it.

"They came to me and wanted me to ask him to resign. I told them, 'Hell no! He's old enough to know when his health can't take it. If he doesn't know enough to quit, that's up to him. I just think he's smarter than that.' So Frank came over to see me. He told me what was going on."

So Leahy looked straight at Father Cavanaugh and asked him for an explanation of what was happening to him. In his heart he knew exactly what was going on, but it was far too painful to face.

"Well, Frank, they're trying to get rid of you," said the priest. "You might as well resign. In fact, if I were you that's exactly what I'd do, because they'll fire you otherwise. Nobody wants that to happen."

A day or two later, Leahy returned, filled with anguish. This was Father Theodore Hesburgh's first year as president of Notre Dame, but Father John Cavanaugh was still acting as an advisor.

"How much influence does Father John still have?" asked Leahy.

"Quite a bit," said Frank Cavanaugh.

"Then he agrees with Father Hesburgh?" asked Leahy. "He thinks I should resign?"

"He's still calling a lot of the shots."

"In that case, I guess I have no choice," Leahy said, hanging up without even one gracious comment. Within seconds he was talking to John Cavanaugh, giving him every assurance that a typewritten resignation would be on Father Hesburgh's desk as soon as possible. Rockne's life was ended in an airplane crash in a Kansas wheat field; Leahy's was ended by executive action. The trouble was that they could bury Rockne. Unfortunately, Leahy still had two decades left to wander, forever a coach without a football team.

They made it so attractive. The five Leahy boys were given scholarships to Notre Dame. The family took a six week vacation. A lot of pretty words were said for the appreciation of the press, which had a tendency, at the time, to believe the Notre Dame sports publicity department even if it announced that Snow White would be the quarterback and the Seven Dwarfs would be the offensive line.

"You can't control your personal life when you're the head football coach at a school such as Notre Dame," said Leahy. "You belong to the people, to the priests, to the radio. I found myself a little more fatigued each day. My family would be pleased if I discontinued coaching entirely. During the fall, I have been getting home roughly two nights a week. The other nights I work late and stay at the University. One season there was a stretch when I was home only six nights out of ninety. That isn't fair and I recognize it. When I look in the mirror I must take a critical look rather than a look of admiration. I fear becoming an egotist and Knute Rockne once said that egotism is the anesthetic that deadens the pain of stupidity. I do not wish to hide my own stupidity."

On the way back to Randall's Inn from Father Frank Cavanaugh's cell, the sports information director at Notre Dame, a small Italian elf named Roger Valdisierri talked about his four years as Leahy's student manager. Like Joe Doyle, he was never sure whether to say hello or genuflect, so he normally did both.

"The Coach could terrorize you without even trying," he said. "But he could be so kind. One time he took me on the trip to Southern California and there was a cocktail party after the game. I showed up in oatmeal colored slacks and a gray jacket. It was a crummy combination. But I was just a dumb Italian kid and I didn't know any better. There was The Coach, staring at me out of the corners of his eyes. I could tell I looked like hell. A couple of weeks later I got a Christmas gift certificate for $50 from Leahy with the notation that I should buy a different coat if I were going to make any more trips with Notre Dame.

"When I was in school there were these twins who came out for football and they just plain busted their tails for Leahy. They were just walk-ons. Leahy tried like hell to get them scholarships, but they weren't good enough. But The Coach loved them. They ran out of money and it looked like they were going to have to drop out of school. You know what Leahy did? He fished around until he found some magazine that would pay him something like $5,000 for a story in the first person. He got somebody to write it for him and he used the extra money to pay tuition for those twins. I don't think they ever knew what he did. They thought that suddenly God had smiled on them and they had qualified for athletic scholarships."

Snow began to dance in front of the car, falling against the hood and turning to water. The public relations man struggled with his thoughts.

"Frank Leahy could be a hard-driving son-of-a-bitch when he wanted to be," he said. "But he was interested in succeeding only if he could be of service to somebody else. He was a wreck that final year. His nerves were in terrible condition. Physically, he was shaking apart. He absolutely had to get out of coaching."

The car turned the corner and moved down the highway toward the inn. The snow was moving faster, even though the particles weren't sticking to the ground. The air was clear with the deadening cold of advancing winter.

"You know something?" Valdisierri asked.

"What?"

"He was damn close to being a saint," he said. "That's assuming a football coach can qualify for canonization."

AN EPILOGUE:

"Pray, sir," said the goatherd, "who is this man who talks so extravagantly? For I protest I never saw so strange a figure in all my life."

"Whom do you imagine it should be?" asked the barber. "It is the famous Don Quixote de la Mancha, the establisher of justice, the avenger of injuries, the protector of damsels, the terror of the giants and the invincible winner of battles."

"The account you give of this person," returned the goatherd, "is much like what we read in romances and books of chivalry of those doughty dons, who, for their mighty prowess and achievements were called knights-errant."

**PART TWO
OUR LADY**

EPISODE 1

In the warm security of late afternoon with the dying sun outlining the spires of tall pines on the far side of Oregon's Lake Oswego, the old man began to talk into a tape recorder set up on the night stand next to his bed. He had returned from a trip, received a transfusion of blood and literally fallen into bed. Whatever diseases infected Frank Leahy's body, they had done nothing to his mind. It still crackled and snapped.

"There are those people," he said, "who felt that Col. Red Blaik and I had a feud going. Whereas I would not say that we were intimate friends, it was never as fierce as the newspapers tried to make it sound. Both of us were highly competitive individuals. When Notre Dame played his Army teams feelings were high. But, I suspect, we both respected one another.

"Not many people know but during the terrible cribbing scandal of August 1951, when a number of fine Army football players were dismissed from the Academy, I received a call from Joseph P. Kennedy and he offered to send the twelve best boys on the West Point team to Notre Dame. I thanked him profusely and hung up. Then it occurred to me that some people might take it the wrong way if players moved between such confirmed rivals as Notre Dame and Army. Then, too, I had just solidified my relations with Col. Blaik and there was an excellent chance that we might resume our series, which had been interrupted.

"Therefore, after much consideration, I called Ambassador Kennedy back and, with deep regret, told him that I was forced to reject his most generous offer. If the Army players came to Notre Dame it would be the sad duty of Moose

Krause to declare them ineligible for football. It took a great deal of courage for me to reject the offer. I genuinely enjoyed bringing worthy lads to Our Lady and as I understood the situation the guilty cadets in most cases were not actual cheaters. They knew it was going on and could not bring themselves to tell on erring classmates.

"That is a violation of Army's very strict military code. I think that it is, ah, rather a pardonable sin, especially when committed by young lads. The dozen players that Ambassador Kennedy wanted to send me all fitted into the category I mentioned."

He paused for a moment and took a deep breath to ease the pain. Then he grinned widely. A thought was crashing through Frank Leahy's brain.

"I dedicated myself to that final season as I had never dedicated myself before," he said. "I contributed to my own collapse by over-working when I should have eased up. When I had to be helped out of the stadium at the halftime of the Georgia Tech game, I had the strangest feeling that the most important chapter of my life had ended. I did not think I would die. Quite often I thought that I would like to go back and change certain aspects of my life . . . but I know this now: Given such an unlikely opportunity, I wouldn't change a thing. No man would."

For a moment, he looked as if he wished to repudiate the statement. His eyes grew narrow and he bit his lower lip. The bed was cluttered with old clippings, magazines and books about Notre Dame football. On the wall was a picture of Frank Leahy after a round of golf with Eisenhower. There was another picture of him posing with Gary Cooper and a plaque commemorating some speech he had made. There, in a box on the floor, were canisters of game film from Boston College's 19-13 victory over Tennessee in the Sugar Bowl, the game that clinched the Notre Dame coaching job for Frank Leahy. It had been preserved, all those years, like an ancient ikon.

"No," he said, reaching for his pills, "I suppose I would not change a thing."

EPISODE 2

The town of Winner, South Dakota, squats on the gritty plains like the wretched remains of a Hollywood set. In the year 1911, it is only briefly removed from the Great American West. This is the land where only recently Wild Bill Hickok and Calamity Jane roamed. The smoke from Indian camp sites still curls in the distance as it escapes from the flues in the tops of the tents. There are swinging doors on the fronts of saloons and no pavement on the streets. Cowboys ride into town on Saturday evening. This is, says one contemporary writer, still the era of bullwhackers, mule skinners and road agents in South Dakota.

The sons of immigrants are on the prowl, spreading out with their families, looking for both living room and a living. Frank Leahy's father, also named Frank but with a different middle name, is a rough man with a violent streak in his soul. His own father, Michael Leahy, had run before the potato famines, settling in Peterborough, Ontario, where so many Tipperary Irishmen had fled. He married Bridget Torpay in 1861, and in 1869, went creaking off in a wagon for Lost Nation, Iowa. They didn't find it there, so they moved on to Nebraska, stopping in a place called Wisner and raising their ten children to maturity while Michael Leahy worked as a peace officer, a genuine Wyatt Earp with a silver star on his chest.

In the meantime, the Kanes had been moving slowly across the landscape from Scranton where many of the Irish had come to work in the coal mines and found only ruthless exploitation and vigorous religious prejudice. They had simply climbed on a railroad and asked for a ticket that would take them to the end of the line. They got off in O'Neill, Nebraska. It seemed that the Irish were always moving, just ahead of persecution, either by nature or by the Anglo-Saxon. One of their children, Mary Winifred Kane, married Frank Leahy, whose father was a policeman in Wisner and who already had a reputation as a man who would rather swing his fist than chat amiably.

It is a matter of record that the man who later coached football at Notre Dame had a maternal grandmother whose reputation as a handler of pistols and shotguns was remark-

able even for the times. But then, hardly anyone went anywhere unarmed. The editor of The O'Neill *Frontier* was indignant about "the indiscriminate shooting of fire arms on the
streets of our town."

There was a restlessness on the land and the elder Frank
Leahy left his wife and six children behind and struck out
for Roundup, Montana, telling the family to join him whenever it could. Dutifully, his wife sold their Nebraska home-
stead and left with twelve-year-old Gene, ten-year-old Jack,
eight-year-old Anne, five-year-old Marie, three-year-old Eileen
and the baby, Francis William Leahy, born, according to some
records, on August 22, 1908, or on August 27, 1908, according
to others. The elder Leahy built a cabin and then sent a letter.
His wife and children took the train. After one year, he decided that the high altitude would be harmful to everybody's
health. They moved again. This time he selected acreage in
Tripp County, South Dakota. An act of Congress had opened
an area forty miles wide and sixty miles long for homestead-
ing. Land was parceled out by means of a lottery. The Leahys
were among the winners.

The town had come by its name in quaint, frontier-fashion.
There had been a competition to determine a county seat and
the contenders were Lamro and Colome. Whatever community
won would also get the Chicago and Northwestern railway
terminal. There was a place two miles north of Lamro that
seemed suitable when a railroad executive conducted tests. It
was a small town, owned mostly by a pair of practicing capitalists named Jackson. They hauled the railroad man aside,
made certain offers and the terminal was built on their land.
Since it also got the county seat, the inhabitants decided that
it ought to be called Winner.

The Leahys spent their first winter there in a tent, huddling
at night under piles of blankets and buffalo hides.

In the spring of 1911, just as the first train was rolling into
town, the elder Leahy finished his house and his barn. After
that everything deteriorated. The hot winds of summer
smothered the crops and a cattle stampede completed the
destruction. When it seemed that nothing worse could happen, the elder Leahy came down with blood poisoning and
Frank Leahy the younger set fire to the barn.

The latter act was accomplished simply, efficiently and without malice. It was Sunday morning and an eight-year-old daughter, Marie, was watching her three-year-old brother while her parents and the rest of the family went to mass. The boy wandered into the barn, struck a match and left it near some hay. Deeply afraid of what his father's reaction might be, the future architect of character at Notre Dame simply toddled on out, returned to the house and, when the smoke started pouring out of the eaves, pointed out the problem to his sister, who was not actually equipped to do much about it. Even when he brought the subject up, several years later, only a few members of the family thought it anything more than childish fantasy.

Now life grew more difficult and the elder Leahy, already remote and bitter, grew even more so. He moved into the freighting business, using teams of horses and mules to haul liquor for the taverns in the Dakotas. It was, he said, "a hell of a way to serve the Lord." He arose at 3 A.M. during the summer because the afternoon heat sucked the breath out of his animals. It was necessary to ford most of the streams in order to pick up his cargo in Dallas, South Dakota, a two day trip. The weather was nearly always miserable and in the winter the freighter would walk beside his wagon so as not to overburden the mules and horses. As he plodded along, Frank Leahy, Sr., blazed with frustration.

"He was a man of great power with a strong aggressive streak," said his son. "He wanted to be a boxer. And don't forget that the sport was very big and very lucrative in those days. He could have been a champion or at least a prominent contender. But my mother was on the puritanical side, not an uncommon trait among, ah, Irish Catholic women. She refused to permit it. He smoldered because he felt he could have done much better in life if he had had an opportunity to make the ring his career. He would tease my mother most cruelly. He would encourage all of his sons to fight and he would do it in front of her. But he was most fair. He refused to permit us to fight anyone smaller or weaker. He truly loved it as a sport and I believe it was good for him because it gave him an opportunity to relax whatever tensions he had inside of him."

It was common practice for the elder Leahy to stop each of his boys and ask them if they had been involved in a fight at school that day. They would deny it. Then he would grin malevolently and say: "Get in one tomorrow. It'll do you some good." The frontier was neither glamorous nor exciting. It was a cruel, debilitating existence and Frank Leahy, Sr., no expert at using hand guns, did what he thought would turn his three sons into iron-backed, clenched-teeth versions of himself.

"On one occasion, another man came into the trading post my father later opened and accused Jack of beating up his son," said Frank Leahy. "He used abusive language and he was probably quite correct in what he, ah, said. But my father leaped at him and beat him badly. He might have killed the man if my brother Gene had not pulled him away. By this time, Gene was a grown man and my father was quite pleased that he had strength enough to restrain him."

By now the story of the barn burning was beginning to be believed. The mules had perished, even though the family's mare had become one of the few horses in history ever to voluntarily leave a burning building. As he grew older, the animosity over the incident between father and son grew more intense.

"I finally told my mother, 'If you can get him to keep quiet over the barn burning, I'll build you a new barn someday. If I can't do that, I'll take care of both of you. I mean that,'" Frank Leahy the younger shouted, almost as if it were still happening. Then his voice dropped in volume. "I meant it, too. My father was dead. And when I was able to, I brought my mother in to live with us. She stayed for 19 years. I made up for the barn burning."

Freighting had come close to ruining Frank Leahy, Sr.'s, mental health and he opened a trading post, exchanging grain with local farmers for produce and then selling the produce to the townspeople. He also worked part time as a law officer. Some of the nearby Indians had been rustling cattle, shipping them out of Winner at night.

"There were these three brothers with the tribe who were absolute experts at the business," said Leahy. "We had become a much more quiet town. The whites and the Indians got along quite well. But these brothers tried to bully everybody, with no regard for which race they belonged to. My father warned them that he would have to arrest them if they persisted. They continued and, like a scene from an old movie, they attempted to take control of the town. My father told them they would have to do it over his corpse. They tried and he thrashed them all. They said they were going to shoot him down. But they never tried. They knew better."

Before puberty, Frank Leahy was a working cowboy. In one of the few acts of intimacy between the two, his father bought him an elderly horse, a meandering swayback puckishly named Devil Dan. Along with a friend, he contracted to escort two dozen head of cattle some 100 miles across the Badlands. The pay was $5 a day, which was not exactly bad money for a child in those days. They camped out at night, a coffee pot boiling on the embers of the camp fire and their heads propped against their saddles. It was almost romantic until one morning when their horses broke the tether line, found a vegetable garden and destroyed most of it.

"The lady who owned those vegetables was most unpleasant," he said. "She impounded our horses and demanded payment before permitting the sheriff to release them. That stripped us of funds. For the next three days, we rode across the Badlands with nothing to eat. We tried our hands at shooting game, but neither of us was able to hit a thing. Water was dangerous to drink because one never, ah, you never knew whether it was spoiled or not. We found some berries. Oooooooh, it was like fiction, but it was happening to us. Fortunately, my partner had relatives—an aunt and uncle, as I recall—at our destination in Washaba."

When they came drooping in, the aunt and uncle stuffed them full of food, scolded them for their stupidity on the trail and gave them both a job at a dollar a day, as working cowboys, despite their age. It was typical of the times. Range hands were quite often mere children, barely able to shave. The only requirement was an ability to work 12 hours at what was an exceedingly dull job, cattle being poor company at best.

"At the end of the summer, I grew quite lonesome for a certain young lady. I believe that her name was Dorothy or something similar. Oooooooh, I was quite taken with her. I decided that it would be best to return home to her as soon as possible, because I believe that I had serious doubts about her loyalty," he said. "I pushed that poor horse, riding night and day. I was back in Winner inside of four days. Unfortunately Devil Dan was not up to the journey. An average day for a young cowboy was supposed to be from 5 A.M. to 5 P.M., but often we worked close to midnight. He was far too old. I found him dead within hours after my return."

Life was slow and entertainment nearly extinct in Winner. Workdays were long and agonizing. Food was home grown, which meant the residents had to cultivate it themselves at the risk of utter ruination. These were the good old days, so fondly remembered in the plastic corridors of Walt Disney's imagination. If they were good, it was because people made them that way. They were not simple. Survival rarely is.

"We had sports in Winner to keep us amused and not much else, except maybe for the local saloon," said Gene Leahy, his voice drifting back over the expanse of the decades. "There was boxing and wrestling. Because we were all driven to it by our father, we were good at it, although Jack was not really strong enough. But he participated. There was a place we called 'The Winner Pavilion.' It was a green painted wooden building, not very impressive. By now our youngest brother Tom had come along and the Leahy sons were supposed to participate. There was father pushing us along. He wanted a champion in the family. He wanted one so badly."

Frank Leahy was barely 16 when he boxed his older brother Jack at the Pavilion. He was 160 pounds, strong to an impressive degree and, sadly, quite slow. For five rounds they boxed delicately. In the audience, their father screamed at them to forget brotherly love. In the sixth, Frank Leahy swung hard and dropped his brother with a right to the jaw.

"For God's sake take it easy with Jack. He had a rough time of it in the war. You can't punish him like that," said Gene. "He's your brother. Now take it easy or you'll have to fight me on the way home. Understand?"

So the seventh round began and there was no fraternal affection anywhere in the hall. Jack Leahy blazed, throwing combinations that left the younger brother smeared with his own blood. Grimly, he found his way back to his corner, looked at his oldest brother and said: "I'm glad you told me to take it easy on Jack. Now I'd appreciate it if you'd march around the ring and give Jack the same advice about his brother. I think your advice stinks." The match ended a round later with Jack Leahy battering Frank into the floor and walking away with a hurt expression.

"Most of Frank's waking moments were spent thinking about sports," said Gene Leahy. "I can't remember a single popular sport he didn't try. He even went out for track and he couldn't run well enough to catch a blind mare. I know how awful he felt when he realized he wasn't quick enough. He'd get tears in his eyes. I had to take him aside and explain that toughness and courage were just as important. 'Someday these kids who are out-running you will be reading about you. You've got something they don't have. You can think things out and you're tough.'

"Still, when he tried to play baseball I knew that wasn't his sport. One afternoon, he hit a home run. I asked whether he hit a fastball or a breaking pitch. He told me, 'Hell, Gene, it was just a baseball.' I knew right then that his aptitude was in another direction. A real baseball man can tell you within an eighth of an inch where the pitch broke and how. Frank liked the game well enough. He just wasn't passionate enough about it. If he had been he would have been the greatest major league manager who ever lived. He could get obsessive about things.

"Frank was only a substitute on the high school baseball team, which I coached," said Gene Leahy. "But he was the only one who learned the proper technique for bunting. He was crazy about strategy and was always reading some book on the technical aspects of baseball.

"Although he took some courses in public speaking later on at Notre Dame, it was in those days that he started his love affair with big words. Father and Frank were never close. But Frank admired him tremendously. He was always impressed by the fact that father had very little formal education but had taught himself a fantastic vocabulary. In fact, father used to bet people that he could define any word in the dictionary. It was a means of identifying with father and Frank took great pride in him."

By the time Frank Leahy was in high school, the town of Winner had grown to a population of 3,000, mostly Swedish and German Protestants, who had a tendency to view Irish Catholics as sort of a curiosity as if, at any minute, they might break into a jig and start singing with a stage brogue. The

Leahys, who had come to town and lived in a tent with wooden sides their first winter and whose first farmhouse had been so small that the two oldest boys slept in a stall in the barn, had now risen to the awesome comfort of a five bedroom clapboard house just off the main street of Winner. They even had indoor plumbing, a status item which made Tom Leahy feel downright snobbish. There was a Catholic Church now and a Catholic grammar school.

There were more cars and trucks, but range cowboys still rode into town on their horses and there was still a fragrance of the old West. Because of the railroad, Winner was prospering and Lamro, which had lost both the county seat and the railroad terminal, was withering away. Gene Leahy had gone on to Creighton University to become an outstanding halfback. He returned one holiday to discover that Frank had been using his monogram sweater until the arms were stretched out past the knuckles. During the course of the ensuing argument, the older brother learned that because of his success at the sport, Frank Leahy was now trying very hard to imitate a football player.

"He was out playing all the time, in scrub games, wearing my sweater. Dad was miffed because it meant he might be losing interest in boxing, which he was. So I gave him hour upon hour of instruction in how to play football and then sent him a technical book," said Gene Leahy. "He read it like it was the Bible and he wanted to go to the seminary to become a priest. He wanted to learn everything he could about football strategy. By the time I was out of Creighton, there was Frank getting ready to play high school football."

Because of its reputation as a boom town, Winner had been able to hire, as the head football coach at its high school, a former Notre Dame teammate of George Gipp. His name was Earl Walsh and, like Rockne, he was able to think big, winning all ten of his games his first season in town. In a sense it was a matter of survival, losing coaches were not tolerated for long. In a town not far from Winner, a man clumsy enough to lose four games in one season was escorted to the train station by a group of irate citizens who had already packed his bags.

The fields were often barren of grass, torturously dry early in the season and frozen solid long before the schedule ended.

This was a time of leather helmets and lightly constructed padding. Living through the season was a challenge. Fortunately, eligibility rules were rarely considered very important and Frank Leahy was permitted to go out for the high school team while still in the eighth grade, for the sweetly simple reason that he weighed 155 pounds and looked big enough.

"This was the year before Earl Walsh came in from Notre Dame and our high school team was coached by a man named Arthur Neff and if you examine the results of the final game you will see why his services were no longer required. There was precious little toleration for defeat in Winner. Life was so hard and the land so bleak that people were anxious to find something to, ah, be joyful about," said Frank Leahy.

"That first season, coach Neff saw very little about me that he liked. So it was that I sat there on the bench watching all the older fellows play. Quite naturally I took a considerable needling because of my inactivity. I had boasted some about my prowess to other eighth graders, who were first jealous that I was on the high school team and then scornful of me when I wasn't used."

On the evening before the last game, against Gregory High School, another former Creighton football player, Jack Crowley, who owned a store in Winner and also officiated at most of the games, had a house date with Marie Leahy. They were sitting in the living room when Frank conceived of a masterful piece of strategy.

"You are going to work that game between Gregory and Winner tomorrow, aren't you?" he asked.

"Yeah, Frank," said Crowley. "What about it?"

"I've got to get into a game and coach Neff will never use me. If you could throw out one of our players near the end, maybe I could play for at least a few minutes."

"Get out of here, Frank," said Crowley. "You know damn well I can't do a thing like that."

But then they kicked off and the Winner team not only failed to make a first down, it couldn't stop the other team from scoring touchdowns. When the score hit 108-0, favor of the visitors, with six minutes left to play, Crowley looked over at the bench where Frank Leahy had been writhing uncomfortably all through this grotesque afternoon. The crowd was understandably restless and coach Neff was struggling furiously to keep from going under. He was in no emotional condition to give an eighth grader a chance to make the score even worse. Crowley figured it couldn't hurt, so ejected one of the Winner regulars. Neff shrugged, figuring heaven was against him. His only hope now was that nobody in the crowd was sufficiently angry or drunk enough to open fire, always an occupational hazard for high school coaches in the Dakotas.

The Winner team was lined up for a kickoff, a formation they had been using frequently during the game, when Frank Leahy came charging out onto a football field for the first time. His glands were churning like turbines and his veins were pumping blood so furiously that when he saw a shape loom out of darkening dust of late afternoon, he did the instinctive thing—he threw the hardest block of his high school career, knocking down one of the Winner players who happened to be pursuing the kick return man.

"I believe that there were some townspeople who were more furious at me for that one act of blatant stupidity than they were at the rest of the team for getting beat by such an atrocious score. The others had been inept. I was an out-and-out blunder. It was only through the threats of my father and the sternest urgings of my mother that I even consented to return to school the next Monday," he said. "It was many years, right up until the time that I was at Notre Dame, before some people in Winner would actually let me forget my youthful indiscretion."

It was indicative, perhaps, that civilization was spreading through the Dakotas, that coach Arthur Neff was not only permitted to peacefully resign from the chair of football at Winner High School, but was actually hired back as a teacher.

EPISODE 3

Until the new head football coach jumped down off the train, where a number of his new players had gathered to meet him, there were two ambitions burning holes in the brain of Frank Leahy. He wanted to go down to Omaha and play football at Creighton and he wanted to return home someday and coach the team at Winner. His father had sent him to Omaha to take boxing lessons and he had visited the school where Gene had become one of the finest small college backs in the nation.

Now Earl Walsh had arrived. Here was a man who played with people like George Gipp, Eddie and Hunk Anderson, Norm Barry and John Mohardt, athletes whose names had appeared in headlines as far away as New York. Oh, Leahy had been aware of Notre Dame. There wasn't a young Catholic athlete anywhere who didn't know about Knute Rockne and the legend he was constructing in South Bend.

"I have often seen it written that when I went to high school for awhile in Omaha that I heard Rock speak and was instantly converted," he said. "It's true that I went to a banquet where he was talking, but I had made up my mind where I wanted to play football long before I saw Rock for the first time. Ooooooh, he was a most impressive, most persuasive man. That was long before he became my patron saint. But I knew what I wanted to do. Coach Walsh told us stories of Notre Dame. It seemed like a mythical place sometimes.

"When I saw Gene I asked him if he wanted me to go to Creighton and he said, 'No, I have bigger things in mind for you.' He told me that he wanted me to build myself up physically. My father was already taking care of that. Quite often he would wake me in the morning at 4 A.M. and bring me down to his place where I would spend the hours before school lifting 100 pound sacks of grain. In those days, everyone was expected to help the family. Nobody argued. Discipline was rigid."

What Gene Leahy envisioned was Frank Leahy playing football for Notre Dame and when Earl Walsh told wondrous stories about the school, he encouraged Frank's enthusiasm. Before a man leaves on a mission somebody has to have perception enough to push him in the right direction. And for that, Frank was thankful for his brother Gene.

"My two older brothers were fascinating men," he said. "Gene was sensible, strong, self-disciplined and very determined. Ooooooh, but Jack Leahy with his swagger, his style, his mad dash through life, his strong language, his drinking and his adventures . . . there was something to that, too. There were times when I felt it would be wonderful to be like him, even though I knew that to be like Gene was the right way to live. Oooooooh, but that Jack Leahy."

In what seems more like an incident from a dime novel of the time rather than documentable truth, Earl Walsh was almost instantly impressed by Leahy's football intellect, something like Philip of Macedonia listening to the young Alexander explain battle tactics. Instead of using him in the line where his lack of speed would be overcome by his mobility, Walsh put him at tailback where he called signals. There were plenty of strong young men in Winner, young men who had been doing hard labor since they were ten. But only one of them could figure out another team's defense so swiftly and so devastatingly. The school stopped losing football games almost entirely. Shortly before graduation there were two developments in Leahy's life. Walsh recommended him to Knute Rockne and his father turned him over to his brother Gene, who was now living in Omaha.

Despite his enthusiasm for the school, Leahy discovered that the actual thought of getting on a train and heading to Notre Dame terrified him. He drove out into the Badlands with his best friend, Clayton Balfany, the team's outstanding fullback. They drank beer and seriously discussed their futures. Balfany had been approached by Rockne and Leahy wanted to know what he planned to do.

"Aw, Frank," he said. "Notre Dame sounds great. But it's a hell of an important football school. I could get buried there. I'd rather go to Springfield College. I know I'll play there and that's important to me. You can talk all you want to about 'meeting a big challenge.' That's not what I'm looking for. I think you're making a big mistake. Notre Dame's too big for small town guys like us."

Leahy stared off into the hills. Then, with Tom Swiftian firmness, said: "I'm glad you said that, Clayton. Now I know I'm going to Notre Dame. It's not going to be easy, but if I make it I'll be prouder of myself."

When Frank Leahy arrived in Omaha to spend the summer living with Gene and working on construction, he discovered there had been a drastic alteration in his plans. His brother had decided to keep him out of college for one year, a not altogether uncommon practice, especially in the Midwest.

After all, Gipp had waited until he was 21 to enter Notre Dame and the great, sainted Rockne himself worked in the Chicago Post Office and ran the half-mile in AAU track meets for three years before first enrolling at Illinois and, then, switching at the last minute to Notre Dame because somebody told him it was a good school for poor boys because they wouldn't be embarrassed.

Unaware of these important historical precedents, Leahy exploded in a blast of temper that would have stunned even his father. Picturesquely, he cursed Gene for being a perfidious fool, an unmitigated liar and the Godamned underhanded snake who was about to ruin his own younger brother's life for no reason except that he wanted to show who was in command.

"Frank bawled, bucked and raved at me for nearly half an hour," said Gene, stoic and steady in moments of crisis. "He never stopped for an explanation until he grew red around the cheeks and literally ran out of breath. I have never seen him so upset. I was convinced that he was going to punch. I think only the fact that I was as strong and maybe stronger than he was held him back."

Finally, Frank leaned back against the wall, quivering with rage, tears pouring out of his eyes, unable to push another word out of his mouth.

"All right, here are my reasons and you can damn well listen to them, because I'm the boss," said Gene. "First of all, you're still physically immature. You'll never make the varsity at Notre Dame if you start your freshman year now. Second, there are some subjects they didn't offer at Winner High School that you'll need in order to get into Notre Dame and stay in Notre Dame. Live with me in Omaha, build yourself up and take some classes at Central High School. It might also give you a chance to grow up a little emotionally, if that outburst was any indication of what a damn kid you still are."

EPISODE 4

A very wonderful thing has happened to the coach of football at Omaha's Central High School. There he is sitting in his cramped little office where the steam from the shower room wilts the papers on his desk and the odor of sweat pours from the gymnasium. The door creaks open and there stands this muscular young Irishman with droopy spaniel eyes. He is asking if he can come out for football. He explains that he is taking classes at Central and, ah, well he kind of had this overwhelming urge to put on a helmet and, ah, well hit somebody.

He says that his name is Frank Leahy and that he did, ah, play tailback for Earl Walsh up in Winner, South Dakota. He explains that he used to live there and that now he lives with his brother, Gene, in Omaha. It is not exactly a lie. Somehow Frank Leahy leaves out one important fact, mostly because he suspects that, having already graduated from high school, he is probably about as eligible for the Central High team as Billy the Kid would be to sing in the heavenly choir.

Unaware of this small, but important detail, the coach immediately issues him a uniform, somehow resisting the urge to kiss his manly young cheek. Halfway through the first practice, coach Bud Schmidt decides that, no matter what they think in Winner, South Dakota, this is no tailback who has fallen so magically into his fingers. Noting that he has here a young man weighing 180 pounds whose speed is fairly good until he gets ten yards past the line of scrimmage, he makes the logical conclusion. Frank Leahy is a tackle who moves off the tee smartly and hits with enthusiasm.

The conversion is a stunning success and coach Bud Schmidt looks up toward heaven and concludes that God is being good to him. Trouble is the conversion is too successful. The reporter from *The Omaha World* witnesses Central's opening victory over Beatrice High and writes the following: "Frank Leahy starred for the Purple in the line. Leahy, who is a newcomer to Central, proved to be the main cog on defense. Many times the big tackle would break through the line and nail the runner in his tracks. On offense, he blocked fiercely, clearing large holes for Central's ball carriers."

For the next five games, the local newspapers continue to splash gaudy adjectives all over Frank Leahy. They are convinced that he will be all-State. Unfortunately, the Omaha papers occasionally get up to Winner, South Dakota. Somebody tells somebody else and pretty soon another coach, who has Central coming up on his schedule also knows. The whistle is blown.

"Why didn't you tell them you were a post-graduate student?" asks Gene Leahy.

"They didn't ask," says Frank Leahy, stifling a snort.

One newspaper, covering up its own embarrassment, makes no mention that Leahy never was eligible in the first place. It reports that this brilliant young tackle they have been braying about has been suddenly called home to South Dakota, which isn't true. And to make the citizens feel better about his loss, they report that he plans to follow his brother Gene to Creighton, which also isn't true. God is no longer being good to coach Bud Schmidt. And so this odd little playlet ends.

EPISODE 5

The summer heat was blowing down the streets of Winner like blasts from an open furnace door. Frank Leahy, a year older, heavier and stronger, with six extra high school football games on his record, was home to pack, getting ready to begin the love affair of his life—with an institution.

This was an especially tender moment between the two brothers. They were walking along the familiar main street and Frank was explaining exactly how grateful he was to Gene for convincing him to sit out a year.

"You have absolutely vindicated yourself in my eyes, Gene. I feel so much more confident. I am convinced that I can play football at Notre Dame and make the first string. I wish it had been two years. I have talked to some college players and they tell me that boys with a little age on them stand up much better."

Near the Catholic Church they ran into Father Arthur Nepper, one of those now-nearly extinct clergymen who believed that rigid self-discipline and piety were essentially the same thing. He had heard that Frank Leahy was getting ready to go to Notre Dame. Fine school, run by the Congregation of the Holy Cross, priests with an excellent record in the field of both religion and education. With such a start in life, it might be years before the devil got his hot hands on young Leahy.

"I suppose you've already registered him, Gene?" said the priest.

"Well, no, not yet. I have the papers filled out, I simply haven't sent them off."

"Why, then, you're too late," said Father Nepper.

"What?" screamed Frank Leahy. "What?"

"Oh, yes, by this time they're all filled up. I doubt if you were a second George Gipp even coach Rockne couldn't get you in for another year."

"Oooooooh, Eugene Leahy!" said Frank, advancing with clenched fists. "Why do I listen to you? Oooooooh, Eugene Leahy! I do not care if you are my brother. I don't care if we are of the same blood and flesh. I don't care if you are a Leahy. Ooooooh, Eugene Leahy! I am going to kill you. Right here in front of this man of God. No jury on heaven or earth would convict me. Oooooooooh, Eugene Leahy!"

Despite his own great strength and proven athletic ability, Gene Leahy retreated all the way down the street to the Western Union office, sending a telegram to South Bend. Outside, Frank leared menacingly. After several long, agonizing hours, the answer came click-clacking back over the wires. Upon receipt of Frank Leahy's registration forms, he would be formally and firmly enrolled for the spring semester.

"I never told you this, Frank, but I always wished that I had gone to Notre Dame. Oh, not that I didn't enjoy life at Creighton. It was a fine school," Gene confessed on the way back home.

"Mother wanted me closer to home as she would undoubtedly have you go no further than Omaha. As fine a football career as I had at Creighton, nobody knew my name beyond Council Bluffs. It would have been different at Notre Dame."

With that 1920-Swiftian bravado, which he never fully lost, Frank Leahy replied, "In that case, I have yet another reason for succeeding at Notre Dame!" There is a small school of thought that suggests Leahy's curious speech patterns came not from imitating his father's vocabulary mania nor from courses he took in college, but from reading too many pulp magazines as a teenager.

EPISODE 6

The train churns eastward through the prairies and Badlands, throwing soot into the shimmering winter air. Seated on a hard wicker bench, Frank Leahy is wearing the young man's uniform of the day, a flat cap with a short visor, a Winner High School letterman's sweater, a high collar, narrow tie, baggy tweed pants and wingback shoes. A bulky overcoat is thrown over a straw suitcase whose straps are beginning to fray. In several hours, the train will come to a halt at the station in South Bend. Frank Leahy was openly terrified.

"I was a very shy young man, who could barely talk to strangers and I was heading off into what was really the unknown," he said. "I did not have my father's blessings. He had paid for boxing lessons when I was in Omaha. His proudest moment was not when I played football, but when I boxed the great Ace Hudkins in a four round exhibition and Hudkins said that I had a terrific punch. My father was very bitter indeed about my choice."

In his back pocket was a wallet with $19 in it, given to him by friends who had attended his going away party. It was all the money he possessed. An athletic scholarship at Notre Dame consisted of free room, tuition and board. There was never any discussion in those days, at least for most players, about whether they would receive laundry money, free books and a surreptitious charge account down at the local men's store.

"That was all the money I had in the world. At that time it was a large sum, equal to $100 or more now. I sat there in that railroad car, which was heated by a pot belly stove that did not throw enough heat down the aisle to where I was. I was hardly aware of the cold. I did not know what I would say when I finally met Knute Rockne. I did not even know if he would recognize my humble presence with a single word. I wanted to either throw up or get off the train."

Other than the power of prayer, which few Irish Catholic

boys were taught to doubt, Leahy had only one comforting thought. The year before, his brother had taken him down to the train station to meet the Notre Dame team as it stopped in Omaha on its return from a victory over Southern California on the coast. Gene Leahy was there to see his old Creighton coach, Tommy Mills, who had gone to Notre Dame to instruct the freshman team for Rockne. Inside of an hour, Mills had become fascinated by Frank Leahy's observations on the technical aspects of football.

"I certainly hope you're planning on a career in coaching. I'd hate to see you behind a teller's window in a bank."

"Don't worry, coaching is exactly what I have in mind," he said and Tom Swift couldn't have said it any better. There was still a sense of nobility to the profession in those times. Sports had not yet risen to the status of a heavy industry and, perhaps, in Frank Leahy's own particular case, football actually did build character. But this was long before Joe Namath and the athlete-as-supreme-hedonist.

EPISODE 7

Striding through the barren chill of South Bend's gothic train station, it suddenly struck Frank Leahy that he was nothing more than a 19-year-old Dakota cowboy with no great talents to offer except an ability to play tackle with a notable lack of speed and to speak several Indian dialects. He was not even sure of himself as a student. His marks had been good, but hardly notable. There he stood, hoping to play football on one of the nation's best known college football teams. Despite his academic ambitions, he was part of a growing number of young men who had come to a university with the idea of majoring in a sport.

"I made great protestations about being a great scholar, but there was only one thought in my mind," he said. "I wanted to learn all I could from the great master, Knute Rockne, so that someday I could send young lads into battle and help them emerge victorious. It was a consuming passion and, in 1927, it was not considered a shameful thing. The people who knock sports as a force for good in our society were not yet born. There were some who said that an athletic program was needless. But they were few in number.

"As I walked through that station, looking for Tommy Mills, who had promised to give me a ride to the campus, I would say that my character was largely unformed. There were several ways that I could have gone, but the years under Rockne showed me the proper direction. This is true.

"However, as much as I believed in the character-building aspects of sports, I stopped and had a beer while waiting for Mills. I even lied about my age. Shameful!"

The hours passed and Mills did not arrive. Finally, Leahy went outside and hired the first taxi of his life. The fare through downtown South Bend, up the shady boulevards and onto the sycamore-lined campus was a horrendous 35 cents. With a fear that would last an entire lifetime, Leahy handed the driver a nickle and hoped he wouldn't be cursed entirely.

Somehow he managed to find Mills' house. The freshman coach had been off on a speaking trip and had somehow mistaken the day Gene Leahy's younger brother would arrive. In the morning, Frank Leahy was awake at 6 A.M. He moved down the stairs and walked up the avenue toward the college. It was abominably hokey, but it actually took place. As the sun came up to the east beyond Cartier Field, he could see the gleam off the Golden Dome. It could happen only in a cheap movie or in real life. And it did. It happened to this terribly shy, overly sensitive boy.

"A young man makes a pledge to himself. I'm sure that every young man does," he said. "I stood there and I looked at the Golden Dome and the buildings that were covered with ivy and I swore that I would never forget what Clayton Balfany had said to me. I did not want to be a big man in a small community. I wanted to be a small man trying to be a big man in a big community. To me there was nothing larger than, ah, Notre Dame.

"Oooooooh, I tell you, it was love at first sight. I never felt so Catholic in my life as the first time I saw that school. I never felt so proud to be an Irish Catholic. That may sound awfully strange, but it is true. At the time neither group was wanted. But I saw that school and I knew I was wanted. They could never tell me that being Irish or a Catholic was a wrong thing to be in America. And I was determined that if everything else in my life should be a total failure, ah, I would be the truest, finest Irish Catholic I could be. And I would try to show other young men that it was not wrong to be a Catholic in America.

"You know that we had to pay a terrible price in pride in order to be accepted," he said. "It was not easy. We looked like everybody else. We talked like everybody else. We could not be any different than anybody else. I did not truly know that there was prejudice against either the Irish or the Catholics until I went to Omaha with my brother Gene. I know exactly how it feels when a black man tries to do something and somebody tells him he cannot. It was not easy interesting young black athletes in Notre Dame because so few of them were Catholics.

"I would tell them that there were many Protestants attending Our Lady's school. In fact the only way I could tell was at Mass. The Protestants would always be in the back.

"Whenever I would suggest to a mother and father who were black that their son should associate himself with Our Lady, they would always say to me, 'Coach, it is so difficult to go to an integrated state university and expect to get a straight deal, why should we send him to a school where the student body must be almost entirely white and Catholic?' They had an excellent point. In 1927 I would have been terrified even more so to have gone to a Protestant college, even though most of the people in Winner were Protestants and our friends. Many years later, black people of the highest caliber would ask me why my great teams at Notre Dame were always totally white. I would give them the best answer possible. There were so few black Catholics. I would have welcomed any lad, you know. Any lad whatsoever."

The Notre Dame of Frank Leahy's freshman semester was not imaginative architecturally. Other than the dome and the statue of St. Mary, it was not much different than any other college, with its neo-Tudor buildings and its frowzy clumps of hanging ivy. It was as if the Holy Virgin were simply presiding over a piece of Princeton set down on the Indiana plains. This was an Ivy League college for non-Protestants, unless that particular group chose to send a stray member of its flock to the arms of the Vatican. It was sheer heresy, especially in the fundamentalist Midwest. But Jess Harper, the first great

Notre Dame coach, was an Episcopalian who loved this incredible school. He brought to its football team a 5' 8" end named Knute Rockne, who was an Augustian Congregation Lutheran and it was Rockne who recruited that son of a Methodist minister from Michigan, George Gipp. In a sense, Notre Dame started out with an unyielding desire to make Catholics in the new world proud of their heritage and it ended up being the first step toward ecumenicalism. In so doing, it won an amazing amount of football games.

There was once a fourth string tackle who came rushing into a game against Methodist-oriented Northwestern only to hear the man across the line scream: "Who the hell is Rockne going to send in next? The damn Pope?" And in return the Notre Dame player shouted: "Don't give me that crap, I'm a Congregationalist and let's not hear any shit about the Pope, good man that he is."

It was almost impossible to define this strangely mystical school. New entrants almost always expected it to materialize out of a fog, like some kind of magic kingdom. In reality, it was a harsh place where the priests from the Congregation of the Holy Cross confidently expected that everyone would work their tails off even if they didn't happen to be members of the football team. And this was in an era when baseball was still an extremely important sport at the school.

In order to be certain that Notre Dame continued to be the finest, fittest college football team in the nation, Catholic businessmen, as a point of pride, regularly subsidized players. In fact, just before he left, Frank Leahy was told by Denny Lannon, a Notre Dame graduate from Winner with a few dollars in his account, that if he did well and finances became tight there would be a place to go to for comfort.

"Don't call unless you really need the money," Lannon said. "Notre Dame is good for you. It won't offer you a lot of leisure. But I don't want you coming home because you don't have the money. You can almost always get it from me. However, I'd rather have you work hard so you know what the school means to Catholics. Nobody ever gave us anything in this country. We all had to work for it.

The line at the administration office stretched down the hall and up against the door. The registrar glanced up at Leahy and asked: "Halfback?"

"Right now I guess I'd say I was a tackle," Leahy said.

"Not big enough for a tackle," the man replied. "Hope you grow."

They assigned him to Carroll Hall, where most of the Notre Dame football players were asked to spend their time. The priests in charge were all firm in their belief that this one single sport would be the best thing possible for the university. The athletes lived in monkish simplicity, a factor which Rockne insisted upon. Desperate players were the best players. Somehow it seemed to work out nicely. The walls were stark and institutional. The beds looked like they had been borrowed from a hospital. The desks were straight and stiff. Outside, the snow was starting to drift across the walks. Frank Leahy felt desperately alone. He had come a quarter of the way across the nation. He was at a school he had envisioned as being a whole lot more gaudy than it had turned out to be. And the registrar had decided he was a halfback, which he knew quite well he was not.

"In the years ahead, I doubt if any lad who came to the University of Our Lady ever had less confidence in his own ability to make good," he said. "I was simply frozen. There was no place to go except straight ahead. I was totally lost. And if it hadn't been for Knute Rockne, I probably would have gone back down to the train station, put myself on board a coach and got back home to Winner. Chances are I never would have left South Dakota again and nobody would have ever heard of me again."

The next afternoon, though, Frank Leahy went down to the gym and met Knute Rockne.

EPISODE 8

Even in an age of giants, when every sport has at least one immortal it can show the press, there is no one who stands as tall as Knute Rockne does in college football, not even Babe Ruth in baseball nor Bill Tilden in tennis. Those people have competitors. But there is nobody who can even compare with Rockne. He lives on another planet. Even after the passage of years, there are athletes who played for him who cannot believe that he is or was real. The incredible thing about the man is that he looks like nothing at all.

When he arrived at Notre Dame, a Norwegian Protestant in this great Catholic attempt at true WASP-style respectability, he was so painfully shy that he made the Frank Leahy of 1927 seem like a bubbling extrovert in comparison. Few remember the fact that he was only 5′ 8″ and there are those historians who insist that he wasn't quite that big. Rockne had stayed out of school for three years and by the time he was pushing 21 his hair was already starting to leave. He had this sad, beagle look about him. His voice was so high pitched that old recordings make it seem absurd that any team ever got excited over what he had to say. But he was larger than his legend, no matter what folks said.

"I would have hated to have followed him on a speaking program," said Will Rogers. "He was my dear friend and he told me so many stories which I later retold and got all kinds of laughs. If there ever was somebody to whom I owed royalties, it was Rockne. He was the funniest man I ever met." He was the head coach from 1918 through 1930 and he won 105 games, lost 12 and tied 5. He was rumpled, unattractive and unhealthy. Knute Rockne became a football coach because there was something about working around a laboratory that sickened him. He went to Notre Dame because (1) he could afford it and (2) he wanted to become either a doctor or a chemistry professor.

"I had never had much chance to talk to people," he explained. "I lived a very quiet life and before I went to college, I had a job in the post office in Chicago sorting mail. It actually hurt me when the time came and I had to communicate with others."

Rockne had a staccato pitch to his voice and he stammered sometimes because his mind was working far ahead of his tongue. He talked, though, of his boys in much the way that Leahy would later come to speak of his lads. He was as much loved, for no good reason, as Leahy would come to be detested, also for no good reason. Knute Rockne left you overwhelmed, just as Frank Leahy would leave you confused and amazed. You would go away wondering why you had loved Rockne so much and Leahy so little when, in effect, they were the same sort of man.

After a practice, Rockne would come walking up to a man and say: "I hear you're doing better in your French courses." Leahy would say, "They tell me, lad, that Father O'Boyle thinks you will do very well in English this year. I am much pleased." Somehow, Leahy would sound less sincere and there were those who insist it might have been the other way around.

Like many other Americans born in the last century, Rockne spent his early years in Europe. He was born on March 4, 1888, in Voss, Norway. His family name wasn't even Rockne. It was spelled Rokne and pronounced Rock-Nuh. His father, Lars, was a carriage maker who came to America originally because one of his creations was placed on display at the Chicago World's Fair. He sent for his family and the Rocknes settled in the Logan Square section of the town. The oldest son went to Northwest Division High School. He failed to make the football team until his senior year, although he was an outstanding track man. Knute Rockne was a dropout.

"Once," said Leahy, "he told me that he got so wrapped up in sports that he absolutely forgot about his academic life. He wanted to become a great pole vaulter and he just stopped going to class. When it became obvious that he would not graduate on time, he dropped out of school and took a job as a postal clerk. It is a matter of record that he never received a high school diploma. He worked mostly at night and took classes at the University of Illinois extension. He never let his mind become idle, even during that period. He was making $100 a month when he decided that it was time to go to college. He always showed that kind of courage. It never struck him that he might not be able to go to college because he didn't have a high school diploma."

He was accepted at Illinois and then decided to go to South Bend. Rockne asked the priest who enrolled him to show some mercy. He was, he said, a Lutheran and not terribly bright. He was right in one case and wrong in the other. They gave him a high school equivalency examination and he passed it with a 92.5 percent grade average. In college he was remarkable. In ten subjects he had a 100 percent grade, meaning that he didn't miss a question all semester long.

"I had saved $1,000 to see me through college and I felt I could get through Illinois on that," he said. "But two guys I knew, Johnny Plante and Jack Devine, whom I ran track with, told me that even if I was Protestant I should go to Notre Dame. Those Catholics knew what hard times were and they wouldn't over-charge a boy. And I was as poor a Protestant as they would ever see. I felt right at home. Protestant or Catholic, it didn't make a bit of difference. Not a damn bit. We were all the same people. Poor!"

There was a charming, almost slummish sort of look about Rockne, as if he had just stepped out of the line at a soup kitchen. It was said by a close friend that he could take an expensive hat and make it seem as if it had just been purchased off the counter at a charitable organization. He was the common man personified, which is why he was the right man for the right time at the right school, Notre Dame. He didn't have to be a Catholic, not until he wanted to become one. It was probably best for the school that he wasn't one. It increased the Plebian image.

"He looks like an old, punched-up preliminary fighter who becomes door-tender in a speakeasy," wrote Westbrook Pegler, the noted literary assassin for the Hearst newspapers. "He sits at a shadowy table in a corner near the door at night, recalling the time he fought Billy Papke in Peoria for $50. No one would ever suspect that Knute Rockne was a great football coach. He simply refuses to act or look the part."

It was a clever description. Rockne read it and never talked to Pegler again, which did not exactly make him unique. Truth is that Rockne tried hard to do something about his image. He honestly did. When his hair started leaving him, he spent hundreds of dollars on restoratives. When his nose collapsed, because of a foul tip off a bat, he went to a plastic surgeon in Chicago. The man just shook his head, the science being somewhat primitive at the time. With characteristic courage, he turned to boxing with Gus Dorais squatting in his corner. The idea was that the two of them would split what money they made. And they made very little.

"The first time I saw Rockne, he looked like a man far too old for college," said Dorais who made a national reputation throwing passes at this gnarled little end. "He was wearing blue cord pants, held up with white leather suspenders. He had on a light blue jersey with a black cap. He could have passed for a race track tout. At least, that's what I thought he might be."

As it turned out, Rockne was something of a prude. He believed that Notre Dame was the best place to coach football because there were no female students and the latter only provided a terrible distraction. Rockne detested social events, although he continually gave the impression that he was something of a party-lover. People who couldn't control themselves after hours were put away as "lounge lizards." He insisted that his players wear corduroy pants and sweaters. Nobody was permitted to drink, talk nasty or think ugly thoughts. Anybody caught co-habitating with a lady during the regular season was unspeakable and therefore highly eligible for dismissal from America's best known Catholic institution. When he drank, it was strictly within moderation and he sometimes acted as if he were being poisoned.

He was a genius at understanding his own worth. While the rest of the nation groveled at his toenails, Knute Kenneth Rockne was enormously self-effacing. They said he was a genius and a master of his craft. He said he was simply the right man in the right place. Football had been important at Notre Dame long before he arrived. The school was not unknown when he arrived. The man he played for, Jess Harper, had been one of America's best known coaches. During one stretch, between 1910 through 1914, the school had won 26 games without a defeat.

Why, Notre Dame had defeated Army, with the injured Dwight Eisenhower sitting on the bench. The score had been 35-13 and this was not one of West Point's weaker teams. It was accomplished with a passing game no one had ever seen before. The summer before, Harper had suggested that Dorais and Rockne work on throwing and catching the football. Working on the hot sands of Cedar Point, next to Lake Erie, they made history. It was a beautiful scene. Dorais would take the snap from center and aim the ball straight at his runt of an end. Twice he completed passes for 40 yards or more. Army spread its defenses and fullback Ray Eichenlaub ran up the middle. They say that modern football was born that very afternoon and it is quite possible that was not an excessive statement.

On that day, Walter Camp, holder of the sacred keys, had named Eichenlaub to his second All-America team and Rockne to the third. Henceforth, Notre Dame would always be considered part of the college football elite.

Because working indoors in a chemistry laboratory made him ill, Rockne asked for a more healthy assignment. They made him an assistant football coach under Harper in 1916. It was just one of those insane occurrences. There had to be something the school could do with a graduate who showed such remarkable promise.

"Even as an assistant, Rockne was an outstanding speaker," said Chet Grant, quarterback for the 1916 team. "Once, before the game with Wabash in 1916, he gave such an impressive talk that we went out and defeated the enemy by a 60-0 score. Our feet never hit the ground once on the way out the door. You have never felt such a tingle in your soul. It was obvious even then that Rock was something special."

Almost from the start, Rockne was unable to accept the fact that he had any ability to charm, soothe or stimulate by speaking. When people praised him for his oratory, he looked at them as if they were quite mad. As late as 1921, he addressed the student body at Notre Dame before a game. When the undergraduates were still shouting, he turned and asked a friend, "Do you think I reached them?"

"When my mother was dating my father, they sometimes doubled up with Rockne and the woman he married," said Ohio congressman Sam Devine. "My mother truly liked Rock and she was always amazed that anyone went out with him a second time, despite the fact that he was a fine man. It was just that he was so shy he hardly said a word all evening and he certainly wasn't the most handsome man around. My mother acted like a big sister to him and she said in later years that the reason people were drawn to him was because he had been able to develop poise and warmth, which he did not naturally possess."

Even after he became successful, Rockne always sort of stumbled around the campus. Never did he make more than $10,000 until the final few years of his life when outside affairs pushed his income up around $30,000. As an undergraduate, he wore a monogram sweater around the grounds at Notre Dame and always seemed to be borrowing an overcoat from somebody. When he became the nation's best known college football coach, when he was a walking, talking legend, he always seemed to be wearing a crumpled sweat shirt and, despite his success, he still seemed to be borrowing an overcoat from somebody.

"Rock had a mind that touched genius," wrote Francis Wallace. "He had a blow torch spirit, physical courage, infectious humor, rare charm. He was a hungry, talented immigrant, eager to prove that he belonged. He was a battlefield of emotion, intellect, moods and feuds. He could be petty, secretive, suspicious. But there was in him neither malice nor hate. Mostly, he was generous, kind, naive. He had no great design, lived from day to day, doing the things he thought should be done. When opportunity came, he was always ready. He usually won because he could think more quickly and more swiftly than bigger opponents. Had he been consistently wrong, he could have been in much trouble because he dared so far. He became a football coach by necessity, remained a football coach by choice. He dignified all sports beyond logic by proving sports could demand and absorb just about every mental, emotional, spiritual and physical resource a human might have. His football was a skillful blend of science and art."

And so Frank Leahy whose actual father never understood him any better than Frank Leahy understood his actual father went walking through the gymnasium one winter's day in 1927 moving closer, closer, closer to Knute Rockne, the man to whom he bore a more stylish resemblance than any other man on earth. Both were shy lions. Both were blazing perfectionists. Both brought to an otherwise prosaic athletic endeavor a touch of nobility. Both of them destroyed themselves physically over a sport lesser men would laugh at. No two men would ever coach football so successfully, yet Rockne would remain a beloved father figure and Leahy would always be an enigma. And no one would ever be able to say just why it happened that way.

EPISODE 9

"When I saw the man it seemed that he should be a whole lot taller and a whole lot more handsome. But the

more I watched him as he came across the gymnasium floor, the taller he seemed and the better looking he got. By the time he was reaching out to shake my hand I thought he was the tallest, best looking man I had ever met," said Frank Leahy. "I guess that's what hero worship can do to you, if you aren't being very careful."

By rights there should have been some sort of dramatic flourish. There should have been trumpets and drums. But in real life, matters tend to be less exciting. There was Frank Leahy, young and shy, standing in the middle of the gymnasium floor at Notre Dame, talking with his brother's friend, Tommy Mills; Rockne came striding out of his office. Mills went through the formality of an introduction.

"Coach Rockne," said Leahy. "I'm from South Dakota."

"Oh, yes! It's Leahy, of course. Heard much about you from Earl Walsh. Hear you play football pretty well. They tell me you don't run as well as you hit people. Don't worry about speed. No trouble there. Speed isn't everything. You can play for Notre Dame if you want to hit people and win football games. You're a fine looking boy. Just fine."

There was an awkward pause. Rockne somehow sensed Leahy's discomfort. He lowered his voice and switched from the staccato stammer. Once upon a time he had been equally ill at ease. The rapport between the two would never change.

"Feel scared as hell, don't you, Frank?" he asked. "It's got to be tough. You'll get over that lost feeling in a couple of days. I did. Oh, God, did I feel like there wasn't a friend in the world! There are a lot of other fellows who feel just the same way. In a couple of weeks, when the snow's off the ground and Tommy here has you out on the field with the other freshmen, you'll think you never left South Dakota. If you need to talk to me in the meantime, I'll be around. I'm not one of those coaches who hides in the office. Four years from now when you're a senior, you'll see freshmen like yourself and you'll know how scared they feel. I never forgot."

"Yes, coach," said Leahy.

"Oh, by the way," said Rockne. "You've got football player's legs. That's for sure. See that you take care of them. Tommy, make sure he sees the statue of Our Lady."

Both Mills and Leahy turned to leave.

"Oh, Frank," Rockne called.

"Yes, coach?"

"Saw your grades from Winner High school," he said. "Better plan on enrolling in the school of physical education. Be the best thing for you."

On the way through the gymnasium door, it occurred to Frank Leahy that he had traveled all the way from South Dakota without a clear idea of what it was he wanted to major in. Previously, school had simply been school. All academic classes had a tendency to look alike. He had come to Notre Dame not so much to study as to play football and be a part of the University subculture. Now somebody had brought up a nagging point. He was going to have to study things like zoology, biology, theory of football coaching and kinesiology. It was a severe jolt to his nervous system.

"Athletes were not so well prepared for college in those days," Leahy said. "It probably did not occur to coach Rockne that I might not have any idea what kind of course of study I wanted to pursue. Athletes came and they went. It was the era of the great tramp athlete. Coach Rockne himself knew dozens of them. His good friend, Emil Hauser, played at Haskell Institute under his own name. Then he came to Carlisle and played four more years as Chief Waseka.

"These people roamed the nation, playing a semester here and a semester there. Sometimes they wouldn't even bother to enroll in the school. They'd just show up for football practice. They'd leave after the schedule was over. There was a lad I knew briefly that first semester who said he was Tim Foley. He bragged that Notre Dame was his sixth school and that he had played for eight years. Coach Rockne was good at rooting out this sort of person. One day he recognized Foley as an end who had played the previous season, either at Wabash or Drake. His name then had been George Marchikowski. I must admit that he had a better chance at Notre Dame as Tim Foley."

That evening, Frank Leahy had his first meal at Carroll Hall, met another freshman player named Lawrence (Moon) Mullins who was to become a lifelong friend and learned that first year men were not eligible for second helpings. When he reached his room, he made another discovery, one that was even more distressing. Here he was at this noble Catholic institution. He had not only met the Great Rockne, he had had a pleasant conversation with him. His heart should have been full. It wasn't. Somebody had stolen his wallet.

EPISODE 10

In the spring of the year, darkness settled early on Cartier Field, leaving it a murky pool of dark, swirling figures. Notre Dame football had grown so large and so important that in this grandiose period, no man wanted to be anything but the last man off the practice field. It was a point of honor and, in this era of American knighthood, the trappings of honor were still important. Because he had taken two vows, one for his brother and one for the meek hearted Clayton Balfany, it was impossible for Frank Leahy to leave at a decent hour. Even Rockne himself would be home eating and there would be Leahy, working one-on-one with some other young squire.

"No one wanted to admit that he was either tired or bored," said Leahy. "It just wasn't the thing to do. It is fashionable now for players to make demands upon their coach. In that period, it was considered the low point of cowardice to quit. I could have used more time to study, classwork not coming easily to me. But I did not want to admit that I was anything but the best tackle on the Notre Dame freshman team. It was a whole different way of looking at things. To fail was to be dishonored. And we actually talked that way.

"The players of my day had their jokes. But they were never, ah, cynical. Oooooh, there was griping about how hard we had to work. But there were few players who, when the day was finally done, didn't feel as if they hadn't contributed something to the University. Glory and honor are lightly considered now. But they were really important things when I was young. To struggle to make Notre Dame pre-eminent in football was noble. Being asked to sacrifice one's own good time for the sake of the school was also noble. To hurt and bleed a little for Notre Dame made a lad feel strong.

"Now, I suspect, it is just the opposite. To defy the school is to show strength. To work hard is to be weak. Wearing long hair and smoking marijuana are not the true problems. They are symptoms. I don't know that wearing long hair is bad. I am told that marijuana is not as dangerous as some people insist that it is. Maybe it is, maybe it isn't. I don't think it is good. As a young lad at Notre Dame, even having a beer was considered sinful. To have a date was to break training, although I must admit that I was often tempted along those lines.

"A football scholarship was not entirely free in those days. One was also expected to work. I was given a mop and broom and told that cleaning up the locker room was part of my chores. Others chalked the field or sold programs at other sporting events. Free rides were not truly free rides."

These were frustrating times for Leahy, who confidently expected that simply because he was willing to work harder than anyone else he would be given the opportunity to start for the freshmen. It wasn't necessarily so. Rockne worked the varsity in the middle of the field and the freshmen were sort of pushed off in a corner, where, hopefully, none of them would get lost. Despite his devotion to duty, Leahy opened his first year at Notre Dame as the second string offensive tackle behind Art McManmon, whose brother happened to be one of the freshman assistants. So Leahy did exactly what he thought was best. He stayed out on the field later and hit harder. Strive and succeed. There was no other course, or so he was now firmly convinced.

One afternoon, Rockne came hustling down to the enclosure where the Notre Dame freshmen were beating each other raw in order to demonstrate their love for the Mother of God. It was not Rockne's habit to speak at length with subordinates. He slammed out sentences as if they were bullets escaping from the muzzle of a gun and the enemy was getting closer.

"Try Leahy at center," he shouted. "See what he can do for us there. You'll like the position, Frank. Know you will."

It was done that quickly. There was no arguing, no discussion. Frank Leahy who had never made a center snap in his life suddenly had his hands gripped around the snub nose of a football. Not once did he suggest to Knute Rockne that he had been dehumanized. Instead, he took yet another vow. By golly, he would become the finest center in Notre Dame history. He even asked the trainer to let him take a ball back to his residence hall. After his evening meal and before he settled down to explore the mysteries of freshman zoology, he would practice centering the ball. Tom Swift, Frank Merriwell and the Hardy boys would have done no other. Those times really existed and young lads actually behaved that way.

There was absolutely no reason given for moving Leahy to center. It's just that Rockne operated that way. He might have had as many as a dozen complete units at practice. He never kept a depth chart but always knew exactly who was playing where and who might be switched from fullback to guard or from quarterback to end. Chances are he had given the change far more thought than anyone imagined. Convinced that he had been moved from tackle to center by some act of God, Leahy returned and spent most of the evening whipping an old practice ball back at Adam Kosky and John Sullivan, two of his roommates, who cheerfully endured the project, mostly because they were now used to Leahy's fanaticism over the game of football.

"No matter what the rest of us did on the football field, Frank always made us seem like we weren't putting out. He worked so hard that a lot of us who really liked him, complained about him privately," Moon Mullins once said. "You'd practice until your fingernails would sweat. There would be Frank giving it something extra. He was such a perfectionist that it scared you. I think that's why Rockne loved him so much—and did you know Frank was just like him. Oh, Rock was warmer personally. And it took a little time to understand what a warm person Frank was down inside his soul. But they were so much alike. Both were shy and refused to settle for anything less than a perfect football team."

Since the varsity started practice an hour earlier than the freshmen, Leahy would stand and watch Tim Moynihan, the dark curly-haired son of a Chicago police chief, who was the first line center on the Notre Dame varsity. He bothered poor Moynihan so much about football theory that Leahy was finally ordered to keep still and just observe. With no one to turn to, Leahy decided to work on his own textbook. Slowly and analytically, he broke center play down into a series of movements. The single wing was the fundamental truth of the decade. Centers did more snapping and less blocking. They looked at the world upside down.

"There was the drag play and the flip to the quarterback," said Leahy. "There was the float pass to the fullback for a plunge. Then you had to throw a leading pass through your legs to the tailback who might be moving on an end sweep or an off-tackle play. Then you had to get a spiral back to the punter. Everything had to look the same and you had to move quickly to make a block. I even diagrammed the moves. I wanted to think that Rockne moved me to the position because I was, ah, able to think quickly and innovate. Because this was my conviction, I developed a fetish for, ah, fundamentals."

One evening, he hunched over the ball, pretending that the man down the hall, John Sullivan, was actually a Notre Dame football player back in punt formation, struggling desperately to remove the Irish from a delicate situation against Army or Michigan State. With strength and speed, he sent the ball spinning backwards. Unfortunately, Sullivan was just a student. The snap soared over his head, through a window which was closed at the time and into the yard outside where Father Vincent Mooney caught it on one bounce.

"I suppose I should pay for the broken glass," said Leahy, who didn't own a dollar at the time.

"Many exceptions are made for Notre Dame football players," said Father Mooney. "And, for your sake, I sincerely hope you are a good one."

While there was still a window left in Carroll Hall and while there was still a class remaining that Leahy hadn't cut in favor of extra football practice, they voted him the Hering medal for outstanding play at center. These were awards given by a former University of Chicago quarterback named Frank Hering, who had been an assistant coach at Notre Dame while attending the law school. They went annually to players who worked hardest in practice. The coaches sat down and voted on which end caught passes the best, which tackle moved across the line of scrimmage quickest, which guards pulled out of the line and blocked the best and which quarterback acted most intelligent at reading defenses. They gave the one for center to Frank Leahy just before he killed someone, either himself or somebody on the defensive unit that had to scrimmage against him.

"It was the proudest moment of my entire life," he said. "I cannot explain what that medal meant to me. It meant that I had achieved something of value at Notre Dame. I had labored very hard and I had won something worth winning. I could take it home and show it to my brother Gene and let him know that his faith in me was not wasted. I had mastered a strange position."

Leahy had also come down with the first truly disturbing illness of his life. In the midst of a practice, he had been kicked in the eye, requiring several stitches to close the wound. The next day, he hitch-hiked to Ontario with Adam Kosky and Frank Carideo. Coming back through Detroit they ran into a serious rainstorm. The temperature fell drastically. Leahy came down with a cold that settled in the injured eye. He spent a week in the infirmary. He came tottering out in time for the annual scrimmage between the varsity and the freshmen.

"That Leahy was superlative," said Rockne afterwards. "There's a young man you can count on. Not the best football player around, but certainly one of the smartest. He'll be on the traveling squad next year. Be sure of that."

The varsity season ended with Notre Dame losing to Army by an 18-0 score. There was Frank Leahy on his bed in Carroll Hall trying not to think about this great natural disaster. A small blond boy came peddling up from downtown South Bend with a telegram from coach Rockne himself. It was addressed to Leahy and he was ordered to get every freshman player he could find in order to bring as many members of the student body as possible down to the train station to welcome the team back the next morning.

"I had been so deeply honored by this telegram. Coach Rockne considered me to be the freshman team leader," he said. "How else would he have selected me to do such a thing? I did not sleep that night.

"I worked continuously on the project. The train was due in at 5:23 A.M. and I had everybody at the station on time. Players ran through the dormitories. I doubt if there was a single student there who wasn't thrilled. Only the sick ones in the infirmary stayed behind and, then, only the serious cases. The band was there playing the, ah, Victory March. When the team swung down off the train, every player's eyes brightened. Right then I knew that I had made the proper choice of schools. Ooooooh, it sounds silly now, when students do not care so much about their alma maters. But at that time, it was as close to perfection as a young man could get. We did, indeed, shake down the thunder that morning. I wore my Hering medal to let them know how I felt."

This was the gilded era, the age of chivalry with great heroes like Ruth and Grange and Bobby Jones and Knute Rockne, about whom no unpleasant words were ever said. There were also despicable villains roaming the land, people with no redeeming social characteristics. There was Bill Tilden to love and Al Capone and Pretty Boy Floyd and John Dillinger and all the others to hate. One either adhered to the code of goodness or he ran the risk of losing his immortal soul. There was no question of what influenced Frank Leahy. He wanted to be one with his God and also play football for Notre Dame.

"Dost thou see that knight that comes riding up directly towards us on a dapple-gray steed with a helmet of gold on his head?"
"I see what I see," replied Sancho. "And the devil of anything if I can spy but a fellow on such another gray ass as mine is with something that glistens on his head. It seems to be a shaving basin, for he must be a barber."
"I tell thee, that is Mambrino's helmet," replied Don Quixote. "Do thou stand at a distance and leave me to deal with him? Thou shall see, that without trifling away so much as a moment in needless talk, I will finish this adventure and possess myself of this desired helmet."—from Cervantes, who could have been a sports writer, if he had tried.

EPISODE 11

Young men of the 1920s who did not care about developing their character spent their summers away from college in idle pursuits. But Frank Leahy had been, he felt, annointed by the blessed Rockne himself and he was burning with a holy fever. He joined his brother Gene, who had now opened an insurance business in Rushville, Nebraska. He could have had an easy job from a Notre Dame alumnus. He could have spent the summer looking for whales on the shores of Lake Michigan. But Rockne despised athletes who insisted on taking life easy, calling them "lounge lizards" and "mezzanine cowboys." So Frank Leahy took a job crushing rocks for a contractor, swinging a sledge in the sizzling heat and feeling very virtuous.

He limited himself to no more than two beers a day, a terrible handicap for an Irishman, he said. He pitched baseball and played right field next to his brother Gene for the Rushville town team. On one memorable afternoon, he started against a touring group of black stars and won, 4-2, defeating a scrawny young pitcher from Mobile named Leroy Paige, whom everybody called Satchefoot. History does crazy things like that. No one in the 1940s would ever associate the finest football coach of the decade with baseball's most celebrated black outcast. But once upon a time, in Hot Springs, South Dakota, they faced each other in an athletic contest. Miraculously the football coach won.

"I had to work hard," said Leahy. "Coach Rockne was, ah, demanding. There were so many legends about him that some of them had to be true. They said that once, when he was still teaching chemistry and working as an assistant coach under Jess Harper, he was asked to instruct a class made up entirely of nuns who had a teaching vocation. One good sister failed to get the point and Rock yelled, 'Sister, that went right off your head like a billiard ball bouncing off concrete.' Nobody in those days ever said anything to a Sister that wasn't respectful. But coach Rock dared to, and they say the nun even grinned."

Never for a moment would Frank Leahy be presumptive enough to think that he could beat Moynihan out of a job, but he desperately wanted to move ahead of Joe Nash who was the second man on Rockne's mental depth chart. The man who had centered the ball for Gene at Creighton, Dr. John Broz, spent an evening coaching Leahy on the refinements of the position. And every Saturday morning before the weekly baseball game, he would go out in a meadow and practice snapping the ball to Larry Chamberlain, who had played quarterback at Creighton the year before.

"Perhaps, in retrospect I may have seemed like a fanatic," said Leahy, "but people have come to forget how truly gigantic college football was in the period I speak about. There were 112,000 present at Soldier Field in Chicago to see Notre Dame play Southern California. That is still, I believe, the all-time football attendance record. Writers toured the campuses doing stories on the top teams. Simply being mentioned for All-America was a most distinct honor. A man could live his entire life profitably on such slight recognition. Professional football was a crowd-pleasing circus, something to be openly scorned. The pros threw the ball on fourth down and long yardage. The objective was theatrics, not sound football. The public believed that college football was the finest entertainment form in the nation.

"In order to succeed you simply had to be dedicated. Coach Rockne was very firm. He was always dropping into the Oliver Hotel where Notre Dame football players regularly took their dates. He felt that girls were a serious distraction. 'You can't be a lover and a football player, too,' he was fond of saying. He wanted his players to spend their spare time in the gymnasium playing handball for agility or boxing and wrestling for toughness. If you dated too often or if he did not see you working out on a regular basis, he would chastise you. And he would do it with a few devastating sentences.

"You felt that you were somehow letting the University of Notre Dame down. And in so doing you were letting down Our Lady, who watched over all of us. I did not know until some years later that Rockne had not always been a Catholic. He had converted only a few years before I arrived at South Bend. You would have thought he had been one all his life. They tell an interesting tale, which may not be true. They say that he asked his 1924 team, the only one that went to a bowl, what reward they wanted for going undefeated and somebody is alleged to have said, 'We'd like you to join us in the Catholic Church.'

"I find that difficult to believe. There was always strict religious tolerance at Notre Dame and no Protestant or Jewish student could be approached by a priest who had conversion in mind. So therefore, I would doubt that Catholic players

114

would approach their Protestant coach in such an open manner. I believe that Rock turned Catholic because he wanted to. He did not even invite the players when he was accepted into the church. He told them that it was far too personal a thing. If he had done it as a reward he would have had them all there. Don't forget that Mrs. Rockne and his children were all practicing Catholics. At any rate, it makes an interesting legend about the 1924 team. Rock was not above creating legends. Oooooh, he did it, you know."

This should have been Frank Leahy's finest hour. Instead it was almost a total disaster. He played only a few minutes all season on what was Rockne's worst Notre Dame team. He never was given an opportunity at center and there were moments when the idea of transferring to Creighton actually came creeping across his brain, but only a heretic would think such a thought, so Leahy dismissed it. He did walk into his room that fall and find Johnny O'Brien, who was going to be part of the Notre Dame football tapestry in a negative sort of way. Here was a cheerful, bright-eyed man with an unshakeable sense of humor who never saw anything dismal about life, who was one of the finest trackmen in the school's history and who grew to endure the nickname One-Play O'Brien with an uncommon grace. Only once in his career as a Notre Dame football player did he distinguish himself. And there are those who suspect that he made the name up as a joke on himself.

"He could be that way," said Leahy. "He knew what a somber, fretful person I was and he did his best to change me. I didn't know I had a sense of humor until O'Brien told me I did. When I would get too serious or too involved in Notre Dame football, he would say something like, 'Hey, Frank, let's go take a walk and not worry so much about life. You're going to be alive tomorrow and you'll work something out. You fidget like my old grandmother.' Do you know that I never really heard that phrase 'One-Play O'Brien' until he used it? I think he made it up himself because he thought it was funny. Ooooooh, Jonathan O'Brien thought everything was funny. I truly admired his ability to get outside himself. Do you know that this wonderfully happy man was killed in an automobile accident? I wonder where God was hiding when that happened."

During the first varsity-freshman scrimmage, it was obvious

to everybody, Rockne included, that this might be a slower year than normal. It was the freshmen who dominated, pushing the older players around almost at ease. Leahy hardly played, sending him into a depression that even Johnny O'Brien had difficulty dragging him out of. Finally, the 6′ 5″ end simply reached down, grabbed his roommate, shook him vigorously and yelled, "Let's forget it, old buddy."

No one was really worried. Rockne was mighty and would prevail. Notre Dame football had reached that point on the evolutionary scale where perfection was expected. It would never change and when Frank Leahy, who understood the legends and the attitudes better than most, actually achieved it, he would be sorely criticized and even driven away. Such is the anomaly at South Bend. And it exists even unto this day.

Matched against Loyola of New Orleans in their opening game, Rockne's players went rumbling through the dressing room door with an emotional charge lingering in the air behind them. They did their sitting-up exercises and then fell over on their manly profiles. No one gave Loyola even a vague chance of keeping the score close. It took a 40 yard run by Jack Elder to break a 6-6 tie in the fourth period. And that's how it ended, with Notre Dame clutching passionately to a 12-6 victory.

"It was obvious to everybody that the sophomores were not going to play much that year," said Leahy. "My heart sank when I realized that the veterans were not really as good as everybody thought they would be. To save the school's reputation, Rockne was going to have to use the regulars as much as possible. In my first varsity game, I played exactly one minute and 36 seconds. I kept track on the stadium clock. Even that was a miracle. As I ran onto the field I realized that I had not adequately prepared myself psychologically. This is something the athlete has to do for himself.

"Certainly coach Rockne couldn't have foreseen my jittery condition. I had visions of blocking my own man as I had done at Winner High or failing completely to accomplish some assignment. I knew I would not get many opportunities to prove myself that year. I realized that I had made the dangerous mistake of under-rating our opponent. I could visualize myself appearing in my first Notre Dame game and being part of a defeat. Ooooooh, I could not stand that idea.

"I made my mind up. Never would I show anything except the greatest respect for an opponent and I would never catch myself on the sidelines unprepared. Ooooooh, they laughed at me when I became a head coach. They said that I was a gloomy person, a man who invented false fears. But I never forgot the lesson learned in the Loyola–Notre Dame game. I became a total pessimist because I believed that caution was the surest route. It is better to fear the worst and be pleasantly surprised than it is to expect victory and be thoroughly disappointed."

There was one small gain. Leahy made the traveling squad and Rockne told him about it with typical coyness. "Ever eat a steak on a Pullman dining car, Frank?" he asked. They went steaming off to Madison for what was supposed to be an easy Notre Dame victory. There was Leahy chewing on a porterhouse as the landscape slipped past. It struck him that he was probably no longer a boy, no longer a child with a hazy future. Whatever else happened to him in his life, he could always say that he went to college at South Bend and made the traveling squad. There was a quiet sort of confidence in that, even if he ended up running a general store in Winner, South Dakota.

"Right up until the time we kicked off, I was living in a world of, ah, dreams. The team went to Mass and Communion the day of the game. I had my ankles taped in a hotel ballroom along with everybody else. Then we all had a steak breakfast and rode out to the stadium," he said. "This was a far better Wisconsin team than anyone imagined. They had agility and a great deal of grit. Notre Dame was known as a school where ball handling was taught. But we gave them seven fumbles . . . or, perhaps, they took seven fumbles. They scored on three of them. It was a badly flawed afternoon and, ah, they won by a 22-6 score."

On the way home, Rockne sat in sullen disbelief. His fullback Joe Savoldi came down the aisle, whistling happily, trying to make his colleagues feel better. "You must think we all just went to see Ringling Brothers, huh, Joe?" snapped the coach. When Notre Dame lost to Georgia Tech in Atlanta by 13-0, it was apparent that this was not going to be one of those thunderously impressive Rockne teams. The great coach grew less fatherly and more concerned over his own reputation. In the sixth game of the schedule, against Penn State in Philadelphia, the Irish barely survived, 9-0. As the team bus pulled away, looking for the train station, it blew a rear tire.

Several of the players took a walk while the bus company mechanic worked with the spare. The others were back in time, but Frank Leahy got lost. As he came puffing up the stairs, Rockne leaned forward and yelled, "It must be tougher getting around Philadelphia than it is finding your way out of a South Dakota bean patch. If you don't want to go back there, Frank, you'd better remember where the bus is."

The following Monday, Rockne went to the church on campus and knelt at the altar rail where only one votive candle was burning.

"What's that for?" he asked Father Mooney.

"I lit it myself," said the priest. "It's for the football team."

"Don't be so cheap with the wax," Rockne said.

The next afternoon, he still hadn't settled the furies flying through his soul. He saw Leahy turned upside down, centering the ball in practice. "See me later on, Frank," he shouted. "It's important. Be at my office."

Life was getting touchy around the Notre Dame campus, he explained. The alumni were starting to think of him as being something less than the incarnation of St. Jude, the patron saint of impossible causes. There was a depth problem at tackle and would Leahy mind switching back? It was an over-whelming suggestion. What was all that work for? Hadn't he won that medal?

"The thing I like about you, Frank, is that you take on any task you're given with great enthusiasm," Rockne said. "We don't have a backup man for Fred Miller at right tackle now that Jerry Ransavage is hurt. It's got to be you, Frank. Got to be."

"Sure, coach, I'd love to try playing tackle again," said Leahy who walked out of the office in a state of total confusion. Someday, psychologists would come to call this an identity crisis. For the moment, Frank Leahy had no idea exactly who he was. He had struggled so hard to become a good center and be part of something that he viewed with a mystic's vision. Now he wasn't quite sure whether he was demoted, promoted or simply pushed aside. No one was ever sure with Rockne. Sometimes when a second team man was ready for a chance to be a starter and it was felt that he might not be able to handle the move without his ego first being deflated, Rockne would drop him to the fifth or sixth unit during practice and then announce, on the morning of the game, that he was now an official member of the first platoon.

"If it had been part of my nature, I think I would have dropped out of school that evening. I was deathly discouraged," Leahy said. "I moped back to my room and there was Johnny O'Brien to pick me up with a joke. I knew I wasn't going to win a Notre Dame monogram now. That hurt me deeply, ah, yes, it did. But O'Brien talked me out of it. Oooooooh, God bless Jonathan O'Brien. If he hadn't reinforced my courage I would not have been with the team on November 12, 1928, at Yankee Stadium. Oooooh, that would have been most unfortunate for me."

On the Notre Dame calendar of feast days, the holiest is November 12. It commemorates that afternoon when Rockne walked quietly into the dressing room at halftime of the Army game and moved from player to player, offering only small scraps of advice and encouragement. This was a brilliant Army team, with Chris Cagle in the backfield and six victories on his season's record. Like a great preacher, Rockne was building slowly to the greatest sermon of his career.

His team was locked in a scoreless tie, one that nobody had expected to exist so late in a ball game that Army should have been winning by a comfortable margin. But there was Jimmy Walker, the song writer who was mayor of New York. There were numerous important people standing along the walls. It was the proper place for a magnificent performance.

Gently, Rockne began to talk. The machine-gun-fire voice had all but disappeared. He acted like a man who could not find the proper words easily. He glanced toward the ceiling hesitantly, while gripping a cigar in his hand. He seemed like a man who had seen a vision of the Holy Grail and was all but transfixed by it.

"Boys, it will be years next month since I visited a mighty sick young man in St. Joseph's Hospital," he said. "He was breathing his last few breaths in this world. He was a fine young man, a man who had contributed so much to the University they named for Our Lady. There he was, on his deathbed, and he had just become a Catholic. He wanted so badly to be a complete part of Notre Dame. But, boys, he had already brought glory to our school as the greatest back in the nation. His name was George Gipp. Remember that name. Never forget it.

"Years after he died, I met a girl named Irene. She was a town girl and she was the girl that George Gipp would have married. I tried to get her to tell me something about him that I might not have known and all she would say was, 'George Gipp was a great gentleman.'

"You know, boys, just before he died, George Gipp called me over close to him and in phrases that were barely whispers, he said, 'Sometime, Rock, when the team's up against it, when things are wrong and the breaks are beating the boys—tell them to go in there and win just one for the Gipper. I don't know where I'll be then, Rock, but I'll know about it and I'll be happy.' Within a few minutes that great Notre Dame gentleman, George Gipp, had died."

Tears flowed down Frank Leahy's handsome Irish cheeks. He peered around the room. Everybody else was in a high state of emotionalism. Up against the door, flanked by two New York policemen, was Jimmy Walker, who was sobbing convulsively. The police were biting their lips.

"Boys, I'm firmly convinced that this is that game George Gipp would want us to win for him. Okay, let's go!"

The atmosphere fairly crackled. These weren't football players, but holy zealots. There was, quite literally, a stampede to the door. For the rest of his life, Leahy would not be able to tell the story without weeping unrestrainedly. This was what Rockne needed. This team would lose four games, one third of the total defeats of his career. He had to do something drastic, especially in front of the New York audience.

So Army kicked off, unaware that it was about to receive an incredible lesson in the value of psychological warfare. With a line whipped to near-fanaticism, Notre Dame drove 80 yards only to lose the ball when Fred Collins, playing with his broken wrist in a cast, fumbled on the two. As the third quarter neared an end, Army was leading 6-0 and Jack Chevigny, a crusader with a strong emotional streak, pulled everybody in the huddle and reminded them that they had a sacred obligation to win. The tears flowed again.

"We've got to score before the end of the period," shouted Chevigny.

So Notre Dame moved another 80 yards. From the one yard line, Chevigny cut to his left and plowed straight into an Army tackle. Legend says that he shouted: "That's one for the Gipper!" The remark is not documented. Nobody knows for sure if, indeed, he said anything. Since Chevigny was killed with the Marines in the battle for Iwo Jima, he can neither confirm nor deny the story. Those who knew him insist that it was something he was apt to have said, and that appears good enough. Leahy never knew. He sat on the bench the entire afternoon.

The winning touchdown was one of those things that should be somehow captured in bronze and placed in a museum showcase. With the ball on Army's 22 yard line, Rockne sent in Johnny O'Brien and the quarterback, Pat Brady, called his number. The tailback took the snap, faked a sweep to the left and then lateraled to another back, Butch Niemiec, who also faked a run and then threw a pass on a high parabola to O'Brien who had moved behind Army's left cornerback. The ball bounced crazily off O'Brien's shoulder pad and then down to his chest. He must have moved five yards before he brought it under control, clutching it to his bosom with his forearms as he rolled across the West Point goal line. It was unartistic, but remarkable. He was "One-Play O'Brien" from the moment he walked off the field where Rockne waited to pull a blanket around his shoulders to the moment he perished in the auto crash.

"There are many mangled facts about that afternoon," said Leahy. "Ooooooh, there are so many. I am supposed to have played in that game. To my embarrassment, I did not. It has also been written that Rockne made the speech before the game. It happened at halftime. He is supposed to have blasted it out in stentorian phrases. He did not do that either. It was very soft, very gentle and very emotional. It has also been stated by many that Gipp did not actually say that on his deathbed. There being no known witnesses, it is difficult to say whether he did or he didn't, but I suspect that he probably did.

"I have heard it said that the year after Gipp's death, Rockne asked the team to win one for the Gipper in the hotel meeting room before the game with Indiana. Yet, I have never been able to locate a single person who was at that meeting who could verify the account that he used the speech in 1921. I have even met people who do not believe that he actually said it during the Army game in 1928. I was there personally and you can be sure that he made the speech. I think that the fame of the scene from the movie may have made people think it was fictional.

"It was not reported in the newspapers the following day, of course. No one knew what had happened except coach Rockne and the players. Naturally, some of us began to talk about it.

"I don't think it was until spring practice the next year when it became something of a national story. There had been a lot of talk among the players and it had been printed in one version or another in the South Bend newspapers. The touring reporters asked Rock about it and he admitted that it was true. But it happened. I was there and I will never forget."

There are two small facts, generally overlooked in the re-telling of the legend, which, although certainly not invented by Rockne, were certainly promoted heavily by him. First of all, even without a Gipper to win this one, Army was on the Notre Dame one yard line and clawing heavily when the clock ran out, there being less time remaining than the West Point quarterback realized. And on the following two weekends of the schedule, the Notre Dame team, absolutely drained of emotion, lost to Carnegie Tech, 27-7, and to Southern California, 27-14. There was only one game to win for Gipper and it had been won.

Did George Gipp ever make that deathbed speech? It seems unlikely. It has been suggested that a South Bend news-paperman was in the room at the time. Certainly, he would have reported it. There are no printed stories anywhere that document it. Considering the mass grief that the death of this brilliant football player caused on the Notre Dame campus, it would have been appropriate to have used such a glorious final wish at the time of the funeral. There is even a serious question that Rockne was with him at his death. His mother, Mrs. Matthew Gipp, a brother and a sister, were present. Gipp died at 3:31 A.M. on December 14, 1920, and the indications are that his football coach visited him somewhat earlier in the evening when the family was out of the room having supper.

The final words that Rockne reported to friends in the

weeks after the athlete's death sound more logical. In his hospital room, as he felt himself losing to pneumonia, Gipp asked to see Father Pat Haggerty. The sincerity of the priests had impressed him and he was bothered by his own cynicism.

"I want to become a Catholic," he said.

"Have you been baptized?" asked the priest.

"In the Methodist Church—my father's church," he said. "Is that okay?"

"I'll give you conditional baptism in the Catholic faith, if that is what you truly want," said Father Haggerty.

"Don't tell my mother. She's coming down to see me and she'd be furious," Gipp said. "She's not crazy about me going to a Catholic University. She's Scotch-Irish and not terribly fond of Irish Catholics."

For several days, Gipp put off the decision, finally telling the priest not to let him go until he was "fixed up" with the Catholic Church. When Gipp lapsed into delirium and the doctor in attendance gave up hope of saving his life, the priest arrived, gave him conditional baptism and the last rites. Rockne had telegrammed the Gipp family and Mrs. Gipp, Matt Gipp, Jr., and Dolly Gipp arrived at St. Joseph's Hospital. His father was unable to attend. It is entirely possible that the last three hours of his life were spent in a coma.

But when he told Rockne earlier in the day, "It's not so tough going," it undoubtedly meant that he was comfortable in his new faith. However, that's not the kind of battle cry that makes a politician weep and a football team want to smash down the door and strangle the opposition for. It was a pardonable lie, suitable to the period. And Rockne would be clever enough not to try it now. If he actually did use it twice in seven years and won two games with it, he was a larger intellect than even the idolatrous sports journalists of the 1920s gave him credit for.

There is one irrefutable fact. On December 18, in Laurium, Michigan, with the snow swirling around the casket and with the church bells playing the Notre Dame Victory March, they took George Gipp's body to the vault on a horse drawn sled, through drifts eight feet high. He was now one with mythology.

EPISODE 12

"This was the worst season Notre Dame football ever has seen. It's the worst for me, too. There are a lot of football folks throughout the country who think I'm finished. The team and the coaches made a lot of mistakes this year. But the team isn't through and I'm not through. After all, a football team should be conducted like any business organization. What happens when the salesmen of a firm find that their merchandise isn't selling? Do they quit? No. They analyze their product for weaknesses they might not have suspected. They change their personnel. They adjust the faults in their product. That's what Notre Dame is going to do. The business of the Notre Dame athletic department is producing an excellent product. If we aren't able to compete properly, then we'll adjust. That's the good old American way and there isn't anything more American than college football. In the next spring practice, we'll incorporate a lot of new stuff. Probably we'll work in a lot of spinner plays. Don't let anyone convince you that Notre Dame or its coaching staff or its players are through. We'll re-tool and come up with a better model,"—Knute Rockne after the end of the 1928 season, his worst.

EPISODE 13

According to the exorbitant literature of the period, Knute Kenneth Rockne was not only without sin, he was reasonably free from error as well. Nobody wanted to admit that he had his moments of temptation. Oh, yes, it really happened. Once when he was in New York, supposedly for a speaking engagement, Columbia University announced that it had signed him to a five-year contract, calling for $30,000 a year. What's more, there was an option that said he could, if he wanted to, be head coach and athletic director for five additional years at $35,000. There was no question but that it was his signature on the contract.

"Why didn't you tell us that you were unhappy here?" asked Father Matthew Walsh, then the school's president. "We would have done something about it. This comes as a complete surprise. There are people who think you *are* Notre Dame. But if you want to leave we certainly won't stand in your way. We just wish that we had had the chance to be competitive with Columbia."

"Father, I was physically and mentally exhausted at the time I signed that contract," said Rockne. "Do what you can to help me get out of it."

"I'll do what I can," said Father Walsh.

There are those who insist that he was simply using the power of his name to get the University to start construction of a huge new stadium in South Bend. There was eager old Columbia, willing to be used as a pawn in the affair. It was. The contract was cancelled and Notre Dame began to raise funds for a modern football field.

All of his psychological ruses were not successful, despite what the movies would have you believe. Before the final game of the 1922 season, he thought he could turn his team into monsters by showing them a telegram that said, in part, that if they beat Nebraska they would have the invitation to the Rose Bowl. At the time, Notre Dame had been slowed down only by a 0-0 tie against Army. It was the wrong thing to do. "I was so sure that we'd beat them and go to Pasadena," said tackle Cod Cotton, "that I went out there and all I saw was red roses and Mary Pickford. I kept thinking how great it was going to be in southern California. I even figured I might end up doing movie pictures. Obviously some of the others had the same feeling because we got beat, 13-7."

Despite his reputation for forcefulness, it was Rockne who trailed after George Gipp and begged him, literally, not to jump to the University of Michigan. The great Gipper remained on the Ann Arbor campus for two weeks while Rockne clawed and whimpered at his dormitory door. At last, Gipp gave in and told Fielding H. Yost that he could not play for him.

But Rockne was a man of the people, stopping at Hullie and Mike's to buy his cigars and to practice portions of upcoming speeches. Like most people who have conquered their own shyness, he was never quite confident that his remarks were as appreciated as they seemed to be. On one occasion, he entertained the clientele for nearly an hour with what was obviously an after dinner talk he had been working on. When he was finished, Hullie whacked the cash register, took out a quarter and threw it to Rockne, saying, "Here, I understand you get paid for speaking now."

Despite the legends, Rockne did not invent the Notre Dame shift. He merely perfected it. In actuality it had been used at Notre Dame as early as 1911 when Jack Marks brought it along from Dartmouth. In fact, it was still being used by Jess Harper when Rockne was an undergraduate.

"Rock was never so much an innovator as he was a perfectionist," said Leahy. "He could take something old and, ah, re-work it until it looked new and exciting. This is one area where I tried very hard to emulate him. When I decided to abandon the shift and go to the modern T formation, I called in the finest experts I could find to teach the system to my lads. Then I sat down and did my best to see where I could improve what they had taught. In that sense, I was borrowing a Rockne technique and, yet, remaining my own man. I invited Clark Shaugnessy and Sidney Luckman, two masters of the system, to come to Notre Dame. I quizzed them constantly.

"What I needed to do was understand all there was to know about the T formation so that I could then begin to adapt it to the needs of the Notre Dame coaching staff. I know that if Knute Rockne had lived he would have become a genius at the T formation and all its variations. He might not have invented the wishbone offense or the pro set formation, but he would have brought them to perfection.

"Rock was such a subtle charmer. My friend, Francis Wallace, the writer, used to like to tell the time that he met Bill McGeehan, the great New York sports columnist, at the train station in South Bend. Of course, McGeehan had written just a day or two earlier that he was going to Notre Dame to see if the football team actually had a university. Wallace, I believe, took McGeehan over to Rock's house and they talked for a long time. When it was over, McGeehan was absolutely spellbound. 'Gee, Rock I sure hope we win tomorrow,' he is supposed to have said. He had become a complete convert.

"Rock had his faults like everybody else. He could be testy. He could sting you sometimes with a remark that he, ah, did not know the impact of. He did things recruiting that would appall a modern coach. In fact, it is said that they were getting ready to move on him when he died. But he was a great influence for good on every life he touched. In business deals, he was an absolute sucker. Somebody once sold him a summer cottage on Lake Michigan which he did not need nor did he use much. But he bought it because he liked the man who was selling it and he knew the man needed to make the sale. No other coach could have brought off the miracle of the 1929 season. All of us were thoroughly disheartened by what had happened the year before. A 5-4 record at Notre Dame was unthinkable. But Rockne brought us back—while he was in a physical condition that would have left a lesser man in a hospital bed. It was then that I learned not to give in to illness, but to fight it aggressively."

For the first time in his life at Notre Dame, Frank Leahy was a starter. It happened soon after he returned to school in the fall. Rock saw him walking toward the athletic department and called out to him, "Something tells me you're going to win a letter this year, Frank." In his mental depth chart, Rockne had Leahy ahead of Dick Donoghue, Al Culver and Art Manmon, although he insisted that Leahy start by working with the fourth unit.

"He could do things like that," Leahy said. "He hated smugness and over-confidence. But all along I knew he'd give me the job. I had an injured ankle for ten days and couldn't practice. It seems like, ah, every time something was going well for me I got hurt or got sick. But when we went to Bloomington to play against Indiana, there I was in the starting lineup. I was a very proud young man. I felt like I earned the money Our Lady's University had spent on me. Both Moon Mullins and myself had become starters on the same afternoon. We took an oath to do our best to give coach Rockne a winning season—no, an undefeated season. He had had a 'winning season' the year before, but it wasn't good enough, not one more victory than the total number of defeats."

The Notre Dame team came filing out of the bus outside of Indiana University's stadium only to be stopped at the gate by a student manager who told Rockne that he could not admit them unless they had the proper pass signed by Indiana head coach Pat Page.

"Good God, boys," shouted Rockne. "This may be easier than we thought. They aren't expecting us."

"I was the happiest young lad alive," said Leahy. "Not only

did we defeat Indiana, 14-0 in an extremely hard game, but afterwards coach Rockne singled me out for praise, not so much my brilliance as an athlete, more for my football knowledge. I felt genuinely blessed. Oooooooh, it was a most auspicious moment."

Not only that, when he awoke and read the Chicago Tribune the next morning at Carroll Hall, he discovered that the following item had been used: "Frank Leahy's tackle play is not sparkling nor sensational. He is quiet and precise much in the manner of Buck Shaw who played tackle at Notre Dame in the early 1920s. Like Shaw, he works so silently that sometimes his teammates get credit for tackles or blocks he actually executes. Leahy is of great value running interference for the ball carrier. Coach Knute Rockne calls him one of the smartest players he has ever coached." If the clouds had suddenly parted and "The Great Football Coach in the Sky" had said: "This is my son, Frank, in whom I am greatly pleased," it is doubtful if Leahy could have been more ecstatic.

After much complaining by Rockne, the University of Notre Dame du Lac was finally adding to its collection of campus buildings a stadium worthy of its football team. The school had originally had merely 2,500 seats at Cartier Field and Rockne found it embarrassing. Even when capacity was raised to 25,000 he still referred to his alma mater as the University without a stadium. Now they were piling brick upon brick and the Irish, who had been called the Ramblers because of their numerous road games, were playing at Soldier Field in Chicago while construction was underway. While touring the work site, Rockne came down with yet another phlebitis attack, a clotting of blood in the legs. It was announced that he would not be able to travel with the team in its game against Navy.

"In a very emotional scene, we were told that Tom Lieb would handle us on the road while keeping in constant telephone contact," Leahy said. "The players couldn't believe what was happening. We were on a crusade to, ah, restore the University's football honor and we wouldn't have Rockne with us. What's more, the doctors said that he would have to spend a great deal of time in bed. He might not even be able to supervise the practice sessions. I recall us all standing around wondering what was going to happen to us."

Rockne put on a magnificent display of grace under pressure, taking advantage of every theatrical opportunity, but in the meantime risking his own life. At any moment, the clot stuck in his leg could have broken loose and shot straight to his heart. When the Notre Dame team arrived at Annapolis, each player was asked to line up outside a telephone booth.

"Boys," said Lieb, "there's a man on the other end of this line who wants to talk to each and every one of you. Listen to what he has to say. Don't break in. He's a sick man and he can't spend that much time talking."

The players listened carefully and then came away from the booth in tears. Now it was Leahy's turn and he moved forward slowly, almost afraid at what he might hear. Good God, Rockne might be making a Gipp-style death bed speech to each player.

"This is an important game, Frank. You're going to start," said the trip-hammer voice. "You haven't played that much, boy. But you can fight. You can fight and win . . . win . . . win. Get out there and fight to live, fight to win. Crack 'em! Crack 'em! You can do it, boy. Yes, Frank! Be primed. Be tough. They think they have your number, but they don't. You can't let it happen to you. You can win, Frank, if you want to."

Well, who on this planet could fail to respond to such a request? Leahy pushed his hand up against those sorrowful eyes of his and left the booth sobbing. At lunch time, he was still throttled by his emotions. Sitting across the table was a young seminarian, John Cavanaugh, whose brother Father Frank Cavanaugh was already teaching at Notre Dame. In one of those amazing patterns where souls would criss-cross throughout their lives, John Cavanaugh would grow in the priesthood, become president at Notre Dame and be both an integral part of Leahy's return as head coach and his leave-taking.

"That Navy game was both a joy and a tragedy," said Leahy. "I was part of an historic occasion, but I also hurt my elbow. Ooooooh, it was an incredible misfortune. I was in on two important blocks that set up the winning touchdown. On one of them, I was opening a hole for Marty Brill and, as I moved forward to block, the defensive man shoved my right elbow back at me. There was this terrible, ah, hot feeling and then numbness. They had to remove me from the game. I came off thinking that, perhaps, I was letting coach Rockne down. They told me the elbow was dislocated. True to his spirit, I asked that they shoot me with something and send me back in. They refused and took me to the dressing room where they did give me a hypodermic needle full of something. I asked to be able to call coach Rockne in South Bend and apologize for what had happened. But they told me Rock would know and understand.

"Afterwards, Father John came to the team bus and asked me how my arm was. Oooooh, it hurt furiously, but I did not want him or anybody else to know that I was seriously injured. So I simply looked through the window and told him it was fine. But it was not.

"I had x-rays the following Monday and they told me I would have to have my elbow in a cast for the next three weeks. I could not permit that to happen. After all, here was coach Rockne coming out to practice every afternoon in a car and sitting in the back seat to instruct us over a public address system. If he could risk his life, why couldn't I play football with a dislocated elbow? Oooooh, these were not easy times in college football. If it had not been for Jonathan O'Brien, I believe that I would have gone quietly crazy. I had finally achieved my goal and he was well aware of the seriousness of my ambitions. He talked to me nightly, trying to comfort me, but he could not entirely. The team continued to win, but I swore I would play football against Southern California. And I did."

Oh, yes, he did indeed and in the best Tom Swift tradition. They removed the cast and the doctors told him not to do anything foolish. As he was coming off the practice field, Rockne summoned him to his car.

"How's the elbow, Frank?" the coach asked. "Coming along all right."

"Couldn't be better."

"In that case, let's see you flex it."

With maximum mental dexterity, he decided that Rockne had not been at the Navy game, therefore he could not be that familiar with the exact nature of the injury. Leahy shoved out his left arm and moved it up and down, looking for all the world like a pitcher getting ready to throw a big game. Rockne shook his head. "Doctors," he said. "What do they know?" Leahy did know that his entire family was coming down to Soldier Field to see Notre Dame play USC and Frank had decided he would play regardless of the pain. He hoped that no one would tell Rockne in the meantime that it was his right elbow that had been injured. Lieb was thoroughly disturbed when he received orders to use Leahy at right tackle. It was the glory of the times.

It was a gallant gesture, but they had to lead Leahy off at halftime in severe pain, complaining his removal was totally unnecessary. He grumbled, swore and complained all the way to the training table where he was lying when the team was told that their best friend in the entire world wanted to talk to them. The door swung open and there was Knute Kenneth Rockne, pale and pitiful in a wheelchair. He was intensely ill. He tried to stand, could not and fell backwards. Leahy leaped up from the table and stood in the doorway, absolutely awe struck. He watched as Rockne held his chin up as high as possible and, in a vague facsimile of his staccato voice, delivered a halftime talk that made the Gipper speech seem like a street corner conversation.

"Boys, get out there and play them hard the first five minutes. They'll hate it, but play them hard. Rock will be upstairs watching you. Go ahead now. Hit them hard. Win! Win! Win! That's the only reason for playing. Crack 'em! Crack 'em! I'll be watching," he said, stopping just short of asking them to win one for the old coach. They had to restrain Leahy, whose elbow was simply too sore to continue. A trainer literally held him back. Such was the power of Knute Rockne in the year of Our Lord, 1929, just before the crash. When it was over, Notre Dame had its seventh victory of the year.

"What kind of team you got?" asked Curly Lambeau, inventor of the Green Bay Packers and the Vince Lombardi of his day.

"Best damn team I ever had," said Rockne. "But I can't tell them that."

"Why?"

"They might believe me."

Absolutely oblivious to his doctor's orders, Rockne supervised practice directly, moving from the back of the open car to a wheelchair on the sidelines. He seemed to many of his players to be a man in a frenzy, desperately trying to vindicate himself for the season before with an undefeated record. Notre Dame took a brutalizing 26-6 victory away from Northwestern and then went on to Yankee Stadium for the final game of the year against Army. All 80,000 seats had been sold.

"I did not know at the time, but this was to be the last football game I would ever play in my life," said Leahy. "And I had to play this one with my elbow in a concrete cast, which proved very helpful in my blocking technique until I fell on the frozen ground and shattered it. Ooooooh, I was moving people out of the way very nicely with it.

"This was the great Chris Cagle's last game for Army and the cadets wanted nothing better than to give him Notre Dame's head on a platter. It was a most bitter game, with the wind so cold it was like playing on an arctic tundra. I'm afraid some of the lads on both sides were less than gentlemanly in their behavior. One lad I faced across the scrimmage line continued to make unflattering remarks about the Catholic Church. I told him that he was not fit to be an officer in the United States Army. Then I made sure that his jaw and my concrete cast made contact. I did not hear him mock the Pope the rest of the afternoon.

"Instead he concentrated on me. I left the game at the final gun with a badly split lip and a chipped tooth. Football was a far more swashbuckling sport in those days."

This was hardly the glorious farewell that all young men like Chris Cagle dreamed of in those days. In the second quarter, he rolled to his left and looked for his end Carl Carlmark who was standing in that wind storm down near the Notre Dame five yard line. This was one of those moments where the truth has been mildly distorted by passage of years and the fading of memories. Some reports say that Cagle simply threw the ball too hard. Others insist that the wind whipped it away from Carlmark. Whatever the facts are, the swiftest man on Notre Dame varsity, Jack Elder, caught it on the three yard line and brought it back for a touchdown, the longest run in the Army–Notre Dame series up to that time.

One yard short of the Army goal line, some cadet, now nameless, took one final shot at Elder, but Tom Conley knocked him down. It was the only touchdown of the game, although twice Cagle seemed to be on the verge of breaking away in the second half. Once he tripped and the second time an Irish defender got in his way. It was a game for young Neanderthals. There was nothing artistic about it.

"The most magnificent part about playing in New York was that Rockne always got his lads tickets to Broadway shows," said Leahy. "Oooooh, that was an enormous treat, especially for someone from Winner, South Dakota, who had been spending his undergraduate days in South Bend, which was not exactly the social capital of the nation. I went with Moon Mullins and Johnny O'Brien to see Helen Morgan in "Showboat." For hour's afterwards, we walked through Times Square and up and down Broadway. We were just Midwestern hicks.

"Back in the hotel lobby we ran into Bob Zuppke, the great coach from Illinois. Even though I was fairly well scuffed up from the game, he apparently didn't think I was a football player. I asked him dozens of questions about strategy. I asked him what he thought of the game. He said that Notre Dame did not deserve to win and that Chris Cagle was the greatest player on the field, although he called him stupid for trying to throw the ball into Elder's territory.

"He finally turned to me and said, 'Is there anything else you'd like to know about the game of football, young fellow?'

"I asked him what he thought of the Army player who had smashed my lip and broken my tooth just because I had objected to his unkind remarks about his Holiness in Rome. Zuppke looked me up and down and said, 'You're a Notre Dame football player?' I felt quite humble. I guess I didn't really look the part."

The train snaked through the wintry hills of Pennsylvania, across the gritty country of southern Ohio and into the soft farmlands of Indiana. By God, the great Rockne had done exactly what he said he would. He had taken Notre Dame from its worst season to one of its greatest. He walked down the aisle, slapping players on the shoulders and behaving as if he had never been sick. In a back row, Leahy joked with Mullins and O'Brien, telling them what a great season he was going to have as a senior. It was fine, bumptious talk from a young man just starting to feel that he might have an important place in life. Confidence is a marvelous quality; it completely ignores the possibility of unrevealed disaster. Frank Leahy never played another football game the rest of his life.

EPISODE 14

Now the golden haze that has surrounded Frank Leahy's student days at South Bend is beginning to fade away. All summer long he has worked for Hugh Mulligan, head of the Chicago Asbestos Workers' Union, for $70 a week, an enormous sum for the time, and it does not especially strike him as unusual that only the ten Notre Dame players on the job are so handsomely paid. The athletes are encouraged to open bank accounts with the understanding that a prize will go to the man who has the largest balance at the end of the summer. Leahy wins the extra $150. Alumni and camp followers have a way of making sure that the livestock are content.

The summer has been one of cruel physical labor during the day and hours of informal football practice during the twilight hours. Leahy has returned to Notre Dame absolutely convinced that these will be his finest hours. He is in excellent condition. He feels a part of the Notre Dame legend. Spiritually, he considers himself one with George Gipp, Jim Crowley, Elmer Layden and all the rest.

"What did you do all summer, Frank?" shouts Rockne. "You must have worked in a tea room. You're getting soft, Frank. Can't have that. This is going to be a big season. A big, big season." Then he turns and greets three other players.

"He's pleased," said Mullins.

"How do you know?" asked Leahy.

"He wouldn't needle you like that if he wasn't," said Mullins.

"Someday I might get used to his sense of humor," said Leahy.

Cold winds were flapping across Cartier Field on the afternoon of October 2, 1930, and Rockne had kept his team on the field well into the darkening hours, getting ready for the opening game against Southern Methodist, a match with an unmistakable religious overtone. Having gone unbeaten the season before, Rockne did not want his troops to grow satisfied in their own ability. So he had been drilling them like a Prussian colonel. Dinner had long since begun to congeal on the plates back at Carroll Hall when the coach finally dismissed the team. Then, almost as a tragic afterthought, he called them back.

"I want to try that end run to the right by Schwartz one more time," he shouted. "Let's go, men. Let's go. Let's go."

So the Irish rumbled back onto the field, tired and hungry and feeling just a little less awed by their coach. After all, there is a limit to such things. The play, after all, had been working well against the second team all afternoon. There seemed to be no reason to try it again. It was simple enough. Leahy pulled out of his right tackle position and went down field ahead of Marchy Schwartz with the purpose of hitting a man in the secondary who might be interfering with the half-back's progress. It was one of Rockne's touchdown plays and he wanted it to function perfectly.

There was Frank Carideo calling signals and there was Leahy pulling back, getting ready to turn for his downfield maneuver, when his right foot came down in a slippery patch on the turf. The cleats sunk in. When he turned the cartilage snapped loose in his knee. He dropped as if a sniper had hit him. Instantly, his friends were standing over him. One of them, he recalled, had tears in his eyes. It is the nature of the beast. Football players risk injury constantly. When one happens that obviously terminates a career, everybody knows without saying a word. They carried Leahy back to the training room in severe pain.

"Oooooh, I knew that it was over," he said. "Perhaps with modern methods I could have played again. But I was out for my senior year. It wasn't fair! It wasn't fair! There was no need having it operated on. I wasn't going to play football after Notre Dame. The professional league was not what it is today. Rather, it was a bum's existence unless you were truly outstanding. They paid little, not more than $50 for an ex-Notre Dame tackle. That evening, I cried. I could not believe what had happened to me.

"If it had not been for my friend O'Brien, I believe I might have gone crazy. Does that sound strange? That playing football meant so much? Perhaps it does now, but not then . . . not then.

"I went to an osteopath in South Bend who absolutely convinced me that I would be well in time to play a few games for Notre Dame. He gave me all sorts of special treatment, none of which worked. I exercised and I ran. Ooooh, the pain was intense, but I was not going to let this last precious year of eligibility slip past me. I had convinced myself that I could not get a coaching job if I did not play my senior year. Suddenly, I could see myself returning to Winner in disgrace and being forced to spend the rest of my days running a feed store or farming. I had tasted just enough success to know that this was not what I wanted from life."

While the 1930 varsity worked on the main practice field, Leahy limped along the edges, a lonely silhouette in the dark Indiana afternoons. One day Rockne called him over and asked to see him after practice. It was one of those fascinating turning points in a man's life that seems so ugly at the time but, when taken in the context of future developments, seems so logical. Rockne wanted Leahy to quit football, to stop ripping his innards out and to stop tormenting his soul. Leahy wept.

"Frank, I watch you and that knee. If there's one thing I admire in a player it is all out dedication," he said. "But this is madness. You're carrying this thing to the edge of fanaticism. I want to give you some advice. Quit playing. You're through. It's all over, Frank. Face up to it like a man. I want you out there with me every day. But I don't want you playing. I'll crowd you in on the road lists. You'll be with the team. You have to start thinking about your future and I want you to learn all the football you can. Okay, kid?"

Leahy wandered off into the darkness, moving like a shadow through the sycamores on the campus. He passed up dinner, forgot his class work and slumped on his cot and openly considered the possibility of going downtown and drinking too much beer. O'Brien came in, sat down, realized what had happened and didn't say a word. For the next two days, Frank Leahy did not go near either a classroom or a football field. He simply looked out the window.

"Don't you think you've babied yourself enough?" O'Brien asked. "Practice starts at 3 P.M. today. I think Rock expects you to be there. Why don't you stop acting like a whipped dog?"

What Rockne was offering was a course in football coaching, O'Brien said. Here was the greatest coach in the history of the game with one of his noblest teams, quite willing to let Frank Leahy trail him around in the midst of his toughest season and ask questions.

"Why don't you get off your ass, Frank?" he said, in conclusion.

And so Frank Leahy made the most singularly important decision of his career. He turned in his football suit and took up a position not far from Rockne at every practice. He wandered from one coaching group to another, listening to what each assistant was talking about. Leahy studied under the best. There was Tommy Moynihan teaching the centers and Hunk Anderson working with the rest of the line. Ike Voedisch talked to the ends. And so it went. Afterwards, Rockne would answer all his questions.

"The most amazing thing about Rockne was the way in which he masked his own deeply seething emotions," Leahy said. "As a player, I watched the progress of the game. I never paid that much attention to Rock. But being an apprentice coach, I discovered certain things I had never noticed before. Oooooh, Rockne would not let a single detail escape him. There was never anything so large, never a moment too exciting that he could be distracted. He was most gracious to me during a crisis period in my life.

"One afternoon, Al Culver, who had taken my place at right tackle asked him a question and he directed Al to me. I was so flattered I almost cried. I could not believe that the great Rockne had so much trust in me. What's more I gained confidence because I saw Culver taking my advice. I felt that I could become a coach, not just a good one, but an outstanding one, a man, perhaps, in the Rockne mold. I started to dream an entirely different sort of dream. I no longer saw myself going back to Winner to coach the high school team. I could see myself working for a major college, maybe even Notre Dame itself.

"I want you to know that, for the longest time, I would have been happy simply to have been Rockne's line coach at Notre Dame. That became my new ambition. And there was Rock posting the traveling squad list every week and my name would always be on it. I knew that he was taking me and leaving some capable player home. That was a sacrifice on his part, and, ooooh, I yearned to make it up to him.

"One of the interesting things that Rockne always did was

to smile when he sent a substitute into the game. No matter how grim the situation might be, no matter what had happened, he always grinned at a man and either patted him on the shoulder or hugged him before putting him on the field. It was very subtle. It was never an open emotion, oooooh, it was very private, as if he meant to convey his confidence in you. I made a note that if I ever got to be a coach, I would be as calm appearing as he was. They called me aloof, but I meant to stay calm for my players' sakes. I think I did that. Oooooh, I hope I did."

What tore at Leahy's heart, though, was the fact that this may have been the best of Rockne's teams, better than the Four Horsemen and their colleagues, better than the one that went the year before. There was a strange electric current jangling across the Notre Dame campus, as if some great drama was coming down to the final act. The team was overloaded with talent. The backfield consisted of Frank Carideo, Marchy Schwartz, Joe Savoldi, Moon Mullins, Marty Brill and Bucky O'Connor. Every time a man looked up he saw another Notre Dame back doing something heroic. One afternoon, Rockne switched Brill from blocking back to running back, against Penn, and Brill scored three touchdowns in ten carries.

"Why did I do it?" asked Rockne. "It was the psychological edge. Brill was a Catholic from Philadelphia playing against an Ivy League school that was largely Protestant from the same city. Why shouldn't he score three touchdowns?"

They came down to the Southern California game undefeated and here was Rockne at his sly best. The story has been told so many times that it almost seems apocryphal. Savoldi had committed two major blunders. He had gotten married secretly, against the University's rules. He had also gotten divorced, against the Roman Catholic Church's rules. He was dismissed from the team for one sin and censured by the Brothers of the Holy Cross for the other. He went off to become one of the greatest and most prosperous wrestlers of all time. Years later, when he was well into his 50s, he was to earn a degree from Evansville Teachers, quit wrestling and live out his years telling high school children all about science.

"Once again I was permitted to accompany the team to the West Coast," said Leahy. "I stayed very close to Rockne on that trip and he seemed to want to have me around. He was constantly asking me what I thought of this or how I would handle that. It was the last game of the year and I felt as if he were giving me some sort of final examination.

"I sensed that he was terribly worried. One evening in his drawing room on board the train, he confided in me that he felt Southern California might be the best college team ever put together. They played a single wing and they had destroyed everybody in the West. Ooooh, they had beaten California 71-0 and UCLA 52-0 and taken apart an excellent Stanford team by a 41-12 score. They had people like Ernie Pinckert and Orv Mohler and how was he, with Savoldi out of school and Moon Mullins unavailable with a bad leg injury, going to beat these people with no fullback. He looked at me, almost as if he expected me, a mere senior on his team to provide some sort of answer. I was flattered and I also felt powerless.

"It was in Tucson that he pulled one of the most devilish stunts any college football coach has ever conceived of. Now understand that there is a little . . . ahhhh . . . larceny in the hearts of the best of us. The third string fullback, Dan Hanley, lacked game experience, so Rock decided to use Bucky O'Connor at fullback because of his great speed. He did not want USC to know about what was going to happen. So he asked O'Connor and Hanley to change uniforms for the practice in Tucson.

"It was the practice then for Los Angeles writers to come out by train to visit us before a game. O'Connor ran all the short buck plays and never once ran wide, where he was at his best. When a columnist from the *Los Angeles Times* asked him for an interview, he talked just as if he were really Hanley. It seems that coach Rockne had coached him the night before just in case that might happen. Some of us wondered afterwards if it were ethical. But we concluded that if coach Rockne thought it was the thing to do, it couldn't be bad."

The coup was administered the evening before when Southern California made the incredible psychological mistake of permitting Rockne to mesmerize its players at a pre-game banquet. It was something like inviting Hitler in to address the Allied troops just before D-Day. He begged the Trojans for mercy. He praised them as the finest football team ever assembled. His Notre Dame players were good, he admitted, but certainly not in USC's range of skills.

"When that game is over tomorrow—and I know you'll do your best to hold down the score—I'd like to ask you fine young men of Troy to come over and congratulate my boys on a fine game. It will mean so much to them to have a firm handshake and a kind word from a team like yours. Thank you very much and I hope we meet again next year when the odds are a little kinder toward Notre Dame. Bless you and good fortune."

It was a stupendous con job and Leahy, who sat down front at one of the tables, was utterly amazed to see the USC players walk out, strong in the conviction that they would do the decent thing and not mutilate Notre Dame too badly.

"I could not believe what my eyes saw and what my ears heard," he said. "If I had tried anything like that when I was head coach at Notre Dame they would have insisted that I be put away for life. In fact, I was severely chastised for lesser crimes. But Rock could turn an entire enemy camp into a group of contrite children. It was amazing what he did. I never forgot it."

It was overwhelmingly, unbelievably, unrelentingly corny. It was lifted straight out of a 1930 boy's book, which leads one to wonder if fiction might not have mirrored reality a little closer than some people suspect. There were 98,189 people who watched the Trojans being systematically dismantled. Schwartz fired a pass to Carideo for the first touchdown. Then, on a reverse, Brill pitched to O'Connor, who whirled around right end and went 80 yards for the score, leading some writers to believe he really wasn't Dan Hanley. Another lateral, this time from Schwartz, got O'Connor loose again and he went for the third touchdown. The final score was 27-0 and Leahy was never quite the same again.

"It was an amazing trip in many ways. While I was in Tucson, Hughie Mulligan took Judge Carberry, a substitute end, and me to Nogales, the nearest Mexican border town. Neither the Judge nor myself was physically able to play. We hired a driver who told us his name was Mexican Pete. He carried a loaded pistol on the front seat and he introduced us to various forms of sin that I had previously been unaware of.

"After the Southern California game, Rockne told everyone

they could break training for a few days. It was a fantastic time. There were so many parties it was difficult to attend them all. There was wine and women and, I guess, a great deal of song. The odd thing was that when I simply went to Moon Mullins' home in South Pasadena I got into the only real trouble of the trip. I was playing—you may not believe this or you may laugh—tiddlywinks on the floor with Miss Leona Martin, who was Johnny O'Brien's girl friend.

"When I tried to rise, my knee locked. The pain went up and down my entire right side. At first they thought I was joking, but it was nothing to laugh at. Several of the players helped me out to the car and when I got back to the Ambassador Hotel they called the house physician, who packed my leg in ice. Nothing did any good and I began to feel that I might spend my entire life as a cripple. My dear friend O'Brien, who had been with me through all my difficulties, even deserted me. He went back to Leona Martin and let me stay there in my misery. Good Lord, even O'Brien walked away. He was back, quite late, and he helped me dress the next morning. If the knee hadn't locked, I might never have gone into coaching."

It is possible, but not probable. Rockne would have pushed Leahy anyway. In fact, he told a representative of the *Los Angeles Examiner* that he had on his team a young man who would undoubtedly succeed him one day as head coach at Notre Dame. He meant Frank Leahy and the words are right there in the newspaper's files, to this very day.

EPISODE 15

They carried Leahy on board the train at Los Angeles' charming old Movie-Modern Union Station. In such great departure scenes, Rockne was always up front leading his entire company while newspaper photographers puffed away. He did not notice Leahy's condition until he made one of his customary sweeps down the aisle. There was his young apprentice with his leg stretched out on the opposite seat. As the train rumbled through the awesome heat of the Mohave, Rockne bent over and put a hand on Leahy's shoulder.

"Same damn trouble, eh, Frank?" he asked. "Something's going to have to be done about that knee. What are your plans for the Christmas vacation? You going home to South Dakota?"

"I'd thought about it, coach. Then again, I may just stay in South Bend," said Leahy. "I just don't know."

"I'm taking a trip to Minnesota," said Rockne. "I've got to go to the Mayo Clinic in Rochester to have my leg operated on. You know how I hate to travel alone. Come along with me and get your knee fixed up. We can share a room and I'll have somebody to talk to. Maybe I can give you a cram course in football coaching while we're both getting better. What do you say?"

Conversation had ceased entirely on the whole car. The great coach himself seemed to be reaching out and symbolically anointing one of them. For the remainder of his senior year, Frank Leahy, by the unanimous concession of his peer group, would stand a few inches higher than everybody else. Knute Rockne was Notre Dame's secular saint and he literally singled Leahy out as a disciple. It could happen only in a 1930 movie or at Notre Dame where fiction and reality sometimes seem to merge.

EPISODE 16

"On the morning when the train pulled out of South Bend, bound for Rochester, I was a quivering wreck. I was about to make a trip with the famed Knute Rockne, the greatest coach and the greatest leader of young men in the nation," Leahy said. "I arrived at the station fully two hours early so that I would not miss this exceptional opportunity. I could not eat breakfast and I had been awake most of the night.

"I had been close to Rock, but only as a part of the team. Now I was going to be his companion for as much as two weeks or more. I suffered from great shyness in those days, ooooh, I must have had what they later called an inferiority complex. I had taken speaking lessons with a professor Robert

142

Kelley, because I felt that it would be necessary to a coaching career.

"I had done quite well addressing the Chicago Knights of Columbus council several months earlier and I had come to think of myself as an orator of promise. Now I would have to make conversation with the great Knute Rockne, one of the most celebrated talkers of his time. I had felt less nervous on dating a young lady for the first time. On the way to Chicago, I did not say much. Rockne read a lot and he carried on marathon conversations with other passengers who had recognized him.

"Here I was, a football player of only mild accomplishments who was no longer even capable of playing the game and I was in the company of the greatest name in American sports. As thrilled as I was, I wanted to sink into the seat and somehow disappear beneath the rails. When we changed trains in Chicago, I followed him around like a puppy. I would imagine that I was terrible company. There was one long conversation during the ride through Minnesota during which I eagerly asked questions about football. Rockne, of course, knew a lot about literature and science and subjects like that.

"Frank Leahy was never much of a scholar. I confess that I was intrigued by the world of finance and business. I loved sports dearly. But I was not the well-rounded intellect that Rockne was. It only made me feel more and more inferior to this fine person.

"When we arrived in Rochester, where we had to wait four days before being admitted to the clinic, I assumed that we would have separate rooms at the Kahler Hotel. But Rockne had ordered a double. I was now in a state of near-panic. Oooooh, I was one scared and insecure young man."

Finally, Rockne could stand the situation no longer. While Leahy unpacked his bag, he placed a hand on his apprentice's shoulder. Then he shook his hand. He had an exceptional way of placing people at ease.

"Please, Frank," he said. "I'd really appreciate it if you'd forget about me being 'The Great Rockne' and you being just a varsity tackle. I'm not so great and you've got a fine mind for football. I admire you and I think you have a great career ahead of you. Someday you may make them forget old Rock.

You're my friend and I hope I'm yours. How about looking at things the way they really are? You and I are just a couple of broken down football folks up here trying to get fixed up. How's that sound?"

Suddenly, the telephone rang.

"Now," said Rockne. "You thought I paid your way up here and I arranged to pay for your operation because I liked you. The real reason, Frank, is that I need somebody to answer the telephone. Those damn things drive me nuts. They'll be calling asking me to speak at this dinner and that luncheon. Now you tell them that you're Frank Leahy, star tackle for Notre Dame's great 1929 team. Tell them how you played against Army at Yankee Stadium and tell them how somebody split your lip and broke your tooth. You tell them that you'll be happy to come by and talk and you tell them that your coach is too damn tired."

No one realized it, but Rockne had coached his last game only a few weeks earlier. His friend, that charming Irish rogue, Jimmy Walker, mayor of New York, had organized a charity match between the New York Giants and a group of Notre Dame stars dating back even unto the Four Horsemen themselves. The doctors at Mayo Clinic had told him not to go, but he went anyway. The urge to see so many of his former players and coach them one more time was too strong to suppress.

The alumni had gathered four days early at South Bend, where, in their slightly overweight condition, they more or less worked out under Adam Walsh. When Rockne arrived, he was somewhat disturbed by the rapid manner in which some of his finest athletes had managed to get out of shape.

"How long they been working, Adam?" he asked.

"Just a couple of days."

"They look over-trained," Rockne mused.

Even in those days, it wasn't possible for ex-college players to do much damage to the professionals. Notre Dame lost, but Rockne came away pleased, if somewhat worn out. He met Leahy in South Bend and began the trip to Mayo Clinic.

"Those four days at the Kahler Hotel were a great lesson to me," said Leahy. "I wanted to make myself in the image of the greatest coach who ever lived and yet I wanted to retain my own identity. I was a different person than Knute Rockne, yet

144

I wanted to incorporate everything about him that suited me into my own personality.

"I watched him in his graciousness. He never forgot where he had met somebody. He was genuinely interested in the well-being of everybody he came in contact with. For a few days, I pondered whether he was sincere. I concluded that he was. Rockne brightened every life he came into, even if it were just briefly. He made me realize how important it was to remember names and to associate where it was you came in contact with those people.

Rockne's treatment was reasonably simple, but Leahy had a substantial portion of his damaged right knee removed. The nurses came by and gave him heat treatments, while Rockne did his best to remove the younger man from the dark bottom of his depression.

"They got me speaking all over town," he told Leahy.

"That's great, coach," Leahy said.

"Ran into Fritz Crisler, the head coach at Minnesota," said Rockne. "Know what I told him? I said, 'I've got this kid with me who's going to make a great coach someday, Fritz. His name is Frank Leahy and right now he knows as much about line play as any assistant I ever had and you know I've had some fine ones.' How does that strike you, Frank?"

"I'm very grateful, coach. That was most gracious of you," Leahy answered, gazing out the window, almost ignoring what must have been the strongest compliment of his life. His eyes were fixed upon a tree, barren in the awful chill of a Minnesota winter. This was Leahy in the blackest of moods.

"Can I ask why you're so discouraged, Frank? You have absolutely no right to be. I thought our Notre Dame players were trained to fight back against adversity. At least that's what I was telling you to do. Maybe I'm not the coach they say I am. What's eating at you? Still fretting because you can't play football anymore. That's foolish, Frank, just damned foolish."

"This knee cost me every opportunity I ever thought I had," said Leahy, still looking the other way. "I figured if I really played well my senior year somebody would want to hire me as a line coach. Now I'm getting ready to graduate and I don't have a prospect in the world. They've forgotten all about me."

A few minutes earlier, Rockne had picked up his mail downstairs at the clinic's front desk. He shuffled the letters, throwing some aside and dropping others in a thick pile. When he finished, he took seven of them and dropped them in Leahy's lap. With a nervous snap, Leahy turned his head.

"What are those?" he asked.

"Those are letters from other coaches wanting to know who I'd recommend for assistant coaching jobs. Those are just seven requests. I've got about a dozen more on my desk back in South Bend. They seem to think I turn out good assistant coaches. I'll recommend you for any job you like. What's more I think you'll get it. Now stop acting so hurt. Your life's ahead of you."

On occasion legend contradicts fact. There was one letter that specifically asked about Leahy. The others simply wanted to know who Rockne would recommend. But Tommy Mills was now at Georgetown and he had lost his line coach, Clipper Smith. What about this young man from South Dakota? How had he progressed? Was he ready?

"The story has always been that I more or less selected Georgetown at random," said Leahy. "That is not so. I much admired Tommy Mills and he was kind enough to make a specific inquiry. It told me that he truly wanted me to work for him. There were some better opportunities in the other letters. But I was an insecure young lad and I thought it best to go where I was wanted. Also, Georgetown was a Catholic University and I felt the need of such a protective institution. I did not hesitate to accept the offer. The pay was $1,200. Thank God I was able to find an apartment with three other young members of the athletic department; otherwise, I would have starved."

Unable to teach a mandatory physical education class at one of the South Bend schools because he was on crutches well into the spring of his senior year, Leahy was unable to graduate on time. Once again desperate, since the job at Georgetown University required a bachelor's degree, he forced himself through a six week summer school program, teaching boys how to throw hook shots and two hand sets through a basket on a playground. There were modest ceremonies in Washington Hall on August 28, 1931. The next morning, Frank Leahy took a train to the District of Columbia and, for ten years, did not set foot on the Notre Dame campus.

EPISODE 17

In the late winter of 1931, with the chronic condition in his legs beginning to ease somewhat, Knute Rockne took his family south to Florida where he sat in the sun, got himself photographed repeatedly and generally relaxed for the first time since he began his coaching career at Notre Dame. He was still in his early 40s with perhaps 20 good years left. He returned to South Bend physically and spiritually refreshed. He called in Frank Leahy and gave him a long, bubbling lecture full of grandiose phrases and brave clichés. It was straight out of his manual on halftime speeches, designed to get his young apprentice up for a lifetime in the trade.

"Frank, I firmly believe you'll make good in this business," he said, his voice reaching that staccato whine. "Don't let me down. I'll be watching. Need any help, call me."

That evening, Rockne sat in his living room, sipping on a beer and talking with his neighbor, Tom Hickey. Some folks out in Hollywood wanted him to do a series of movie shorts on football. He was taking a train to Kansas City and then flying on from there. Hickey was aware that Rockne took little joy in riding airplanes. But he was relaxed and cheerful, putting his beer aside and rolling on the living room carpet with his children.

There was an appointment in Chicago first and Rockne dined with Christy Walsh, a friend and business partner, who brought along Albert Fuller, a hotel man. When Rockne got into the cab that was to take him to his rail connection with the flight from Kansas City, Fuller leaned over and said, through the lowered portion of the window, "Soft landings, Rock."

"I'd rather have you say 'Happy landings,' if you don't mind," he answered. "They tell me that's better luck." Everybody laughed and Knute Rockne, on the edge of eternity, couldn't help laughing at his new acquaintance's odd remark.

In Kansas City, there was enough time between the train and the plane for Rockne to get on the telephone and call Arch Ward, sports editor of the *Chicago Tribune*. It was March 31, 1931. It was reasonably early on a Tuesday morning

147

and Rockne promised Ward that he would be back in a week or so to talk extensively about his next Notre Dame team.

"Feeling great, Arch," he burbled. "I'm feeling better than I have in several years. I've finally learned how to truly relax. I got so many things going for me now, I don't know how I'm going to take care of them. They paid me $10,000 to do six lectures for Studebaker. They're thinking of coming out with a small car called the Rockne. Can you imagine that? Now they want to give me $50,000 to play the football coach in the movie version of Good News. I figure if RKO has that kind of money, I'd better take it. I can do some good with that much dough. After all these years, I'm not going to have to worry about money anymore. Isn't that great, Arch?"

So he got on board a Ford Tri-Motor owned by Transcontinental and Western Airways. There were seven other people on board. The plane took off into clear skies over Kansas City and headed to the West. In a field, a few miles southwest of a place called Bazaar, Kansas, a farmer looked up in the air and saw an airplane nose down, spouting a long, ugly trail of black smoke. There was an explosion and the airplane came down in sections in a stand of winter wheat. It was hours before anyone knew which flight it was and well into the next day before any attempt was made to identify the bodies.

The managing editor of the *Chicago Tribune* called Arch Ward at home to tell him what appeared to be disastrous news. There had been a report on the Associated Press about a TWA crash in Kansas. Nothing had been confirmed.

"Where's your friend Rockne?" asked Loy Maloney. "There's a report that this might be the plane he was on. You better get down here. There's nothing official, but it looks like Knute Rockne's dead."

On the way to his office, Ward struggled with the dramatic unreality of the situation. Only a few hours earlier, Rockne had been talking about taking a jazz band on a tour of Europe to help raise funds for the mother of one of his players. The lady was dying of cancer and there wasn't any money available. He had mentioned the fact that the Hearst newspapers were willing to pay him $75,000 to quit coaching and just do a football column for their syndicate. After years of living frugally and giving his extra cash away to people who seemed to be in a lot worse shape, Rockne was at last getting prosperous. It seemed like a staggering injustice.

"Mrs. Rockne, there's this crazy story going around," said Ward, calling the family home on East Wayne Avenue in South Bend. "I don't mean to upset you, but the wire services think something awful has happened to Rock."

"It's true," she said. "They just called." Then the phone clicked off.

EPISODE 18

The first day of the month was beautifully warm. The birds were beginning to filter through the sycamores and students sat on benches by the lake. In his room, Frank Leahy was stretched out on his bed, reading a book for a history course he was supposed to have taken as a sophomore. Outside the window, students were gathering on the lawn and he could hear their voices getting louder. The door to his room opened slowly and in walked Johnny O'Brien. His face was twisted backwards in an awkward manner as if someone were pulling on the muscles in his jowls.

"Frank," he said. "I'm sick to my stomach."

"What's the matter, John," said Leahy. "Have a bad breakfast or something?"

"No, God, I wish to Christ that's what it was," he said. "Oh, Frank! They're saying that Rock is dead."

"Oh, dear God, that's crazy!"

Instantly, Leahy was on his feet, struggling to find his shoes. On the lawn he grabbed the first people he could. What had happened? Well, said one of the Notre Dame players, one of the wire services had reported a plane crash and one of the bodies on the wreck was Rockne's. Wildly he turned to another man, a non-athlete, who shook his head. Leahy's brain was burning. Near Sacred Heart Church, he came across students kneeling on the grass praying for the coach's immortal soul.

"Get up! Get up!" he screamed. "It isn't so. I know Rock better than any of you. He'll figure out a way to get out of this thing. He's smarter than anybody. If everybody else is dead, Rock is alive. He'll figure out a way. Get up!"

149

Already, the president, Herbert Hoover, was on the line from the White House, telling Mrs. Rockne, "Every American grieves with you. He was a great man. A true folk hero of our land. Coach Rockne so contributed to the high purpose of sportsmanship in America that your loss is a national loss." There was a call from Douglas MacArthur, the Army chief of staff. And the King of Norway announced that its best known American emmigrant would be knighted in death.

They came and put a hand on Frank Leahy's shoulder and asked him to come back to the room where he had a chance of getting his emotions under control. He had just come to know Rockne intimately and now this gigantic figure had been removed from his path.

"It was an hour of intense personal crisis for me," he said. "I pledged that evening after I returned from the prayer service at the church that, if I ever could, I would try to fulfill Rockne's faith in me. I would attempt to be the coach he was, not only on the field, but off it. I would be my own man, but I would follow his principles as closely as I could."

The telephone lines into South Bend were overloaded. They tell the story of a newsboy in Chicago who picked up his bundle, read the front page with the words "Rockne Dead" and threw the papers into the river near the Tribune tower rather than deliver such incredible news. No modern athletic figure overshadows the nation quite the way Rockne did in his time. When the casket bearing his burned and mutilated remains was taken off the train in Chicago, more than 20,000 people surrounded old Dearborn Street station. Every flag in the city was at half mast. Radio stations played funeral music around the clock.

There were pictures, swathed in black, of Knute Rockne in every department store window and every hotel lobby. Some schools closed out of respect. His ride home to South Bend was every bit as mournful as Abraham Lincoln's sorrowful return to Springfield, Illinois.

"It was fully two days before I could bring myself to believe that Rockne would not walk through the door and say something like, 'Hello, Frank, how's the leg, Can't stay in that cast forever. Gotta get going! Gotta get going!' In every corner of the Notre Dame campus, men were grieving. The priests wore the most somber of expressions. It was as if someone had stolen

Our Lady off the Golden Dome. Gradually, I got back into the main stream of life again. It was years before I was really the same. I always had lingering in the back of my mind these words, 'Frank, if you are ever in trouble or ever need advice, you know my telephone number and I'll do my best to help.' Now there was no need to know that number. I did not return to Notre Dame for fully a decade. It would have been too painful."

And so they buried the legend on the afternoon of April 5, 1931, with six of Rockne's best athletes as pall bearers, Frank Carideo, Marchmont Schwartz, Marty Brill, Moon Mullins, Tom Conley and Tony Yarr. It disturbed Frank Leahy some that he was not selected. After all, hadn't this greatest of football coaches told numerous people in the business that he felt Leahy was someday going to prove to be his brightest apprentice? He told O'Brien of his disappointment.

"If they let everybody be a pall bearer who ought to be, there would be ten million pall bearers, Frank," he said. "Just be happy that Rock singled you out for so much praise. He never did anything he didn't mean. That's honor enough, isn't it?"

So Leahy fell in with the 1,400 who tried to enter a church built for less than 300. The members of his football teams were admitted along with the family, close friends and the Notre Dame faculty. The rest listened on loudspeakers set up on the lawn. There were several eulogies. But it was Rev. Charles O'Donnell, his personal friend for more than 20 years and the president of the University, whose words are still remembered.

"In this Holy Week of Christ's Passion," he said. "There has occurred a tragedy which accounts for our presence here today. Knute Rockne is dead. And who was this man? Ask the President of the United States. Ask the King of Norway who sent a special delegation to this service. Was he, perhaps, a martyr who laid down his life for some great cause, a patriot who laid down his life for his country, a statesman, a soldier, admiral of the fleet or captain of industry, a great clerical leader?

"He was none of these. He was a football coach and athletic director of Notre Dame. I find myself in this piteous hour of loss recalling the words of Christ, 'Thou shalt love thy neighbor as thyself.' Knute Rockne loved his neighbors.

"What was the secret of his irresistible appeal to all sorts and conditions of men? Who shall pluck out the heart of his mystery and lay bare the inner sources of the power he had? When we say simply that he was a great American, we shall go far toward satisfying many, for all of us recognize and love the attributes of the true American character.

"When we say that he was an inspirer of young men in the direction of high ideals that were conspicuously exemplified in his own life, we have covered much that was unquestionably true of him. When we link his name with this intrinsic chivalry and romance of a great college game, which he, perhaps, more than any other man, made finer and cleaner in itself and larger in popular appeal, here, too, we touch upon a vital point. But not one of these things, not all of them together quite sum up this man whose tragic death at the age of 43 has left this country aghast."

So, while the campus bells tolled the Notre Dame Victory March in funeral cadence, they bore him off to the cemetery hard by the trail that Father Sorin walked on the day he and his small group of teaching priests first looked upon the future campus. In the van of the mourners walked Frank Leahy, his dark brooding eyes awash with tears, trying to convince himself that he was not witnessing the death and burial of all that he had found noble and uplifting in life. As he walked along, he found himself becoming one with the Great American Ethic. Never in his life would he consider deviating from it, if not in deed always, at least in word. He had found a whole philosophy and he was ready to defend it until there was no more strength left in an ancient and perishing body.

EPISODE 19

"Do not get the impression that my early years as an assistant coach were all that grim," said Leahy. "I was discomforted by lack of money, but I did enjoy a most marvelous social life. Our group at Georgetown enjoyed numerous parties and it was really quite enjoyable. We discovered that many of the young ladies who came to Washington in various stage

152

productions were interested in football, or at least in football players and coaches.

"Unfortunately, the priests at Georgetown were looking at the sport as a needless expense. This was invaluable training for some of the pressures I was later to experience at Notre Dame. Poor Tommy Mills was constantly having to defend football and, I fear, he spent less time coaching than he did politicking to save the game at Georgetown. In the off-season, I worked part time and attended as many coaching clinics as I could. I knew that I would have to move on shortly and it happened just that way.

"The Georgetown line had performed admirably ... aaaaah, very admirably . . . against Michigan State, which was then coached by Sleepy Jim Crowley, one of the Four Horsemen. I believe we held Michigan State to a 6-0 victory during one of their best seasons. Afterwards, when I returned to Chicago for the summer to pursue a job with a printing company, Crowley called me and asked me to meet him at Tom Dugan's Saloon, an old-fashioned Irish pub greatly favored by athletes and the sporting crowd. By now I began to feel like a permanent part of the ... aaaaah ... world of sports. I knew I was secure in the coaching profession and that I was doing exactly what I wanted to do with my life. I knew I would never be head coach at Winner High School. I knew that I would do more than that with my life. I sensed that I had a mission and was filled with noble purpose.

"Crowley told me, 'Frank, you're a fool if you stay with Tommy at Georgetown. They are only going to drop football, either that or make it such a minor sport that nobody will care about it. Come up to East Lansing with me and take a look at the facilities. If you like what you see, sign a contract to coach the line for me this fall. What do you say?'

"Needless to say, I was impressed and I signed even before I could send my resignation to Georgetown. My salary went up to $2,200 and Michigan State got me a job working as a councilor at Camp St. George, a Catholic boy's camp. I worked there for two more summers, even after I left Michigan State. They treated me as well as I have ever been treated and 1932 was a marvelous year at East Lansing. Our line was easy to coach, so I certainly had every chance to look good. Michigan

State lost only one of its nine games and that one went to a Michigan team that didn't lose all season.

"When the season ended, Crowley was offered the head coaching job at Fordham, which was sort-of the Notre Dame of the East in those days, as far as football was concerned. It was a tempting offer and he could not turn it down. He wanted me to come with him as his line coach, but I was nearly 25 and very anxious to become a head coach. Years later, I thought Terry Brennan too young at 25 to replace me as head coach at Notre Dame. But at the time, I thought I knew enough to take Sleepy Jim's place at Michigan State. I went to the president of the University, no less, and offered my services.

"He looked for all the world like a man who had lost the power of speech. He told me that he would look into my credentials. In the meantime, he told me that my name would be placed alongside those of other serious applicants.

"I comforted myself with the knowledge that Rockne had been only a few years older when Jess Harper resigned as head coach at Notre Dame and recommended that his assistant, Knute Rockne, be named as his replacement. I figured that if Rock could be head coach at Notre Dame when he was 29, there was no reason why I couldn't lead Michigan State at 25. I waited and waited to hear. Suddenly it struck me that it might be best to join Crowley at Fordham. The good people at Michigan State had taken my application as something of a joke. But, ooooooh, I meant it. I believe even now, in all modesty, that I could have done the job.

"It was interesting how Fordham came to hire the entire Michigan State staff. Our team had come to the Polo Grounds as betting underdogs. This was Major Frank W. Cavanaugh's final year. His health was very poor and he was almost blind. Well, on the first play from scrimmage, our finest halfback, a lad named Bob Monnett, ran 80 yards for a touchdown behind what, I must confess, was excellent line blocking. Michigan State went on to win by a 19-13 score.

"It seems that Fordham had decided to pirate—that is the only word that comes to mind—the coaching staff that did the best job against them. It was not unheard of in those days. Only one of our assistants declined the invitation. That was a fellow named Miles Casteel, who wanted to stay at Michigan State. Immediately, I thought of my old high school coach,

Earl Walsh. He had left Winner and was working at a prep school somewhere in southern Illinois that was considering the possibility of dropping football. Crowley remembered him well as a man who had played halfback at Notre Dame before he had.

"Earl was pleased to accept, and he and I and Judge Carberry took a three bedroom apartment together in the Bronx. Oooooh, I felt like I had made the big time, even though the money wasn't much better and the prices were higher. Both the depression and prohibition were ending and New York was starting to be an exciting place again. Oooooh, I was something of a South Dakota hick even then. While we were scouting for an apartment, I stopped at a bar on Concourse Plaza, ordered a beer, gave the waiter a $20 bill and kept waiting for the proper change. The man kept insisting that I had given him a $2 bill. Oooooh, by sundown, I was something less of a rube.

"I had been to New York before, but only with football teams. I took long rides on the subways and walks in Central Park. Oooooh, you could walk around the city without fear in those days. I would go into some of the famous bars and eating places I had heard of and just stand there watching the people. I was part of something important. It was somewhat like going to Notre Dame for the first time.

"It was difficult teaching those Fordham lads the Notre Dame system. They had been used to the single wing with its power backs and straight ahead blocking patterns. Now we came to teach them the shift. We came to teach them the proper use of the pulling linemen. It seems to have worked. During the six years I was at Fordham as an assistant, we won 35 games, lost 8 and tied 7 others. Never again was football at the school so great. I would like to say that I learned a great deal from Crowley, but I did not. He was excellent at teaching backfield play, but as a head coach he left a great deal to be desired. He did, however, delegate a great deal of authority to his assistants.

"Jim Crowley enjoyed his social life and when practice was over that was it. He liked his cocktails and he wasn't much for putting in long hours. I liked him personally and I have ever been grateful to him for giving me a chance. But his great success was based mostly on the fact that he had a group of young, vigorous assistants all of whom were willing to work hard to succeed.

"In addition to the extra work which was necessary to cover up the lack of real leadership on our coaching staff, it was necessary to find outside employment. No assistant coach of the time could afford the luxury of just teaching football. I would spend my summers at Camp St. George and then return to New York to find employment. I worked for an advertising firm, selling billboard space. But it meant getting up very early, riding the subway downtown, spending the morning talking to clients, getting back on the subway, getting off just in time to prepare for practice and then working until quite late getting ready for the next week's game.

"Often when I was at Notre Dame, they would ask me if I minded such long hours. I would tell them that from the time I was old enough to haul grain for my father at 5 A.M. in the morning, I had been doing just that. Sacrifice is not difficult if that is all you have ever really known.

"If it had not been for the United States Rubber Corp., I doubt if I would ever have had the opportunity to travel around the country and better myself by attending coaches' clinics, I doubt I would have had enough money to get married and I doubt if I would have risen to the position where either Boston College or Notre Dame would have wanted me as their head coach. That is the, aaaah, important part about American industry, there is always room for a poor lad who wants to work hard. He can always get ahead. I learned that much from US Rubber before I was 30.

"Tom Young, the sales promotion manager, came to me and asked me what I thought I could do to promote the sale of rubber soled, canvas-topped shoes among adults. Sneakers, as they were called, had always been thought of strictly as a child's shoe. Basketball players wore soft leather shoes that often gave them terrible blisters. I threw myself into the project because I saw it not only as an opportunity for outside income but as a means of going to as many clinics as possible at the company's expense. I had decided to make a reputation among other coaches as a student of the game. I did not care about outside publicity. I wanted it to be mentioned around at clinics and coaches' conventions that 'this Leahy is a comer, a potential head coach.'

"I presented US Rubber with some structural ideas which their designers immediately adapted. In a sense, Frank Leahy was the father of the modern basketball shoe, a designation that does not necessarily come to mind when my name is mentioned. The company was most gracious. They sent me nearly every place I wanted to go to promote it.

"Aaaaah, let me give an example of the manner in which Notre Dame men tended to cooperate with each other in those days. It was like one large, national fraternity. The most famous basketball player that Notre Dame ever had was Moose Krause. He had been an impressive football player as well, but his reputation hinged more on basketball than football, despite his proficiency in both sports. He had become coach and athletic director at St. Mary's College in a small Minnesota town. I was putting on a very important demonstration in Chicago. I called to see if he might be available.

"Moose informed me that he had to spend the evening at St. Mary's because there was an important faculty meeting. I decided that the only thing I could do would be to hire male models who might be able to impersonate basketball players. Even then, male models did not look even vaguely like athletes. I met them at 7:30 A.M. to try and teach them to be as much like basketball stars as they could. It was not easy, but I had over one thousand coaches present and I could not afford to lose their attention.

"I was in despair. As it came closer and closer to my 9 A.M. demonstration, I decided that God simply did not want Frank Leahy to succeed at this business venture. Then, the door opened and there was Moose with several other ex-college basketball players. He had driven all night from Winona, Minnesota, and he had gone around Chicago rousing other basketball players from their sleep, because I needed help.

"Instead of having to send some fop out there onto the stage to dribble a basketball with our shoes on his feet, I was able to grab a microphone and say, 'Gentlemen of the basketball coaching profession, it is my intense pleasure as a graduate of Notre Dame to present Ed Krause, the man we call Moose, who is probably the greatest basketball player Our Lady ever had.' That single act of loyalty saved my position with US Rubber and enabled me to have some sort of financial latitude in my life when I desperately needed it."

EPISODE 20

A clipping, only recently unearthed from a mound of moldering memorabilia located in the storeroom of a Lake Oswego, Oregon, apartment house in August of 1973:

"If the Four Horsemen of Notre Dame were the most famous backfield unit in the history of college football, then the Seven Blocks of Granite at Fordham are the most famous assembly of linemen. The man responsible for their proficiency is Frank Leahy, an assistant coach whom Knute Rockne once said would someday be a great head coach. Young Leahy has a tremendous start toward that goal."—*The New York Sun*, October 26, 1936, after Fordham and Pitt had played one of those 0-0 ties.

With only a couple of exceptions, their individuality has been sacrificed to history. They remain forever interlocked as the Seven Blocks of Granite. The name had been used to describe at least two other lines coached by Major Cavanaugh, but in 1936 it finally took. Even the most ingenious trivia expert would have difficulty naming more than three of them and it sometimes comes as a shock that one of them was Alex Wojciechowicz, possibly the finest center who played the game up to that point, and another was Vincent Lombardi, whose true fame was still a quarter century away.

"There never was a more aggressive man who played for me than Vincent. There were times when I genuinely worried that he might be too aggressive. There is a point where, aaaaah, competitiveness ends and fanaticism begins. Oh, Vincent was always treading a thin line. In later years, I was pleased to see that he had harnessed all that energy.

"Vincent was so intense. When a play worked against us, he considered it a personal affront. When one of our plays failed, he would come back to the huddle like a madman, looking for the lad who made the fatal mistake. He had a flash-flood temper. He might have been a greater offensive guard if he had simply been able to contain his emotions more. It actually hurt his concentration. I had long talks with him about it and he prayed always to St. Jude that he could overcome this weakness.

"Football was not as commercial then as it later became.

We played for the satisfaction of bringing a winner to our school and for personal satisfaction. It was manly combat and for a good cause. We stimulated people and we entertained them. Vincent took it far more seriously than was really good for him at the time. You had to eat with the game of football, sleep with it and live it. It must be impossible for some kids today to understand how we felt, but football at Fordham was not an individual thing. We played for the team, for the school. It was a great moral crusade. We could never shrug off a loss. It was a great disaster. That's how deeply we felt.

"Our individuality was sacrificed for the larger contribution to the school. We were making people proud of Fordham, to go to Fordham, to donate money to watch Fordham grow. I don't think there was a man on that team that didn't realize that by making people interested in the school, he was helping it progress. We didn't say as much, but we were playing for better chemistry labs and a finer library as well as for ourselves.

"What Vincent later applied to the Green Bay Packers, he had learned at Fordham. I was there to be a part of his life. Oooooh, he was a vicious one. On a certain afternoon, I did as Rockne used to do. I went out onto the field in shorts and a sweat shirt and gave Vincent one-on-one instruction. He became so angry at me that he slammed me to the ground and chipped a tooth. Years later, he apologized, but he could not apologize at the moment. He was so filled with the desire to win.

"They never recognized his genius. Fordham could have made him head coach at a time when football was dying there. But they only gave him an assistant's job. Army could have had him when Colonel Blaik retired. The New York Giants, in their abject stupidity, could have made him the replacement for Jim Lee Howell and they failed.

"One day after he took the job with the Packers, we had dinner and I asked him why he had chosen to hide away in little Green Bay when I knew him to be one of the finest head coaching prospects in the nation. He looked at me across the table and said, 'Coach Leahy, I'm 46 years old and nobody has ever asked me to be a head coach before. This is my first offer. Can you God damn well believe that, coach?' I could hear his teeth grinding together and, ooooh, it was an awful sound. There he was, nearly 25 years after I had coached him and he was just starting to control that temper.

"And you know, I admired him more. Vincent waited so long. I am sincerely pleased that, before he died, they recognized him for the great football mind and great leader that he was.

"Vincent was a man of strong religious beliefs. Some young people think that rigid religious beliefs and strong self-discipline are opposites. But they are wrong. Oooooh, they are very wrong. They talk about love. But the ability to love an enemy, a strong religious tenet, indeed, is the result of strong self-discipline. It is easy to love a friend, but football teaches the kind of strength it takes to walk off the field with your arms around the shoulders of a man who has just been, aaaaah, trying to beat you into the ground.

"Love comes through sacrifice. Sometimes the route is strange and twisted. But that is how life is. That is what Vincent learned at Fordham and what he preached later on.

"I, personally," Leahy said, wincing, "have not practiced self-discipline as much as I should have."

EPISODE 21

A small recollection, suitable for framing on your office wall, or at least over your mantlepiece at home:

"There were times when Vince (Lombardi) was doing so well with the Green Bay Packers and Frank knew that he'd never coach again because he was getting too old and too sick that he kind of thought he was the keeper of some sacred flame. Old Rockne had patted him on the head and told him to go out and beat everybody he could and, somehow, he convinced himself that he'd passed the power onto Lombardi during those years he coached him at Fordham. Maybe he did. All three of them came from poor immigrant backgrounds or close to it. They all came from rigidly disciplined families. They all found winning at football a means of expressing themselves. I'm just surprised that Lombardi didn't find his way to Notre Dame."—Rev. Frank Cavanaugh, August 29, 1973.

EPISODE 22

The players came and went, the parts being largely interchangeable, but the real Seven Blocks were, as Frank Leahy remembered them, Leo Paquin at left end; Ed Franco at left tackle; Nat Pierce at left guard; Alex Wojciechowicz at center; Vince Lombardi at right guard; Al Babartsky at right tackle and Johnny Druze at right end. There was an underground effort in later years to discredit Leahy's part in assembling this incredibly swift, strong and mentally aggressive line. It came when he was at Notre Dame and journalists were saying that he was far more skilled than Rockne ever was.

It is a matter of record, however, that one of his underlings decided to call his first male child by the implausibly un-Slavic name of William Francis Leahy Wojciechowicz. This anonymity was having a curious effect on Leahy's inner pride of accomplishment and his outer humility. As much as he liked Sleepy Jim Crowley on one level, he was struggling to get away from him on another.

"I was constantly seeking a head coaching job," he said. "Oooooh, I never applied directly, but I kept seeking information on possible openings. There was a time when I was quite willing to go to a small college and establish myself with hope that a larger school would eventually call for me.

"Do not misunderstand me. Jim Crowley was a wonderfully kind, sentimental man with a very optimistic attitude toward people. He simply hated to share credit with other people. For instance, he and Don Miller, one of the other horsemen, were the finest of friends. Somehow Crowley felt that Miller received too much attention at Notre Dame and he had not received enough. Now Miller was one of the most forgiving souls I have ever had the pleasure of associating with.

"Crowley got in the habit of referring to Miller as 'the man who used to block for me at Notre Dame.' In fact, once Don was kind enough to come to Fordham to work with the backs in spring practice and Jim was most sarcastic. He introduced him in the following manner: 'This is Don Miller, boys. He used to play right halfback and block for me at Notre Dame. He is going to give you backs some coaching tips. When he is through, I want you to forget everything he said.'

"It reached the point where Miller had heard himself described as Crowley's blocking back so often at banquets that he eventually wrote to Mrs. Rockne and asked her for a copy of a letter Rock had sent to the *New York Times* in which he stated that 'Don Miller was the greatest open-field runner I ever had at Notre Dame.' It was written just before Rock's death. Miller had it photostated and sent out to everybody he knew. The whole thing caught Crowley completely by surprise.

"Even then, Jim Crowley was marvelously funny. Ooooh, he could have been a great actor. He was a master of the art of mimicry and he was a deadpan comedian, the equal of Buster Keaton. I often thought while I coached under him that he should have gone into show business.

"I was determined to have my own team and I spent a great deal of my time at coaching schools and clinics. Our defensive line gave up only 33 points in its first eight games in 1936 and our only loss was to New York University by a 7-6 score. Our offensive line was the best known in the nation. In all modesty, I felt that I had come close to mastering the technique of line coaching. During the summer of 1937, I set out to learn as much as possible about coaching the backs. It occurred to me that the widest-open, most exciting offensive football was being played in the Southwest Conference. I signed up for seven clinics in that area so I could absorb everything I could.

"This was a critical point in my career. I felt that if I could prepare myself for a head coaching job and get one, perhaps, I would be better off than going with United States Rubber. I was spending roughly half of my work time with them, anyway. I had taken a medical course in podiatry, the study of the human foot. This was to be my last drive toward my life's dream. I, aaaah, did not want to be an assistant coach much past my 30th birthday and I was just short of 28 when I went on my tour of the Great Southwest.

"It is curious. These were exciting years at Fordham. There were the amazing string of three 0-0 ties with Pittsburgh. There was the undefeated team of 1937 that went to the Sugar Bowl. But I strained to get out. I was in a limbo, possibly of my own making. Still, I associated with some wonderful people. There were two men who went with me when I finally got my chance, Johnny Druze and Joe McArdle, who played the line at Fordham under me, and there was Ed McKeever. Aaaaaah, there is an interesting story.

"I had gone to a coaching school at Lubbock and one of the speakers was McKeever, who was then an assistant at Texas Tech. I was much impressed by this young man and I asked Pete Cawthon, the head coach to introduce us. I was surprised to hear McKeever tell me, in his thick southern drawl, that he had not only been at Notre Dame but that I had hit him especially hard during the 1929 varsity-freshman scrimmage. I had always associated him with Texas Tech, where he had been an outstanding back.

"But he had thrown in his lot with Our Lady and had played only in spring practice as a freshman. His father had taken ill and he returned to Texas and entered Tech. I spent many hours talking with him at the clinic and he said, 'When you get a head coaching job—and you're going to—I want to be your backfield coach.' I told him that I was much appreciative of his most gracious confidence, but that so far there had been no great rush for my services.

"I came home from that clinic exhilarated. For the first time, I felt like a true leader, somebody in the Rockne tradition, perhaps. Already in my mind I could see myself forming my own staff, preparing for games, devising a game plan, exhorting young men to play to the best of their ability for their school. Ooooooh, I felt like a man with a mission. When the 1937 season ended, I had my first contact about a head coaching job. With great relish, I leaped onto the train and went to Lafayette, Indiana. Ooooooh, I was a very excited young man. I had come all this way from Winner, South Dakota, and now I might be offered the job as head coach at Purdue.

"Well, it was a most unsettling experience. I had purchased a new suit and hat for the occasion and I felt that I had as good a chance as anyone. For two days, I met people connected with Purdue. It was a fine, sociable time. I had not made an application there, but several Notre Dame graduates had recommended me highly. I was most flattered, of course. Eagerly I kept waiting for some offer. But nothing was said to me. I was driven to the train station and told how happy they were that I could visit them. No offer was ever made to me, ever. No explanation was ever made.

"You can imagine my mental depression. I felt myself ready to be a head coach. I knew exactly which men would be the best assistants. For more than a year I had been outlining an entire program for putting a college football team on the field. For a long time, my outlook changed from day to day. First I would ponder the possibility of trying to find a job at a small college. Then I would decide to hold out for a major school. And people were forever telling me, 'Ooooooh, Frank Leahy, you are going to make a great head coach someday.' Then I would tell myself that it might be best to simply forget my dream and go with US Rubber. The business world had always been a source of keen interest to me.

"It is most difficult to feel yourself a football coach and have no team to command. But the company seemed to offer the most security. After all, I was married now and my family was started. This was a bright spot, the only light in the darkness of my inner turmoil."

EPISODE 23

It was naturally supposed by a number of people examining the man's surface qualities that Frank Leahy was something of a 1930s-style sex symbol. Indeed, he was mournfully handsome, far more in keeping with the stereotype of the dour, unhappy Highlander than the mental image of a whistling, finger-snapping, party-ravenous Irishman. Then again, Americans never could come up with a decent, accurate stereotype.

In a massive effort to overcome his natural shyness, he had concentrated on being courtly and charming around women. Since he seemed to have the ability to instantly turn women on, it was presumed that he was a lover of magnificent proportions. It wasn't necessarily so.

"Oh, as a young man, Frank had a healthy interest in women," said Tom Leahy. "But he was terribly shy around them. He could turn a waitress to mush by giving her that wistful little Irish smile and saying something polite. He'd eagerly pursue a young lady and, then, when he caught her not know exactly what to do with her. Frank never was that much of a swinger, although, God knows, he loved a good time. In his later years, he could work like hell for weeks and then decide it was time to relax. Then you couldn't get him to bed by 5 A.M. Even when he was older, he could still be a charmer."

The most fanatic of Fordham football freaks was John Abbatermarco, who had been a freshman at Notre Dame when Leahy had been a senior. He was part of Brooklyn's Irish-Italian-Jewish upward mobile society. His father owned a paper mill and he lived on Ocean Parkway, the proper place for all the successful sons and grandsons of the later immigration waves to go when their bank accounts hit a certain level.

For weeks, Abbatermarco kept inviting Leahy to dinner at his parents' house. He was going with an Irish girl named Ann McCafferty who had an equally Irish girl friend. Well, there was always work to do on an entirely new basketball sneaker Leahy was thinking about and there were sports dinners to go to and luncheons to attend and some sophomore guard who hadn't looked that well in spring practice to fret over. So Leahy kept putting Abbatermarco off. There was always something more important.

"Are we friends, Frank, or aren't we?" Abbatermarco asked one afternoon.

"Why, friends, Jonathan, of course."

"Don't you know it's a personal insult to turn down an Italian's invitation to dinner?" he asked. "If you refuse again, I will have to consider you an enemy."

"Oh, my goodness, Jonathan. I had no idea."

As they rode across Manhattan bound for the Brooklyn Bridge, Leahy listened to what amounted to be a scouting report. It was Abbatermarco's belief that his friend would be thrilled with Florence Reilly. Reddish-blond hair, he said, and on the slender side. Not exactly beautiful, but pretty and prone to smiling a lot. Very refined. Nice, well-to-do, Irish Catholic family.

"Mmmmm," said Leahy. "How well-to-do?"

"Her father is Sanford Reilly and he's president and owner of the Ferguson Furniture Company. See, I told you I was fixing you up with something special."

"Ooooooh, Jonathan," he said. "I fear you have been too zealous in my behalf. Oooooh, I don't think this will work out very well. A furniture company, you say? I'm afraid all we'll have in common is our religion and the fact that we are both Irish. Ooooh, I'm afraid you've over-matched me. Yes, I am."

Dinner passed in agonizing silence. Leahy made a few courtly remarks to Miss Reilly, noted that she did indeed have an astonishingly pleasant smile and thinking that Abbatermarco had underrated her looks somewhat. On the way to the movies, he loosened up some, made a few small, but witty remarks. He brought up the subject of football and then wished he hadn't. What would a girl from a refined Irish Catholic family from Brooklyn know about football? Not much.

Over cards at the Reilly house later on, Leahy grew quiet again. Indeed, his date's family were living considerably better than anybody in Winner, South Dakota, ever considered possible. It struck him that some of the Irish in America did not start out life in a tent with wooden sides in the deadly inhumanity of a Dakota winter. Nor did their fathers drive teams of freight wagons 100 miles to the next town and fight drunken cowboys in the streets. It was weeks before he called again, and only with a great deal of quivering insecurity. If Leahy hadn't been prodded, he might never have asked for another date.

"What's the matter with you, Frank?" asked Abbatermarco as Leahy was winding up his affairs at Fordham, getting ready to leave for Camp St. George in a couple of weeks. "That Florence Reilly really liked you. She's hurt because you haven't called back. Didn't you like her?"

"Ooooh, yes, indeed," he said. "A most charming and interesting young lady. Very nice, indeed. I don't think I'd fit in with her family, though. Very well to do."

"And I thought you were a Notre Dame man," said Abbatermarco, snickering.

"I am worried about what her father might think. I am, after all, a South Dakota cowboy."

It was not necessary to wait too long to discover exactly what Sanford Reilly thought. A man whose notion of fun was going to a solemn high Requiem mass, he ran his household and his children with that peculiar style of Irish Catholic puritanism that utterly confounds non-Celts.

It was obvious that Florence Reilly was thoroughly taken with this darkly handsome, laconic frontiersman whose wit kept crackling out of his somber moods like lightning flashes from a thunder cloud. He did not smoke and drank moderately. Then again, he did not read great books either. One moment he was totally pessimistic about his future and the next he was telling the Reillys about this great quest for football victories he was going on, when the moment was right. Despite a brilliant mind, he seemed to have no real intellectual leanings. One moment he was the truest-type lace curtain Irishman. Minutes later it was possible to detect the rawness of the Dakota Badlands in his soul.

To Sanford Reilly, just as he was to hundreds of sports writers only a decade later, he was a bewildering enigma with no real clue to the complexities of his personality. One thing was quite certain. The elder Reilly was not completely enchanted with the notion of having a football coach for a son-in-law. Somehow, it didn't set quite right. Leahy was far more popular in the parlor when he talked at length about his business involvement with United States Rubber.

That summer, the mail poured back and forth between Camp St. George and 1123 Ocean Avenue in Brooklyn. In the fall of 1934, Frank Leahy came back to Fordham convinced that he was in love and wanted to get married. At last, there was something besides football and business in life. Florence Reilly was in third place and closing fast. Seeing each other was somewhat troublesome. Since refined Irish Catholic girls from nice families in Brooklyn were not permitted to visit bachelors at their quarters in the 1930s, it was necessary for Leahy to spend a nickle every day after practice and ride 31 miles from the Bronx to Brooklyn on the Eighth Avenue subway.

Somewhere around Christmas, it became understood that they would get married. There was no eloquent halftime-style speech proposing marriage. As it so often happens, it was just sort of decided. Sanford Reilly took it with as much grace as possible. On Florence Reilly's birthday, February 14, 1935, Leahy gave her a ring, thereby covering a Valentine's gift, an engagement gift and a birthday gift with one present, an overwhelming vindication of Celtic ingenuity.

There was a drawback, as there so often is in these small romantic stories. Reilly, himself, believed in the ancient code of letting the daughters get married in order. He had just spent himself into one financial pit for Eleanor and, now, Edna wanted to get married.

The wait was becoming intolerable. Sanford Reilly kept talking about putting the marriage off until 1936, the Irish traditionally being in no hurry to start raising families. About a week before the big Fourth of July weekend at Camp St. George, councilor Francis William Leahy told the director that he had to return to New York on an emergency. Quite possibly it was. The Rev. Joseph Scanlan, rector of Our Lady of Refuge parish in Brooklyn, agreed, somewhat against his will, to perform a quiet, non-family ceremony. He understood the ways of the Celts, who marry their daughters off in order. There was no wedding trip. In fact, it was three months before Leahy could explain to his father-in-law that he was, indeed, his son-in-law.

"I was so nervous and worried that I would have, aaaah, preferred to send the man a telegram explaining that Floss— my own nickname for Florence—and I had been married," Leahy said. "When at last it became necessary to explain what we had done, I believe that I was as nervous as I was before any football game I played or coached in. He looked at me and said, 'Were you married in church, son?' I told him that we had been and he seemed to relax and accept me. It was not easy being taken into an Irish Catholic family as a son-in-law in those days."

There is evidence that Reilly relaxed somewhat after the news had broken across his parlor. He invited them to use a couple of upstairs rooms in the family's house until they could find a suitable apartment. Florence Reilly Leahy was delighted. Francis William Leahy was not, but he accepted the offer anyway and lived there a year. One evening, just before they turned out the lights, he turned to his new wife and said: "I don't mind it here. I adapt very easily. If I had to live in a jail for a year, I'd probably come out loving it."

Eventually, they found three rooms on the Grand Concourse near 196th street, not that far a commute from the Fordham campus. They started having all those fine, healthy children, the ones the public used to see praying around the Christmas tree every winter in publicity stills sent out by the University of Notre Dame. There were eight children, the Master Coach and the Perfect Catholic wife. It was the Perfect Catholic family, complete with a live-in mother-in-law and a great aunt who came to stay a few weeks and wasn't gone after eight years. It was the most beautiful Catholic family in the world, or so they said.

No one ever doubted that the Master Coach wasn't the Master Parent. It was a myth that prevailed right up until the last three years of Florence and Frank Leahy's life together.

EPISODE 24

The autumn of 1938 was exceptionally balmy and soothing, the great hurricane of the summer before having crashed through the upper Eastern states, uprooting old trees that had been standing when Washington went to rendezvous with the French Admiral Rochambeau. Gone forever were old houses and old ways. The Fordham football team finally lost to Pittsburgh. It tied two other games and won six—until Pitt scored 24 points against it. Leahy's line had given away only one touchdown in a 6-6 tie with Purdue, which most certainly must have wondered why it had not given the young Fordham assistant the courtesy of a return call.

In Boston, life was not entirely grim. The brothers who ran Boston College had hired, a few years earlier, the redoubtable Gil Dobie, a major league football coach if one ever existed. He had done a remarkable job, especially in the area of recruiting. Young men from all over New England seemed to be drawn to this unsmiling, somber man. A morbid fascination with the stock market had made him a millionaire by the time the country was just moving out of the Great Depression. He was sour and pessimistic. He trusted no one in particular. He was given to darkly disturbing remarks about the most sacred of American institutions.

"The story was once told of the much sought-after campus queen who promised that she would marry the first football player who made All-America. Whereupon the football gladiators fought so valiantly for alma mater and for their sweet young thing that four of them made various All-America selections picked by the football critics. Naturally, this unforeseen circumstance caused considerable discomfort to the sweet young thing, as well as the players. It was decided to relieve her of her promises to unite in wedlock with them," Dobie said. "She did not wish to hurt anyone's feelings by marrying just one and if she married them all, she'd be promptly arrested for polyandry. The moral is: Don't believe that everybody who makes All-America does it just because he loves the game of football."

Gilmour Dobie had all the qualities that Francis William Leahy had, except for two. He was not young anymore and he was a Presbyterian' Scotsman working for a school that was largely populated by Irish Jesuit scholars. Even though they are first cousins and blood brothers, the Scot and the Irishman are not always compatible, suffering from the feuds that often divide separate but equal branches of any family.

Dobie did his very best to be respectful. He undoubtedly respected a Catholic priest with as much intensity as he ever admired a Presbyterian minister. It was just that he failed in nomenclature.

As hard as he struggled, he never could quite understand that he was taking his players to Mass, rather than to services. Dobie tried to think of the priests as priests, but he always ended up calling them ministers, which suited his tongue better. Lord knows he wanted to call them Father, but he was just too much of a Protestant. Few Jesuits really enjoy being called parson, no matter how well-meaning the man addressing them is. On one occasion, he had been asked to speak with Father Patrick Collins, faculty moderator of athletics at Boston College.

"Parson, how many of these boys here are receiving athletic scholarships?"

"Oh, about 24 of them, Gil," said Father Collins.

"Yes, but how much money are they getting?" asked Dobie, looking as bleak as a Scottish moor.

"It comes to about $1,000 all told," the priest explained.

"You parsons don't care how you spend your money, do you?" Dobie said. "And you Irish agree with everybody else when they say we Scots are cheap." Even though his three year record at Boston College had been 16-6-5, Dobie was ready to forget the whole thing at the end of the 1938 season. He had been a coach of great reputation at North Dakota State,

Washington, Navy, Cornell and Boston College. He had a law degree and he was becoming more and more disturbed by the constant use of the tramp athlete that many schools were recruiting. He would not use them. What's more, he felt that college players as a group were becoming softer. Some of them had even refused to practice that summer at Alumni Field as the vanguard of the hurricane went crashing across Boston.

"So Gilmour Dobie is gone from Boston College," wrote one Boston columnist. "Never again will our city be subjected to his gloomy pessimism, which we have come to think of as 'Gildobian remarks.' His equal as a doomsayer may never be seen again."

This was a choice piece of nonsense. The columnist in question had not even heard of Francis William Leahy, who one day on his way to an astounding victory over Tennessee in the Sugar Bowl would honestly admit that he was terrified over what St. Anselm's would do to Boston College.

EPISODE 25

In the reception room high above the great brass boilers at the Ruppert Brewery, all the best and brightest brains in eastern college football were gathered, celebrating the end of another glittering season. They did not know that another world war would soon end their dominance of the game.

Just past his 30th birthday, and thoroughly convinced that he was doomed to be somebody's line coach forever, Frank Leahy drew a glass of beer and moved through the crowd, smiling graciously at everybody he saw. He stopped and talked to a couple of groups and then pushed on, filling his beer glass again and looking around for somebody to talk football with. Near the bar, he discovered Father Patrick Collins and Jack Curley, the athletic director at Boston College. They chatted pleasantly.

"Surprised a man like you hasn't had any offers to be a head coach," said Curley, knowing fully that Leahy knew Dobie was leaving. "How many have you had, Frank?"

"None at all," he admitted. "I did talk with Purdue a year

ago, but I didn't receive any offer. I guess I'm going to be somebody's line coach until I decide it's time to go to work fulltime for United States Rubber."

"Don't be too sure," said Curley. "I keep hearing rumors about you."

"Ooooh, rumors are all I've ever heard about myself," said Leahy, grinning. "That's the way it goes when you work for a successful head coach like Sleepy Jim Crowley. Everybody says you're going to get a head coaching job because you work for a guy who's doing well. Maybe it's the head coach and not his assistants. Ever think of that? Ooooh, I do. All the time."

The party ended and Leahy went home. It was February 6, 1939, and Leahy was sitting at home watching his first born, Frank, Jr., and his second, Susan, while his wife completed a novena at the parish church. The radio was on and Frank Leahy was reading the records of a recent coaching clinic he had attended when the telephone rang.

"This is Jack Curley, I believe we met a few weeks ago, just before Christmas," said the voice. "Frank, I won't string you out with a lot of crap. Would you be interested in coaching at Boston College?"

"As line coach, Jack? I'm . . . aaaah . . . I'm afraid that I would not be interested in leaving Fordham for another assistant job. I'm happy enough here doing that. I'm only interested in bettering myself. I have no other objective. If the good Lord has meant me to be an assistant, well . . . I can do that here until I find something better in business."

"Oh, no," said Curley. "Boston College wants you to be its head coach. We're damned interested in you. Everybody who talks to us says you're not only ready, you're more than ready. Now, here's what we want you to do. Can you get a train first thing in the morning? Now I know the weather's getting bad, but we want you up here as soon as possible."

"If you aren't joking, Jack, I'll fly up there," said Leahy. "I'm ready. I've been ready for a long, long time. If you want me to, I'll fly to Boston and be there tonight."

"Tomorrow will be just fine," said Curley. "The job is yours if you want it. Frank, you might as well know that you are the first person on our list."

Early in the morning, after a nearly sleepless night, Leahy jumped out of bed, being careful not to wake the two babies.

Floss turned fitfully and went back to sleep. Somewhere in the murk of night she heard a terrible pounding on the kitchen floor. There was Frank Leahy slamming a hammer against a metal bell, which contained all of Frank, Jr.'s, savings.

"What are you doing?"

"Floss," he said, grabbing nickles and dimes and quarters, as they scattered across the kitchen linoleum, "I don't have any cash to buy a train ticket to Boston. This is the only damn money we have in the house. Ooooooh, Florence, get that half dollar next to the fridge."

Somewhere, Florence Reilly Leahy found a check that her father had given her to buy a new coat with. She put on her old coat and went down to the men's store on the corner of 195th street and bought her husband a new pair of shoes and a muffler, both of which he needed. Somehow there was enough money for a ride to the railroad station.

"I hope that they plan to pay for my meals and my hotel room," Leahy said. "If they don't, Floss, I'll have to hitchhike back from Boston. As your sister's husband says, it's easier to get a job that's better than the one you have when you've got a good job already. Now, have confidence. I have been a line coach for eight years. I am considered one of the best in the country. It is not a bad living, although I know we aren't getting rich."

At old South Station in Boston, with its gothic arches and ancient soot, there were three priests waiting along with Curley and Father Collins. One of them was Father Francis Low, a former baseball player who had joined the Society of Jesus and risen to the presidency of Boston College. For reasons which were readily apparent to ethnic-minded people of the period, he was anxious to replace the strongly Protestant, thoroughly Scottish Dobie with a coach whose appeal to the Irish-Catholic Bostonian would be unmistakable. Here was Francis William Leahy, husband of Florence Reilly Leahy, graduate of Notre Dame and an assistant at Fordham. Only William Butler Yeats could find someone more identifiably Irish.

They put him in a cab and took him across town to the Hotel Kenmore, a melting brownstone edifice that was one of the more elegant boarding houses of its day. This was the hiring committee and it cross-examined Leahy as if he had kidnapped somebody important. They especially wanted to know why Fordham's defensive line had been so brilliant the past four years, which was good, and what Leahy thought of this T-formation insanity that seemed to be sweeping across the nation like a plague. Was he that much of a Notre Dame man that he couldn't adapt to another school?

Deep inside Frank Leahy there arose a mighty clatter. All of his life he had been waiting for this moment. He battled constantly within himself, humility versus vast confidence, bordering at times on arrogance. Here was a man with a basic shyness who still had a strong sense of manifest destiny. Rising up, he asked to be permitted a few remarks.

"Gentlemen," he said. "Holy Fathers, I am very interested in becoming a head football coach. I believe that I can bring something important to Boston College and to the young men that you bring to your school. I am not at all reticent to talk about my qualifications. I am the very best head football coach you could hire. I promise you that. Oooooh, but I have other matters in the back of my mind. I want to name my own assistants. Most of them will be from Fordham. There will be some Notre Dame influence. I also want to know what kind of players that Gil Dobie left behind? Are they as good as I have been led to believe?

"I also want to know what kind of money will be available for recruiting? As I am led to believe, it is not that high. I want to know how cooperative the alumni will be when it comes to helping out with recruiting. I want $12,000 a year and a similar amount for my three main assistants, to be split among them. If you can give me answers to these questions, I am quite willing to become the next head coach at Boston College."

The room was blessedly still. Two members of the committee stared straight down. One priest looked at another and the other shrugged. Finally, the president of the college rose and in tones that only a Jesuit might employ said: "I think we have our man." The rest of the afternoon was given over to specifics. When it ended, Curley and Leahy went out and drank a couple of beers. Then Leahy called home.

"I put it over, Floss," he said. "I put it over. I hope you don't mind leaving New York. Oooooh, Boston is not as bad as you might think. I did not tell them yes, but I have them more excited than I ever dared hope was possible. I am coming home and I am to sign a contract a week from today. Don't tell anyone at Fordham, for they will try to talk me out of it."

Not a single person on the Fordham campus was unaware of what had happened and no one, certainly not Sleepy Jim Crowley, wanted the football team's line coach to leave. There was a solemn meeting in the coach's office. Crowley's tone was suitable for use at funerals, floods and other great disasters.

"Frank," he said, "you aren't 31 yet. Consider what would happen to you if you failed at Boston College. You could easily be washed up at age 32 or 33 and nobody would want to hire you again. And what would US Rubber think? They don't want a former Boston College head coach representing them. They want the man who built the Seven Blocks of Granite. I'm thinking of what's best for you, Frank. I really am."

"I'm sure you are, Jim," said Leahy. "But I have to do what's best for me. I'm ready to be a head coach and if they meet my demands I'm going up there. It isn't fair of you to talk me out of it. I've talked with Tom Young at US Rubber and they are very enthusiastic about this chance. They will continue to employ me through their Boston office. Jim, they may not meet my demands. If they don't, what can I say?"

One week after the conference at the Kenmore, Leahy received a telephone call from Boston. All of his demands had been met. Would he be able to come to New England the next morning for a press conference? This time the train ticket would be pre-paid. He was the new head coach at Boston College and it would be a long time before he would have to hammer a piggy bank apart in order to be able to afford something.

This time they met his train at the depot with a huge entourage. Photographers were running up and down the dock, popping flashbulbs and asking Leahy to turn one side and then the other. Reporters, many of whom had no idea who he might be, were asking questions about his home life in Winner, South Dakota. One of them, columnist Bill Cunningham, admitted that he liked what he saw.

"This man isn't coming here to lose. He may be only 30, but he's pretty mature for his years," he wrote. "Just because he looks like a Hollywood actor doesn't mean he can't coach.

At Fordham, his lines were the best in the nation. If he has only a fair idea of what it takes to make an outstanding back, he's a success already. They say that Leahy is a little arrogant. That remains to be told. If he is, that's exactly what Boston College needs to win games. It's always better to have a man who has too much confidence than a man who stumbles around looking for it."

The real Frank Leahy had emerged. He was flesh and blood, not merely an insecure blob from the dusty plains of a distant state. On the ride up from Central Station he discovered that he had a passer at Boston College who might be the finest, strongest arm in the nation. There was a man sitting next to him on the wicker seats, a fellow named Bill McCarthy, who was an irrational lover of Boston College football. It seems that there was this sophomore the Eagles had, named Charlie O'Rourke. In a later incarnation, he would have been a T-formation quarterback of vast ability. But the times, being what they were, demanded that a man be a hard-running single wing tailback. Football was, unfortunately, still locked into a castle-mentality.

"You must take a look at this lad," said McCarthy, using language that Leahy instantly identified with. "Oh, Frank, this lad has it. He's about 6′ 2″ and he weighs about 180. His name is O'Rourke and something has to be done with him."

In the afternoon, Leahy signed his contract. That evening, he addressed one thousand alumni at the Boston Athletic Club. His stomach was located someplace under his chin. He stood and talked at length about Boston College football, a subject that wasn't exactly his strongest. Still, he did his damnedest.

"Ladies and gentlemen," he said. "I know that we have a great football team. I mean a *great* football team in the making. I am aware of such brilliant players as Ernie Schwotzer, Gene Goodreault, Pete Vignetti, Vito Ananis, George Kerr, Henry Toczylowski and, above all, a young man in whom I have the greatest confidence, next year's passing star, Charlie O'Rourke. Where are you Charlie? Stand up and let the people see you."

For a few minutes, Leahy babbled on about how close he and O'Rourke were and how much he wanted the Boston public to know this outstanding lad. Finally, the kid in the white jacket who had been filling Leahy's water cups and pouring coffee, pulled at his sleeve.

"Please," the kid said, "don't ask for me to stand anymore. Coach, I'm Charlie O'Rourke. This is the only job they could get for me."

"How much do you weigh?" said Leahy out of the side of his mouth.

"It's pretty close to 140, coach, but don't worry about a thing. I'm on a weight building program," he said. "You aren't mad are you?"

"How can I be?" said Leahy. "I've just told everybody that you're my new sensation. Couldn't you at least get your weight up to about 155 pounds so I don't look entirely stupid."

EPISODE 26

Words that only appear when the family is around and nobody else is listening:

"I loved my uncle Frank. He was a great man. He was a mean son-of-a-bitch, but a wonderful man. I never knew a guy who was as brilliant as he was. I never knew a guy who could push you so close to insanity as Uncle. He had this crazy thing about being called 'Coach.' I used to call him Uncle Frank, because I was proud of him. I knew exactly how much he thought of my dad, Jack Leahy. I kept calling him 'Uncle Frank' and he kept telling me to call him 'Coach.' Finally, one day I went to him and I said, 'You mind if I call you Uncle Coach?' and he looked at me for awhile and said, 'Jackie, you do whatever you feel is best for you.'

"So one day Uncle Coach asked me to go over and scout Holy Cross for him. Now I was going to a prep school near Boston College and he knew I'd played some football. So Uncle Coach paid all my expenses to scout Holy Cross. He didn't give a damn about my athletic scholarship or anything. As long as I could get over and scout Holy Cross all season he was happy. That was his first year at Boston College and he had to beat Holy Cross or forget about it.

"The closer the game got, the more paranoid he got. He kept calling me on the phone and saying, 'Aaaaaah Jackie, aaaaaah,

177

how does the Cross look?' I was supposed to send him detailed scouting reports, but I was only a kid, what-in-hell-did-I-know? So finally, about a week before BC was going to play Holy Cross, he sends me over to spy on them. I'm supposed to sit upstairs in a factory across the river from the HC practice field.

"Well, I don't care what Uncle Coach wants, I can't see the field. I do everything a man can do, but I can't get a good shot at the field. By now, the field patrolmen know that I am Uncle Coach's nephew and they will grab me and throw me in the river. So I see this great big pile of snow at the edge of the field. So I sneak across the frozen water. I tunnel under the snow and I get real close to the chain link fence, where I can see through this God awful little slit, this view of the practice field. Nobody knows that I'm there.

"I take real detailed notes. I mean, there isn't a thing that Holy Cross does all afternoon that I don't have some idea of. I take the whole thing back and Uncle Coach looks at me and says—honest to the Pope!—'Aaaaaaah, nice work, Jackie, but what about the spacing of their backs?' Just this minute, he doesn't give a damn that I almost froze my ass off, all Uncle Coach wants is the spacing of their backs."—Jack Leahy, Jr., 1974.

EPISODE 27

All that Frank Leahy ever wanted from life was suddenly happening to him. In the spring of 1939, he began to assemble his command. He called Pete Cawthon at Texas Tech and asked, with graciousness, of course, if stealing Ed McKeever would be an unforgiveable sin. Leahy was able to offer more money and Cawthon said he couldn't meet the price. Johnny Druze had played one year of professional football with a team called the Brooklyn Dodgers, hadn't liked it and was in business in Manhattan, which he also wasn't fond of. One afternoon, while Leahy was cleaning up his New York apartment and getting ready to move, he opened the front door to fierce knocking.

"Where the hell do I fit in?" asked Joe McArdle, one of the later Blocks. "I hear you're taking everybody else to Boston College with you. What's wrong with old Joe?"

So they assembled in late March and spent a weekend making plans. The snow was whipping around the building and the moving van was due any hour. They plotted and they schemed. For continuity, Leahy had retained Ted Galligan who had worked under Dobie. On the 13th day of the month, they all jumped into Leahy's car and headed up the parkway to Boston—three assistant coaches, one wife and two small children. They had planned to start spring practice on the 15th, but a blizzard stopped them. In fact, they were lost for several hours in the storm while the Massachusetts Highway Patrol searched for them. They found the Leahy party in a snowdrift, happily talking football while Floss fed the children and waited to be rescued.

"Officer," said Frank Leahy. "We aren't crazy, we're football coaches."

On the morning of his arrival, Leahy asked to speak before a convocation of the student body. He asked that the football team be seated in front of him. He walked to the lectern like a man who had just taken over an important military post in time of war.

"This is not going to be one of those stale pep talks, lads," he said. "There is a genuine apathy toward not only the football team, but Boston College as a whole. That will end. My assistant coaches are passing out instruction sheets to members of the football team. Copies will be distributed to non-football playing students on the way out. There are faults that the coaching staff will not tolerate. Football is going to be fun at Boston College. It will also be hard work. It will be a source of inspiration to the entire group of students.

"Let me list the things we do not want our football players to do—First, don't report late for practice. This is a stern requirement, one that we shall not take lightly.

"Second, there will be no insubordination. No dirty play will be tolerated. Slugging is absolutely cowardly. No alibis are acceptable. There will be no loafing. Aaaaah, am I going too fast? Don't play easy just because the man across the scrimmage line happens to be a friend. Don't develop the habit of hitting easy. Griping is justifiable, but only in small doses. And, finally, the best lads play on the first team. There will be no playing favorites. Skill and enthusiasm are all that get you anywhere.

"Here are some of the things that we will do. First, players will refer to coaches as 'coach' because this is a mark of respect for what a man has had to sacrifice in order to reach his position. All players must trot to and from the field. Players must go to work as soon as they arrive at the field. All players must strive constantly for improvement and they must learn to work under pressure. Because of classwork requirements, players are on the field only a short number of hours each week, therefore, they must not waste a moment.

"All Boston College players are expected to watch their diets and get the proper amount of rest. When the teams line up, players are expected to run to their positions. Everybody must develop the urge to excel. You are also expected to give the game everything you have on each play. Everybody is expected to work to make the first team. Are there any questions from anybody in the student body?"

There was total silence in the auditorium. The undergraduates had somehow expected a stimulating, win-for-the-old-school speech. Instead, they had received a cold, calculated list of orders. Everybody had been made to feel like a part of the football team. It was as stupefying as it was terse.

"Oh, yes," said Leahy. "Non-football playing students are expected to attend practices whenever possible. The more practices you attend, the better effect you will have on your team. Thank you. Now to introduce your football coaching staff . . . that is Coach McArdle, that is Coach Druze, that is Coach McKeever and that is Coach Galligan. I hope that when you meet them on campus, you will address them that way."

Leahy stopped short of declaring martial law in Boston. He announced that because of the snow, indoor practices would begin at the Brighton High School gym. Buses would be available to bring the players back and forth. Parking would also be available for non-football playing students. So much for the orders of the day. Henceforth, football would be considered compulsory at Boston College. Several academic-minded priests twisted uncomfortably inside their Roman collars.

EPISODE 28

The cartoon in the sports section of the *Boston Post* showed an effeminate Frank Leahy dressed in drag on a throne chair. In front of him was John P. Curley, athletic director of Boston College, placing a glass slipper on one dainty foot while a group of big name coaches, also wearing evening gowns, departed in the ballroom in disgust. It was a far more innocent era, one in which a new head football coach would not get upset about being portrayed in a dress.

"They call him 'Unknown Leahy' but that won't last too long," wrote Boston columnist Arthur Sampson. "The man, although he looks almost too young to be a player, has this incredible knack. He looks you straight in the eye and memorizes your name. Whenever he sees you afterwards, he does not forget you or where he met you. He won't have to use the trick with too many people in order to make himself popular."

There was fear and trepidation that Leahy would turn Boston College into a duplicate of Fordham, which played hard-scab defense and depended upon God to score points. Those long hours in the Texas sunshine hadn't been a total expense account write off. What Leahy had in mind was some Southwest Conference theatrics. There would be some Rockne-style shifting, but basically the Eagles were going to do things that literally defied disaster.

"How can we be sure you just aren't saying that?" somebody asked at an early press conference. "At Fordham, you didn't exactly excite many people."

"I did what a good assistant coach always does . . . I followed instructions," Leahy said. "I didn't want to lose my job so I did exactly what Sleepy Jim Crowley told me to do. I expect the same sort of loyalty from my assistants, too. But I have offensive ideas of my own, ones I have never had the opportunity to put into operation.

"In fairness to Crowley, it should be said that he hasn't always had the type of material it takes to put over a flashy attack. There's no sense throwing the ball all over the field if you don't have a decent passer. There have been some brilliant linemen at Fordham over the years and it has been my pleasure to coach them. There have also been some good, hard running backs available. But the really outstanding runners have been few and far between. The talented passers have been noticeable by their absence. That's the reason Fordham has looked better on defense than on offense.

"Crowley did say that he was pleased to have me leave because he felt I was upstaging him at sports banquets. That's pretty tough to do. You have to work hard to be a better talker than he is."

It was essential to conquer the alumni next. Marching into a dinner where roughly a thousand of them were present, he looked around the room and said, "My fellow coaches." The place exploded in laughter.

"I know you wanted somebody with a larger name than Frank Leahy, who actually played only one season as a starting football player at Notre Dame and has never been anything more than a line coach. Boston College has a tradition of great coaches. I have come here to succeed and to win football games. My only regret is that my old coach from Notre Dame is not here to see one of his tackles step into such an important job. Somehow, I feel that he is with me in spirit. I can almost feel his hand touching my shoulder."

In one smashing paragraph, Leahy had shown (1) a sense of humor, (2) a sense of humility, (3) a sense of purpose, (4) a sense of destiny, and (5) flattery toward the school. What's more, he had established his spiritual link to the sainted Rockne. He had also displayed a remarkable ability to cloud men's minds, an absolute necessity for survival in the coaching business.

And, oh yes, henceforth, the Eagles would not only be using the Notre Dame shift with offensive gimmicks taken directly from Texas Christian, they would also be wearing new uniforms, more stripes and a lot more color. Every time the crowd looked down on the turf at Alumni Field, they would know that something dramatic had happened.

The Boston papers, which have always had a tendency to either crucify or sanctify, with equal vigor, responded as if they had caught Leahy taking a stroll across Boston Harbor. "Knute Rockne Lives Again In Frank Leahy!" shouted the *Boston Globe*. It could not have suited Leahy's purposes any better if he had set the type himself.

EPISODE 29

"In all modesty, let me say that when Gilmour Dobie left Boston College, he left a vast amount of talent on the football team. He was a master recruiter. Ooooh, we were truly blessed with backs like Charlie O'Rourke, Lou Montgomery, Bob Jauron, Ed Cowhig and Frank Davis. There were linemen like John Yauckoes, Chet Gladchuck, Ernie Schwotzer, George Kerr, Dick Harrison and Gene Goodreault. Aaaah, I shall never forget Lou Montgomery. A fine lad, one of the first black players to appear at a major school in New England. He was a fine football player. He was one of the first blacks that I had ever come into personal contact with and it was an enriching experience for me.

"Because of my connections with US Rubber, I was able to get a recruiting edge on some of the other coaches. Ooooh, it was perfectly legal. I was able to put Coach Druze, Coach McArdle and Coach McKeever on the payroll as members of the US Rubber staff. They went all over the East, conducting clinics at various high schools. It had the desired effect. Whereas my associates never directly mentioned coming to Boston College, it was obvious to the youngsters at these schools that BC had a young, attractive and very aggressive group of coaches. And we also stimulated the sale of rubber soled shoes as well.

"From the start, my intention was to go undefeated at Boston College and to attend as many bowl games as the team might be invited to. Let me explain my attitude toward total victory. There is no other attitude to take. I don't think there is a coach who honestly wants to settle for any less. I think it is a wholesome attitude. Unless you have total commitment to excellence, you have a flawed attitude toward life.

"Practice sessions at Boston College and, later, at Notre Dame were not as gruelling as some people have suggested. Ours was a constant search for perfection. It is a wise coach who knows when he has overworked his players. This I learned very early in my career. That second season I drove our players through an exceedingly hard week in my zeal to win a certain game. The result was one of the two losses we suffered in our two years at BC. The next week the team looked sluggish on Monday and even worse on Tuesday. On Wednesday afternoon, I had a bus parked outside the gymnasium.

"I told the players not to bother to dress. I put them all on board the bus and we all went to an afternoon movie in downtown Boston. Everybody went, the players, the coaches, our trainer, our student manager and Billy Sullivan, our publicity director. The next afternoon, the players went out and we had our finest practice of the year. The next game was won by a 55-0 score. The worst thing a coach can do is convince himself that he isn't making any mistakes.

"That is why I always had a secretary next to me taking down what I said during the games and why there was always a long session in our preparation for the coming game in which we discussed the players' mistakes, the assistant coaches' mistakes and, most important of all, head coach Frank Leahy's mistakes. The fault did not end with me, it began with me."

EPISODE 30

On the morning of his first game as a head coach, Francis William Leahy, ex-cowboy, former boxer and child of the vanishing frontier, arose from a solid two hours sleep on the couch, threw up from sheer nervousness and then went to Mass.

Earlier in the week, Florence Leahy had leased a house for the family in Newton Centre and there were packing crates all over the apartment. When the nation's newest head coach returned from church, his skin was the color of a shroud. Sullivan who had dropped by offered him a cup of coffee and a roll. He pushed them aside and sat back staring like a man without a soul or any hope of ever getting one.

"William," he said, somberly. "I am quite worried about this football team that we meet today. They do not have a man under 210 pounds on their offensive line and their backs have speed. Boston College could easily be beaten today, William. Oooooh, it could happen."

"Get beat by Lebanon Valley State?" asked Sullivan, who

acted as if he had just learned that the Pope had joined the Masons. "Oh, Frank, you must be joking."

"No, it's true, William," he said. "Boston College has some injuries. Ooooh, I am not sure about Charlie O'Rourke. I do not know if that lad is . . . aaaahhh . . . durable enough to stand the punishment. Henry [Toczylowski] is a fine quarterback, but he seems to be injured a lot. We have so many sophomores, William. Much of our reserve strength is untested. We could get beat."

"By Lebanon Valley State?" asked Sullivan, who was beginning to get the ugly feeling that he had been locked in an apartment with a madman. Florence Leahy came into the room, holding Sue, the younger of the two children. Sullivan looked at her wildly. She shrugged.

"I am wondering about Lou Kidhardt," he said. "I like the lad. He is a letterman at tackle, I know. He does not have much speed. And I am not sure about his blocking capabilities. About the only thing that I really admire about him is his determination and his willingness to make any sacrifice in order to make first string. I wonder if I am making a mistake using him on the first team. One oversight could cost us this game."

"Lose to Lebanon Valley State?" said Sullivan, growing slightly feeble.

"Ooooh, William, you must not take anything for granted in this business," said Leahy. Teams have come up to their openers overconfident in the past. And, generally, they have lost those opening games."

"But not to Lebanon Valley State, Frank," said Sullivan in cringing disbelief.

It was far worse than anyone imagined. Boston College came charging out in its new uniform with the gold helmets, the white jerseys with the maroon letters and gold stripes, the gold satin pants and the maroon stockings with the white and gold stripes.

Out came the visiting team wearing a motley variety of jerseys and pants. Poor dear Lebanon Valley had ordered new uniforms from a mill in Britain and because of the war in Europe the material had been held up. They looked laughable and Leahy, on the sidelines in his gray fedora and trench coat, got physically ill when some of his players grinned and made

185

jokes. There were 17,000 people in the stands and the press box was filled with journalists who were there largely to tell the world what a genius Boston College had hired for a coach.

Leahy was running some plays from a Texas-style single wing and some from the Notre Dame formations that Rockne used. There was one innovation that had been rattling around in his head for a long time, although he had never suggested it at Fordham. Once, in the Mayo Clinic, Rockne had told him that he planned to sophisticate the Notre Dame system to the point where not only did the ends move at more advantageous blocking angles, the tackles would as well. Lebanon Valley watched Lou Montgomery run for 45 yards for a touchdown and O'Rourke pass for 462 yards. The result was a 45-0 victory that left the Boston press completely fanatical.

"This could be one of the most powerful football teams in the country," wrote John Gilooly, who apparently thought he had seen Notre Dame on the field rather than Lebanon Valley State. "This Boston College team is a tribute to Leahy's genius. Leahy is young and believes in new methods. He has the daring of the modern school of coaches and he has convinced his players they can't be beaten. For several years, Boston has been looking for another winner at Boston College such as existed in the palmy days of the Iron Major, the immortal Frank Cavanaugh. This man Leahy has the aura of immortality about him."

One victory over a team so wistfully bad that the last periods had to be shortened to ten minutes each had brought Leahy close to canonization. Ironically, there was another athletic figure moving toward Boston at about the same time who would not be treated with such reverence. His name was Theodore Williams and nothing he ever did suited a single person in that most curious of American cities.

Even when Leahy contrived to lose the Eagles third game of the schedule, to Florida at Fenway Park, the sabre-toothed tigers in the press box were strangely docile. The tailback Bud Walton had thrown a 27 yard touchdown pass to an end, Leo Cahill, in the first period and the Gators had stopped Boston College five times inside the Florida five yard line. Considering this was the first major college Leahy had faced after defeating Lebanon Valley State and St. Joseph's, it was clearly time to denounce him as a fraud. Nobody touched him.

In fact, columnist Bill Grimes of the *Boston Evening American* fell on his typewriter in a fit of compassion rarely seen among the nation's sports writers. It was a remarkable example of kindness under pressure. "Just because Boston College lost a 7-0 verdict, don't quit on the Eagles. After studying Ed McKeever's report of the Florida-Mississippi State game, Frank Leahy knew he was in for a beating. Naturally, he did not divulge his prediction to the Eagles," he wrote.

"Leahy is installing the Notre Dame system at Boston College. During spring practice, the Eagles were drilled on the fundamentals of that style of play, the kind that made Knute Rockne famous. They were fairly impressive during the scrimmages, but a long way from perfection. In the Notre Dame system, blocking is done with the shoulders and as soon as the Eagles reported for practice this fall, an epidemic of shoulder injuries hit the squad. Those injuries were responsible for the failure of the Eagles to make a better showing than they did against the Gators.

"At first it was believed that these injuries were due to defective shoulder pads, so new ones were ordered. In the meantime, many of the key men were on the hospital list. The Eagles could not register against Florida because they could not block properly. They missed enough assignments to have lost overwhelmingly. Instead, it was only a 7-0 loss, from which they can easily recover."

Truth was that Florida had used a five man defense line against Boston College that nobody was looking for. In his third game, Frank Leahy had been out-coached and he knew it. He and McKeever ate a sandwich after the game and went home slowly, hardly saying a word. Morosely, Leahy opened the door to his new house at 620 Daniels Street in Newton Centre, mumbled something to his wife, kissed her on the cheek and wandered in to say goodnight to the children.

"Daddy's team lost, Frankie," he whispered to his semi-asleep son.

"Buy a new one," said the boy.

"Mmmmmmmm, son, I'm afraid that wouldn't set very well with the NCAA," he muttered.

In the living room, Leahy slumped down on a corner of the davenport and looked like a man in the terminal stages of some awful disease. His wife walked back and forth, offering to fix some tea or open a can of beer. The folds on Leahy's eyes sunk down to his cheekbones. His voice seemed to be echoing out of some distant cave.

"Oooooh," he said, sounding more Victorian than ever. "What a fool I was, Floss. What a total, ignoble fool. Do you recall last spring when I became the head football coach at this fine Catholic institution? Do you recall that I took films of every game and made a complete analysis of every player? Do you recall that I spent hours talking with returning lettermen, asking them about themselves and about everybody else on the team? Do you recall me spending days discussing personnel with Jack Curley? Do you recall that something in one of the films made me believe that a third string fullback named Joe Zabilski could become the fine guard he is right now?"

"Oh, yes, Frank," said Florence Leahy, fluttering just a bit. "I remember all of that?"

"Then why was I such a fool? I did not prepare properly for Florida. Oooh, they are not a worthy football team. They did something against us that I was not prepared for. I let my lads down. Floss, it is the truth. That defeat was my fault. I do not enjoy losing football games. There is no reason for it. No reason!"

"Frank, it's not possible to win every game," said Florence Leahy, immediately aware that she had selected the wrong platitude. Leahy's eyes widened. The pupils became larger. He seemed to be fighting intense anger.

"Where is that written, Floss?" he asked. "In the Bible?"

EPISODE 31

A small sliver of information, found in a yellowing scrapbook:

"Have you noticed, incidently, that the Fordham line is not what it used to be? When Frank Leahy was the line coach there, Fordham annually came up with seven blocks of granite and annually won their way to the national ranking through the play of a superlative line. It may be that Leahy mixed the mortar which joined seven young men into a moving line of great strength and skill and now that his mixing machine is

up the turnpike in Boston with the BC Eagles, *poor Sleepy Jim Crowley isn't quite the genius we all thought he was,"*—taken from the *New York Herald Tribune* and dated October 30, 1939.

EPISODE 32

Now the city of Boston, which long ago decided that it wouldn't be impressed with much of anything, had lost its precious sanity over a college football team. Students crowded the practice field, cheering almost witlessly at mere dummy drills. Pep rallies which had sunk to the excitement level of reading the dictionary, were wildly popular again.

When Kidhardt tore up his knee and was lost for the season just before the game against the University of Detroit, the entire city was distressed. It was just one of those incredible conditions where everything comes smashing together at once. There was Frank Leahy, darkly handsome and seemingly brooding. He prowled the sidelines like something out of a detective movie, his face half hidden by a Sam Spade hat. The Eagles threw the ball and did things not normally identified with Eastern college football. They were simply too entertaining to be cynical about. They rolled over everybody and it was even possible to dismiss the Florida game as some sort of nonsensical freak.

"I have an idea that Frank Leahy is deliberately following the road taken by Rockne," wrote Colonel Dave Egan. "Spirit, instilled by Rockne was responsible for the great success of Notre Dame. Somehow Leahy has managed to do the same thing with his first Boston College team. It is an attitude never before felt at College Heights. Boston College football has always been important, but it has never had that fanaticism usually associated with Notre Dame. You will note that the good colonel is getting behind Boston College football early this year. The suspicion here is that BC is going places and Frank Leahy is on his way to becoming the greatest coach the game has known since Rockne died in a Kansas wheat field. They say it is comfortable riding on a bandwagon and I want to get a good seat as soon as possible."

In the stilted rhetoric of the times, it was an open license for Leahy to take over the city. Boston sports writers never gushed like that. They sat back and said ugly things about people. But there was Boston College defeating Temple, 19-0, after Leahy personally scouted the Owls in an attempt to atone for his blunder against Florida. On the morning of the game with St. Anselm's, he called Billy Sullivan and carried on as if Lebanon Valley State had returned wearing prettier game pants. The score was 28-0, in favor of Boston College. The season turned on the game with Auburn and two of Leahy's strongest running backs, Vito Ananis and Pete Cignetti, saved it.

There were the Eagles behind by a 7-0 score in the final period when they moved down the field to score the tying touchdown. Then Ananis and Cignetti pounded straight ahead and Boston College had a victory that left the newspapers asking such circulation-titillating questions as "Rose Bowl?" and "Are Eagles Headed For Heavy Sugar In New Orleans." As it turned out, they were doing neither, but that is second guessing long retired newspaper deskmen.

They rolled over Detroit, Boston University and Kansas City, running their record eight victories and one defeat. News stories had them in every bowl on the NCAA schedule. All they needed to do was defeat Holy Cross, in a game that had all the lack of emotion of say a game between Texas and Oklahoma, California and Stanford, Auburn and Alabama, Israel and Egypt or Irish Catholics and Irish Protestants.

"Notre Dame has no real natural rival," said Leahy, looking back. "Our staff was, shall we say, Notre Dame–oriented. Every team that plays Our Lady wants to defeat it. In a sense, Notre Dame had nine or ten or eleven natural rivals. It was difficult for us to understand how important it was for Boston College to defeat Holy Cross. As the weeks went by, we began to understand. Here were two strongly Catholic schools located not more than 65 miles apart.

"They were the two largest Catholic colleges in New England, an area founded by Protestants and still largely dominated by Protestants. There was Yale-versus-Harvard in those days, but those Ivy League schools had a strong Protestant image, as well they might. But Boston College–Holy Cross was the Catholics answer to the Ivy League and, oooooh, it was not wise to lose this game.

"As luck would always seem to have it, two Notre Dame men were running the Cross. The head coach was Joe Sheeketski and Moose Krause was on the staff. The pre-game buildup was quite a bit more than I was prepared for. They dragged us in front of a football writers' luncheon the Monday before the game. Sheeketski was ready for it and, I fear, I was not. They were a marvelous football team with the great Bill Osmanski, later a brilliant fullback with the Chicago Bears, running the ball and Ron Cahill, a marvelous passer playing tailback. They had only lost one game and everybody said that the winner of the Holy Cross–Boston College game would most surely go to either the Rose Bowl or the Sugar Bowl, although it did not turn out that way."

There Leahy stood next to Sheeketski, trying very hard to be both gracious and clever. This was his first year as a head coach and he lost so resoundingly that some of his idolators in the Boston press corps sat out front and winced. The luncheon was supposed to be a test of wit and intellect. Instead, Leahy was badly out-talked.

"Cahill is the best I have," said the Holy Cross coach. "He's the best blocker, the best tackler and the best punter. You know, Frank, that he's the finest passer in New England. I'm convinced that he's far better than your Charlie O'Rourke."

"Don't you have any great sophomores behind him?" said Leahy, weakly. "I keep hearing you have nothing but great sophomores."

"Oh, yes, we have a tailback named Jack Sullivan who ran wild last weekend. He looks like another Cahill, Frank. I'm really sorry about that."

"Then we'll cancel next year's game and play this one under protest," said Leahy, desperately looking for a funny line.

"I have another kid named Roger Trichon. He's very fast, too. He can really travel, Frank. I think you'll like seeing him in the years ahead. I really feel sorry for Boston College," said Sheeketski, smirking badly now.

"Is he a sophomore, too?" asked Leahy.

"Just a sophomore, Frank, I'm afraid you're in for a lot of trouble. Don't you wish you'd stayed at Fordham where Sleepy

Jim took all the blame for your mistakes? I hope that Rockne doesn't know about what you've been doing at Boston College. Beating Lebanon Valley State wasn't that big a deal, Frank, and the Cross has all these fine young sophomores. Too bad, old friend, too bad."

"No sophomore linemen, eh, Joe?" asked Leahy, praying that Sheeketski would be merciful. He was wrong.

"Oh, Frank, plenty of young linemen. Good solid linemen who know how to play football. Good centers, good guards, good tackles, good ends. The best is my young sophomore right tackle. Much better football player than you were at Notre Dame, Frank. I'd call him an all-around mean son-of-a-bitch, Frank. That's what I'd do if there weren't so many Holy Fathers here today. Now tell me about that nice little team you have at College Heights, Frank. They tell me it isn't half bad."

"Please don't tell me about Cahill again," said Leahy. "I think I've had about enough."

Afterwards, Leahy went scuttling back to Newton Centre, his mood so low it scraped across the pavement. He threw open the front door, slammed it behind him and sat down on the davenport. He sighed loud enough to crack the plaster. "Ooooh, Floss," he shouted. "Ooooh, Floss, I think I have disgraced myself in public once again."

"What went wrong?" she asked, coming out of the kitchen, all apprehensive.

"I let that Joe Sheeketski make a fool of me in public," he said. "I did not come prepared. When in hell am I going to learn?"

The newspapers were convinced that the Leahy-Sheeketski confrontation was a smash. Gushing and gooing, they suggested that this was the start of something great. Decades would pass and these bright young men would be eyeball-to-eyeball every autumn. It would not work out that way, but at the time it seemed sensible.

The skies were choked with unspent snow when the two teams met before 41,678 customers at Fenway Park. The storm struck shortly after kickoff. Snow flakes dotted the air and then the temperature began to rise. The rest of the afternoon was hidden behind a curtain of drizzle as Jesuit battled Jesuit with coaches trained by the Congregation of the Holy Cross.

The first time Boston College had the ball, the Eagles found themselves on their own eight yard line. Two plays went nowhere and O'Rourke punted for 80 yards. The match went down to the final period with no score. Then Boston College moved 56 yards with Pete Cignetti running inside tackle for three yards and a go-ahead touchdown. A few minutes later, Gene Goodreault did a most amazing thing. There was O'Rourke running around in his own end zone with no particular hope of getting out. With a masterful concept of the situation, Goodreault came charging back and tackled his own man, thereby giving Boston College a touchback and preventing a sure Holy Cross safety.

Then, with minutes remaining in the game, Ernie Schwotzer slammed a punt back in Ron Cahill's face on the Holy Cross 15 yard line and Goodreault leaped for it. The ball squirted away from him in the muck and Schwotzer fell on it in the Holy Cross end zone. The final score was 14-0 and as the seconds ticked away, the clock at Fenway Park drove the citizens wild. "It's 15...14...13...we want a Bowl Game... 12...11...10...we want a Bowl Game."

On the sidelines, Frank Leahy slumped forward and held his forehead in his hands. Near him was Billy Sullivan, taking notes on what the head coach said during the game.

"William," said Leahy, when he could speak. "Please remind me to be calm in the dressing room afterwards. I must be gracious to the press. They cannot see how excited I am just this moment. Stay right next to me, if you...aaaah... would, please."

Inside the Boston College dressing room, the players were awash with enthusiasm.

"Bring on those Bowl bids," shouted O'Rourke. "We'll go anywhere...the Rose Bowl, the Cotton Bowl, the Sugar Bowl, the Sun Bowl, the Orange Bowl. We'll go and we'll beat anybody." Nearby, Leahy was pulling at his uniform, pleading with him to be still while the reporters were wandering through the bathhouse.

"I will do anything to get these lads a bowl bid," said Leahy, grandiosely. "A feeler would not surprise me. I suspect that our lads have earned an opportunity. They haven't traveled much this season and they deserve the chance to take a trip.

I would not be surprised if we hear something in the next few hours, in fact. Oooooh, it would not shock me at all."

In the opposing team's dressing room, Sheeketski said all the proper things to the reporters. He praised everything about Boston College. On the way out the door, he turned to an assistant coach and muttered, "That God damned Leahy outcoached me. Don't ask me how he did it. He just did. The Eagles acted so cocky it made me sick."

The newspapers were hopelessly drunk on Leahy and the Eagles. No amount of self-doubt by the coach could alter the absolute optimism of their headlines. Here Boston College had barely outlasted Holy Cross in what was a mentally and physically excruciating game and the verbs on the sports pages made it sound like a great natural disaster. The Eagles had "drubbed" and "crushed" and "flattened" the Crusaders. Down the pike in New York, the columnist for the *New York World-Telegram* was telling everybody that Frank Leahy was the coach of the year, despite the fact that his only loss was to a team he should have defeated. A 9-1 record was smashing and Boston College probably had the finest football team old New England had ever seen. When somebody called Lou Little at Columbia, he said approximately the same thing. If Leahy hadn't made just one small blunder, the Eagles would undoubtedly have been the undefeated, untied national champions.

"The greatest coaches make mistakes their first year out," said Little. "And I have long considered young Leahy to be one of the greatest football men in America. Everyone knows that Knute Rockne himself thought Frank to be his equal."

It was news to Leahy who was in Newton Centre making the third and final blunder of an otherwise brilliant rookie year. There was word from the Sugar Bowl. The committee did not feel that Boston College was that good a team because it had lost to a Florida bunch that wasn't worth thinking about. The Rose Bowl crowd heard all the talk from New Orleans and decided essentially the same thing. There were less bowls then and committees tended to be extraordinarily picky.

On December 9, 1939, the telephone rang in Leahy's house. Would the Boston College Eagles like to play Duquesne in the Cotton Bowl? Call Jack Curley and Father Patrick Collins.

There was a long discussion over how well received a football game between two Eastern colleges that happened to be Catholic would be in overwhelmingly Baptist Texas. The people at Boston College suggested that it might be better to invite a Southern school with a strong Protestant identification. Professionalism and economics were, by far, the forerunners of ecumenicalism. Father Collins heard back from Curtis Sanford, a wealthy Texas oil adventurer, proposing a match between BC and Clemson University of South Carolina. That sounded more like it. In the Associated Poll, the Eagles were rated eleventh and Clemson was twelfth. No one seemed to care that Duquesne was tenth.

"It was a proper match," said Leahy. "But I made a stupid move. Oooooh, I was young then and learning a great deal about my profession. I was 31 when the 1939 season was over, but I felt as if I were 51. I decided that it would be best for Boston College to practice at home and make the trip to Dallas four days ahead of the bowl game. It was a terrible mistake.

"There were ten Pullman cars leaving Boston for Texas. Many of them were occupied by well-wishers, who kept telling the players how well they were going to do. They were telling me how brilliant I was, but I was so smart that I didn't realize how badly it snows in New England in the wintertime. Most of our workouts were in an armory and the soil on the floor was terribly soft. It wasn't possible to have a decent workout because I was afraid of having somebody tear up an ankle during one of our frequent shifts.

"I insisted that they learn ten new plays before the Bowl Game, which was absolute nonsense. They should have given the head coach an F for the manner in which he handled that whole thing. Our team arrived in Dallas in the midst of a warm Texas winter. Oooooh, I had been told that north Texas was not that warm in January, but it was far warmer than Boston. We arrived on Wednesday. We had two workouts on Thursday, one on Friday and another on Saturday. The morning of the game we had a long blackboard instruction. The temperature did get down for the game on Sunday, but it was almost like spring in New England. I should have been there two weeks ahead of the Bowl. Now all coaches are required to do that. I wish that such a rule had been in effect then. Ooooh, I tell you, Frank Leahy would have been the genius they said he was if there had been such a rule."

On the train ride across the nation, Victor Jones of the *Boston Globe* did one of those fascinatingly inane stories on the coach's wife that left Florence Reilly Leahy just a little bit confused about why anybody would actually want to know what she thought about the game of football.

"I don't know a thing about football," she confessed, almost helpless. "I don't discuss the subject with Frank at home, ever. It's his business, not mine. I get excited over the games, of course I do, but my father can't figure it out. He keeps asking me, 'Why get so worried, it's only a game?' I tell him, papa, it's the way Frank makes his living. Except for the Christmas picture with the children, I would just as soon stay out of the newspapers. I'm not that type. Frank is, but he won't admit it."

As if no Catholic had ever ridden the range or got drunk in a Western saloon back when cowboys were in flower, the Texas press had a huge laugh over all those fine young Polish, Irish and Italian lads coming to Dallas. They gave them all ten gallon hats and posed them in awkward ethnic groupings. The Texas papers made fun of New England accents and the Boston papers got a huge laugh out of the way Southerners spoke. Only one person asked Lou Montgomery what he thought.

They made little mention of the fact that Boston College's only black was not permitted to play against Clemson in Dallas. Nor did anyone on the coaching staff, not Frank Leahy or anybody else, make that big a deal out of the fact that the fastest runner on the team was home working in the Boston post office when the Boston College Eagles headed south. After all, how many black Catholics were there?

One writer went out to Montgomery's home where he and a friend were making spaghetti and meatballs for two dates. This was a time when blacks took what they could get and didn't make noise.

"This is a grand guy," said Murray Kramer of the *Boston Daily Record*. "He's taking adversity with a grin. This could easily be the story of a man who is upset because he can't play in his team's biggest game. But he's too big for that. Instead, he and a friend were making dinner for two ladies before going to the theater.

"Don't kid yourself," Montgomery said. "Boston College doesn't need a climax runner to win this football game. The Eagles can't miss with Toz clearing the way and O'Rourke passing the ball. Boston College is a cinch to win. Sure, I hate not being there. But I know there isn't a man on that team that doesn't hate the fact that I can't be there."

The mighty *Boston Post* did say that Montgomery was making more friends by staying home than by going. It wasn't necessarily his fault or Leahy's that they were both 20 years before their times. It just happened that way, a long time ago, but yet so close.

On the morning of the game, Lou Montgomery walked to the Postal Telegraph office in Philadelphia and sent a message: "Drove halfway to New Orleans so I could hear the game better on radio. Expect you fellows to take this one for Boston College, coach Frank Leahy and for me. He told me he wanted me to come, but there was nothing to be done. Will be with you in spirit while listening to the game from Philadelphia. Good luck and God bless you, Lou Montgomery."

The Postal Telegraph operator looked at it and said that it was not necessary to keep the message to ten words. Montgomery smiled appreciatively and attempted to pay for the original telegram. The man behind the counter kept shaking his head.

The football game itself wasn't quite worth all the grief. A substitute end named Alex Lukachik kicked a 25 yard field goal for Boston College and Clemson's brilliant passer Banks McFadden threw a touchdown pass to end Charlie Timmons. Even though two of O'Rourke's passes were batted back at his eyelashes from the eight yard line as time elapsed, Boston College was a 6-3 loser. Naturally, Leahy blamed himself. It could have been no other way. His brothers Gene and Jack had both come to Dallas. It had been a fine family brawl with Jack being outrageous, but not destructive in any major sense.

The Eagles wept loudly in their dressing room and did not talk to anyone when they got on board the train. Leahy himself behaved like a king-in-exile from his throne. Finally, he emerged, looking terribly tragic. His words had a prophetic sound.

"This has been a wonderful trip," he said. "I do not know of a single man on this team who did not consider this a glorious expedition in Boston College's behalf. I do not know of a man who did not do his best to win. They gave us black-eyed peas before the game because they said it was a symbol of good luck in Texas. Apparently, that doesn't hold good for people from Boston who come to Dallas, especially not Irishmen."

There was a Cotton Bowl ball that evening after the game and a number of the Eagles attended. They were greeted with a copy of a book entitled, "Mr. Garner of Texas," a miniature bale of cotton and a felt hat that looked suspiciously like it might have been worn by the Rebels in the Civil War. Only Pete Cignetti was willing to say anything to a reporter.

"No damn way in the world we should have lost that damn football game," he said. "I'm at this damn ball tonight and for the life of me I can't figure out what I'm doing here. That's a hell of a lot more than I ought to be saying. Hope coach Leahy isn't angry."

When the train came hissing into Boston, there was Lou Montgomery standing on the platform. Behind him were several thousand fans and a genuine brass band. One of the players leaped off and embraced him. Another waved a cowboy hat he had made sure the Cotton Bowl people had put aside for the racial exile.

"Louis," said Leahy, "if they had let us bring you along we wouldn't have lost."

"I'm always going to believe that, coach," said Montgomery. "Always!"

EPISODE 33

On the patio of his apartment on the shores of Lake Oswego in Oregon, the rapidly aging Frank Leahy turned away from the tape recorder and looked unhappily at his diabetic's lunch. No ice cream, he said sadly, and damn little beer. He picked at the bland chunks of food and pushed most of them aside. Past events were suddenly far more appealing.

"Aaaaah, that second year at Boston College," he said, "I hadn't the slightest idea that I would ever leave. My salary was $10,000 with numerous side benefits. There were offers from other schools. Both Tulane and Mississippi State offered me $15,000, which was a vast amount in those days, roughly worth about $45,000 or $50,000. But I was not interested in going elsewhere. The attitude of those Boston College lads was far more spirited than anything I had seen at Notre Dame under Rockne. I felt that it might be better for me to build a coaching reputation in an entirely different section of the nation than the Midwest.

"They were making comparisons between Rockne and me. It was not a fair comparison. In the back of my mind, I guess, I could see myself returning to Notre Dame, but it was only an alumnus dream. There was a very successful coach working for Our Lady. His name was Elmer Layden and I had not heard that much criticism of him. His teams had lost something like 13 games in seven years. He was involved in a number of highly exciting games which Notre Dame won, all in the last five or six minutes.

"Not only had Gilmour Dobie left us with a rich legacy of athletes, but our recruiting had been most successful. We had discovered at Norwich Free Academy a 6′5″ demon named Gilbert Bouley. In one scrimmage against the varsity, he sent three guards to the sidelines hurting badly. Ooooh, he was a monster.

"It had been decided by the coaching staff to revolutionize Rockne's system. We were using flankers and men-in-motion. The line was charging from an unset stance. In fact, we were doing many of the things the T-formation teams were doing, only with a tailback instead of a quarterback standing over the center.

"It is interesting to note, I believe, that the Boston College Eagles used what has long been called the Notre Dame Lecture Huddle that second year, with the quarterback standing with his back to the opposing team and lecturing—if that is the proper word—the two lines of players who were facing scrimmage. We had lost players like Pete Cignetti and Vito Ananis, but we had totally renovated our backfield with Mick Connolly, Teddy Williams and Mike Holovak. Crowds of 15,000 showed up at our spring practice scrimmages.

"This was a fantastic football team, one that far surpassed my somewhat meager expectations. Ooooh, Boston College defeated a brilliant Tulane team in the worst Louisiana humidity imaginable during the regular season. I shall never forget standing in the dressing room after that game, which I believe we won by a 27-7 score. Fred Digby, a New Orleans sports editor, came running up to me and said, 'I've just seen this year's Sugar Bowl team and it's got to be Boston College.' It was most difficult to convince our lads that the season wasn't over.

"It was, ah, most difficult indeed. But the lads defeated Idaho by a 60-0 score that was most refreshing. It came down to Holy Cross, of course, and they defeated them by a 7-0 score to remain undefeated—ten straight victories. They attempted to throw their coach into the shower, but I convinced them that my suit was the only one I owned and it might be best not to shrink it before the Sugar Bowl game. They were most merciful to me, most merciful."

Into the dressing room stepped Brother Peter, president of St. Stanislaus College in Bay St. Louis, Missouri. Aware of what happened to the Eagles the year before, he invited Leahy to bring his team to St. Stanislaus. Courtly to the end, Leahy declined with thanks, because he had not yet received a bowl invitation and any move toward establishing a training camp would be presumptuous. The man who did the Boston College post game show on the radio yelled to Leahy. The report had just come down. Abe Goldberg of the Sugar Bowl committee had just called Curley and asked the Eagles to be Tennessee's opponent.

"I accept your kind offer, Brother Peter," he shouted. "Circumstances have just been altered to our liking."

Off the Eagles floated on one of the wildest bowl trips in the history of college football. Mary Leahy had come to live with her son in the family's new house in Waban, Massachusetts. Reluctantly, she stayed behind to care for the third child, Florence Victoria, born the day after the smashing triumph over Tulane.

"Name her Florence for your wife, Frank," she decided, "and Victoria because you were victorious in the game. Makes sense, doesn't it?"

Roughly a week before the game, she called long distance to Bay St. Louis. Mary Leahy was quite concerned. The evening before she had had this disturbing dream.

"Son, I'm afraid that Boston College might not be in Tennessee's class," she said. "I had this dream where they ran up a big score on the Eagles. Also tell Charlie O'Rourke to be accurate with his passes. I'm afraid he might be intercepted a lot."

What she really had to worry about was one of her older sons, Jack, who had been careening through New Orleans for more than a week, getting drunk in lobbies, passing out and getting half his mustache shaved off, getting one shoe stolen on Bourbon Street and suggesting to every fine looking woman who passed by that she would go to her grave in a state of unrequited love if she did not immediately follow Jack Leahy back to a hotel room. In playful New Orleans-style, the police let the visiting coach's brother go about as he pleased, as long as he didn't murder anyone.

The days at Bay St. Louis were about as cheerful as two weeks at a French Penal Colony. Three of Boston College's finest players, Joe Zabilski, Chet Gladchuck and Mike Holovak had taken to griping among themselves, but in Polish—the language they had learned at home as children. By the fifth day, Leahy was catching on.

"I want your attention, Chester. Aaaaah, you too, Michael and Joseph. I want you lads to know that I have purchased a Polish-English translation book and I will be listening with care to what you, aaaah, say the next few days," said Leahy, grinning happily.

No one ever complained of being over-fed at a Leahy training camp. Breakfast was cornflakes, juice and one glass of milk. Lunch was salad and protein items like cheese and cold cuts. Dinner was steak and cottage cheese. Young knights going into battle had to have a lean and hungry look.

"In a sense," said Charlie O'Rourke, "that particular young coach and that particular college football team were meant for each other, because it was a perfect marriage. Gil Dobie had recruited an outstanding team, but he was at an age where he was past caring. Along came Frank Leahy like a man trying to spread the gospel in a heathen land. He took us on a holy war of conquest. He was a real messiah figure as far as we were concerned. He was one of the first head coaches to break the team down into groups and then bring us together for a workout just before the end of practice.

"There was one play we worked hour after hour at Bay

St. Louis. I was supposed to shove the ball under my arm as if I were carrying it on a run. I was supposed to go as far right as I could and then throw at the last second. We went over that play until I didn't think I'd ever be able to wing the ball again the rest of my life. I think we used the play once against Tennessee, but he wanted us to have it, regardless.

"They said he was a slave driver at Notre Dame, but I doubt that. He loved to make jokes on the practice field and he permitted us to have our own personalities. He drilled things into your mind so hard you couldn't forget it. I think it was part of his frontier upbringing. A man had to be resourceful in times of emergency. He was preaching a kind of ethic that was beginning to fade even back in 1940. As players, we had an enormous respect for Frank Leahy. I wouldn't say we idolized him or loved him. He wasn't that kind of man. You just sort of watched in awe at his grasp of strategy and technology.

"I can't believe that Rockne saw much of himself in Frank, not from what I've heard about Rockne. I think that he saw a rare kind of genius. Leahy was crazy over details. Later, when some of us became coaches, we began to appreciate his struggle for perfection. He would have made a great chess master. There was a lot of back-biting criticism of him from people who didn't really know him. I think he must have had a few lazy athletes on those Notre Dame teams of his, because only a lazy man would knock him and some of them did. He was no slave-driver, no brow-beater and no evil, self-serving egomaniac. He was a real man, tougher than hell. He never asked anything more of his players than he was willing to give of himself.

"Why that man took a group of individualists at Boston College and turned them into the greatest athletic team New England has ever seen. There hasn't been anything like the 1940 Eagles since and there certainly wasn't anything like them before. I wouldn't lie and say I loved Frank Leahy. But, good God, there hasn't been a mortal I've respected more, forgetting his faults, because he had them and they weren't that important. He was a man to look up to. You don't meet many of them. Just one will do for your whole lifetime."

A couple of days before the Sugar Bowl game, Mrs. McKeever bore twin daughters which, in her ignorance, she named Mary Susan and Mary Jane. Her husband had other ideas. He stood and shouted at the evening steak dinner, the men who score the first two touchdowns against Tennessee can name the babies. Everybody applauded. The players kept shouting that they were going to win this one for the McKeever girls. It was a charming thought.

Sportswriters kept arriving at the Boston College training camp to discover that the players were out on a fishing adventure or playing golf or being romanced at a Christmas party or being pampered in some unusual manner. They became thoroughly convinced that nothing good would become of them. The odds on Tennessee kept getting fatter. They did not realize that every time the Eagles were out late at night, their kindly coach roused them for a 9 A.M. practice. It was part of his charm. Only Fred Digby was unconvinced.

"I think that Boston College will win easily," he wrote in the *New Orleans Item*. "Nobody has a passer like O'Rourke. The Eagles have the most incredible morale I've ever seen. And they are in such excellent shape, they will be strong when the fourth quarter comes."

So with three minutes left in the game, O'Rourke threw three passes and then ran 24 yards for a touchdown that gave the Eagles a 19-13 victory and sent New England writers into spasms. The *Post* absolutely declared that Leahy was the greatest coach since Rockne and maybe greater. The *Globe* insisted that there could be no other national champion but Boston College. The *Record* was convinced that Eastern college prestige had been ransomed. And Frank Leahy told Maurice Tobin, mayor of Boston, "I pledge and I guarantee you that this is just the start of things. I told these lads at halftime that they were upholding the honor of dear old New England. I told them that I knew they would be ashamed to return home to that most pleasant part of the nation losers. I told them that they had a permanent friend in their head coach. I told them I would always be with them. They can always call on me, and that I would come with whatever help would be necessary. I love Boston College and I will never leave it. That is my pledge and my promise."

Leahy said that he felt that he had actually succeeded in that most wistful of coaching myths. He had, indeed, built character. His players were now true citizens of a better society. In the gathering darkness of a New Orleans evening, he fairly glowed.

On the train ride home, he turned to a Boston newspaperman and said: "I missed my calling. I should be in Hollywood doing scenarios. This was more exciting than anything you will ever see on the screen. To think I was responsible for making it happen. Ooooh, I get a strange feeling of power when I think about it. Maybe it isn't good for me to dwell on the subject too long."

The writer, George Carers, stopped taking notes, bit hard on his pipe and agreed. "Nothing ruins success like feeling too powerful at the wrong time."

"True, George," said Leahy. "Very, very true."

At the train station, Mrs. McKeever sent word that she would hold still for a slight alteration in her daughters' names. After all, Mick Connolley had decided upon Anne and Mike Holovak admitted that he preferred Helen and they had scored the first two touchdowns in the game. This was some sort of sacred pledge. So she made one girl Sue Anne and the other Jane Helen. It made no sense, except in the context of the times and the times they were a'changing.

Before he could even get home, Leahy had a job offer from Fred Mandel, the owner of the Detroit Lions, a professional team. This was a period when only a man with unique tastes would admit there was such a thing as the National Football League, let alone tell reporters that he had been offered a job by them. Working for the big name colleges was the only thing and Frank Leahy was aware of this obvious prestige factor. There was the telephone call before he could even leave the station. Leahy promised Mandel that he would go to Detroit and at least talk to him.

"Can I bring my wife?" he asked.

"Certainly," said Mandel, "and stay as long as you like, both of you. If you want to go to Miami afterwards with your three kids and your mother, you can be my guest as well."

The meeting was held first in the Cadillac Hotel and later in Mandel's home. The price for Leahy would be twice what he was making at Boston College, some $20,000, although it was printed in the *Detroit Times* as $12,500. The people at Boston College came back with an offer of $17,500 and a bonus from alumni every time the Eagles made the Bowls. There was talk about giving Leahy part of BC's $75,000 Sugar Bowl share. The talks dragged on and on.

"So, who's gonna get you, Frank?" yelled Jack Leahy over the telephone. "Is it gonna be the Jebs at BC or that Jew from Detroit? I'm going crazy, Frank. Who is it, the Jebs or the Jews? Either way, I figure an Irishman is in trouble."

The entire offensive line was leaving and Leahy was starting to get panicky. He told Mandel that his offer was most gracious, but that there had to be something better. What would BC be like now that he was forced to recruit a team of his own? It had been one thing to take Gilmour Dobie's last creation and turn it into an honest football team. Now Leahy wasn't sure what would happen when the team belonged solely to him. He was, as the moderns say, suffering from an intense identity crisis.

The Leahys went south to Miami, with Mandel's financial blessing. A reporter for the *Herald* asked him what he thought of professional football and he replied that it was not legitimate.

"It is not good football," he said. "The professionals do too many things that are not sound. They pass on fourth down and do many things that are not in keeping with the best interests of the game. I have a big enough job at Boston College. My line is graduating and so is Charlie O'Rourke, who is probably the best passer that New England has ever produced. I do not think I will be leaving College Heights. I am happy at Boston College."

In such a way did Fred Mandel discover that the Jesuits had seemingly won the struggle for Leahy's intellect. If he was bitter, that bitterness did not last long. For weeks after his return from Florida with his wife, Leahy made sounds as if he didn't plan to sign with Boston College either. Poor Jack Curley was under intense pressure from alumni who didn't quite understand what it was like to have a 32-year-old coach of such fiercesome national appeal. Some of them kept wondering why he was alternately described as being 33 and 34. Nobody really believed that a man of his ability could be so young.

One afternoon, Leahy and Sullivan were getting ready to board a train and head south to Atlanta where the universe's brightest young football coach was being paid good money to address the Touchdown Club. The alumni were getting nasty and Curley looked as if he hadn't had much rest in some time. There was talk that Leahy might replace a couple of Horsemen, either Harry Stuhldreher at Wisconsin or Sleepy Jim Crowley at Fordham. Everyone was anxious.

"Frank, I have to get some kind of commitment from you," said Curley. "They're after my job. Can't we please talk?"

"I'm trying very hard to catch a train, Jack. Wouldn't it be possible to discuss this sometime later?" said Leahy. "I'm in no hurry to leave Boston College. I've told you that. There's only one other job I'd take and that would be . . . well, aaaaahhh . . . it would be at Notre Dame. Naturally, I would want to go there. But I am not at all sure the job would ever be offered to me, Jack. I think you can understand my position in the matter."

They talked on and on while Sullivan waited outside with the bags, eager to find a cab and make the proper train connection. Didn't Leahy appreciate what Boston College had done for him? Indeed, he did. Didn't Boston College understand what he had done for the school? There is a decrease in morality when football coaches stop building character and start asking for more money.

"Would you sign a five-year-contract with Boston College, one that will give you what you feel you need?" said Curley, not begging but coming frighteningly close.

"I will sign whatever you want me to sign in order that I can get away on this speaking engagement, Jack. I do want one consideration in the contract that I did not have when I came here. I want an 'Alma Mater Clause.' Now I realize that this is a standard thing for successful coaches. If Notre Dame should ever call me, I would want to be free. I do not think that will happen. I am pleased and now if you'll make that concession, we will sign and we will leave," he said.

In a small office, Leahy sat at a desk and wrote his name on an agreement. Curley laughed and shook his hand. "This saved me a fine job, Frank," he said. "I know things will be fine between us."

While Leahy was chugging across the frozen landscape, Elmer Layden was pondering an offer of his own. The alumni had been growing surly. They wanted him to win every game. They were thin-lipped and unamused. They had heard the joke about Layden's tailback, William Shakespeare, flunking

English so often that they were actually starting to believe it. Now the National Football League was looking for somebody with a name in order to stay close to the baseball people. The deal was that Layden would get an unbreakable five-year-contract, calling for $20,000 to start. He listened carefully and he understood the weather forecasts.

"There's some bad news," said Father John Cavanaugh to his brother and fellow priest, Father Frank Cavanaugh. "I think we're losing Layden."

"The man to get is Frank Leahy," said Father Frank.

"He's one of several that are being considered," said Father John.

"Then let's stop thinking of the others who are being considered," said Father Frank.

"You have an agile mind," said Father John.

When Leahy got off the train from his speaking tour, reporters rushed up to smother him. He looked mildly confused, which he was. The paper he had signed was an informal agreement and not a true legal contract. However, he had told Curley that if Notre Dame called him home he would go. After all, there aren't too many opportunities like that.

"Jack," he said to Curley. "I am going to the testimonial for Gene Goodreault up in Haverhill. I know we haven't signed a real contract. But the fact remains that I have an agreement with you. I have heard absolutely nothing from Notre Dame and everybody tells me that I am not the leading candidate to replace Elmer Layden. If I had heard a word, I would tell you. Now, I must go home to Floss and the children and I will call you on my return from Haverhill."

EPISODE 34

The evening before, Frank Leahy had driven back through the snow and ice, roughly 65 miles from Haverhill. He was sleeping late when the telephone rang in his home at Waban. In the kitchen, Florence Leahy was feeding the three children and wishing she didn't feel quite so queasy. She assumed that it was Charlie O'Rourke calling to see if his coach could attend a testimonial they were giving for him. It seemed that 1,500 residents of Malden had given one dollar each and the Boston College tailback was interested in having Leahy present. He planned to take the money and give it to his mother, who worked nights in order to assure him of spending money while he was in school.

"Charlie?" asked Mrs. Leahy. "Don't worry. Frank will be there."

"No," said the operator, "Mr. Eddie Dunigan is calling from Palm Beach down in Florida. Is Mr. Leahy there?"

Up the stairs stomped the coach's son. Down came America's newest hero. He pushed the hair back out of his eyes and listened. This was the same Dunigan who had been a friend of his during his undergraduate years at South Bend, the same man who had helped him stay in school. Inside, Leahy knew what the call was all about, but he acted as if it were a total surprise.

"Frank, I'm not going to joke with you," he said. "You know that the job of athletic director and head football coach is open. They have four candidates and you're first on their list. The other men are all good, but you're the youngest and you're the man they want. Now, you have to play it cool. Father Hugh O'Donnell wants you and so do both of the Cavanaughs. Now, here's what you have to do if you want the job. You have to go under an assumed name to the DeWitt Clinton Hotel in Albany, New York. You'll be met there by Father Frank Cavanaugh.

"This can't get in the newspapers. Notre Dame wants you, but it can't look like it's stealing a coach, especially from another Catholic school. They are so damn sensitive about that you can't believe it. Now, are you interested in the job? Hello, Frank? You there?"

"Ooooooh, yes, Edward, I am here" said Leahy. "Dear mother of Jesus, I am here indeed. Tell me, Edward, why do they want me, please. I want to know why it is Francis William Leahy they want and not somebody else. It is very important to me."

"They think you're the best man. They also think you're another Rockne. Oh, they don't think you're just like Rock. They think you can be just as successful in your own way. How about it, Frank? Can you be there? Hello, Frank?"

"I have to speak at a dinner for one of our lads tomorrow

night, but I'll be in Albany the day afterwards. Ooooh, I should be there early Wednesday morning. Eddie? Ooooh, Eddie, I cannot tell you how thrilled I am. I have a clause in my new contract here at Boston College that releases me in case Notre Dame calls me. Oooooh, Edward! I cannot believe that Notre Dame wants me. Oooooooh! I'd better get something to eat now. Tell them that I am most interested, most interested. Oooooh."

Leahy placed the receiver down on the cradle and turned to his wife who was standing only a few feet away, holding the baby and looking apprehensive. She waited for some small word.

"Oooooh, Floss, they want to give me Rock's job," he said, hardly remembering Hunk Anderson or Elmer Layden who had the position of football coach at Notre Dame in the ten years since Knute Rockne's death. "Aaaaah, I cannot imagine it. They want to give me, Frank Leahy, that job. Oh, I can't stand the thought of leaving Boston College and all these fine lads, but I am going back to South Bend. Ooooooh, Floss, they want to give me Rock's job. Can you imagine that?"

Thus, began the homecoming, the long return to Alma Mater, the spiritual fulfillment of one man's life. Whatever else he might be, Francis William Leahy was charged now with upholding an ideal. Never again would he be the same person. The torch had been passed. To him, there would never be another Knute Rockne, but there could be a Francis William Leahy greater and stronger and more resourceful. In the simplicity of his heart, he could see himself symbolically picking up a quest and any means would justify the end. Rockne wanted to go undefeated. So would Leahy. He would make it a holy mission. He would move forward as if God were nipping at his heels, demanding that he succeed. From this point in time, Frank Leahy was no longer a father or a husband or a coach. Rather, he was a zealot, burned with the fire of a zealot's urge. He was going to be head coach at Notre Dame. He would represent Our Lady in sacred combat. When he put the telephone away, he was not so much a changed man as a man who finally understood his manifest destiny. He was going home to Alma Mater and he would obscure everyone, from Father Sorin on to Knute Rockne. He would out-Rockne his own coach. He would become greater.

"Ooooh, Florence, it will be difficult," he said. "But I must accept the task. I must. It will not be easy, but I must make the sacrifice. You know I must make the sacrifice and so does the University of Notre Dame and so does Our Lady. This is going to be difficult and I must not fail. Our Lady will not let me." That is exactly what he said and, let history know, he meant it.

It has been written that there were a battalion of candidates for the job. Supposedly Notre Dame had a list that included Dr. Eddie Anderson, Jim Crowley, Harry Stuhldreher, Buck Shaw, Frank Thomas, Charley Bachman, Clipper Smith, Dutch Bergman, Mal Edwards and Harry Mehre. It was not extensive. It consisted of Frank Leahy and Buck Shaw, in that order. The others were merely afterthoughts.

"There were just those two, Frank Leahy and Buck Shaw," said Rev. Frank Cavanaugh. "They talk about all the rest. But they didn't count for anything. And Shaw was No. 2 on the priority list. Father O'Donnell, who was president of Notre Dame at the time, came to my brother Father John Cavanaugh, who was vice-president of the University and director of the faculty board of athletics. He asked Father John who he liked and my brother said, 'Why there's just Frank Leahy and maybe, Buck Shaw. But I like Leahy the best. He'll do the job.' And Father O'Donnell nodded his head. That's all there was to it, except to call Dunigan and have him make the contact, which he did."

The two brothers spread out, Father John moving West to talk to Shaw and Father Frank going to Albany for his rendez-vous with Leahy. Both men traveled under assumed names. John Cavanaugh arrived in Santa Clara and called Shaw on the telephone.

"This is Jimmy Egan, you remember me from 1923 at Notre Dame?" he asked.

"I don't know any Jimmy Egan," said Shaw. "Who the hell is this?"

"It's John Cavanaugh, but I'm registered at the DeAnza Hotel as Jimmy Egan and I think that it would be good for us to have a talk," said Father John. "Can you meet me at the train station at 7:30 P.M. in Salinas and take me to San Jose? Oh, I think we can talk on the way."

It was winter in northern California, when the winds swept

down off the arctic ice pack, bringing rain clouds that slammed against the shore. The two men sat in a black Ford near the railroad station for nearly two hours in a smashing storm. They discussed the matter at length.

"Am I the first choice?" asked Shaw.

"You are one of two first choices," said Father John.

"Am I the first of the first choices or am I the alternate?" Shaw demanded.

"It's down to two men, you and Frank Leahy of Boston College," Cavanaugh said.

"I think I know where I stand," said Shaw. "He's pretty hot right now."

There was Frank Leahy, going by train across New England to Albany. When he stepped down off the train, he saw a copy of the *Knickerbocker News*. "Shaw New Head Coach At Notre Dame, West Coast Source Reports," the headline said. It was based entirely on guesswork. A *Los Angeles Herald-Express* writer had called Notre Dame and had been told that Father John Cavanaugh was on a working trip in California. Since Father John Cavanaugh had been long identified as a friend of Buck Shaw and since Shaw at Santa Clara had been a magnificent lineman under Rockne, it was natural to call Santa Clara, which the writer did. The person on the other end replied that Shaw was out talking to an old friend from Notre Dame, a fellow named Jimmy Egan.

Two plus two equalled the fact that Jimmy Egan was probably John Cavanaugh, the priest. So the story went slithering all over the nation that Shaw was the man and that Leahy was out.

"I was stunned," said Leahy. "I had been led to believe that the job was mine if I wanted it and that Shaw was the alternate choice. I was tempted to get back on the train, return to College Heights and enjoy the security of a five-year-contract at Boston College. It was never my intent to become a gypsy. I proceeded to the DeWitt Clinton Hotel anyway. Only a day or two earlier, I had told the gathering at Goodreault's testimonial how pleased I was to be rehired and I had been profuse in my praise for Boston College. I had pledged to do even better at BC. Now I was running off looking for a job that, aaaaah, might or might not have been filled.

"I felt like the worst sort of hypocrite. Word had gotten

around about my five-year-contract. Ooooooh, I guess that Jack Curley told the story to a newspaperman who told everyone else. Pretty soon it was in all the Boston papers. I had no choice but to act gracious, even though I knew I was being considered for the Notre Dame job. I had asked Jack Curley to keep the news a secret until the Notre Dame matter had been settled one way or the other, but he was far too anxious to show Boston College what he could do, so that he would be able to retain his job.

"In fact one of the first questions that Father Frank asked me was whether I could get out of the new contract gracefully. I told him about the Alma Mater clause and he relaxed. He told me the job was probably mine and that I had first refusal. He also told me that if I turned it down, it would go to Buck Shaw and if he didn't want it, it would probably then be offered to Clipper Smith.

"Upon my return, Curley was most upset. He said that he couldn't release me from my contract and that the faculty moderator of athletics, who was, by now, Father Maurice Dullea, was out of town, and he didn't know how soon I could get out of it. He indicated that he wanted to try to talk me into staying. I explained to him that I had turned down three offers during the season and two after it, all for more money. The only reason I wanted the Notre Dame job was that it was my Alma Mater and I had, aaaaah, long dreamed of replacing Rockne. He did not seem to understand.

"The release was very slow in coming. There was always some excuse why it could not be issued. The people at Notre Dame were pressing me for a final word. They did not want to be accused of stealing me from another college, especially another Catholic one. The matter of the missing release became crucial. It was necessary to do something. So, I engaged a suite at the Kenmore Hotel and invited the press and sports announcers to come up and have a drink on Frank Leahy. Then I called Curley at Boston College and said, 'I have all the football writers and radio men in town in this suite. I have told them that Boston College has promised me my release to go to coach at Notre Dame. They plan to print it and put it on the air. If I drop out there now, will the release be available? What do the good fathers at Boston College say?'

"Well, what could they say? I got in a cab, picked up the

release and was on a train to South Bend within the hour. Some of the people in Boston professed to be mad at me. I heard very little talk along those lines. Father Francis Murphy, president of the school, expressed sorrow at our leaving and Joe McArdle said, 'Well, Father, what would you do if you could go to another area and become a Cardinal-Archbishop? That's what they are offering Frank.'

"On February 15, 1941, at about 3:15 P.M.—I shall not forget either the date or the time—I walked into that same administration building where I had registered for classes some 14 years earlier and signed a contract with Father Hugh O'Donnell to coach football at Notre Dame. My three assistants could come with me. They had given me everything I demanded, that is to say, asked for. The money wasn't as good as I could have received elsewhere, but it made no difference. I was at Notre Dame under the Golden Dome with Our Lady for protection, and I was determined to make a success of myself."

In order to ensure the probability of his success, Leahy made certain that a dozen fine young athletes that he had placed on loan to various New England prep schools and had been marked for delivery to Boston College in the fall went with him to Notre Dame. Some say the number was as high as 27. That is a lie. It was only a dozen. Of course, one of them was Angelo Bertelli.

EPISODE 35

Old wounds never heal and the scars never fade away:

"I don't give a damn if he's sick and carrying on like a champion. I was a member of the class of 1942 and I thought he did Boston College a terrible disservice and I know dozens of other alumni who feel exactly the same way, even after the passing of 30 years. Nobody gave Frank Leahy a better deal than BC did before he left. What's more, he took all kinds of great talent with him. I'm bitter and I'm mad and no amount of time can ever make me feel any different toward the man. He ruined Boston College's taste for big time football. The school would still be a power now, except for what one man

did,"—Arthur (Bud) Crosbie, general manager of the *Willimantic* (Connecticut) *Daily Chronicle,* April 13, 1973.

EPISODE 36

The players were seated, all prim and preened like proper schoolboys, in the first few rows. The student body had grouped itself around the perimeter. It was a scene taken from Boston College only two years earlier. There on the podium was the new head coach, looking somewhat like a priest fresh from the seminary and giving his first sermon as a curate. Except for glasses, Frank Leahy didn't seem much different than he had ten years earlier when he left the sacred turf at Notre Dame and went off to become as great as Rockne. And there was hardly anybody now who did not agree that he at least had a chance at it.

"Men," he said, letting his voice fill the microphone. "Men . . . men of Notre Dame . . . this is a momentous occasion for all of us. For you today, as well as your new coaches, we begin to write another chapter in that great volume of history that is Our Lady's University. This is a great challenge, a great quest. We are searching for perfection in football, the same way that we seek perfection in everything we do at Notre Dame. The football team is a symbol of what the entire University should be like. Perfection is the goal, in Our Lady's Holy Name.

"It was not too long ago that Frank Leahy was a student here. I was never accused of being too swift on my feet, but when it became obvious that somebody else was coming out on the field to replace me, I somehow found myself getting quicker and quicker. I have nothing against tackles. They are essential to the welfare of the nation. I used to be one myself. If it weren't for ex-tackles, food stores in this nation would be much poorer.

"Many people have the wrong idea about tackles. Some of us are not too smart, that's true. But we are usually dumb enough to tell the truth. That is exactly what I will always tell you lads on the football squad. You will hear nothing but the truth from us on the coaching staff.

"One month ago, I received the greatest surprise of my entire life. For it was just about four weeks ago that the authorities at the University of Notre Dame saw fit to ask me to coach the football team at my Alma Mater. My meager vocabulary lacks the words to describe fittingly the monumental feeling of joy which permeated my entire body and soul. As I rode out here on the train to sign my contract, some writers said that 'we had a rendezvous with destiny.' I do not subscribe to that. I feel like I am coming home. Here I am at the University consecrated to Our Blessed Mother. I am home . . . home at last.

"Notre Dame leaves a mark on its sons. It is an indelible mark. There is the football team. Only 11 men can be on the field at the same time. Every other student is the 12th man. You must encourage the football team to greater heights. Every team in America wants to play Notre Dame and beat it. I am happy to be back home. I love this University, its traditions and its wonderful campus. When I was away, at Georgetown, at Michigan State, at Fordham and at Boston University, I could strain my ears at evening and somewhere . . . somewhere deep in my mind I could hear the bells in the great church on campus. I could see the students walking by the lake.

"To be honest, when I was here I never appreciated how marvelous Notre Dame really is. After starting the game of life, I know far better than words can tell just what Notre Dame means. Notre Dame has thrown us a flaming torch. I hold it proudly and I hold it high. Help is needed from everybody. You will be proud of your Alma Mater, as I am. Now let us call on Our Lady for assistance as we progress along the paths of goodness and truth, for these are the roads to genuine happiness. Pray along with me and the other coaches for Our Lady's divine blessings."

Everybody pitched forward on their knees as Leahy stepped back from the microphone, tears rolling down his smooth cheeks. Not a single person in the audience was unwilling to believe that a Holy War against the Infidels had been declared. Not a single soul doubted that, after all these years, the power and the glory of Knute Rockne had been restored to Notre Dame. This was truly the Second Coming and Frank Leahy went off to meet some heavy duty alumni at a cocktail party.

EPISODE 37

Before Frank Leahy decided that it was his holy mission to return home and serve Our Lady by recruiting the finest, fittest livestock in the nation, he made contact with Angelo Bertelli, who played hockey well enough to interest the Boston Bruins, baseball well enough to have St. Louis Cardinal and Detroit Tiger scouts waiting outside his house in black sedans and basketball and football well enough to make every head coach between South Bend and College Heights think he was worth kidnapping. He was the single most important athlete ever to attend Springfield Cathedral High School. He listened very carefully to Ed McKeever, who insisted that he spend his formative years at Boston College. He talked over the telephone to head coach Frank Leahy. He talked to Leahy in person. He became convinced. The papers kept insisting he was going to Boston College. Then they said he was going to Notre Dame because Milt Piepul, a neighbor, had been the captain at Notre Dame.

"I genuinely like coaches McKeever and Leahy," he was quoted as saying to a representative of the *Springfield Union*. "But there is something special about Notre Dame. I wish coaches McKeever and Leahy were at Notre Dame instead of Boston College, not that I have anything against Boston College, understand."

By the merest of chance, they saw each other at Leahy's first spring practice in South Bend. With whimsy floating through his brain, McKeever walked up, tapped Bertelli on the shoulder and said: "Doctor Bertelli, I presume? What are you ever doing at Notre Dame?"

They could not complain about Bertelli or any of the others that Leahy had shadowed away in various obscure prep schools. They were, technically, fair targets. When Gil Bouley came to South Bend and asked to transfer, he and Leahy talked for several hours. He received a meal and a tour of the campus. He was advised to go home and play good football for Boston College.

There was something remarkable about Bertelli. He looked like O'Rourke, thin and vaguely malnutritious. He smiled a lot and threw a football with speed and accuracy. He punted brilliantly. He could not run as well or as far as O'Rourke, but he gave a splendid imitation of a tailback. What he was, oddly enough, was a T-formation quarterback, but such a word was heretical at Notre Dame, a school where an entire system of offensive play had been designed under the Great God Rockne. It was said that he was so unimpressive physically that a student saw him walking across campus without his football armor on and tried desperately to cancel a $5 bet on the Northwestern game.

"No lad ever worked harder than Angelo did," said Leahy. "He could not have been much more than a fourth string tailback when I first saw him in spring practice. He worked hard and what he got he earned. A most ambitious lad. He took a job as a painter on Campus because he had the notion that it would strengthen his right arm. He painted everything that didn't move. He painted the kennel where they kept Clashmore Mike, the school's Irish terrier mascot. He would have painted me if I had stayed still long enough. After he got through, he would spend the twilight hours passing a football to George Murphy, our varsity end.

"I kept nudging Coach McKeever, telling him to watch this lad. Oooooh, I doubt if I would have been the same man if it were not for Angelo Bertelli, a blond Italian, of all things. He practiced so much with Murphy that I knew they were made for each other. They were like Gus Dorais and Knute Rockne, who made forward passing a national craze by doing it so well against Army. I knew that they would do well together in the Georgia Tech game my first year.

"Ooooh, Angelo threw a very bad pass, one of the few really bad ones I ever saw him throw. I was convinced it would be intercepted in the other team's end zone. Instead, Murphy stuck up a hand and caught it. It was a magnificent combination. You know, it is said that Dorais and Rockne spent one whole summer throwing the ball while they were both lifeguards, but that is not true. Only Dorais was a lifeguard. Rock went up on weekends and they practiced only a few hours each day."

There was one tactical achievement that first season that most football people forget, or at best, ignore. Frank Leahy invented pass protection blocking. When Bertelli took the snap, he never got back more than seven yards. The line fell back and protected him in what the Notre Dame public relations department described as 'a pocket.'

"It is possible that Angelo might not have received the attention he deserved if he had not been addicted to gangster movies," said Leahy. "He would walk around campus with a slouch hat, imitating Humphrey Bogart. I'm sure if the rules of the day had permitted it, he would have had a cigarette dangling from his lips. The other players thought it most amusing and, after first chiding him for presenting such a poor image to Our Lady, I was forced to admit that it was simply innocent fun and that he meant no disrespect by it. Eventually, I found myself laughing, too.

"Naturally, the Chicago sports writers picked it up and they had a marvelous time with it. They nicknamed him The Duke and he became their special pet.

"Angelo was a delight to coach. Very cooperative. The coaches used to say that he had ice cream for blood. His only fault was that he could not run the way a tailback should. In fact, he was the finest passer and worst runner I had ever seen. This made me, aaaaah, ponder the possibility of going to the T-formation, where a pure passer could excel without having to worry about other skills. I sensed a definite change toward specialization in football and away from the triple-threat left halfback who could do everything. There weren't that many around."

EPISODE 38

The newspapers and their resident mythologists began to work Leahy into the fabric of the Notre Dame legend almost as soon as he moved into his cramped little office, the one with the massive picture of Rockne smiling benignly from the rear wall like some sort of holy icon. Perhaps Frank Leahy went home to Notre Dame to be his own man, but he quoted Rockne as if the dead man's words came from sacred scriptures. The style may have been Leahy's, but the act was Rockne's, unquestionably.

His first spring practice was a perfect model of a forced labor camp. Several linemen appeared with drooping beltlines. They were turned over to McArdle for punishment. From the time that he reported to the opening game, lineman Wally Ziemba was converted from a 268 pound tackle into a 218 pound center. Position changes came hourly. A couple of slow fullbacks, Bernie Crimmins and Harry Wright, became a guard and a blocking back respectively. One morning Dipper Evans was a 168-pound tailback. By twilight he was one of the nation's lightest, but swiftest fullbacks.

The summer wasn't half over before the first of hundreds of complaints was lodged against Leahy. Over the years, they would build and build in number, most of them based on false reports, some of them based on the natural paranoia of coaches who knew that if they played Notre Dame they would only be beaten and a few based on truth. The sports editor of the *Chicago Daily News*, Lloyd Lewis, traced rumors that most of the Notre Dame players were practicing illegally in a pleasant little campsite on the Indiana portion of Lake Michigan's shores. The entire starting backfield, Bertelli, Wright, Evans and Steve Juzwik had jobs at Notre Dame Stadium, which consisted basically of emptying a few trash cans and then working on such assorted janitorial duties as practicing handoffs and throwing passes.

"I do not deny that some of the boys may have got together," said Leahy, roguishly, "but strictly on their own and without coaching supervision."

When practice started officially, none of the athletes were permitted to feel they were undertrained. They were back at South Bend before classes and Leahy had them reporting at 6 A.M., working through to 8:50 A.M. and taking coffee and cornflakes in the dressing room. They broke down into groups and watched films and took instruction until noon, just before the lunch break. Off everybody went for a two and a half hour nap and then back to the practice field at 4:30 P.M.

"This labor is necessary as our lads endeavor to obliterate the defects," he told newsmen, who were suddenly aware that Leahy's public speech was becoming more and more ornate. "These lads are worked hard—very hard—and there is a point to it. Only through stringent practice can perfection be achieved. I want Angelo Bertelli to throw a certain pass in an important game with utter confidence because he has completed the same pass so often here on the practice field at Notre Dame. Perfection is the residue of hard work."

In his early years at South Bend, it was Leahy's practice to dart about the field, rushing from group to group, sometimes illustrating a point himself, getting down in a crouch and charging straight at some startled 240 pound tackle. In later years, he rose above the masses, directing the entire scene from a 30 foot tall wooden tower, which gave him the image of an Oriental war lord reviewing his troops attacking some nearby kingdom. He took to standing there, baseball cap on his head, stiff and stern, yelling at everybody over a battery of microphones connected to loudspeakers placed on various parts of the field.

Preparing for his first season at Notre Dame, he was not so still nor so imperious. Moving rapidly, he would move up very close to some sophomore running back and inquire, "Perhaps, Our Lady erred about you. Perhaps, you lack the character to see the job on through." Sometimes, he would sprint up to a senior tackle and suggest, "Maybe you are unwilling to make the necessary sacrifice for Notre Dame, which has treated you so wonderfully these past four years. For shame!"

As if to demonstrate his spiritual kinship to Rockne, it was Leahy's custom that first season to invite writers into the Notre Dame clubhouse to listen to his fight talks. That splendid old Boston curmudgeon, Colonel Dave Egan, listened to one and swore that he had seen a trance medium bring back the voice of Rockne. There he stood in the back, by the door, thoroughly impressed by what he saw and what he heard, the era of enlightened cynicism still being some years away in American sports writing.

"There in the bowels of Notre Dame Stadium sat 54 young men, in attitudes of prayer," Egan wrote. "The silence was thick and heavy, the tension was that of a tight-wire. It was like wading through a soundless surf. I met McKeever back in the recesses of the room. We were surrounded by the trunks that have covered so many a mile, that have gone to New York to Baltimore and to Atlanta and to Evanston. They are blue trunks, and the legendary name of Notre Dame, in golden letters, is printed on the side.

"We were among the tall, green lockers when Leahy steps

into the middle of a silent circle of players. 'Men,' he says, 'watch for a play like this.' And he describes a play. His voice is charged. He's straining at a leash. This isn't the soft-voiced, polite, gentlemanly Leahy I know around the cocktail circuit. This is a different Leahy, stripped naked of all his inhibitions. This is the real Frank Leahy, the one the public never sees. He diagrams a play on the blackboard and demands that everybody memorize it instantly. He stabs at the board with his chalk.

"His eyes grow even more intense. 'Watch for this! Watch for this!' he shouts. 'The center is liable to pretend to be fixing his laces or something. Then he'll snap the ball. Get set for it, lads. Get set for it!' His voice moved up a notch. His face is straining. His eyes are burning their way into the souls of 54 dedicated, passionate young men. He isn't asking for perfection. He is demanding it!

"It seems that Southern California has some flanker plays and Leahy strenuously orders that they be stopped. Every ounce of him seems to be straining. Then the lesson ends and the clock moves toward the starting hour. Then the voices from outside, so loud before, are strangely stilled and there is a shroud of silence in the big locker room. Leahy is poised like a man ready to deliver a great sermon.

"'All right, lads,' Leahy says, and it surprises me that three such homely words could be the lash of a whip and the roll of a drum and the ring of a trumpet. He weighs every syllable with doomsday importance. What an archbishop this man would have made. 'All right, lads,' he repeats. 'In four and a half minutes, you will be out there defending the honor of Our Lady. The following lads will start . . . Dove, Brutz and Maddock! Ziemba, Crimmins and Wright!' He makes it sound like an honor roll. 'Kovatch and Lillis!' And then, in one quick burst, 'Bertelli, Evans and Juzwik. This is a hard game. Make no mistake. Anything worth winning is worth paying the price for in sweat and sacrifice, and, if need be, in blood.

"'This will be exactly like last week's game against Northwestern. I don't think you can win it in the first half. But I know you can pull it out in the fourth period. I know that, lads! I believe in you, lads! Our Lady believes in you!'

"His voice, by now, was the roll of thunder," Egan wrote. "'You're rougher than they are! You're tougher than they are!

You're a whole lot tougher! This is my team!! It's a tough team! It's a fourth quarter team and I like a fourth quarter team. I say this to you, gentlemen of Notre Dame, I say this to you. Oooooooh, I say to you—hit hard! I say to you—stay with them and then beat them. I say to our backs—go! go! go! hard! Our Lady is watching from Her heavenly throne!'

"His voice had filled the room with its battle cries. Suddenly it stopped. For a few seconds that seemed an eternity, there was nothing but silence again. Then he turned, like a tired and defeated old man. No longer was he a handsome, black-haired young man of 34. The weight of all the centuries was on his soul. He turned and addressed himself to his captain, Paul Lillis.

" 'Paul,' he said in an ordinary tone of voice that carried to the darkest, smallest corner of the building. 'You gave a nice speech at the pep rally last night. Oooooh, lad, you gave me the happiest moment of my life. I appreciated it, Paul. Oooooh, I appreciated it far more than you will ever know. Just a few simple words you said, Paul, but they touched this heart of mine, and I'd like to show my appreciation to you and the other seniors. You and they are leaving us today. Never again will you labor for the glory of Our Lady and for Her beautiful university.

" 'I have never worked with a greater group of boys. Oooooh, I was thinking of you and the seniors, Paul, as I listened to your touching little talk. I said to myself, 'Oooooh, if I could help Paul and the boys. Oooooh, I wish that God would grant me the strength.'

"His voice was strident now," Egan reported. "Now he was the master of this quiet, tension-taut room again.

" 'If I could help you! If I could block with you! If I could run with you! If I could stand next to you and fight with you! Oooooh, if I could do those things with you, Paul and the rest of the lads, I think you'd know just how much I appreciated you and your most gracious words. But I can't. That time is past for me. It's your game—to win or lose.'

"His voice broke," Egan said. "The words were emotion-drenched and forced.

" 'Good luck, Paul! Our Lady is with us all!' "

Their emotions churning, the young gentlemen of Notre Dame pushed their clanking armored bodies through the door, filled with the righteousness of purpose that goes with the knowledge that they had been touched with the Holy Spirit. Which holy spirit? Well, it might be difficult to identify which one. In the third period, Bertelli faked a reverse to Dippy Evans from the USC 18 yard line and then threw to the fullback on the flat. Despite the fact that he had severely cut his knee the evening before, chasing a colleague through the hotel halls after being subjected to a practical joke, Evans caught the ball, broke three tackles and put Notre Dame ahead 20-12. Mindful of the fact that Our Lady was with them and that Frank Leahy would have loved to have been on the field with them, they allowed a touchdown in the fourth period and held on and won 20-18.

It was Notre Dame's first unbeaten year since . . . well . . . since Rockne's last team. And there wasn't a reporter plowing through the steam of the Irish dressing room who wasn't mindful of the fact that Leahy had been associated, if not actively, with the 1930 squad.

"Weren't you sort of an unofficial assistant coach that last year, Frank?" asked a man from the *Chicago Times*.

"Coach Rockne was most gracious to me my senior year," said Leahy. "But I was not an assistant coach. He permitted me to observe the coaching staff and it is true that some of the players did ask for my advice, which I was most proud to give them. But it would be most pretentious of me to take much credit for that 1930 team's success."

"How does this team compare to that team?" said the writer from Chicago.

"Most favorably," said Leahy, still stressing his own humility. "We did not have much reserve strength this year. And, if you recall, the 1930 team went untied. As you know, this team had a 0-0 tie with Army. We strive to go unbeaten and untied."

In three years as a head coach, Leahy had lost exactly two games and tied another. His somber face with the snap-brim hat decorated nearly every newspaper and magazine in the country. They were already telling anecdotes about him, as if he'd been a prominent professional for 20 years. His family was getting large enough now for the wire services to group around the Christmas tree or to pose on their knees saying the rosary.

Yet, on the Tuesday after he had taken his first Notre Dame football team to an unbeaten season, he read the headline of a new series by J. Ray Hunt, which was starting in the *Chicago Times*. "The story of Frank Leahy—A chip off the old Rock. South Bend critics Accept Leahy, Ready to Admit He's another Rockne."

Everybody in South Bend, the writer explained, was talking about the new Notre Dame coach. Naturally, they were already comparing him to their dead hero.

"They said there would never be another Rockne," said Hunt. "But when Leahy's victories marched through Arizona, Indiana, Georgia Tech, Carnegie Tech and Illinois, they began to change their song. When the rain and mud grounded the Notre Dame passing attack, the experts were willing to concede that not even Rockne could have saved a scoreless tie against Army. The New Rockne chant became louder and louder as the Irish sank the Navy, out-pointed Northwestern and defeated Southern California.

"After the final game, there were alumni in the dressing room shouting, 'Our search for another Rockne has ended. We've got his prize pupil.' It's obvious that Leahy absorbed much more of the Old Master's philosophy and psychology than anyone else. This is Rock's legacy. There are some differences. Rockne's practice periods were more relaxed, but as the game approached, he frowned on levity. Leahy's methods are exactly opposite. His boys work in businesslike efficiency, but the week ends in loud, hilarious pep rallies. Rock was a humorous man with a serious side. Leahy is a somber man with a sense of humor beneath his gloom.

"Leahy has many of the Rockne mannerisms. He folds his arms during conversation much like Rock did. He's quick on repartee, too. And, like Rock he is a marvelous speaker. His face occasionally sets itself like Rock's. For want of a better word, he has a certain quality about him that can only be referred to as 'the Rockne Touch.' A young man has come to replace the Old Master. There is a new Rockne."

Quietly, Leahy pushed the newspaper away and rubbed his chin while his eyes narrowed to thin brush strokes. That curious kaleidoscopic collection of emotions and characteristics was moving and changing, humility and pleasure at being compared to Rockne were giving way to stubbornness and ego. Inside of a month, he committed the unthinkable. Frank Leahy announced that he was doing away with the basis of Rockne's genius, abandoning that method of offense and defense that had come to be known as The Notre Dame System.

Dear Lady, Queen of Heaven, standing there on that Golden Dome! He was going to the T-formation! Frank Leahy was nobody but Frank Leahy.

EPISODE 39

It is not necessarily true that the Doctrine of Papal Infallibility could be altered or eliminated with less trouble than Frank Leahy experienced when he decided that it was time to drag Notre Dame football kicking and screaming into the modern era. For weeks after he made his decision, he talked to no one about it. Finally, he mentioned the possibility to McKeever, who looked at him as if he were playing devil's advocate to Francis of Assisi.

"Do you want me to talk you out of it?" he asked, weakly.

"No," said Leahy, snorting with laughter, "I want you to help me in my plot. We must make a careful study of the system and make sure that the priests and alumni, who are sure to oppose it, realize that we are well-versed in the subject. I plan numerous innovations on defense, which may not sit too well, either. Please collect as much information on the T-formation as possible."

A couple of days later, he called Bertelli into his small office, which he had hardly left in several weeks. There were empty milk bottles in the wastebasket and sandwiches scattered among the charts and graphs on his desk. It was late February, long after the season ended and still some time before the snow would be off the ground in Indiana so that Notre Dame could begin spring practice. Bertelli slumped down in a chair and waited for Leahy to rise to greet him. His spinal column automatically stiffened when the coach stuck out his hand.

"Ah, Angelo," he said. "Ah, lad, you're looking fine. To get straight to the point, because this concerns you as much as it does anyone, quite succinctly, lad, you are the finest passer in the nation. You are also about the slowest running tailback I have seen since I played the position at Winner High School many years ago. How would you like a situation where all you had to do was concentrate on your passing. You would simply hand the ball off to the others and let them worry about the running."

Bertelli nodded his head and acted like somebody had shown him how to stand in the middle of an interstate highway and not get hit by a truck.

"What you will do in the T-formation, which is what we are planning to install this spring, is take a direct snap from center, drop back about seven or eight yards and pass. There's not as much deception involved, but it is better suited to the times and to many trends which are developing. New defenses are making it difficult for the center to stand on his head, make a long snap and still be useful as a blocker. I also believe that it will be easier to find good T-formation quarterbacks than it will be to look for triple-threat tailbacks.

"With the center able to block for the T-quarterback, the passer has more coverage from enemy tacklers. With perfect timing, far more faking is possible. The backs arrive at the holes exactly when the linemen initiates the contact. Thus, Angelo, we can employ man-for-man blocking and allow the linemen on the opposite side of the line from the hole to release their blocks and head downfield to remove the linebackers and safety men from the scene of activities.

"Assuming that the timing is perfect, the best that the opponent can do is grab the ball carrier and employ an arm tackle instead of a full shoulder tackle, which is, of course, much more difficult to break. Man-for-man blocking enables blocking assignments to be switched quickly at the line of scrimmage with a minimum number of men having to make the change. The wear and tear on personnel is lessened because faking and deception are stressed more than naked power. This is it, Angelo, football's future."

Bertelli smiled. "I handle the ball on every play, right?"

"Very true, Angelo. On every play."

"How many new plays do I have to memorize next month?"

"About 80 or 100," said Leahy. "But you'll do splendidly, lad. Splendidly."

EPISODE 40

The car pushed its way through the smoky phantasm of Gary's steelmills, heading for a sports banquet in Chicago. Outside, small lights blinked helplessly like lost souls and Ed McKeever who was driving the car noticed that Frank Leahy was less talkative than usual on these trips from South Bend. Sitting in the back seat were Father John Cavanaugh and his brother, Mike Cavanaugh. Perhaps he was thinking of a speech. Maybe some recruiting problem was wedged in his intellect. Even when Leahy was home with his family, his mind was always wandering off to football.

"Father John," said Leahy. "I wish to bring up a football game that we both witnessed last summer. Do you recall the match between the Chicago Bears and the College All-Stars? Do you recall that the All-Stars, with my former lad, Charles O'Rourke playing so well, had a 16-13 deficit to work on with only 12 minutes left to play? Do you recall how they seemed to be closing that three point gap and what happened when the Bears saw they might be threatened?"

Cavanaugh, strengthening himself for the inevitable long lesson in football he knew was coming, closed his eyes, nodded his head and admitted that he had. Well, did he know why the Bears had been able to rout the All-Stars in the final 720 seconds of play?

"I have a fair idea, Frank," he said.

"Father, you are a most perceptive man. I knew that you would see it and still remember it. You are absolutely correct. It was the T-formation. I would like to hear your opinion of it. I respect your opinion on such matters."

"Well, I think it's quite a thing, Frank," he admitted, realizing that it was useless to resist. "Why do you bring it up?"

"Frankly, Father John, I think we can use it at Notre Dame. Now I'm not junking Rockne's system entirely. I'm just interested in retiring the shift, aaaaah; but I, aaaah, wish to point out that Rockne used the T-formation in the early 1920s, long before the Bears adopted it. I think it is most important we all remember that point when we discuss this further."

"If you think it's better for football at Notre Dame, I'll

recommend it to Father O'Donnell tomorrow," said Father John. "He'll have a lot of questions for you, so I hope you've done your homework as usual. There are a lot of alumni and a lot of synthetic alumni who aren't going to understand or like this and you'd better be ready for the pressure."

"Oooooh, I will be, Father John," said Leahy, slouching forward in the front seat and smiling happily. "You can be sure of that."

EPISODE 41

A letter from an irate alumnus that still exists after the passage of three decades:

"You may have been the best coach in the country last year, Mr. Leahy, but junking the classic Notre Dame box formation for the questionable T-formation is, in my humble estimation, a stupid move. You are known as a gambler. Remember a gambler's luck runs dry after awhile. The T-formation that Rockne used was far different from the modern Bears' T and you know it. This is a foolhardy experiment. Going to the T after an undefeated season makes as much sense as breaking up a fullhouse to draw for four of a kind. Stand pat, coach, and play the cards you have. That's what a real gambler would do."—Jerald Herndon, Class of 1921.

EPISODE 42

In the hallway, the maid stood talking nervously to the house detective. She had come on duty seven hours ago and witnessed a most amazing scene, one that was shocking even for the Statler Hotel in Detroit, one of the Midwest's busiest hostelries at the time. Three grown men had entered Room 620 carrying only a football and some notebooks. They had not emerged since and the noises inside sounded as if they might be beating each other to death.

"Anything wrong in here?" asked the detective, exhibiting his badge.

"No," said Leahy, remembering to be gracious. "We are just holding a practical demonstration of the T-formation."

"What the hell is that?"

"Football!"

"Isn't that an outdoor game?"

For weeks, the Notre Dame coaching staff had taken a crash course. McKeever and McArdle had gone to Chicago where Bear coach-owner-ticket manager, George Halas, had opened his files and his facilities to the gentlemen from Notre Dame, which was not unlike the Kremlin giving aid and comfort to the *Wall Street Journal*. Had it been any other institution but Notre Dame, the chances are excellent that Halas would have told the amateur competition to go invent their own T-formation. But the legend has the power to cloud the toughest of minds.

McKeever had permission to view films and examine the Bears' playbook. When the regular season started, he was free to attend practice at Wrigley Field and ask questions. Halas recommended one of his spare T-quarterbacks, Bob Snyder, to Leahy as an assistant coach and he put him in touch with both Frank Shaughnessy, who had helped install the system with the Bears, and with quarterback Sid Luckman, who ran the system for Halas.

Now Luckman and Leahy and McArdle were in a Detroit hotel room. The furniture had been shoved against the walls. Notebooks were spread everywhere. McArdle was bent over, centering the ball to Luckman who was dodging, faking, dropping back, handing off and practicing deception, while Leahy asked endless questions. Then Luckman stepped back and showed Leahy how to take the snap from center, pivot and handoff. They worked until midnight. Both Luckman and Leahy were traveling for business firms. They agreed to meet again at the Commodore Hotel in New York, where Leahy promised to rent one of the larger meeting rooms so that a more thorough demonstration would be possible. Luckman, somewhat bemused, agreed.

"This was a monstrous undertaking," said Leahy, recalling the past at his Oregon apartment for the benefit of a tape recorder. "The T-formation is such a basic part of football now that hardly anyone under the age of 45 can remember the Notre Dame box or the single wing. But at the time, it was a major revolution and we were greatly criticized. The letters ran seven or eight to one against us. That is why it was necessary to make sure that we did not miss a single point.

"I met with Luckman on two other occasions. Once at the Commodore and again in a vacant loft on Sixth Street in New York. It was necessary in order to be able to throw the ball. The East was blanketed with snow at the time and there was no place to go outside. Sidney was most patient with me, answering every question in great detail. From there I went to College Park in Maryland where I renewed an acquaintance with Clark Shaughnessy. He had gone from the University of Chicago to great success at Stanford and was now coaching at Maryland. He was the absolute master of the modern-T. Despite his own heavy schedule he would work with me until 4 or 5 A.M.

"Upon my return to Notre Dame, I felt satisfied that I had at least a fundamental working knowledge of the system. By now there was a storm of criticism. Much of my popularity which came about because I was 'The New Rockne' was now starting to fade because I had made the mistake of altering a tradition. I explained that Joe Sheeketski, another of Rock's pupils, had gone to the T-formation at Holy Cross the year before and I was convinced that Knute Rockne himself would be doing exactly what I was doing at Notre Dame. In fact, had he lived, he might have installed it sooner. This placated them some, but . . . ooooh . . . it was not a simple task.

"You could not believe the nonsensical stories that were making the rounds. They said that when word got out that I was switching to the T-formation, a huge crack appeared in the marble bust of Rockne that was sitting on a pedestal in the fieldhouse. They said that it had to be rushed out for emergency repairs before anyone saw it. Ooooh, that is what they said. Unbelievable, but true. They said it. Some also said that pieces of the Golden Dome slipped loose and showered down on the students These stories were designed to show that Our Lady was displeased with Frank Leahy.

"One rival coach condemned the move, but in a much different manner. He said, 'With his penchant for swift backs and strong throwers, Leahy will be even more dangerous. He doesn't just want to go undefeated and untied, he wants to murder everybody on his schedule. That's what the T-formation will enable Notre Dame to do.' So you see, I was either a destroyer of tradition or a destroyer of everybody else's football team.

"My only regret that spring was that I spent so little time with Floss and my mother and the family that some of my children wondered if I'd died. It was not unusual to work after hours and look up to discover that it was 7 A.M. and time to meet the lads for practice. I ended up in the hospital twice that second season. Ooooh, they said it was colds or the flu or arthritis, I fear now that it was overwork. At the time I would not admit it."

EPISODE 43

The practices were longer, more tedious, more confusing with so many intricate new details to learn. They had begun while there was still snow on the ground and the turf was so hard from winter's hammerlock that even a man's hair hurt when he fell on it. Only one thing helped the players retain their sanity. They knew that Holy Week was almost here and, surely, the brothers of the Congregation of the Holy Cross would not let them work during the time of Christ's passion. They could go home and rest, try to collect their wits and then meet Leahy the day after Easter Sunday. They talked about little else.

"He hammered us like nothing I've seen before or since," said Bob McBride, a guard who later became Leahy's first assistant. "He was absolutely driven to make the T-formation a success. The Coach thought of nothing else but work. Now, the players didn't mind the work, but they had other thoughts than football on their mind.

"All we dreamed of was going home for Holy Week. That was going to save our lives. While The Coach drilled and drilled us, we'd say things out of the corners of our mouths like 'only two more days' and 'the parole comes on Sunday.' Then he called us all together in the dining room. He was so happy, he was almost shining."

Eagerly, Leahy flipped on the microphone and began to talk excitedly. It was an instant or two before the players actually understood what it was he was saying.

"Ooooh, lads, I have such fine news for you, news that will gladden your hearts as it did mine when I learned it just a few minutes ago," he said. "Yesterday, I asked the good Brothers of the Congregation of the Holy Cross if they would permit us to stay on campus during Holy Week and continue to work out."

No one groaned, but one undisciplined lad did gasp before he realized what he was doing. Fortunately, he was in the rear of the room and The Coach never heard him.

"They deliberated until just now. Lads, we have their permission. I know you are as excited as I am. Now, let's have our finest practice of the spring this afternoon."

The players left the dining hall like condemned prisoners. Holy Week was worse than anyone imagined it could be. All the furies that were burning in Leahy's chest exploded. He moved between groups faster. He talked more. He scrimmaged everybody harder. On Holy Thursday, the Irish scrimmaged in the morning and again in the afternoon.

"No way in the world, will they let him work us out on Good Friday," whispered McBride to tackle Lou Rymkus.

Back in the dressing room, Leahy called for attention. As long as they were up early enough and off the field before Good Friday services started, it would be permissible to work again in the morning. No one muttered. And no one moved in bed that night. The practice began at dawn and it was even more brutalizing than the others. They even lined up and scrimmaged again. When it was over, the players literally wobbled their way back to their lockers. Most of them simply slumped on the floor in piles of blood, bandages and sweat-drenched uniforms. Nobody quivered. There was McBride, back against a bench, groaning in pain. On the floor was Rymkus, his arms outstretched, his feet together in a distressingly irreligious pose.

"Mac," he gasped.

"Yes, Lou," said McBride.

"I think I know how Christ felt on the Cross."

EPISODE 44

The mandate Frank Leahy had received from Notre Dame was clear. He was to win. To some people, with lesser drives and weaker ambitions, that might have meant winning most of the games or the vast majority of them. To Leahy it meant winning every weekend and never executing a play that was less than flawless. It is doubtful if Father John Cavanaugh, as well as he knew this man, realized the intensity of his zeal. Leahy, even in the year of Our Lord 1942, with Europe burning and the Pacific an angry ocean of dying men, was a moral crusader, seeking an unknown ideal and sacrificing anything to achieve it. He was not quite a fanatic, but the wall was thin.

With Notre Dame idolators everywhere watching a man whom they now suspected of being a heretic for disposing of the sainted Rockne's offense, the Irish went off to play Wisconsin, coached by one of the Horsemen, Harry Stuhldreher, who had not swerved from orthodoxy. The Chicago papers did not miss the point. The result was a 7-7 tie that left Leahy devastated. Oh, Angelo Bertelli had missed the train and hadn't arrived at Madison until the kickoff and Dippy Evans had injured a knee that removed him from combat. But it was obvious that Notre Dame, while it could gain yardage out of the T, still wasn't sure exactly what it was playing with. The following week, Georgia Tech beat them 13-7 at South Bend. There were three rude fumbles and Bertelli was able to complete only six passes. They not only muttered in the stands, they booed.

Afterwards, Leahy drove home, parked the car uncertainly and told Florence Leahy that he needed to go to bed immediately. He was weak and his back hurt. What's more, there were deep grooves worn in his brain and he needed rest.

For the first time, but hardly the last, the public saw pictures of Notre Dame's glamorous young coach lying in bed listening to the game on the radio with a telephone in his hands, ready to call the bench at South Bend. They cured Leahy's flu quickly at Mayo Clinic while Ed McKeever took his team to three straight victories. They were not sure exactly what the pains in his back and neck were caused by. They thought he might have the beginning symptoms of spinal arthritis. One doctor suggested that he was suffering from severe nervous tension. Somehow the phrase made the newspapers. It was interpreted as a "nervous breakdown," a sickness much in vogue at the time.

"I had worked on too little sleep. Indeed I was exhausted," Leahy recalled. "But it was hardly a mental breakdown and neither was it arthritis, because that problem did not manifest itself until many years later. I had simply driven myself too hard. I returned too soon, but it would certainly not look good to have the head coach of football at Notre Dame out for the entire season. We had trouble defeating both Army and Navy and just barely lost to Michigan. There were two more very close games, which we won, against Northwestern and Southern California. The season ended with a 13-13 tie at the Great Lakes Naval Training Base. When it was over, I felt empty."

And when it was over, Leahy withdrew to a friend's home in Miami Beach, along with his family and attempted to sort out what had happened. Even though he had lost only four games in four years of coaching there were increasing complaints about him. The newspapers no longer gushed up so many lurid adjectives. They did not fawn quite so obviously. When threatened, Leahy became more insular. For years, Notre Dame had depended upon a group of alumni with as much enthusiasm as money to help with their recruiting. In his final years, Rockne rarely had to leave the campus. He simply sent out word that he was interested in this or that player.

By Layden's time, the network of so-called "bird dogs" was large and influential as a group. Notre Dame had so many volunteers it was difficult to control the flow of talent. It became a source of pride for each of them to out-recruit Michigan or Northwestern or Illinois or, even, Southern California. A bird dog could feed his ego by bringing in a great prospect. He immediately rose above his peer group and stayed there the rest of his life if he fetched a super hero. "That's Jack Murphy, the man who got us Bronko Beefhead back in 1934," they would whisper as he walked up the aisle to his stadium seat.

"I was all-city in my senior year, but that didn't mean much because there were only three high schools in the city," said Johnny Lujack. "I had a lot of offers and I liked making the trips. They took me to West Point and I never did meet Red Blaik. The coach who took me on the tour didn't seem too enthusiastic. I was only 160 pounds and I figured that a place like Notre Dame was way over my head. Then a fellow named Henry Opperman asked me if I'd like to go see Southern Cal play Notre Dame at South Bend. They acted interested. Opperman made sure I had a summer job and he helped encourage me in a lot of ways. Every place I turned, I seemed to see another Notre Dame man who was interested in doing some good for me. I went."

In the winter of his discouragement, as he tried to relax in Florida, Leahy decided that it might be better to organize a smaller group of extremely influential alumni, people like his close friend Fred Miller of the brewing company, and recruit more efficiently. Other than his illness, Leahy blamed the fact that his second season wasn't as overwhelming as his first on the fact that when important players were injured, Notre Dame was short on replacements. Now he had a solution.

It was an understandable blunder, but a blunder just the same. Frank Leahy had been associating more and more with great capitalists. He loved their life-style. He was, without actually knowing it, removing himself from the dust of the Dakota Badlands, losing his awkwardness, and beginning to see himself as the leader of a corporation, namely the Notre Dame football team. It was the start of a national trend, the coach-as-captain-of-industry as well as an architect of character.

In so doing, Leahy began to create an entirely different climate at South Bend. Despite the numerous acts of kindness toward players in trouble or in need of a job, despite the warmth and roguishness of his humor, despite his own firm belief in the rightness of his quest for perfection, he would live under constant cricitism, a criticism that would eventually drive him to the edge of physical ruin, alienate some of his children, push his wife into the fog of alcoholism and lead to his own departure from the University which he loved with an unquestioned strength of purpose.

No longer was Notre Dame football a participation sport. Leahy took it away from the great mass of alumni, who complained to newsmen who listened. The bird dogs no longer pushed their way into the dressing room after the game to personally congratulate their boys. Their letters went weeks without being answered. He did not answer their calls personally,

Francis William Leahy was, once again, ahead of his times. Modern college coaches, tangled in the tenacles of rising athletic costs, constant demands for excellence and intensive pressure, operate exactly the way Leahy did 30 years ago. But they are not the keepers of the shards of Camelot. And Leahy was. He recited all the proper litanies, because he was the legitimate heir to Rockne. If there had been no Rockne there would have been no comparisons. But there were and in the comparisons, Leahy suffered. The times they were a'changing and, as Rockne had, Leahy knew what to do. Other coaches, weary of getting destroyed annually by Leahy's machines sensed that he was, from a personal standpoint, more vulnerable with the alumni and with the priests who ruled Notre Dame. They did what they would never have done to Rockne because the latter's image was too firm. Sensing Leahy's weak under-belly, they fought him in the press and dropped him from their schedule.

As he sat there in the Florida sand, taking one of the few honest vacations of his life, he made the first truly tragic miscalculation of his career. It seemed small. But in retrospect, it was that one infinitesimal act that all coaches, all captains, all crusaders fear.

And when he had made it, he excused himself. He left the family and drove to the place where the Boston College Eagles, under his replacement, Denny Myers, were practicing for their Orange Bowl game with Alabama. He insisted that he was there as a spectator, but Myers had no choice. Leahy was invited to address the team. They went out and lost, 37-21, mostly with players Leahy and his staff had recruited.

"I'd like to think this trip was strictly for pleasure," said Floss Leahy, laughing cheerfully among friends on the beach. "Knowing Frank, he probably picked Florida because Boston College was training here."

She never really was sure.

EPISODE 45

"If there was a lad whose memory pleases me the most," said Frank Leahy, "I would have to look back to that team of 1943 and select Creighton Miller. Ooooh, there was a young man of great impishness. He kept me well prepared for the advent of Zygmont Czarobski. He was the son of Red Miller and the nephew of Don Miller. Now, I must admit that I coached for Jim Crowley, I coached against Harry Stuhldreher and I succeeded Elmer Layden as coach at Notre Dame. Ah, but that Don Miller. Of the Four Horsemen—he was the finest man that God ever gave ten toes to.

"Ah, Creighton was high spirited, with an unpredictable sense of humor. Very refreshing. Once when he was a sophomore, he bet his roommate that he could remove more than 40 pennants from the wall without touching one of the tacks. He got most of the lower ones by winging his sneakers at them. But the ones on top were more difficult. So he took to running up the wall and trying to kick them off. He won his bet and the wall collapsed, keeping him out of practice for some time.

"I looked at him when I had heard the story and I said, as seriously, as I possibly could, 'Ooooh, Creighton Miller, I am forced to report your erratic behavior, lad, not only to your parents, but to your Uncle Donald. The latter would grieve me mightily, for I respect him as much as any man I ever met.' But there was no real harm in his nonsense.

"He was a magnificent running back. If he had been born 25 years later, he would have been worth a $150,000-a-year contract. However, he did do incredible things. As the records show, Notre Dame was the national champion in 1943, losing only one game. But against Navy, Creighton performed the most amazing act of forgetfulness I have ever witnessed. He was running alone, when he mistook the five yard line for the end zone. He slowed down and started to wave one arm. A Navy tackler caught him. Fortunately, he had presence of mind to speed up and take the man in with him for a touchdown.

"I feigned utter anger. When the game was over, I took him by the arm and dragged him down the field. 'This, Creighton

Miller, is the five yard line and that, Creighton Miller, is the end zone. Never, never in your life confuse one for the other. Our Lady is watching.' He listened to my speech and repressed a snicker. I knew that the lesson had sunk in, because his normally cheerful face suddenly got grim. He said, 'I think I know what you mean, Coach. I gotcha. Don't worry. I'll stay alert.' I knew that he meant it."

In five seasons as a head coach, Frank Leahy has accounted for three undefeated teams, one national championship, two bowl appearances, one Heisman trophy winner. He was 36 years old and had four children, a wife and a mother to support. But there was a war on, as they used to say, and he seemed strangely unsettled. His health alone could have disqualified him, but he applied for a commission in the Navy. It was mid-April of 1944 and he could stand it no longer. Something larger than football was going on. They made him a full lieutenant, the equivalent of a captain in the Army. Leahy went off to the South Pacific in a submarine with only five football defeats behind him. He was never shot at, although he did almost drown when the submarine began to submerge without warning.

He was one of America's great celebrity-officers, people of national importance who traded their civilian occupations for a comfortable tour of duty. Leahy was in charge of athletic programs under Pacific Submarine Commander, Admiral Charles Lockwood. Most of his time was spent on Midway, Guam and Saipan, after those islands became safe. The country did not want to lose a single important name. Mostly Leahy talked football with submarine sailors, put on some softball games and posed with other celebrity-officers in propaganda photos that pointed out to America that everybody was "doing his or her share for the war effort." It was not difficult for Leahy to receive permission to leave the war zone to fly home and listen to Mickey McBride's offer to join the All-America Conference, which he refused when Father John Cavanaugh, now president of Notre Dame, took him out on the lawn, pointed to the statue of Our Lady on the Dome and made him feel disloyal, if not to say sacrilegious.

While he did his patriotic duty, first Ed McKeever and then Huge Devore, took Notre Dame football teams to consecutive winning seasons. (Well, they were satisfactory from a South

Bend standpoint, 8-2 and 7-2-1, but hardly spectacular.) When it was over over-there, Leahy took his discharge on November 15, 1945, and headed back to Notre Dame as quickly as possible. The post meat market would create an unusual situation in college recruiting. Literally thousands of fine athletes, back-logged for as many as four years, were swinging down gangplanks and getting off airplanes. There were fine prospects who graduated in 1942 as scrawny teenagers. They were returning as hardened adults. There outstanding athletes who who had played a year and then went off to crusade in Europe. They were free, now, to attend any college without skipping a year of eligibility.

This would be college football's all-time shopping spree and Frank Leahy, intelligent man that he was, did not want to be late in the line at the supermarket. He dropped out of the Navy, rushed home, kissed Floss, said hello to the children, embraced his mother and promised to go on a long vacation. Then he re-occupied his office, reassembled his staff and began the great manhunt.

EPISODE 46

Stories that never grow old, no matter how often they are told:

Leahy to Illinois halfback Julie Rykovich upon his mustering out at Great Lakes Naval Training Station: "Julian, lad, everyone at Notre Dame, from Father Cavanaugh down to the lowliest janitors in the fieldhouse would like you to come with us."

Rykovich: "I'd love to attend Notre Dame, Coach, but I'm an agricultural major and that's not a course of study at your school."

Leahy: "Aaaaah, lad, you are most observant. It is true that there is no agricultural school in South Bend. However, I will hire a special tutor for you and someday you can tell your children that you were the first man in the history of Notre Dame to graduate with a degree in agriculture."

EPISODE 47

Gone is the hellishness of war. The good times are rolling so fast that hardly anyone can keep up with them. The Studebaker car which seems to be going both frontwards and backwards at the same time is not the biggest thing in South Bend, although it is awfully close to the Notre Dame football team, which acts as if it never intends to do anything more clumsy than tie, which it does only rarely. There are five Leahy children now, Jerry and James have joined Frank, Susan and Florence, the younger. They no longer live in South Bend. The family has gone from a renovated summer cottage, with grandmother, to a white colonial house on the edge of a golf course called, with some irony, "Happy Days." At least that is what the sign insisted. It was a hangover from the cuteness of the 1930s when all summer cottages needed a name tacked over the door.

By now, the people were willing to admit that in order to obtain perfection from their favorite football team, they were going to have to accept an entirely different sort of coach. The celebrities drove the miles to Long Beach, on the shores of Lake Michigan, to see this man who functioned with the mechanical aloofness of General Motors. If he was warm and humorous, which he was, Frank Leahy withheld those qualities for the people who counted.

There were cocktail parties at Happy Days. But they were for princelings of the church, for important people and for captains of the financial armies. The common herd rarely saw Frank Leahy at Hullie and Mike's and the other places where a man in a more pastoral setting, such as Knute Kenneth Rockne, might suddenly appear. The Notre Dame football coach was a celebrity now, a hundred thousand light years removed from the eager young man who ran the Boston College team as if he were an undergraduate himself. He stood above the players on the practice field on a high tower, overseeing the entire operation and coaching from a distance.

No longer did he have to fret about the details of the athletic department. He had hired Moose Krause as an assistant coach. When it became obvious that he would simply be the football coach, the determined, but outwardly amiable Moose became athletic director.

"Those post-war teams of ours were the greatest over a four year period that any school has ever produced," said the aging Leahy. "They compare with the best professional teams I have ever seen. I have had all sorts of chances to coach in the professional ranks. I could have been coach of the Detroit Lions when I was at Boston College. And soon afterwards I received a most attractive offer from George Preston Marshall, who wanted me to handle his Washington Redskins. After the war, I could have had the Los Angeles Rams on two occasions. I could have been the founder of the Cleveland team. I nearly had the Anaheim franchise in the American League in 1966, if the merger hadn't come. I was offered a position as head coach of the Philadelphia Eagles at a time when Leonard Tose had taken them over and I was far beyond the point when I could effectively coach a professional club.

"They said that I attempted to build up scores strictly for position in national polls. That was, aaaah, cheap talk. I had so many fine young lads on our football team at Notre Dame that I simply could not hold the third team back and tell them not to do what they had prepared all week to do. This was the complete culmination of my entire coaching philosophy. How do you tell a lad that his duty is to achieve excellence and to win, win, win by perfect execution and then instruct him to go out and take it easy because his team is leading by a healthy score. It was my policy to put my best team on the field and wait for them to do their duty.

"Should they perform expertly and should the opposition appear feeble, then the honorable thing to do was to place my next best players on the field. If they should be as adept as the first line, then it was incumbent upon me to go to my next best grouping, to give them the chance to play for the honor of Our Lady. It was not my fault if the fourth string continued to score touchdowns after that."

EPISODE 48

In the years immediately after the war, the two best football teams in the nation belonged to Notre Dame and Michigan, two ancient tribal enemies. They fluctuated back and forth in the rankings. The schools were only 181 miles apart. They had played together and they had dropped each other from each others schedules. Leahy began to needle Michigan after it barely pushed the Irish out of the 1948 championship. The athletic director, Fritz Crisler, could stand the situation no longer. He responded angrily.

"If Frank Leahy wants a game with us again, why doesn't he just drive up from Long Beach, Indiana, and ask me if there is an open date? I'd be willing to talk to him. Why is he shy?"

Crisler was genuinely puzzled, mentally and spiritually.

"I don't know why I don't like Frank Leahy. I don't know why I do like Frank Leahy," he told a reporter from the *Detroit Times*. "He's a total enigma. One morning you see him and he's full of fun, full of life. The next morning you see him, he's morose and gloomy. One day you think he's going to fight fair. The next day he's telling you how he's going to destroy you. Some say his teams play rough, but don't play dirty. I'm never sure what Leahy thinks is the difference between rough and dirty. I just don't know what to make of the man."

In a sense he was a modern re-creation of Dr. Fell, the hero of a poem: "I do not like thee, Dr. Fell, / The reason why I cannot tell; / But this I know, I know full well, / I do not like thee, Dr. Fell." Nobody really knew why they did not like thee, Francis William Leahy. It just happened. Perhaps, thee won too damn many times with a vengeance nobody else could really understand.

"Fritz Crisler said all those things and he probably meant them at the time," said Leahy, recalling the circumstances. "But in 1944 I asked him directly if we could resume the series. He looked me straight in the eyes and said that Michigan was willing to meet Notre Dame any place, any time and any Saturday. I believed him. I repeatedly asked him for a date that we could meet and he never could make room on his schedule for Notre Dame. Ooooh, they grew afraid of us in those post-war years. Notre Dame had the players, by far the best there were.

"It was a source of pride that we attracted so many outstanding players. It was a credit to Our Lady that such a large number of great ones wanted to come to her University. The more games we won, the easier it was to convince young men that their future was with us. There were a number of things that we could guarantee, or at least attempt to guarantee. No lad ever went to Notre Dame without being assured of moral guidance from the faculty. Every attempt was made to secure a summer job for a Notre Dame football player and then make sure that he was well situated after he left the University.

"Our lads got their degrees . . . well, almost all of them. It was a matter of principle. Ooooh, you did not ask a young man to sacrifice so many hours that could have been expended in fun. They gave of themselves to play football. They were worked very hard. They were driven. But they got their education. They received jobs. When they were out in life on jobs that suited them, other Notre Dame men saw that they advanced through life as rapidly as possible.

"Recruiting at Notre Dame was, in fact, a moral responsibility."

It was such a matter of morality, some people said, that Notre Dame had its own professional football franchise in 1947. It seemed that way. Considering the times, when young men only dallied at playing games for a living, when a Johnny Lujack would sign for four years with the Chicago Bears and then retire, it was probably the equal of anything in the National Football League. Most certainly it was the best college team ever assembled. Consider the case of a fifth string tackle named Al Zmijewski, who sweated a lot on Cartier Field and made only one trip all year, a tribute to his integrity rather than his ability as a football player. Leahy sent him in for one play against Southern California. Somebody threw a sloppy pass and it was intercepted by Zmijewski, who brought it back 30 yards for a touchdown, making himself the Slavic version of "One Play O'Brien."

This was the coldest, most efficient team that Notre Dame ever produced. It was crushing and relentless. The first string was not that much better than the second string, which was only an inch or two ahead of the third and fourth strings. The post-war recruiting binge had produced predictable results. When Notre Dame defeated Army with such absurd ease that 27-7 didn't seem like the real score, Leahy and Red Blaik met in the center of the field. They shook hands and then walked off toward the same exit, ten paces apart, absolutely unwilling to talk to one another. One man's enormous drive had crippled the other's enormous ego.

"They didn't really hate each other," said Frank Leahy, Jr. "They just disliked losing to the other. There was talk about a feud. It wasn't so. My dad didn't want to lose to a man he considered his equal and he hated to think any coach was his equal. Blaik was the same way. He didn't want to lose to an equal and he didn't want the world to know he thought of Frank Leahy as an equal. Coaching football on a big time level is an ego trip. That's why many coaches didn't like my father. Their egos were bruised.

"Both dad and Red Blaik were big golf nuts. Dad couldn't play worth a damn but when he found out I was pretty good at it, he drove himself until he was better than I was. Of course, he made me pay the price. I'd go out there and shag balls by the hours. He'd play with me and he wouldn't rest until he could beat me, at least by one stroke. One day, he got an invitation for him and Moose to go up to West Point and play Colonel Blaik and some member of the Army athletic department in a foursome. It was raining and Blaik wanted to call the game off. Dad insisted that they play. He lost by one stroke and he spent the entire year practicing for the re-match. He was strictly a believer in competition. He didn't want anybody to whip him in anything."

In reality, Blaik was a soldier and a gentleman in comparison to Tulane's Henry Frnka, a Hungarian who looked up at the scoreboard, noted that his team was behind at the closing gun by a 59-6 score and when Leahy came over to offer his hand all but pulled out a gun and shot the victor. His language was decidedly not gracious. Leahy turned and trotted in the opposite direction with something less than compassion warming his chest. The loser stood there, transfixed by anger. The legend of Frank Leahy as an un-loved winner was firmly a part of American mythology. Opponents insisted that he taught his lads to play dirty football and, if that wasn't exactly true, he at least looked the other way when they started to gouge, kick and thumb.

"That never was true," said Stu Holcomb, coach and athletic director at Northwestern and later vice-president of the Chicago White Sox baseball team. "I was no close friend of Frank's. I don't think he had that many or wanted that many. But I liked him. What wasn't there to like about him? He was warm and pleasant off the field and he wanted to beat you on it. As far as dirty play was concerned, the Irish were just the opposite. Oh, God, they'd hit living hell out of you, because that's the way Frank wanted them to hit. They were tough and they were rough, but they never did a thing illegal.

"There were problems involved getting a team ready for Notre Dame. You see, Frank was always one up on you. That was something you knew before you went into the game, so you made your own players prepare so strenuously for the Irish that they burned themselves out in practice and just weren't ready for the football game. Frank was so technically superior that he made the rest of us, no matter how good we were, feel somehow inferior. It's a tough thing to consider yourself one hell of a coach and then turn around to discover that somebody has made you look downright dense. Notre Dame teams hit harder, not dirtier, but harder. That came from heavy scrimmaging. They were so deep in personnel after the war that they could scrimmage by the hour.

"Not many teams could afford to do that sort of thing. Those great Army teams with Doc Blanchard, Glenn Davis and Arnie Galiffa could do the same thing. Why? Well, they had people around that could withstand the punishment. Ask how many people loved Red Blaik in those days. Ask how many really loved Vince Lombardi until he was dead and couldn't hurt them. Why did they come to hate Frank Leahy in those days? It's simple. He beat people. He beat them regularly and he figured to keep on beating them. It hurt a lot of folks, but Frank had this desire to succeed.

"It was always, 'Follow me to Mt. Excellence.' Some of his players thought he was excessive. But he always won. His 1947 team was the greatest in college history. No second pick."

By now Frank Leahy was standing so tall that not even the sun or the moon could eclipse him. Newspapermen, who had once drooled over him in print, now acted as if he had given atomic secrets to the Commies. He had become one of those national figures who have such stature that attacking them seems the only sensible thing a writer can do for his paper. They said that he spoke in riddles, that he was vainglorious, that he used the royal "we" too frequently, that he discussed the chances of Notre Dame defeats more than was seemly during a period when nobody had a chance of beating the Irish. In short, he committed the unpardonable sin of being exactly what a football-dizzy university ever dreamed of—a coach who not only couldn't be beaten, but thought of every way possible to fend off such a tragedy.

"They paid him to win football games and, by damn, that's exactly what he did for them folks," said Wallace Butts, head coach at Georgia and the only truly close friend that Leahy had among college coaches. "They're always getting on Frank's fanny about one thing or another, but I'll tell you this about that man: He's gonna win some games and he's gonna make every man who went to that school think he's made a commitment for the rest of his life. A boy plays for Frank and years later, whether that boy peed a drop or not, old Frank is gonna come and help him out. You can't beat that kind of loyalty. Say, that's the kind of loyalty that Frank demanded, but that was also the kind of loyalty he gave. That's what coaching is all about."

If Creighton Miller was the best loved player Francis William Leahy ever coached and Angelo Bertelli was the greatest passer and Ziggy Czrobski was the funniest, then John Lujack was the most versatile. He arrived at the wrong time. He was the last of the truly magnificent triple-threat tailbacks. But he came to Notre Dame just when they were switching over to the T-formation. He could pass. Oh, he could pass. He could also run. But in senior year, Leahy did not necesarily deem that proper. He was a brilliant defensive player, a man who could now make all-Pro as a strong safety. Lujack was a field commander. He gave orders and other players listened carefully.

As running backs, Lujack had people like Emil Sitko, the perfect model of a modern fullback, and Terry Brennan, fast as hell and a thoughtful lad who spent a lot of time taking notes in Father Theodore Hesburgh's philosophy classes. There were so many replacements that nobody ever thought of relaxing. There were Bob Livingstone, Coy McGee, Mike Switowicz, Billy Gay, Lancaster Smith, Ernie Zaleski, Corwin Clatt and Floyd Simmons. The second string quarterback was Roger Brown and there wasn't a single soul who couldn't have started for Indiana.

Life was so comfortable that year that Leahy had planned to use George Ratterman as his quarterback and place Lujack at left halfback, where he could run or pass on his own option. What's more, he could even go downfield and catch what Ratterman threw. Lujack was clearly the more remarkable athlete, but Ratterman was the better pure quarterback. He was superior at faking and he had a stronger arm. Somehow his mind didn't seem to be as finely tuned to football as Lujack's was.

"Still, I had this dream of Ratterman throwing long and Lujack running and passing off the option. I could see the opposition going, aaaah, mad trying to stop us on offense. Unfortunately, George did not apply himself to his scholastic load in the manner that would have impressed Our Lady. When the 1947 season opened, he was playing quarterback for the Buffalo Bills and Notre Dame was using Lujack at quarterback. The unusual thing was that writers always referred to George as being a 'second string Notre Dame quarterback.' He was never that in fact. When his turn came to play the position, he was first in line. He would even have made a running back out of the great Lujack."

It really made no difference, because Notre Dame ruined everyone in its path. It shutout its first three opponents and then it got ready for Army. While Leahy had been off teaching submarine men how to do push-ups, the United States Military Academy had done phenomenal damage to Celtic grace, winning 59-0 against McKeever and 48-0 against Devore. In the first post-war year, there was a 0-0 tie.

"Our entire season was dedicated to the destruction of the Army football team. There is no denying that," said Lujack. "The students really got into it, too. They sent letters to Blaik warning him 'that the war is over and the men are back at Notre Dame.' They called the Army players 'draft dodgers' and stuff like that. The only real disappointment was that Columbia broke Army's undefeated streak with a 21-20 win before the Irish could get at the Cadets. God, how we hated

Columbia for doing that. It took the edge off the game for a lot of people. They said, 'Well, if Columbia can beat Army, anybody can.' I tell you, we wanted to win it by a 60-0 score. And all week long, The Coach was driving us like I've never seen him drive before."

Before the match at Notre Dame Stadium, Leahy turned to Blaik and said, "Earl, I believe your players will be very happy after this is over. I do not see any way that you can fail to defeat Notre Dame this afternoon."

"Oh, Frank, save the poor-mouthing for somebody who believes you," said Blaik. "Your team is favored because it deserves to be favored. However, you can be sure that the Cadets will give you a battle. That is my only opinion on the game and it's an honest one."

The blood was pounding through Frank Leahy's body so fast that he could barely make his way to the dressing room. He sat in silence for long, lonely minutes, massaging his temples with his palms. Then he went forth to exhort the troops. Leahy spoke of the wartime humiliations. He discussed the 0-0 tie of the year before. He spoke of the fact that many Army players did indeed hide behind the solid gray walls at West Point while Notre Dame players were slogging across the mud of Europe or suffering in the tropical heat of the South Pacific. His voice leaped to the tops of great mountains and descended into calm, soothing valleys.

"Remember, young men of Notre Dame, that a tie is the same as a defeat when you play for Our Lady," he said, softly and reassuringly. "Let me recall a line from that most stirring of songs, the Notre Dame Victory March. The words entreat us to 'Shake Down The Thunder From The Sky.' This afternoon, you play Army. You must redeem the honor of our school, which has suffered. Now, I ask you, in the sacred name of Our Lady, to go onto that field and . . . 'Shake Down The Thunder!' Go and persevere . . . Our Lady demands it!"

There were 59,171 fanatics in the seats at South Bend that afternoon. The first kickoff went out of bounds. The second one settled into the arms of Terry Brennan on the Irish three yard line. Running expertly behind his blockers, he went all the way for a touchdown. Blaik turned and shook his head. Army punted after making only one first down and the Irish went 80 yards for another touchdown. A great deal of thunder was being shaken down. But the Army defense stiffened its spines. Notre Dame scored again in the third quarter and, after giving up a touchdown to Cadet halfback Rip Rowen, smashed some 80 yards with Larry Coutre and Mike Switowicz carrying the ball. It was Coutre who went over the line for the score. Leahy looked at the scoreboard, grinned thickly and clapped his hands together. Across the way, Blaik saw the tableau and ground his teeth together.

This was the final match in a continuing series that reached back 34 years. Even though it would be revived in another decade, the great Army–Notre Dame vendetta had ended. Blaik grouched off the field and told reporters, "They beat us 13-7 in the final 51 minutes of the game," a classic example of early Pentagonese. He alluded to the fact that Leahy had used some semi-sneaky maneuver in the game, such as using Lujack occasionally at left half and having him take direct snaps from center.

"It was quite obvious that Leahy didn't want to rub it in," wrote Gene Kessler, columnist for the *Chicago Sun-Times*. "The game was decided in the first nine minutes, but it seemed that Notre Dame could have run up the score if it wanted to. The coup de grace was Brennan's kickoff return. After that it was merely a matter of seeing how many points the Irish would score. Leahy should be complimented for showing restraint. He didn't do what the wartime Army teams, with Doc Blanchard and Glenn Davis did. He didn't try to demolish the opposition. Cadet coach Red Blaik had no complaints because Notre Dame used 39 players."

Outside the Notre Dame locker room, a broadcaster was finishing his post-game show when he saw Red Grange, the glimmering football-style immortal from Illinois, marching toward Leahy's office. Would he mind being interviewed? Grange shrugged.

"You know why Notre Dame is the best college team in the country?" he said. "It's because Frank Leahy is the greatest college football coach who ever lived. He's greater than Knute Rockne ever thought of being and I'm not knocking old Rock. But Leahy is just the best. Frank's a total perfectionist. Consequently, his players never make a mistake . . . well, they seldom make a mistake.

"They complain and say that he teaches dirty football and all that silly talk The reason they complain is that Leahy is superior and he wins. They stay clear of Notre Dame for one reason: Frank Leahy. They don't want to get beat. Why do you think Red Blaik wants to get off the schedule? He knows if he plays Notre Dame he's going to look bad. He's an egotist. So's Frank. The war's long over and the kids are going to be going elsewhere. Army isn't going to be the juggernaut it was. Leahy's success is the result of long hours of work. They say he's a sour person and he can be, when he's preoccupied with football. But when he's got nothing else on his mind, he's the nicest guy I ever met. I hate this silly criticism of him.

"I don't think Notre Dame offers more inducements to a player than any other school does. Oh, they've got alumni who like to see kids come to South Bend. But I think, from everything I've heard, that Notre Dame players probably get a little less than most kids. But they know they are going to play for the best—the very best. And they are going to win."

It sounded like a paid political announcement. The radio man was mildly amazed. Grange and Leahy weren't that close friends. To know Frank Leahy was to fear him. He had grown that strong.

EPISODE 49

A rain squall has come slashing down from the great woods to the north, churning the waters of Lake Michigan and snapping branches off trees on the south shore. Power company trucks cannot get through the debris and everyone in Frank Leahy's neighborhood huddles in the darkness. There are candles on the tables at Happy Days. Even though there is a football game on Saturday, the head coach at Notre Dame is at home. This is an anxious period. Florence Reilly Leahy is pregnant for the sixth time and, as she stands to open the bathroom door, she is reasonably certain that the birth could come anytime. A pain rattles her entire body.

"Oh, God, Frank!" she shouts, dropping to both knees. "For heaven's sake, get up here as quickly as possible. Oh, God! Oh, God!"

There is a stampede of humanity up the stairs, sons and

daughters, husband and mother-in-law and husband's aunt. They arrive at the door at approximately the same time. It is one of the fastest deliveries on record. The coach gets his wife to their bed, makes her as comfortable as possible and witnesses exactly one contraction. Plop! There lying on the comforter, in less than 30 seconds, is Frederick Leahy. There is another stampede downstairs. Frankie Leahy gropes in the darkness trying to find a home remedy book that might tell how to tie an umbilical cord. Everyone gives orders, a Leahy family failing. Mary Leahy telephones the doctor, who insists that the roads are impassable because of flooding. He will stay on the line to give instructions.

Somebody sends Sue Leahy to boil some water. In the darkness, she trips and fractures one of her big toes. Frightened to the point of slavering at his jowls, the friendly family dog attempts to bite one of the forms moving past him, trying to help an eleven-year-old girl who thinks she has broken her entire leg.

"I think Sue has broken her toe or her leg or something," shouts Frankie Leahy.

"Thank God it wasn't one of the players," mutters the Coach, who gets criticized by his aunt for his total lack of sympathy for Sue Leahy's pain.

Now the doctor is ready to give Frank Leahy lessons in how to be a mid-wife. He listens while nine-year-old Florence Victoria holds the receiver up next to his ear. "All right, doctor, I'm ready. Oh, by the way, can you also tell me how to set a broken big toe. No, no! Not my wife's, my daughter's. Well, I'll explain it to you later. What do you do first?"

In the midst of the operations, Jimmy Leahy, not yet three years old, shoves his redhead inside his mother's bedroom. "Is it a boy?" he asks.

"Yes," says the Coach, "it is a little brother. Aren't you happy, Jub?"

"He isn't sitting in my high chair and he isn't using my football," said kindly James (Jub) Leahy, slamming the door hard enough to hit Auntie Sue in the rump.

Sometime the next morning, the doctor arrives along with an ambulance. Everybody goes clanging off toward a Michigan City hospital, a trip which Florence Reilly Leahy insists isn't necessary. After all, she's fine. She's done this thing before, although not at home. Fred Leahy is healthy. In fact, he's overly healthy. She is not gone more than a few minutes before the telephone rings. The resident public relations genius in the Notre Dame athletic department, Charlie Callahan, is on the line. Covering the Leahy family is an adventure, similar to reporting on wars and street riots.

The newspapers have been alerted to the fact that the masterful coach at Notre Dame has delivered his sixth child himself. What sex was it, Callahan asks.

"A fullback, I hope," says Leahy, ever mindful of what looks clever in headlines. "That would be excellent because we might be weak at that position in 18 years."

The story hits the wires and the nation loves it. America's best-loved Irish couple—well, next to Fibber McGee and Molly maybe—have done it again. Newsreel cameras grind at the hospital and football fans everywhere chuckle. There is one more face for the annual picture around the Christmas tree, the one so deeply loved by the International News Service photo editor. That makes six children and there will be two more.

Only two years later, Florence Reilly Leahy goes charging up the stairs in pursuit of Fred Leahy who has committed some sort of domestic atrocity. Her foot catches on the top step and she falls back down, fracturing her lower left leg. It is the second day of practice and she is forced to call from the hospital.

"Frank," she says, "I'm sorry to call you off the practice field. But I'm in the hospital."

"What happened, Floss?" he asks, deeply concerned.

"I broke my left leg," she says and then pauses for dramatic effect.

"Frank?" she continues.

"Yes, Floss! Yes!"

"Better me than Johnny Lattner, huh?"

EPISODE 50

Little scenes from history that might otherwise be lost to history, if people didn't frequent old book stores:

"It was always my impression that Frank Leahy was the most pessimistic, most gloomy human being I had ever met. They

told me that he picked up this mannerism from his father, but I suspect that it must have been a thorough family trait. Frank had a brother named Tom Leahy, who was a very successful insurance man. Tom ran for the Indiana state senate and on election night, I happened to run into him. Naturally, I asked him how he was doing and he said that he wasn't terribly optimistic. He was leading by 3,600 votes, but two precincts hadn't reported yet. I wondered right then and there what it would take for a Leahy to admit that he had a sure thing,"—Francis Wallace, author of *Notre Dame, From Rockne to Parseghian,* 1966.

EPISODE 51

"I think," said Frank Leahy, "that it is an interesting endorsement of Notre Dame football to know that after our lads had been acknowledged as national champions in 1947 three of our players, John Lujack, George Connor and Ziggy Czarobski, could have played another year by simply lengthening their scholastic programs. Instead, they decided to graduate on time. I did not encourage them to remain. They had completed their years at Notre Dame and it was time for them to move toward something else."

By now they are playing numbers games everytime you open a newspaper. They are talking about the number of games Notre Dame has won in a row. They are talking about the numbers in Leahy's record and how they relate to other great coaches. They are saying that if he lives to be 65 and doesn't retire from coaching that he will set a record for excellence unmatched this side of the Roman legions. Moreover, Leahy has moved into higher intellectual circles. He is a practicing member of the Christopher Movement, which believes in lighting little candles rather than cursing dark nights. He is a Knight of Malta. ("I do not understand how His Holiness, the Pope, could have considered me for such an honor," he says, although there are those who insist that Leahy has been campaigning for election to the order among American Catholic laymen for some time.)

The Notre Dame victory streak stretches on and on. As it gets longer, the rumors about Leahy's impending departure grow stronger. Lou Perini, owner of the Boston Braves baseball team, will be awarded a professional football team if he can prove that he has Leahy under contract. Every year, just before the Irish play the Trojans, it is freely predicted that the next coach at the University of Southern California will be Frank Leahy, who admits that he enjoys the company of numerous gracious celebrities in the movie industry,

"I was approached by them on three different occasions," he recalled. "There was a man who had played football at USC who had become very important in the entertainment industry. He was quite willing to pay me as much as $50,000 and make sure that I had a retirement house in Palm Springs. He guaranteed me that if I were as successful at Southern Cal as I was in South Bend that I could easily quadruple that figure. So many offers were dangled in front of me that my, aaaah, head fairly spun. It was most flattering . . . most flattering indeed.

"There was a time when I considered the possibility stronger. I believe it was 1950. I would have carte blanche to do what I wanted as far as recruiting was concerned. They assured me that I would have the finest talent in the nation at my disposal. I told them that I already had that at Notre Dame.

"Do not misunderstand me, I did not altogether care for the means whereby players were induced to attend our school. There were some things that occurred at Notre Dame that I did not wish to think about. They happened. I knew about them. I did not care for them. But in the pursuit of excellence, one learns to make important compromises. They are not tasteful ones, you understand. But they do become necessary.

"I enjoyed the last few years at Notre Dame because recruiting had become so much more pleasant. This business of going out after boys and then flying them to your campus for an inspection tour may work out well sometimes. On the whole, you can't count on it. It's a poor way to create a winning spirit. I never wanted a boy who had to be sold on Notre Dame. What I wanted was a boy who was already sold on Notre Dame. Lads are more coachable when they have a burning desire to play football for your school. When I was offered the Texas A&M job in 1956 I decided that I had found another unique situation, one not that much different from the one I had in South Bend. That is why I considered the possibility.

"The lads loved Texas A&M, the same way my lads loved

Notre Dame. The atmosphere was similar and I was intrigued. I did not consider the Southern California people to be sincere at all times.

"I discussed with them many things that genuinely stirred me, such as our country's struggle against Communism, the rising crime rate, the venereal disease epidemic, the continuing problem of illegitimate children. I talked with them about the possibility of combating these evils through the use of movies. I was aware of the good that the film industry had done during the war to fight Fascism. I only hoped that they would do the same to battle Communism. I told them I would work for less if they opened these facilities to me. I never contemplated a thing without weighing the moral value of what I was doing."

Not many people were aware of the matter, but some 160,000 babies were born every year out of wedlock to girls under 14. Somehow, someway Frank Leahy wanted to do something about that. By going undefeated every year, he seemed to feel that he was making a contribution to the halt of moral decay in America. Those thoughts were always on his mind, floating just below the surface.

EPISODE 52

Few laymen understood exactly why Frank Leahy, a mere football coach, should be one of the 245 men in the world selected to be a Knight of Malta, although it was said at the time that both Henry Ford and Cardinal Spellman had a great deal to do with it and that Leahy had not exactly kept his desire to become a member of this exclusive organization a secret. The nation was aware that nobody had come close to ending the 39 game streak since Southern Methodist, with a Roman Catholic lad playing quarterback and several others in the offensive line, contrived to hold the Irish to a 27-20 victory that was depressingly close from Leahy's slightly jaundiced viewpoint.

"They ran from a triple and double wing offense that we certainly weren't prepared for," he said. "The man that we expected to give us the most trouble was, quite obviously, Doak Walker. They used this offensive formation that I had never seen before and never saw afterwards. Walker had been injured the week before and we had no idea what they might do. There was even some inside talk that Walker might play. Oooooh, those were secretive times. More so than today.

"The coach at Southern Methodist was Matty Bell, a most pleasant man, but a clever one. He took his lads behind closed doors and came up with a spread that was entirely confusing. There was Kyle Rote back in Walker's spot. In most cases, the backs were flanked behind split ends. They went from a double wing to a triple wing and back to a double wing. I recall my players coming off the field saying, 'Coach, what is that they're using?' I was at a loss for an answer, perhaps, for the first time since I burned down the barn in Winner, South Dakota.

"Afterwards they asked me who the greatest back I had ever seen was. Well, there had been Kyle Rote, threatening to end our streak. I looked at the reporters and told them that they had me at a disadvantage. If they asked at any other time I might give some consideration to the matter. But at the moment, I could think of only one person—Kyle Rote. That winter I went to a banquet in Houston and took Frankie with me. The victory over SMU had been our tenth of the 1949 season and it ensured another national championship for us.

"Morris Frank, the sports editor then of the *Houston Post,* asked Frankie who his sports hero was, expecting that he would say that his father was. Instead, Frank, Jr., said: 'Oh, it's Kyle Rote.' I did not attempt to strangle him, but the thought later came to mind.

"Few people remember that Notre Dame led 14-0 near the halftime against Southern Methodist and, on the last play of the second quarter, we scored again. They had not even come close. But Rote was superhuman in the second half. Oooooh, he was magnificent. I never saw the Great Gipp, but I can't imagine anyone playing any better. He gained at will. There was nothing we could do to stop him. Kyle scored two touchdowns and was responsible for a third that made it 20-20. I was genuinely frightened. I was sure that Notre Dame would lose right up until the moment that somebody kicked off. This time I was genuinely panicked, although I tried not to show it in front of the players.

"Often a coach is given credit for giving a quarterback

prudent information pertaining to how to win the game. But the Cotton Bowl was filled with people going crazy, ringing cowbells and making loud noises. Bob Williams, a truly wonderful quarterback, came over. He had the entire offensive unit with him. He asked me for advice. I said, 'Bob, don't ever enter the coaching profession.' The offense laughed and I believe those lads thought that I was calmer than I was. They scored with two minutes to go. I was convinced that Rote would get them back in the ball game and he very nearly did. He ran and he passed and he ran some more. Jerry Groom, one of my finest young lads, intercepted a pass in a crowd and we had the game by a 27-20 score.

"Afterwards, I was invited to have dinner with several people including Harlan Ray, who was a very fine booster of SMU athletics and one of the school's most enthusiastic alumni. The party lasted until 3 A.M., at which time I begged that I must return to my hotel because I had planned to go to Mass on Sunday with my players before returning to South Bend. He said, in that fine booming Texas-style voice, 'Why, y'all have to go to Mass with mah wife and I.' It suddenly struck me what a fine world it was. This great Southern Methodist alumnus was . . . a Catholic."

When the season ended, they asked Leon Hart, never a loud Leahy lover, what he thought of his coach. The answer was somewhat unusual, even though this was not a time when players dared speak their minds in public. Here was one of Notre Dame's finest players, an end, a fullback, a defensive tackle and a rare athlete.

"He worked my tail off and I guess I grumbled a lot," he said. "But he wasn't a phony. People said he was, but he wasn't. He acted like a phony because of those mannerisms. But those mannerisms were the truest thing about him. His enthusiasm overflowed. He damn near choked everyone with it. He wanted the eleven most savage men in the starting lineup. He didn't want dirty players, he wanted the toughest, hardest-hitting men he could find. The Coach had a way of making you more aggressive.

"When I was a freshman, he noticed that I wasn't practicing as hard as I should have been. So he came running out with that, 'Leon Hart . . . ooooh, Leon Hart . . . you are disgracing this fine Catholic Institution.' I wasn't entirely lazy, though. I was a 17-year-old freshman and I was opposite George Connors. So, I figured I'd better take a few shots at Connors. First time out of the blocks, I whacked the great Connors a good one and dropped him on his back. There was the coach out on the field yelling, 'George Connors . . . ooooh, George Connors . . . you let this man, a mere freshman, beat you like that . . . for shame . . . ooooh, for shame.' So the rest of the afternoon Connors and I stood there trying to beat each other into the ground

"Every now and then, we'd get even with him. When Lujack got married, Connors was one of the ushers. For some reason, the Coach and his wife got there late. So Connors whispers out of the corner of his mouth, 'You're late, Leahy, take ten laps around the church before I seat you.' Those were the days."

Indeed, they were and Frank Leahy's whole life was reaching its apex. The unbeaten streak kept climbing higher, higher, higher. Sports writers ran out of great coaches to compare him to. A few said that he was the greatest who ever lived, better than Rockne, better than Amos Alonzo Stagg, better than anyone. The Master Coach they called him, just as they had called Rockne. And hardly anyone knew that Leahy was seriously undermined by the anti-football priests, who cringed whenever Notre Dame's football success was mentioned in the press, who fretted endlessly when the school's fame was measured in yards-gained-rushing instead of brilliant-scholars-graduated. They managed to bring enough pressure to reduce the number of football scholarships from 32 to 18. Stunned, Leahy begged for suitable explanation and received none that he could live with.

"The pressure had become enormous," Leahy recalled. "I was being blamed for the fact that Army discontinued their series with Notre Dame. I was being blamed for the fact that several Big Ten schools either dropped us or wouldn't schedule us. They said that I was unpopular with every other coach in the country, which wasn't true. Several times I went to Father John Cavanaugh. The first time I asked him if the administration felt that I was responsible for the scheduling problems. If it did, I was prepared to resign immediately. I told him so and he explained that I was not being blamed directly. That is to say that it had nothing to do with me personally. He said that it was obvious that I had simply created football teams that were too good for some opponents' tastes. But that is what I had been hired to do and I had done it. He said that one Big Ten athletic director had told him that Notre Dame belonged in a class of its own and that by putting together a string of great teams so soon after being away in the Navy, I had scared everyone.

"I accepted that explanation. Soon afterwards, Colonel Blaik said that one of the reasons for discontinuing the series was that 'Army has no hope of ever beating Notre Dame again,' which I thought was a curious thing for the coach at a military academy to admit. There were other factors. Enormous sums were being bet on the Army–Notre Dame game. I heard from a man in Chicago once that as much as $30 or $40 million might have been wagered on the 1946 game. Ticket scalping was thoroughly out of hand, which is one of the reasons the 1947 game was switched to South Bend so that it might be easier to control such things. Yankee Stadium had become unmanageable.

"Most of the criticism, I could stand. Ooooh, some of it was shabby, indeed. It is true that my closest friend among the coaching profession was Wallace Butts and we enjoyed each other's company immensely. Because we were seen together constantly at coaching conventions and other professional gatherings, this was taken to mean that I did not have other friends in the entire country.

"When I was suffering the torment that went with the realization that not everyone at Notre Dame was as firmly committed to excellence as I was, I told Wallace about my misery and the fact that I was questioning my own Catholicism because I did not believe Our Lady would let such a thing happen to a team that had done nothing but bring Her honor. Wallace looked at me and said: 'Frank, did you ever consider the possibility that you are simply too good for college football and, maybe, you'd be better off with a professional team? If you won every game for four years, there wouldn't be a single priest telling you to stop.'

"I told Father John that I might leave after the 1949 season. The Los Angeles Rams had made inquiries as to my availability and I was tempted. Ooooooh, I was sorely tempted. But I considered it an honor to be head coach at Notre Dame. To me it was a sacred trust. How could I give it up to join the professionals? It seemed indecent.

"Do you know that I still have with me a letter from Jeff

Cravath, the former coach at the University of Southern California. When I was being savagely attacked for causing Notre Dame's scheduling problems, he wrote to me and said, 'There never will be a time when USC drops Notre Dame from its schedule. The Irish play football the way it was meant to be played and it is a distinct privilege to coach against Frank Leahy. Let's preserve the classic USC–Notre Dame series for our grandchildren. The Trojans are proud to play Notre Dame. Never would I criticize boys who fight with all their hearts and souls for their school. Hopefully, that is the same spirit we have here at USC.'

"Soon afterwards I noted in *The St. Louis Sporting News* that he had said essentially the same thing to the Los Angeles press. I got along very well with Mr. Jeff Cravath. Unlike some of our contemporaries, he was not transfixed by the possibility of losing at football."

The drum beats continued, some softer than others, but they continued ceaselessly, until just before the 1950 season when Father John Cavanaugh issued a public statement, making him, perhaps, the first college president ever to be forced to explain how proud his school was of an undefeated football team. It was a devastating indictment of the American sporting ethic, a contradictory code which demands all-out, bloody-jowled dedication to victory and then condemns the Boston Celtics, the New York Yankees or Frank Leahy's Notre Dame football teams for achieving the ultimate.

"Leahy is blamed for wrecking the Notre Dame schedule by developing teams that are too strong," he said. "But that is what he was hired to do. He was brought here to win and to achieve excellence. If he didn't win they would be asking to fire him. His is, indeed, an unsolvable position. At Notre Dame we have no apologies about wanting winners. We want our students to win in debates, on the basketball court, on the baseball diamond, in the classroom and in the more important battles of life. The football team is a great example of how perfection may be attained. We shall always want Notre Dame men to play to win so long as there is a Notre Dame. Frank Leahy is the greatest man in American athletics today."

Concessions were made and the number of scholarships allotted to football began to rise again, but never to the pre-retrenchment level. And when the horror of the 1950 season was over and Frank Leahy began to see more and more quality sophomores and freshmen appearing on the holy green grass at Cartier Field, he could feel his religious beliefs returning stronger than ever. The beautiful Lady on the Golden Dome was favoring him again. Some afternoons he could feel the benign warmth of Her smile and feel the touch of Her hand upon his soul.

EPISODE 53

Proof that even the righteous and the morally proper have their moments of sin:

"It was during that 1950 season when Leahy was suffering through the only really bad season he ever had. He came walking into the dressing room for a post game press conference. He had his head down and he was obviously in anguish. Leahy had been given a really bad time by the officials and he was seething inside. I was the last one to get up to leave and he motioned for me to stay. There was obviously something he wanted to get off his chest.

"He said: 'Joseph ... oooooh, Joseph ... you are aware that I attempt to avoid profanity, with the exception of an occasional 'hell or damn'. That is true, is it not?"

"I agreed and he said: 'Joseph, please forgive the use of the unpleasant expletive. At the moment, it is the only word that seems to fit ... Joseph ... we got fucked!'

"Then he asked me to make sure that the word did not appear in the newspaper, as if any editor would let it pass."—Joe Doyle, sports editor, *The South Bend Tribune*, September 1973.

EPISODE 54

Outlined against a cold, gray October sky, the anti-football faction at Notre Dame rode tall in the saddle. The victory streak had gone to 39 and now Purdue, largely a sopho-more football team, had come to South Bend a 20-point betting underdog. There seemed to be no reason why Leahy's reign of terror shouldn't continue. As usual, he was gloomy. He talked with great pessimism, but that was natural. The public and the press had become immune to it.

This was the second game of the season and John Carmichael, sports colmumnist of the *Chicago Daily News,* came down to lunch with Leahy on Thursday.

"John," he said as they sat overlooking Lake Michigan, "you are about to witness one of the greatest debacles in the history of intercollegiate football. Purdue is going to defeat us easily."

"Cut out the bullshit, Frank," said Carmichael, "and get out the bottle."

For once, Leahy was correct. It wasn't even close. Purdue was so absurdly loose for the game that the players came on the field, smiling and talking eagerly among themselves. There were 56,716 communicants present and the victory was easy for the Boilermakers. A child named Dale Samuels, just an 18-year-old sophomore, passed for three touchdowns in the first half. On two other occasions he moved deep into the Notre Dame half of the field, getting stopped on the one and the seven yard lines. If anything, the officials seemed to be favoring the Irish. There was an 86-yard touchdown run called back on a Purdue clipping penalty that nobody could see in the game films later on.

Gone, mysteriously, was Notre Dame's brilliant offense, although quarterback Bob Williams did pass to Jim Mutscheller for one score in the third period and John Petitbon ran ten yards for another just as the final period opened. That made it 21-14 as the rain began to slice down the slopes of Notre Dame Stadium. Some people got excited, but Purdue was simply dominating the game. When Samuels threw to halfback Mike Maccoli on a pass play that covered 56, it was obvious that the victory streak would not hit 40 games. Leahy himself sat down on the bench, pulled his hat forward and bit his lips.

Afterwards the students milled around, talking among themselves and looking at the scoreboard. They did not know how to respond. No one had seen a Notre Dame defeat before, not even the seniors. The Irish had not been beaten since losing to Great Lakes Naval Training Station on December 1, 1945, when Leahy had been in the Navy. Only a 0-0 tie with Army and a 14-14 tie with Southern California had come in between. It was only the fourth loss Leahy had suffered in his entire eight-year coaching career. And the Irish had not been beaten at South Bend since 1942 when Michigan won 32-20. It was like the fall of the Roman Empire.

Some of them marched to the dressing room, where for all of their undergraduate lives they had set up a clamor for the winning Coach. Now they shouted for Leahy who finally came out and stood there in the rain, looking terribly noble in defeat as the water poured down over his hat and down the back of his heavy arctic coat.

"Gentlemen of Notre Dame and ladies who have accompanied them to today's football game," he began in utterly formal style, "defeat is inevitable. It must come eventually, no matter how hard you try to avoid it. I promise you this . . . we shall reciprocate against Purdue. Let us have no tears in defeat. Rather, let us show the world what Notre Dame gentlemen are made of."

Inside the press asked him to comment on the situation. This was a fine opportunity to strike back at the opposition. The timing is perfect. The football monster is breathing hard and bleeding from both nostrils. For once, he, Frank Leahy can represent himself as a humble loser. It has not happened often in the past decade.

"Once, coach Stu Holcomb pointed out an interesting thought," he said. "He told me that you cannot beat Notre Dame if you refuse to play them out of fear of losing. To me this is a most courageous attitude, one unshared by many other institutions of learning. I admire coaches that are willing to take a chance. I like the attitude, too, of Dale Samuels, the young gentleman who played so well against us today. He was quoted in the newspapers as saying that it was the dream of every young football player to either go to Notre Dame or to play against Notre Dame. That is a wonderful compliment to our athletic program. He said that one of the reasons that he was convinced he wanted to go to Purdue was that he knew he would be playing against Notre Dame. I can't help wishing, gentlemen, that he had chosen to play for us."

In one magnificent sweep, Francis William Leahy, the consummate coach, had turned a football defeat into an advertising campaign for his own personal integrity. He made a Purdue victory at South Bend seem like an endorsement of his own, renewed recruiting program. Other coaches reportedly hated him, mostly because he stayed one giant step ahead of them. Jealousy burns holes in a man's brain.

"On the long ride home to Long Beach that evening, two thoughts were running through my mind. Where had I failed, as a coach, in preparing for the game against Purdue? Certainly that had to be part of it. I couldn't blame the defeat on personnel problems. It was true that we had inexperienced juniors and seniors and a paucity of fine sophomores. But that couldn't be the whole answer. I told myself that if I were as great a coach as the newspapers said, I would have done something more with lesser talent.

"The second thing on my mind was the personal sadness at our first loss in five years. The pain was indescribable. I wondered if, perhaps, I was simply a creation of my own recruiting. Oooooh, could it be that I simply was sitting on top of a situation where fine young players went to Notre Dame because it was Notre Dame and not because they respected me as a coach or because I was an especially good coach. I suffered much self doubt that autumn . . . much self doubt."

It would grow worse. The Irish lost to Indiana, Michigan State and Southern California. They saved a tie with Iowa and ended up 4-4-1, close to the first losing season Notre Dame had seen in 17 years.

EPISODE 55

The story progresses from year to year until almost every Notre Dame player firmly believes that it happened the year he was a senior:

It is the morning of an important football game and Leahy is trying hard to figure out exactly how to motivate his team. Inspiration stikes him between the eyeballs. He charters a bus and takes everybody out to the cemetery where Rockne is buried. They kneel at the grave, Protestants and everybody. Suddenly, Leahy looks up and sees that two of his players (fill in the blanks according to the year you think it actually happened) are through at Rockne's grave and are praying at the burial place of George Keogan, a former Notre Dame basket-

ball coach. "Lads, lads," he shouts to the two wanderers, "we'll pray for Keogan during the basketball season." Maybe it did happen, although nobody, not even Leahy, can substantiate it. But it is part of the legend regardless of whether it was Creighton Miller or Lou Rymkus or Johnny Lattner at Keogan's grave. It sounds good and that is what Notre Dame is made of.

EPISODE 56

"The newspapers wrote so many unfair things. Oooooh, it was almost as if any rumor about Notre Dame was fair game for their pages," Leahy recalled. "They said that when Moose Krause became athletic director I was upset. It was not true. Running the department had become an incredible extra burden, one that I was anxious to be rid of. It was accurate that I wished to retain the title. But I wanted Moose to run the day-to-day affairs of the department. I expected that they would make him 'executive athletic director' or 'associate athletic director.' That was my idea. In fact, I insisted that he be moved up.

"It was also written that Father Hesburgh and I had some problems. He was faculty chairman of the athletic board and it was said that I angered him by making him wait outside my office while I watched football films and he was anxious to see me on some matter. I do not remember this ever happening. Knowing Father Hesburgh as I do, I would suspect that he would have called me to let me know his displeasure. There were many areas where we disagreed on athletic policy, but I don't think that I was ever discourteous to him at any time. He saw Notre Dame in one light and I saw it in another. But our objectives, I think, were the same. He never was one of the anti-football priests. I think he had an open mind on the subject.

"What distresses me is talk that Father Hesburgh somehow fired me. That never happened. It never did. He was one of the first to congratulate me on the 1952 season, which was probably the finest achievement of my entire life. It could have been one of Notre Dame's worst seasons. It could have been a total disaster. The schedule was finally tough enough to satisfy the worst of my enemies. It was the best job of pure coaching that I ever did and it helped me forget my worries that were left over from 1950 about my own possible incapabilities. The material was a year away from fruition. The schedule was far more difficult than anyone thought Notre Dame would have under Frank Leahy. Somehow, we survived.

"I knew that Our Lady was with us once more that season when Purdue fumbled eight times—the first eight times it had the ball. It was incredible. The best we could do was a 26-14 lead. When the Irish met Oklahoma that year, they put the game on television. It was the first really big television audience they had for a college football game. Somebody told me that it was 50 million afterwards. Notre Dame had just recently gone to the Oklahoma-style split-T offense, a modification of our original Chicago Bears system. They had one of the greatest backfields ever assembled, Eddie Crowder, Buddy Leake, Buck McPhail and Billy Vessells. Our backfield was just emerging, but it was, at its maturity, just as good, Ralph Guglielmi, Neil Worden, Joe Heap and Johnny Lattner. They were not quite ready. They were so close. Ooooh, they were as superb as the Four Horsemen in many ways.

"Lattner was an amazing football player. He made mistakes, oooooh, but how he hated to make them twice. He defeated Oklahoma neatly in what must be considered one of the great Notre Dame victories. The Oklahoma lads were undefeated. They were considered the year's national champions. And Notre Dame defeated them 27-21. I was embraced by a friend of mine, Fred Miller. I asked him, 'Have you ever wondered why I never took a job coaching professional football?' He asked me why and I told him, 'It is moments like this.' Jonathan Lattner was the key. Ooooh, he was better on defense than offense that day. He intercepted a pass and ran it back 27 yards that set up our second touchtown, the one that tied the score 14-14. When he came off the field I told him, 'You are a game saver and a credit to Our Lady.' Late in the game, when we were ahead, Jonathan Lattner made a recovery of one of our fumbles that was so important . . . soooooh, very important.

"That was a most brilliant season. We won games because of our defense and because of our alertness in keeping our mistakes from turning into disasters. That is an important part of coaching.

"Ooooh, we lost two games and tied another, but those lads produced. I believe that Dan Shannon should have received a letter from all eleven teams that we played. On defense, he was in the opponents' backfield more often than their players were. What a fine lad was Daniel Shannon. A dark Irish type, wild and reckless and one of the most enthusiastic players I ever had the pleasure of coaching. He was superb, especially in the final game of 1952. Notre Dame met Southern California—a team that was most bold about remaining on our schedule— and it was a heroic contest. The young men of Troy were undefeated, untied and already champions of their conference. They had scored in every game they played, but we shut them out by a 9-0 score. What a fine opponent USC was. On the occasions when we defeated them, their band gallantly saluted us with the Notre Dame Victory March, a most wonderful gesture, one that never failed to bring tears to my eyes. Our series with USC was most dear to me, a constant source of inspiration.

"I coached very hard and I worked far too hard. I found myself almost incapable of taking time off. I was treated in the off-season for nervous exhaustion and was ordered by doctors to relax in the off-season. This was most difficult. I could see my new seniors ripening into outstanding athletes. I was anxious to work with them. I rested for awhile. Our whole family took a vacation. I placed much of the recruiting in the hands of other coaches and remained away from the campus for several weeks before the preparation for spring training began. But it was not easy. In fact, it was more agonizing not being involved. I knew that this would be my greatest team and I was eager to begin assembling it."

EPISODE 57

"Lad, lad! Leap to your feet and resume the struggle for Our Lady,"—Frank Leahy, at a frantic Notre Dame practice shortly before the opening of the 1953 season.

"We can be proud of past glories, but we cannot rest in them. The worst attitude would be to assume that this is just

another hour, ushering in just another year in a history already 111 years old at Notre Dame. As this new page is unfolded, let each of us consciously reach for it and think what we shall write upon the page this year. Now, as for the matter of football . . . we shall never de-emphasize the sport so long as I am president of Notre Dame. Frank Leahy is a great credit to this institution."—Father Hesburgh, September 1953.

There were stories everywhere, in the *New York World-Telegram,* in the *Saturday Evening Post,* in the *Chicago Tribune,* that said that Francis William Leahy was in his final season at Notre Dame. Nobody paid much attention because that news had been reported so often before. They said that he was going to coach the Chicago Bears. It was on national radio. Harry Wismer said it and George Halas did not deny the possibility. What's more it seemed to make sense, even though Leahy insisted that he wanted to die on the bench at South Bend. His legend was now secure at Notre Dame. His identity was wholly separate from Knute Rockne's. He was handsome, hard-working to the point of ruining his health and the perfect Irish Catholic father.

His name brought forth an instant image now. There were those eight children grouped around (a) the Christmas tree (b) the hearth at the mansion he had purchased for $30,000 from an Oak Park, Illinois, Mafiosa or (c) the backyard swing. His eldest son, Frankie, had passed for 18 touchdowns and kicked 18 extra points for Campion-Prarie du Chien and made all-district as a quarterback.

"Your greatest coaching job is in your own house," he told columnist Hal Boyle of the Associated Press. "All Notre Dame football players are taught that when they meet a person they should look him in the eye, pronounce his name clearly and then address him as 'sir.' That is what my children are taught to do. I run the house much like a football team. About once every two weeks I line the children up and grade them on five points—neatness, courtesy, respectfulness, cooperation and unselfishness. Even Chrissy, the baby, and Mary, who is one-year-old, are included. We have eight children and we want more. I was never one to hold down the score, you know."

Confident that the Blessed Virgin was smiling down on him, Leahy opened the season with his finest football team. It could easily have entered the National Football League intact. The line was Dan Shannon, Frank Varrichione, Ray Lemek, Jim Scrader, Menil Mavraides, Art Hunter and Don Penza. A future all-Pro named Dick Szymanski did not even start. The backfield was Guglielmi, Heap, Worden and Lattner and Francis Wallace wrote, in *Saturday Evening Post*, if they were named All-America as a group hardly anyone in the country would complain, and he was right.

"I have tried to refrain from undue public optimism since I was coaching at Boston College," Leahy told Dave Condon of the *Chicago Tribune*. "I once professed an encouraging feeling about a game between BC and Florida. We pushed them all over the field and Florida won, 7-0.

"I swore I would never make that tactical blunder again. It was necessary to talk enthusiastically that fall. There was such an incredible furor over the so-called 'sucker shift' of the year before. Everyone grieved because Notre Dame went into a shift at the line of scrimmage against Southern California. Oooooh, it was a standard practice. It happened against us repeatedly and it was merely something that our players had to be aware of. We came out of the huddle and went into the T-formation. It was third down on USC's nine with three yards to go. So we pulled one of the oldest bits of deception in the book. Instead of snapping the ball, we shifted. The Trojans went offsides and we had a first down on their four and we scored.

"It was standard procedure and USC was aware of it. The school made no complaint, probably because the athletic department realized that their coach would have done the same thing to Notre Dame under the circumstances. The original genius at the sucker shift was Fritz Crisler. He invented it, perhaps, when he was at Princeton, although it probably goes back even further. He would have his teams shift deep in enemy territory and the referee would have to be quick to get in the 'one-thousand-one' count before the ball was snapped. When I was at Fordham, I happened to be scouting a game between Brown and Colgate in which coach [Andy] Kerr of Colgate did exactly the same thing. Afterwards, there was a near fight between Kerr and Dr. Eddie O'Brien who was refereeing the match.

"No one could have been more surprised than me when they suddenly made a big noise about it. The shift had been used before when a touchdown was needed against Oklahoma. It seemed at the time no one noticed or they treated it as part of the game. When it happened against USC, it became a raw issue. Notre Dame was not supposed to use means that other teams regularly used. By 1953, Notre Dame was supposed to be so far above the crowd that it would do nothing except show up for the game and take whatever tactics the other team wished to give out. Our style of 'tough play' was accused of being 'dirty play.' It was said that Coach Leahy looked the other way when his lads wanted to do something underhanded. I want you to know what we did when we discovered, in our films, that a lad was not upholding the honor of Our Lady by not playing decently.

"He would be called in and warned. He would be given a copy of our standard rules. If it happened again, oooooh, he would be brought in and chastised severely for his over-enthusiasm. If it persisted a third time, he would be asked to disassociate himself from our group. Dirty playing was cowardly playing and could not be tolerated."

EPISODE 58

The minutes of an historic meeting:

"On one occasion, I watched a posse of powerful brutes going through a scrimmage before a big Notre Dame game. Afterwards, I asked Leahy where he located such powerful specimens. My tribute to his recruiting skills seemed to offend him.

" 'We really have a small squad,' he said.

" 'Yeah,' I remarked, 'you've come up with a race of super midgets.'

"Football players come to Notre Dame in eager droves and 1953 is not any different from any other year. No other school in the country falls heir to such abundance. Leahy has the edge before the season starts. But he is not expected to lose; he must win, despite the presence of a harping throng of anti-football priests on the Notre Dame faculty. He is responsible for me correctly picking the score of the last Army–Notre Dame game. I met him in the corridor of the Oliver Hotel in South Bend on my way to Western Union to file my copy. He asked me what I thought the game would be like and I showed him my column.

" 'James, you will make yourself ridiculous. The lads are not capable of defeating the United States Military Academy by such a score,' he said.

"I took my pencil and corrected the score. He thought I had lowered the margin, but I had raised it by a touchdown.

"Your attitude convinces me," I said. "Notre Dame is seven points better than I thought.

" 'James,' Leahy said, 'you will regret this.' But the score was exactly what I made it. Any time that Frank Leahy admits that he has a team populated by cripples, dim-witted children and assorted humpty-dumpties, you can safely sit down and write that he won't be beaten all season."—Jimmy Cannon, the *New York Post*, September 6, 1953.

EPISODE 59

When Leahy came out of the closet and actually admitted that he might have one of the finer teams in the nation, opponents winced noticeably. They simply hoped that Notre Dame would take prisoners. In order, they rolled over Oklahoma, Purdue and Pittsburgh impressively as the coach ignored his promise to relax. The better the Irish did, the more his fragile new optimism faded. He became morose again. When Notre Dame flattened Purdue with an incredibly powerful infantry attack, he was back in mid-season form.

"I did not see a running back out there all afternoon," he confided to Tim Cohane, then the sports editor of *Look Magazine*.

"Don't know what game you were watching, Frank," said Cohane, waiting . . . just waiting . . . to see if Leahy was putting him on. "I saw a hell of a lot of them. Now I know you're going undefeated. You're agonizing again and you look just terrible. Those are both good signs for Notre Dame."

That evening, Leahy skipped his usual post-game conference with the coaching staff and asked Bob McBride to drive him home. There was a party at the villa in Long Beach, but the master of the house refused a drink. For a few moments, he moved through the rotunda of his home, being gracious with his guests. There were pains flashing through his chest and lower back. When it seemed proper, he explained that he was not as well as he might be and asked to be excused. Florence Reilly Leahy watched him leave with a confused expression on her face. It was not a typical move.

She assumed that he was concerned about the next week's game, against Georgia Tech, which hadn't been beaten in 31 starts. Still, Frank Leahy did not go to bed on important people and the house was jammed with them, alumni, priests and businessmen from Chicago. The game had originally been scheduled for Atlanta, but a couple of years earlier Leahy had decided to begin recruiting black athletes. With sweeping grand eloquence, he informed the press that he felt that he was missing something important because he was not privileged to coach lads who were either black or Jewish. The majority of his players were, of course, Catholic with usually a half dozen to a dozen Protestants on the squad.

In Vanderbilt, Pennsylvania, he found a halfback named Dick Washington and in Cannonsburg, not far away, he learned of a tackle named Wayne Edmonds who expressed a long standing desire to play football for Our Lady. Though neither was a starter, their presence was still an offense to southern mumbo-jumbo as it was practiced in the early years of the century's fifth decade. Having endured the mortification of having to tell Lou Montgomery that he was not welcome to play with Boston College in bowl games at New Orleans and Dallas, Leahy stubbornly refused to repeat the hardship. If Georgia Tech wanted to play Notre Dame, it could come to Indiana and meet the entire squad, Washington and Edmonds being a part of that squad.

"What I was forced to do with Louis was humilating, both to him and to me," Leahy said. "He showed much polish and class. But I swore it would never happen again."

With Leahy fretting mightily on the sidelines, the Irish took the opening kickoff and moved 80 yards for the game's first touchdown, scoring on a smash through the right side of the line by Worden. While the congregation of 58,254 went wild, while the Victory March rattled the October clouds, Leahy went back and slumped on the bench, his head down like a man at prayer. When the second period opened, he did a strange thing. He sent in the second unit. On the seven yard line, the replacement fullback, Tom McHugh, fumbled and Georgia Tech tackle Bob Sherman recovered. On the bench,

Leahy began to gasp for breath. Pains were beginning to knead the muscles in his chest. They grew steadily worse, until he gasped. One of his assistants, Bill Earley asked him what was wrong.

"Oh, just fatigue, William. I guess that's what it is," he said.

As the first half ended, Leahy tried to stand and he felt a severe restriction around his heart. He steadied himself for a minute and thought: "So this is what a heart attack is like." But he dismissed the thought and tried to trot off the field with his team. The pain grew worse and Earley had to help him the last few feet into the dressing room.

"For God's sake, Frank, are you all right," Earley shouted. "You look terrible. Let me get Doc Johns. He's somewhere in the stands."

For a few minutes, Leahy sat on a trunk scribbling notes about what he wanted to tell his players during the halftime talk. The pencil fell out of his hands. Laboriously, he picked it up and tried to write again. This time both the pencil and the notepad flopped on the cold concrete floor. Earley was outside having Dr. Nicholas Johns paged. Father Frank Cavanaugh had witnessed the entire scene of Leahy slumping off the field. When he heard the coach's private physician being paged, he sprinted toward an exit.

As Leahy reached down to pick up the pencil and pad, a dark curtain fell across his brain. He felt himself floating in a dark void. His mind flashed. He was either dead or dying. What an irony to die at halftime with a 7-0 lead over an undefeated team with the national championship at stake. Then he fell into total unconsciousness.

His eyes snapped open again. There he was stretched out on the trainer's table. Nearby, John McAllister was crying. Several football players stood in the doorway, their muddy cheeks stained by rivulets of tears. Good God, Leahy thought to himself, they've already started the wake.

With a great burst of naked will, Leahy managed to sit up. A resident character named Old Smitty had a bottle of raw hootch hidden somewhere in the Notre Dame dressing room. Suspecting a heart attack, the old man recognized that a shot of whiskey might be a vascular stimulant. He pushed a paper cup filled with it under Leahy's nose. The coach accepted feebly. The pain came back and Leahy slumped backwards. McAllister caught him before he fell. There was the figure of Rev. Edmund P. Joyce, vice president of Notre Dame and chairman of the athletic board. He was present to give Leahy the last rites. It would happen six more times in his life.

The others filed out of the room and the head football coach was anointed with oil. After awhile, he began to feel better. He tried to sit up again, only to feel Father Joyce's hands on his upper arms gently forcing him down again.

"Is the team still here, Father Joyce?" he asked.

"Be peaceful, Frank," said the priest. "It's the middle of the third quarter."

"Father!" said Leahy, trying to shout. "I've told my players never to quit on one another. Here I am quitting on them. I've got to get back out there. Where's Father Frank Cavanaugh? He'll help me."

Just before he became irrational, Dr. Johns slipped a hypodermic needle into his arm. Leahy grinned his crooked little grin and lapsed into sleep. As he drifted away from the stadium, he thought to himself, "I will never coach football again. Oh, God, what am I to do with the rest of my life?" Then he laughed to himself. He was probably dying anyway. The word was already raging through the stands. The great Frank Leahy had died of a fatal heart attack. It had happened to Notre Dame once again. He was nearly the same age as Rockne was when he perished in that wheat field. His record was almost the same. They were getting ready for another sentimental orgy at South Bend when the word was flashed: Frank Leahy was alive.

"Coaching burns out a man's insides," he recalled later. "It was more than tensions. Oooooh, it was far worse. I had so many chances to get back in coaching. The Texas A&M job was mine in 1957. I could have returned to Boston College the following year. It seemed that some school was always trying to bring me out of retirement. Oooooh, I loved to coach. I loved to teach young men the tenets I believed in so thoroughly. I felt I was doing something fundamentally good for my country . . . a country that had given me so much and asked so little.

"The pressure at Notre Dame was probably the heaviest in the country at the time. They kept saying in the administration that they did not mind if our team lost a few games. But Notre Dame had millions of followers all over the country. Our football team was a source of immense pride to Catholics everywhere. Most of them were second generation Americans who were just moving out of the slums and into positions of importance. There was still much anti-Catholic prejudice in America. That is why it always made me very pleased to run into a man who was obviously from an old line Protestant family who told me that he was a Notre Dame rooter. We were helping to break down barriers by our successes. I was always conscious of that fact. And there was the tradition of excellence. And . . . I hated to lose. It destroyed me a little inside to lose. I even hated tie scores. Oooh, football was a means to an end."

Assuming that their spiritual leader was either dead or dying, the Irish overcame a quick Georgia Tech tie in the score, 7-7, and went on to bury Georgia Tech 27-14 with the tears of vengeance in their eyes.

"It wasn't even necessary to say anything important at halftime. The players had tears streaming down their faces when they kicked off," said Earley. "I just asked them before we went out for the third period, 'Anyone want to win this one for The Coach?' They did. It was a beautiful moment."

It was not a heart attack, but a case of acute pancreatitis. One more might be fatal. It was caused by tension and a faulty diet. During those long hours of work, the ones that pleased Frank Leahy's soul, he drank soft drinks or milk from cartons. He ate sandwiches or heated cans of Campbell's tomato soup on a hot plate in his office. He was a candidate for diabetes. All of the ailments that would conspire to kill him before his 65th birthday were already present.

"Frank," said Florence Reilly Leahy the first time he could have visitors at St. Joseph's Hospital in South Bend, "you're going to have to get into a more relaxing form of work."

"Don't you tell me what I already know, Floss," he snapped. "Don't tell me. You've wanted this for a long time and now you've got it. I'm through and I guess I know it. You don't have to tell me."

The students gathered under his window, just as they had gathered for the dying George Gipp. They cheered him with the school's sophomoric, but emotional, "He's a man! He's a man! He's a real Notre Dame man!" The record shows that Frank Leahy wept real tears and turned his head into his pillow.

EPISODE 60

A twice-told tale that seems plausible under the circumstances:

It is late in the afternoon of a singularly important Notre Dame practice. Frank Leahy has come tottering back from the hospital. His outside activities have all been cancelled until he regains his health. He still has an undefeated football team which has been coached, generally, by three of his finest assistants. Next on the schedule is Iowa and tackle Frank Varrichione, whose name will live in infamy, is by himself on a distant patch of Cartier Field. He is, allegedly, practicing the art of faking injuries. He is rolling on the turf, feigning a badly stretched knee. Leahy comes up to him and looks down for the longest moment in Notre Dame history.

"Aaaah, no, lad," he says. "Better make it total unconsciousness."

It may even have happened, just the way everybody says it did. Like most Notre Dame fables, nobody took the name of witnesses.

EPISODE 61

Now the stars have become irrevocably crossed. The fates are conspiring against Frank Leahy with a vengeance. It is November 22, 1953, and life will never quite be the same again. Having survived the hurricane that arose over the sucker shift of the year before, Leahy is about to go into life's long, agonizing decline. One miscalculation will serve to discredit him until the moment of his death. Had he either died at halftime of the Georgia Tech game or taken the wrong airplane to Los Angeles, he would have been preserved intact, a total piece of the Notre Dame legend.

Faking injuries to stop the clock date back to the first time Princeton played Rutgers in 1869. It is a largely winked-at piece of brigandage used by every man who has ever been the head coach of a college football team. It is a recognized piece of semi-legal cheating, similar to phantom double plays in baseball where the second baseman does not actually touch the bag on the pivot. As long as he's close, the umpires never complain. But Frank Leahy, who has been scrambling all his life, right from the morning he woke up in a board-sided tent in Winner, South Dakota, doesn't realize that nature has exalted him. He must now be above suspicion, But a hustler cannot stop hustling.

All afternoon Leahy tormented himself on the sidelines, walking back and forth, kicking the turf and, at one point, stomping in the crown of his hat. Iowa dominated play throughout a miserably cold, but sunshine-drenched afternoon. Just before the end of the first half, with the ball on the Hawkeyes' 12 yard line, Leahy made a blunder. Only two plays earlier, the Irish, who were behind, 7-0, at the time, were informed that they had used up all of their timeouts. Now they desperately needed help. It was time for Varrichione's act, standard operating procedure, of course.

As he turned to go back to the huddle, he let out a terrible scream, clutched his back and fell on the turf like a fighting bull who had just been given the *coup de grace* by the matador. It fooled nobody. But the officials were obligated to call a special time out while Varrichione was led off the field whimpering. Up stepped Guglielmi and passed 12 yards to his end, Dan Shannon, in the Iowa end zone. This was one of the first major sporting events to be sent back live to a closed-circuit television audience. The 3,700 people at the Marborough Theater in Chicago laughed uproariously as Varrichione left the field at the half, acting as if he'd never been battered beyond recognition.

With six seconds left in the ball game, Shannon, who had come into the game at right end, rather than at left where he normally played, because Don Penza was injured, caught a nine yard pass from Guglielmi and Notre Dame had brought off a 14-14 tie that literally became the most famous non-victory, non-defeat in the school history.

Leahy leaped to his feet when Shannon caught his second

touchdown, took his crumpled hat off his head and paraded around the Irish bench, smiling and doing a pseudo-jig. Up in the press box they were getting ready to make a big deal out of Varrichione's act. Leahy had just given the anti-football faction a reason to believe that they might eventually get some peace and quiet. They were going to get rid of the most successful coach in the country and do it gracefully, if not graciously.

Afterwards, Varrichione continued to act beautifully. Reporters, who saw him play all but a few minutes of the second half, were amazed to see how healthy he appeared, not an ache anywhere in his massive body. He moved free and happy.

"No use asking questions, because I'm not going to talk about it," he mumbled.

"Don't you think feigning an injury to stop the clock was using your head?" a writer asked. "Or was that play sent in from the bench?"

"I'm not saying nothing," said Varrichione, embarrassing Our Lady's English department.

"The press corps saw you get up after the play just completed, look at the score board and then start screaming and hold your back when you saw that there were only two seconds left before the half," asked Irving Vaughn of the *Chicago Tribune*. "Were you really hurt?"

"What do you think?" said Varrichione, attempting to close all debate on the subject.

In a nearby locker stall, Johnny Lattner listened carefully to a reporter's question. Was Varrichione faking? Lattner nodded his head for a second and said, "Pretty smart thinking, wasn't it?" Nobody felt especially ashamed. Nobody felt damned to hell fires. It was simply part of the code. Leahy had done nothing inconsistent in their eyes. It was Monday before anybody realized that a grievous sin had been committed against the entire moral structure of the nation. Notre Dame had cheated . . . or something.

The papers were filled with vigorous assaults upon Leahy, his character and the basic objectives of the University he represented with such a passion. Only a few people actively supported him, although there was that one Iowa player who admitted to a reporter that he was his team's designated fainter.

There was one on every squad, he said. And Cal Hubbard, the former All-America tackle turned major league umpire, insisted that he was amazed by it all.

"Hell, where do they get off trying to give credit to Leahy?" he asked a man from the *Chicago Daily News*. "I thought I invented that play 30 years ago when I was at Geneva College. They've all been stealing it ever since. Nothing's sacred anymore, not even the good old fainting play."

Leahy was not well served by Iowa coach Forest Evasheski who wrote a snide little poem for the school newspaper: "When the one great scorer comes to write against your name, it's not whether you won or lost, but how you got gypped at Notre Dame." It was not supposed to be even mildly funny. Then the story got around that Leahy had been training the family dog to dash out onto the field to stop the clock. The signal was to be when the coach dropped his hat. Damned if the dog wasn't progressing nicely at the time. Now all the resentment festered. What could have been dismissed, as a bit of wry subterfuge was treated like perfidy in the face of sincere moral obligation.

The letters began to rise in Father Joyce's office. Some of them went straight through to Father Hesburgh, who looked at them unhappily. He sent a note to his adjutant. "This has become a problem that is rapidly growing out of hand," he said and he could have meant nobody else but Frank Leahy when he said "problem." He asked Father Joyce for a proper solution.

The alumni howled in self-righteousness. A sampling:

"Dear Father Joyce:
As a Catholic, my religion has always taught me that the end justifies the means and as a sportsman, the important thing to me was not who won the game, but how it was played. Clearly, I feel Notre Dame was in error. Notre Dame has always been regarded as the number one football institution in the United States. As such, it must be above reproach. Its reputation has definitely been damaged by the conduct of the Notre Dame team in the game against Iowa. I cannot help but feel that it is only fitting and proper for Notre Dame to forfeit the game to Iowa and to publicly censure coach Leahy, just as he was censured last year for his "sucker shift" by the NCAA.

I'm sure that the school's many fans throughout the country would regard Notre Dame in a better light for taking this action."—John A. Andresen, Flushing, Long Island.

"Dear Father Hesburgh:

As a spectator at many of Notre Dame's sporting events during the past years, I feel it my duty to write to you regarding the recent Notre Dame–Iowa football game, which I witnessed. I will not argue with coach Leahy about faking an injury being within the rules, but I do feel that it is morally bad. Sports are fine and Notre Dame is unquestionably one of the finest and most religious schools in the entire country and therefore should set an example to the rest of the nation for clean, good and morally fine sportsmanship. So very sorry, I, as well as many other fans, cannot condone coach Leahy's tactics in the Iowa game."—Mrs. J. M. McCurdy, Goshen, Indiana.

"Reverend Father Joyce:

Frequently at Sunday Mass we are instructed to remember our important function as ambassadors of the Catholic Church. We are told that our example is more important than the words of our priests, since we come into daily contact with so many who never visit ours or, indeed, any church. We are told that we, the laymen, make the church's reputation. I would suggest then that you issue a statement saying, 'We deplore the unfortunate incident that occurred in the heat of last Saturday's game and let the score stand, 14-7, in your favor.' I am interested only in protecting the honor of my school."—Gene Sullivan, Kennedyville, Maryland.

"Dear Father Joyce:

After Saturday's shameful exhibition of low morality and disgraceful sportsmanship on the part of your football team against Iowa, your University won a tie on the football field but lost its sacred honor across the nation and the world. So much, all of it bad, can be said about Saturday's blockout of ethics and morality. And if that wasn't enough, the customarily modest and self-effacing coach Leahy, before a nationwide television audience, had the nauseating bad taste to declare that of all the teams he had ever coached, Saturday's team and its fighting performance were the greatest of all. I think he's sick. Better get him some help."—S. J. Be'Hannessey, Chicago, Illinois.

"Dear Father Hesburgh:

Despite the fact that I am Catholic and a good Hoosier as well—and proud of both—won't you agree that this was a low blow. What was your lineman trying to prove when he feigned an injury against Iowa? If coach Frank Leahy is such a moral man, how could he have done such a thing? Is he a hypocrite? Surely, he must be. This loophole in the regulations must be plugged immediately and Notre Dame should lead the way, first by forfeiting the game as a gesture of good faith and secondly by leading the movement at the next rules committee for a change. You were outplayed by Iowa and you did not deserve a tie."—Jack A. Larsh, Chicago, Illinois.

"Dear Father Joyce:

Varrichione's feigned injury may have helped Notre Dame stave off a defeat, but if this type of sportsmanship is condoned by the school or the coaching staff, Notre Dame has lost more than a football game. I went to South Bend to see my Alma Mater play a good game, but the obvious dishonesty in the closing minutes left a sick feeling on my part. Father, doesn't football policy and attitude need to be reviewed? If character building is to be more than fine words to be printed in football programs, must not the university retain its integrity and intellectual honesty? Johnny Lattner spoke admiringly of Varrichione's quick thinking. After hearing that, I wonder if honesty and fair play aren't both out-moded."—Frank H. Simpson, Wilmette, Illinois.

They did not permit Leahy to go west with his team to the Coliseum in Los Angeles where the Irish dismantled Southern California by a 48-14 score. When the Notre Dame team returned to South Bend to complete an undefeated schedule by whipping Southern Methodist, 40-14, the students—perhaps sensing that something important was happening—came pouring out of the stands. This was Frank Leahy's final game as a coach. They did not know it. They did not particularly care that alumni and administrators were beginning to wonder if he hadn't suffered an emotional as well as a physical breakdown. They ringed him in increasing numbers until there was a thundering crowd surrounding him. They lifted him up on their shoulders, cheering him without loving him. The ride ended at the dressing room. Gallantly, Leahy rose up on the steps to address the crowd. They hardly paid any attention to his words. They simply roared every time he opened his mouth. Rockne had brought the students warmth and recognition. Leahy brought them perfection. They appreciated it, even if their elders didn't. But Francis William Leahy was sinking fast and nothing could save him. He was on a collision course with disaster. Even his old friends with the Boston newspapers were looking at him from a strangely different posture.

EPISODE 62

For several weeks, even as they were taking the picture around the Christmas tree, Frank Leahy pondered his fate. His doctors told him that he was heading for a total and immediate physical and emotional collapse if he did not approach his work from a less aggressive attitude. Not once did they give him a strict ultimatum to either quit coaching or die. They simply suggested that he stop coaching quite so hard. Since he could not run the Notre Dame football team in any other manner, he confused one possibility with the other. There was grim talk that the anti-football faction was closing in on him.

With the bowl games over, he went to Cincinnati where the Scripps-Howard newspaper chain was having a dinner for Jim Tatum of Maryland, who had gone undefeated and been named coach of the year. There was going to be a half-hour national television show. hosted by Joe Williams, columnist for Scripps-Howard's *New York World-Telegram,* and Leahy decided that it might not be a bad idea to get on it and explain what had happened in the Iowa game. He was a nervous man, greatly confused over what was happening to him. The sun was setting on his coaching career and he hardly behaved like a man who was getting ready to give in to his doctors and resign.

"Certainly," said Williams, "we'd love to have you on the show. I'll tell you what I'll do. I'll file a little story for my paper saying that you are going to explain what happened and what Notre Dame's position is on such matters."

"That would be excellent, Joseph," he said. "I would appreciate that opportunity greatly. I am working on my little talk right now. I would also like to add some sort of inspirational message to high school football players in there someplace."

"We'll see about that," said Williams. "I'll have to look at your script before you go on. Bring it down to my room and give me a look at it."

"Yes, Joseph," said Leahy. "I trust that you, aaaah, will do right by the old coach."

When Joe Williams looked at the speech, which had been written on the back of a Notre Dame program, he realized that Leahy would be on the air for more than eight minutes and much of what he wanted to say was mere bombast. So he sat down and revised it so that it would stay strictly to the incident at the Iowa game and would run under four minutes.

Leahy was to say the following:

"Thank you, Joe. It's awfully nice to be here. My congratulations to you coaches for your excellent judgment in naming my good friend Jim Tatum of Maryland as coach of the year. And, of course, my warmest congratulations to you Jim. You did a tremendous job in carrying your team through ten games without a defeat and all of us are very proud to join in this salute to you and your great team tonight.

"Now, gentlemen, I feel this is an appropriate occasion to touch upon a matter which has given me great concern and distress. I refer to stopping the clock in a football game, a loophole in the rules which can be exploited in an emergency situation. I need not tell you that I now have good reason to wish that this loophole never existed.

"Feeling as I do, I am anxious to see that something is done about it. As you all know, stopping the clock in football is an old practice. Just last night Joe Williams had a story in one of the Cincinnati papers in which he told of seeing Yale do this very thing against Princeton back in the middle-30s. All coaches can recount scores of similar instances. We all know that, under the rules, it is perfectly legal. Now it is time for us to agree that, legal or not, it isn't the sporting thing to do. I can assure you gentlemen I have been giving this matter a great deal of thought.

"One of the conclusions I have reached is that it would be a good idea to do something to protect us coaches from ourselves. If there is any practical way that the prevention of faking injuries to stop the clock can be put in words, then the rules committee should do it. If there isn't, I suggest that we, as men of good will and as coaches, take a personal vow that it can't or won't ever happen as long as we are connected with football. This should apply to high school coaches as well as college coaches.

"Frankly, I would prefer to see this problem handled among ourselves on a gentleman's agreement basis; but in any case, we must take some sort of deterrent action. We must keep in mind that our responsibility to the boys is becoming greater and greater. Today we get boys who are better disciplined, better mannered and who have a greater sense of responsibility. They understand the difference between right and wrong. It's certainly up to us to set the finest example possible. This much, gentlemen, I can faithfully assure you: No member of the Notre Dame football team will ever resort to such tactics again. Thank you for hearing me out on this matter."

After Leahy had left the room, a network executive looked at the script and asked Williams what he thought. The executive was plainly in great distress.

"It's weak and hypocritical," said the columnist. "That isn't the Frank Leahy I've known so long. He acts like he's afraid of something. He's running scared and I'm sorry as hell to see it."

In his hotel room, Leahy prepared himself for his television appearance. The telephone rang. It was Father Joyce who had seen the story in the *New York World-Telegram*. His tone of voice was not soothing.

"I must insist that you not make this speech unless it is approved by the administration, Frank," he said. "Would you please read it to me."

Leahy looked at his longhand notes and tried to make them sound like something over the long distance connection to South Bend. He failed. There was a long pause. Finally, Father Joyce found the proper words.

"That can only compound an already serious situation," he said. "I must officially ask you, Frank, not to go on Joe Williams' television show. I do not care what it does to the program. I'm not interested in what happens to Joe Williams or what his problems are. My only concern is the University . . . and you, too, of course. I must forbid it."

It was necessary now to call Williams and explain that a "higher authority" at Notre Dame had made the decision. Somehow Leahy made it sound as if Our Lady had called down from the Golden Dome Herself. Drained of all emotion, Leahy sat in his hotel room feeling centuries old and half dead. This was his one feeble attempt at ransoming his honor and it had failed. When he returned, his wife met him and asked him how it was. "It's all over, Floss," he said. "Whatever it was that was working before, isn't working any more. I fear that I will not be the head coach of football much longer at the University of Our Lady. I am back where I started when I left Fordham." The depression lasted for many days and grew darker and deeper.

Suddenly the thunder stopped. It happened just like that. There was no sabbatical year offered. There was every indication that many people connected with the University would be just as happy to read of his resignation. No one rose to stop him. Nobody truly wanted to fire him, but it was made explicit that if he quit, it might be the best thing. Leave-takings are ugly at best. "Floss," he said, after hearing that Father John Cavanaugh stood with Father Hesburgh in his willingness to accept a resignation for health reasons, "Notre Dame is, aaaaah, bigger than any of us. We must remember that." Even though his very soul hurt, he departed. There was a press conference with Father Hesburgh present. It was very sad and very sentimental, typically Notre Dame.

When it was over, he jumped into a car that Frank, Jr., was driving. They circled the campus, driving past St. Mary's Lake, past the grotto, past the church. Then they stopped under the Golden Dome. With a gesture stolen from a 1938 movie, Frank Leahy got out of the car and stood once more in front of Our Lady. He bowed his head, prayed and then turned to offer a kiss. Then, he was gone from Notre Dame.

He had said the right thing. He had, once again, been gracious under pressure. "I have reached a point where the state of my health frightens me at times and since tension seems to be my greatest peril, I must leave football," he had told the newspapermen. Leahy had reminded his lads that it was necessary to "pay the price in sweat, effort and sacrifice and to strive for perfection in each day's drill. When looking in a mirror, take a critical attitude rather than one of self-admiration. Remember that egotism is the anesthetic which deadens the pain of supidity. Remember this, lads, never, never, never give up. It is too easy to quit, to lie down and say that you are defeated. Go out and win one more victory for Our Lady. I am leaving as head football coach at Notre Dame . . . but I will never leave Notre Dame. Farewell and thank you."

EPISODE 63

It was over and there was nothing but silence. Oh, occasionally, the telephone rang and quite often it was necessary for Frank Leahy to drive to Chicago for a business conference. There were more offers than he could honestly cope with. Floss sat on the arm of his chair, posed for pictures and said the right things. The play-acting was brilliant and nobody doubted that it was anything but true. Leahy was going into the insurance business with his brother Tom. In Chicago, he was going to work on a syndicated sports show with Billy Sullivan; and in Boston, he was going to be public relations director for a major steel firm. Surely, all of those important alumni and noteworthy Notre Dame lovers would provide for him. He was in his early 40s and his career as a businessman was just starting. Maybe he'd coach again, someday.

It was the day after the resignation when Gene Kessler came down from the *Chicago Sun-Times*. He recorded a charming playlet. Floss was absolutely radiant. She moved around the living room like a bird.

"I'm glad for Frank," she said. "He looks so relieved and healthy again—now that he's made the decision. When he took the job at Boston College years ago, he said that nothing important had ever happened to him. He said he hadn't accomplished anything. Well, now he's done it all and they'll always remember him as being Rockne's equal. That's what he wanted. This is so much like it was back in 1941 when we kept waiting around to see if Notre Dame was going to call. Now, we're waiting to see if Frank made the right move."

Leahy put a telephone back in its cradle and slumped in a green lounging chair. "I'm better already," he said. "Say, Gene, there were two factors that dictated my resignation. One was my health. The other was whether the administration at Notre

Dame would take it well. I had two years to go on my contract. But they were great. They set up scholarships for my five sons. Isn't that wonderful. Oooooh, what other school would do such a thing? It was a great thrill when they did that. I am quite content that I will do well in the business world. Quite content."

The conversation dragged. Kessler fell on standard questions. What had been Leahy's biggest thrill during his long association with Notre Dame. A smirk rippled across Leahy's lips.

"Aaaah, you will find this most unusual and most amusing, Gene," he said. "While on submarine duty in the South Pacific, I went on patrol on a native island where few outsiders had ever set foot. The savage-looking horde was enough to scare any well-meaning visitor, but, to my great relief, they were most hospitable, most gracious.

"When the inspection was over, the king of the island had the children assemble and sing songs for the departing visitors. After several lusty renditions, the native guide waved his arms for silence and proudly announced to the Americans that the next number would be from something called a Victrola. A half-hundred naked urchins drew deep breaths and awaited their leader's cue. And then, thousands of miles from the Golden Dome, on this wind-swept, God-forsaken atoll came the familiar refrain . . . 'Cheer, cheer for Old Notre Dame, wake up the echoes cheering her name, send a volley cheer on high, shake down the thunder from the sky.' I stood there weeping."

Once again, right there in his living room, even as Father Hesburgh was selecting a 25-year-old philosophy major to replace him, Francis William Leahy wept again. A telegram had come that morning from Red Blaik, congratulating Floss on defeating Frank's mistress—the University of Notre Dame. It was a nice gesture, but it wasn't true, it wasn't true.

EPISODE 64

The wind was coming up on Lake Oswego, whipping the water to a soft meringue. Along the shore, old black men bent over on the piers, their fishing lines swirling in the foaming confusion. It was growing dark and Frank Leahy paused while another cassette was placed in the tape recorder. He paused a while and then recalled old wounds. They still hurt.

"When it was over, I honestly felt free to answer the critics," he said, pulling the corners of an ancient plaid bathrobe around his neck. "I felt no true remorse at the feigned injury thing against Iowa. They had done the same thing to us two years earlier. In that 27-20 victory over Southern Methodist, they had feigned injuries not once, but three times. They were so realistic that their fans booed us for dirty play. With two seconds to go in our memorable 27-21 win over Oklahoma, one of the Sooners sprawled on the turf as if he had been hit between the eyes with a two-by-four. They wanted to get off one more pass. It didn't work, but nobody accused Bud Wilkenson of cheating. In 1952, we lost a game to Pitt when one of their players did the same thing. I never heard anyone defending Notre Dame.

"Rock used to say that it was important to have a man who was truly capable ready to replace the man who faked the injury. As for the sucker shift . . . well, they censured Frank Leahy for that. But we got the idea from Pitt. They pulled us off five times in our 1952 game. When I decided that it was time for us to use it, the maneuver suddenly became the Notre Dame sucker shift. Good God! I stole it from Pitt!"

On the lake, with the sun a screaming red in the west, a lonely mallard lifted out of the water with a piece of food in his mouth. He headed toward a copse of pines burning bright in color, silhouetted against the sun. At the last minute, he dropped the food. For awhile he circled frantically, looking for what he had lost. Then he streaked off into the sunset and was seen no more.

"Just like a football coach," said Leahy. "Just like a football coach."

The tape spun on relentlessly, catching every noise.

PART THREE
THE FINAL WEEK

EPISODE 1

Oblivious to the warmth of the early morning sunshine, Francis William Leahy, dressed in a faded, out-dated flannel robe, pushed back in his reclining chair and slipped an insulin needle into his arm. In addition to everything else that was assaulting his body and stealing his life, his diabetes had grown far worse. Instead of going to a charity dinner in Chicago, which they had named in his honor, he was forced to spend the weekend in St. Vincent's Hospital. The doctors said that he might call the banquet hall long distance and address the gathering, but for no more than ten minutes. His eldest son, Frank, Jr., or Frank-Junior, which is what everybody called this famous man's child, running it together just that way, represented him at the head table. That wasn't quite good enough. Somebody might have gotten the impression that The Coach was dying. So he summoned up a burst of strength.

With masterful skill, he spoke for nearly an hour, expressing his gratitude, greeting the honored guests, speaking sternly about the moral decay threatening to sweep his America over the precipice, telling stories about his days at Notre Dame, recalling Rockne, talking in such great detail about major league baseball that Chicago White Sox manager Chuck Tanner was shocked at his grasp of another man's game.

Finally, with a weary salute and an invocation of God's blessings, he had reluctantly said goodbye. They brought him home from the hospital in an obviously decaying state. For the first time, Francis William Leahy could begin to see the possibility of his own immediate death. It was not that he had stopped struggling to stay alive, to spread his message, to help save this Great American Ethic that he so fearfully felt was perishing. He was simply facing up to a stern and awful reality. Here was a man who had seen every game his powerful Notre Dame teams were scheduled to play as a potential defeat and yet his optimism about his victory over the grave was a total contradiction. Now his firmness was beginning to fade.

He was on the telephone, dialing weakly, missing a number,

cursing himself and starting over again. In the kitchen, his wife, Floss, was straining to find an acceptable diet lunch.

"Use a menu that has ice cream in it," he yelled.

"Aw, Frank," she said, her voice still haunted by a Brooklyn accent, "you know you can't have ice cream. It's not on the list."

"Make me a lunch with ice cream, anyway," he said, testily as if he were talking to a fullback from Delphi, Indiana.

The day before he had called the man who was taping his biography and asked him not to wait until mid-July to finish the project. This newest disability, he thought, might be his ruination. The writer and his wife had flown from San Francisco to Portland on the first coastal flight. Now he was calling his secretary at Canteen Corp. headquarters in San Jose, asking for some pictures he had in his files.

"Aw, Frank," said Floss, "I got all that junk up from our storeroom."

"Junk?" he shouted. "Junk! That's what you always thought of my coaching career, don't lie to me."

"Junk was just a word I used, Frank," she said. "I'm the one who saved all these clippings and pictures all these years. Why don't you think of that? If it wasn't for me they'd all be gone. I was a one-woman clipping bureau. All the places we've moved, it's a wonder we still have them. Why aren't you ever grateful for anything I do?"

Out in the kitchen, Floss Leahy leaned against the counter and lit a cigarette, puffing on it nervously. She shook her head.

"These last few weeks he's been terribly emotional," she said, softly. "He seems to sense something, like time finally running out on him. He's grouchy. He keeps talking about things he wants to do next year and the year after. He even gets teary. Can you imagine Frank Leahy getting teary? It's true and it would shock his ex-players and all the writers who thought he was a cold mackerel.

"Lately, he's been getting so strange acting. He's always been funny about whether we were wasting food. Oh, he was generous about everything else. Always wanted me to have the best clothes. But he had this funny thing about food. The other day when he returned from his last speaking engagement I caught him down on the floor, looking at the cat's dish to see if I was giving the cat some food we could have eaten. This diet is killing him by inches. He likes his ice cream and his

292

occasional beer. He talks like nature was stealing the last two things he really enjoyed."

The evening before, the Rev. Theodore Hesburgh, the Notre Dame president who did not protest when Frank Leahy resigned from his last coaching job, made a special visit to Lake Oswego Apartments. There was not even the mildest hint of animosity or rancor. Whatever had gone before was totally obscured now by the mists of time. It was like a visit from the Holy Father himself. Few men get to be head football coach at Notre Dame. Few men get to be president of the school. They spoke of many things, even social conditions, arch-liberal cohabiting with ultra-conservative. It had been an extremely warm meeting, a tying-up of long forgotten loose ends. As Father Hesburgh left, he and Leahy embraced. It was a thoroughly unexpected gesture on the part of two undemonstrative men.

They walked together to the parking lot, Leahy wobbling on his arthritic legs and Father Hesburgh moving with firmness and authority. They commented on how unusual it was to find such staggering heat in the midst of a normally rain drenched Oregon summer. Then they said farewell. It was Frank Leahy's last living touch with Notre Dame.

"As ever," said Leahy, "it was a pleasure to see Father Hesburgh . . . a most gracious man."

"Aw, Frank," said Floss, laughing, "if you died and went to hell you'd describe the devil as being 'a most gracious man.' Who are you trying to kid?"

She laughed and retreated to the kitchen. Leahy glared. Then he went back to thumbing through his clippings. He snickered when he saw himself standing there in a Notre Dame uniform again, looking younger than he could ever remember looking. His eyes began to fill with tears and suddenly he was starting to tell the story of Rockne's 1927 locker room speech again. His voice changed and he seemed to be looking straight into the past. The words came faster and faster. Gone was Leahy's own Victorian phrasing. In its place was Rockne's machine gun style. As he reached the point where all fine young Catholic gentlemen were exhorted to go out and win the game for George Gipp, he sat straight up in the reclining chair.

Afterwards, the writer remarked it was an eerie feeling to

watch Leahy slip into the character of Rockne, as if moments in time suddenly came together.

"Awww," said Floss, laughing, "Frank's done that so many times he thinks he *is* Rockne."

EPISODE 2

In the evening, Leahy poked restlessly at a piece of unsalted chicken, which he had obviously rejected on sight. He grumbled about the disastrous lack of ice cream and then pushed the whole meal away. With a shaky hand, he asked to start the tape recorder again.

Halfway through a story about his Chicago sports show, the one that won an Emmy in 1966, he stopped and looked straight at the man who had been asking him questions. Something was troubling him.

"What do you think of Mr. Nixon and this Watergate . . . this Watergate . . . well, this Watergate thing?" he asked.

"Well," said the writer, "if he knew about and let it happen, I'm afraid the President of the United States is dishonest. If he didn't know about it and his assistants set it up, then I'm afraid that he's a poor administrator and subject to severe scrutiny by the public."

"Ooooooh, yes," said Leahy, deeply pained. His Republicanism had been severely wounded. "I am afraid that I have come to the same conclusion. It hurts me that a man who should have been so good for America could get so deeply involved in something so, ah, dishonest. I find it hard to believe that moral decay has gone so far. This is what happens when a society becomes too permissive. I have warned many audiences about this."

He slumped back on his bed and drew a long, labored breath.

"You know I played golf with Mr. Nixon on several occasions. I found him most pleasant. Quite a gracious man. I find this hard to believe."

Into the apartment bounced Frank-Junior, a pony-faced man with quick eyes and a scar rippling across his upper lip. All his life, he has been battling to be his own man. He has done everything to establish himself as his own man. Life has placed him in the awkward position of having to run away from his father when he doesn't actually want to. Frank-Junior hustles for a living, selling stocks and bonds, broadcasting small college football. He moved to Portland to get away from being Frank Leahy's oldest son. Several months later, his father followed him and bought a big house on the hill overlooking Lake Oswego. Just for the pure pleasure of it, he coached a minor league team in Portland. One evening he turned around on the bench and there was one of the two greatest college football coaches of all time marching toward him. It was not Knute Rockne.

"Gotta talk to my dad," he said, excusing himself. "I'm trying to straighten out some of his financial affairs. They are incredible. He thinks he's a great financial genius, but he can't even read a stock prospectus. I give him books on finance and he never touches them. I went through some of his files not long ago and I found uncashed checks dating back to 1952. There was one for $1,000 from a magazine that has long since gone out of business."

The bedroom door closed and Frank-Senior and Frank-Junior talked loudly for several minutes over some complicated stock deal the younger man was proposing. It is a fact that no member of the Leahy family prides himself on his ability to modulate his voice. The door opened and the elder Leahy, his face growing more and more yellow, shuffled forward and excused himself for the night. He was tired and there was nothing more in his head for him to say, no memories to recall, no anecdotes to relate, no football games to recount.

In the smothering heat of the patio, Frank-Junior leaned against the railing and expressed real fear for his father. Tough man, he said, absolutely unwilling to die. But now the son was willing to set a limit: Six months and no more. The battle had to end sometime. Funny thing was that Frank-Junior couldn't envision life without Frank-Senior. They had been father and son, antagonist and protagonist and, to the rest of the family, father and deputy-father. Frank-Junior had been the number one assistant coach at home. His father got him a driver's license illegally at age 14 and told him to take care of his mother and the rest of the children while he went out to batter every college football team on the schedule.

"Funny thing was that I could have played at some small college or, maybe, even at a medium-sized one," he said. "But I had to go to Notre Dame. Now Terry Brennan didn't want any part of me. I wasn't big enough and he was having enough heat without having Frank Leahy, Jr., on his team. I held for extra points and that sort of thing. I kicked some field goals in practice and finally I quit and played hall football. They have this fantastic intramural program at Notre Dame and I was switched to halfback and I had a fine season. A fellow from Marquette came by and told me I was wasting my time. He said I could start for them. So I told Dad I was switching. He looked at me and said, so cold you couldn't believe I was his son: 'Change your name.' He didn't want Frank Leahy, Jr., playing for Marquette. So that took care of that."

It was good, he said, that his father and the Rev. Theodore Hesburgh had been given the opportunity to talk once more. It made a difference, cleared away a lot of the wreckage of the past. It was a nice gesture on Hesburgh's part, Frank-Junior decided.

"The last year at Notre Dame there was a lot of friction between Dad and certain of the priests," he said. "I was a senior in high school and worried about my football career, but I knew that certain priests were barred from the practice field and Dad was barred from the administration building.

"Dad will never say this but after they cut down his scholarships, he went out and raised $50,000 from his group of elite alumni. He got the money from Frank Scobie, Fred Miller, Henry Alberman, big Notre Dame supporters like that. Notre Dame had got this reputation for being a football factory and a lot of the intellectual priests just didn't like it. There wasn't any more hanky-panky at Notre Dame than there was at most schools and, actually, with Dad being something of a prude there was a whole lot less. Notre Dame was a damn good Catholic school and after the war, the money rolled in. There was more outside help available than Dad could use. Hesburgh saw Notre Dame win three out of four national championships and finish second the year they didn't win. He wanted to make the school a 'Catholic Harvard.'

"Hesburgh could never see how he could make Notre Dame a Catholic Harvard as long as the school had the reputation of being a football factory. Who was to blame for that? Well,

Frank Leahy was and he had to go. There was a deep philosophical difference between Dad and the Hesburgh faction. He never wanted to be humiliated as he was in 1950 when he went 4-4-1 and wasn't going to let it happen.

"Dad just plain got fanatic. He wasn't going to let it happen. He was more determined than ever to build a dynasty. It couldn't happen. He went to illegal summer practices. He *did* do it, you know. When they okayed freshmen to make up for the Korean War's drain on manpower, he brought in 22 freshmen. If they couldn't go to summer school he told them, 'Forget it, we don't want you, go to Alabama or someplace like that.' He used something like 13 of them at one time. They scrimmaged at night, right inside the stadium, with the gates locked and no priests who weren't friendly allowed. I couldn't even get in and I was his oldest kid. It was like the CIA. He was totally determined that he would never be humiliated. When Indiana beat Notre Dame in 1950, he was deeply distraught. It was the first time it had happened since 1916.

"That final year, he was in a bad way. I forget what happened, but he was in a hospital and Notre Dame was ahead something like 40-6 and they blew a chance to score another touchdown and he was on the telephone to the stadium. I mean, he was raising hell. He wanted to crucify every team he played. When the end came at Notre Dame, though, he had no financial worries. The financier, Louis Wolfson, was taking care of him. They were going to have the Wolfson-Leahy Insurance Agency and it was going to be his springboard into other ventures. Hell, two years after Dad quit at Notre Dame, if he wasn't a millionaire he was damned close.

"So Dad had that assurance behind him. He was dealing from strength. He thought Hesburgh had only been in office a short time and Dad told me one time, 'I'm not going to let a young, whip of a priest tell me what to do. I've been head coach at Notre Dame since 1941.' Well, a young whip of a priest was not going to let Frank Leahy tell him how to run a university. They reached an impasse. One of them had to go. It wasn't going to be Hesburgh. It was tough. They forced him to resign. He'll never admit it and neither will Hesburgh, but that's what happened.

"That stuff about a one year leave of absence was wishful thinking. Nobody would have taken the job for one year and his assistants weren't eager, either. They wanted their chance to fly. He should have sat out a year or two and then gone back into it. Nobody who ever associated with Dad in business was too enamoured of the way he conducted himself. He was a lamb . . . a real lamb. He still is. But the people who wanted to help him in business either died or got in trouble. But he was no businessman. Fred Miller made him a lot of money, but he guided him all the time. Lou Wolfson made him a fortune in a stock deal. But those people faded out of his life all too quickly and he was left naked.

"The man who helped him the most was Miller. And Leo D'Orsey, the Washington attorney who was a partner of George Preston Marshall in the Redskins. Dad put something like $20,000 in the Capital Bus Authority and came out of it with about $200,000 a year later. I don't think anyone, himself included, didn't think he'd go into the professional league after he got his health back. Dad talked about it all the time. The whole family felt he'd be happier if he ever could shake this stuff about business and be a coach again. Now, Mom didn't really start drinking hard until well after he'd left Notre Dame. She identified with him furiously and when he was miserable, she drank a lot to get away from it.

"Say, do you know what Dad did during the war? He picked up 33 kids in the Pacific who played football for him. He spent that whole hitch recruiting. That's what made him think he was such a sensational businessman. He could sell kids in a war zone on the idea of playing football at Notre Dame if they lived through the war. He picked off people like Jim Martin and George Conners and Emil Sitko. And he figured if he could do things like that, why couldn't he make $10 million in business? Except he wasn't geared for it.

"I can never understand why he didn't leave Notre Dame in 1949? I've asked him a thousand times and he's never known why himself. He'd have had four national champions in his last five years of coaching. The Detroit Lions offered him $1 million, which was an incredible figure.

"Why to get $100,000 a year for ten years in that era was like getting $6 million now. What's more, he was going to get ten percent of the club. He could have been rich and famous beyond belief because he would have been coaching still when the pro football boom started. He was ready to leave. He told

Mom he was resigning. Then Jerry Groom talked him out of it. He said, 'Coach, when you recruited me you said you'd be here my four years.' Now Jerry was young then, but Dad wasn't. He believed that he had a commitment and he wouldn't let it go.

"You know, when he quit he was offended because Brennan got the job and he was only 25, and that hurt like hell. He was in a terrible rage around the house about it. He considered it a slap in his face. But he was also hurt because they didn't go with Bob McBride, his all-time favorite assistant. He was the heir-apparent in Dad's eyes. But they didn't want anybody Dad recommended, because they figured Dad would be calling the shots from 35 miles away at Long Beach, Indiana. Johnny Lujack had come back as an assistant and he thought he was going to get the job. So did Dad. But Brennan wasn't a popular choice at our house. Dad really wasn't that fond of him. Hesburgh knew he could control Terry because he was young and he'd jump at the opportunity. And he did. Dad feuded with Terry. I think Dad was wrong. He had this television show. He had this deal where he wanted to put Paul Hornung on the Friday before a football game. He was going to give him $500 or something. Well, naturally, Terry said no.

"Dad couldn't understand it, but he never would have allowed it himself. He went on saying that the school had lost the Notre Dame Spirit and Brennan came back with what-the-hell-does-he-know, he's the ex-coach. They went back and forth like that. I don't think it ever was resolved. What he told me he wanted to say was, 'All right, Hesburgh, here's the idiot you picked. What are you doing about him?' Brennan deserved a lot of it because he lost total control and Dad knew it. But Dad should have shown more class on the matter. He was hurt and it showed. One day Dad came home and said, 'Do you know what the players call coach Brennan? They call him Terry? That is, ahhh, most disgraceful.'

"Funny thing about Dad was that he not only kept blowing it in business, he never really believed in the American Football League. He had three chances. He was general manager of the Los Angeles Chargers for awhile, but Sid Gillman got him. He nailed him good and Dad had no choice but to resign. He was in with a group that was going to buy Harry Wismer's New York Titans and he was going to be the head coach, but

Sonny Werblin's syndicate got there first. Then we had a franchise in Anaheim in 1966, but the merger ruined that.

"That summer in Los Angeles was terrible, though. Mother was drinking terribly and Dad was drinking far more than I had ever seen him drink. He was never a big drinker. He'd have his few beers or a couple of cocktails. But that summer, he just seemed to let everything go. He spent all kinds of Barron Hilton's money. He felt that the league wouldn't last and maybe the best survivors would make it. So he got pretty reckless. It seemed that Sid just stabbed him in the back. Maybe Sid figured he was just doing his duty. Who knows? Everything that Dad did wrong was reported to Barron Hilton, the owner of the Chargers. For the first time, and maybe the only time in his life, Dad was carousing. He and Mom were separated and they were talking about divorce and Dad was carousing, period. And Barron's ears were filled with that stuff. Dad made his biggest mistake by hiring Gillman, who had just left the Rams, but when he couldn't get McBride the job, he did what he thought was best. He should have got Lou Rymkus. Why, Lou would have been loyal to a fault.

"Poor Dad was terribly confused in those days. His confidence was really shaken. He'd seen Mother slip way down hill and he'd been involved in that tragedy with an oil and gas venture. That was another one of his crazy business deals that fell apart. He sold stock to his own brothers and sisters. Sold it to old Jim McAllister, the equipment manager at Notre Dame. This thing was going to give the little guy a chance to get rich. These two characters got ahold of him and they were forming this company to drill for gas and oil in a western state. The guy who was leading the action was a professional man. I heard the proposition. He claimed that he started with a company at fifty cents a share and it had gone up to $60 a share. That had been his last victory. This was going to be one where you'd buy a share for $1.50 and you'd get rich. It appeared that they used Dad to raise money for them. That's all.

"We still wonder if they ever did drill a gas or an oil well. The other guy involved was a fellow who claimed to have known Gene Leahy once. Well, Dad thought of Gene as being a substitute father, so that was good enough for him. It was a terrible disaster. Dad just barely escaped and his reputation was all but ruined by it. But he went around and, out of his own funds, he repaid people like Jim McAllister and his brothers and sisters.

"When he went into these ventures and didn't have the success he'd had as a football coach, he got irritable and tough as hell to live with. He bought a title company in San Diego in the early 1960s and paid $250,000 for it. He didn't know anything about it and it went down the drain.

"He'd fall for anything. He'd talk to some guy and come home and tell me that some businessman who was trying to bleed him dry was 'the greatest man I've ever met.' I've heard him use that phrase fifty times since he left Notre Dame. People would flatter him and he'd believe every word they said. People have told me that on the sucker list, he's No. 1. He was overly trusting and he wouldn't research things out. A good example of Dad's ineptitude was that title insurance company. He bought it from a guy for $125,000 down. Tom Leahy had begged him to let his company send a lawyer out to investigate. But it was too late. The guy he bought it from waited about 90 days and said, 'Well, we need another couple of hundred grand.' Of course, Dad gave it to him. One day the sheriff came and took the keys to his company car and said, 'You don't own it anymore.' His original investment was about $250,000, but he must have blown another $250,000 trying to keep it going.

"Old Peter Shannon, whose son Dan was such a great All-America for Dad, said it best about Frank Leahy's business sense. He said, 'Frank-Junior, I raised a great football player, I go to all the games and I think I know football. But I'm a businessman and a successful one, because I understand the business world. But I'd make a horse shit coach.' That was Dad's trouble. He thought he knew all there was to know about business and he was just the opposite of Peter Shannon."

The heated winds were ruffling the pine trees across the street from the Lake Oswego Apartments. The doors to the Leahy flat were open. Frank-Junior leaned back against the white concrete wall of the patio.

"For awhile, we had an insurance office together here in Portland," he said, shrugging his shoulders. "Dad was the general agent, in name only. He never had an insurance broker's license. He was afraid of taking the test. He wanted me to go down and take the test for him. I told him that I couldn't do that and he got mad as hell. The thing finally

301

broke up because he wanted the salesmen to wear bow ties, which were his trademark. They said no and that was it. In the 14 months I was with him, Dad made $90,000. I did about 88 percent of the work. Dad just let the business disintegrate. When Dad had a guy like Pat O'Malley of Canteen Corp. taking care of him he was alright. But most of these small promoters just used him to fatten themselves. It hurt my guts."

The conversation turned gently back to football and the obvious comparisons between Rockne and Leahy and Lombardi. Now Frank-Junior was rising to a crescendo of oratory.

"Do you know what made Lombardi great?" he asked, rhetorically. "Do you *know* what made Lombardi great?"

From the master bedroom several yards away from the patio came an almost ghostly reply: "Because your father coached him!" The rest was silence.

EPISODE 3

WEDNESDAY, JUNE 20, 1973

In the morning, Frank Leahy discovered that he could not get out of bed. The pain in his back was too intense and his muscles felt like rotted rubber. Laboriously, he propped himself up and looked in the mirror on the dressing table at the foot of his bed. He saw a yellowed, withering figure who could have been 96 instead of 64. It was, he said, later in the day like something he had seen on a late night horror show. This character had aged prematurely and he looked in the mirror and said, "Oh God, is that me?"

After much deliberation over how it might sound, he decided to call the writer and his wife and ask them to come over around 11 A.M. In two hours, he was convinced that he could bring himself around. When his biographer arrived, he was sitting in a state of near exhaustion in the reclining chair.

"Perhaps, we'd better postpone the taping today. I'll just go over some of your old clippings again to see if there is any ground we haven't covered."

"Ooooh, no, lad," said Frank Leahy. "It is not good to give in to these things. It will pass. Now, if you and your lady will assist me, I would like to go out to the swimming pool. It is not far, just down the corridor and a short turn to the left. It is my custom to take exercise each day. I swim the length of the pool five times and kick 100 times."

"Coach, I'd advise you not to."

"Aaaah, lad," he said, exposing all his teeth in a full grin, "you forget that I am considered an expert in the field of physical education. It is *my* decision, then. Will you help me?" Partially hidden by the kitchen cabinet, Floss Leahy shrugged both shoulders. It was useless to resist. In half an hour, he was ready. The old bathrobe was gathered around him and he tried to stand erect, with his shoulders back. It was nearly impossible because his stiff-legged, arthritic walk had been reduced to a shuffle. He put his arms around the writer and his wife and moved forward in one final act of gallantry.

A number of residents in their early 30's were gathered around the side of the pool, drinking vodka and orange juice and laughing over faint humor, when Leahy turned the corner and shuffled up to the chain link gate. Their voices softened reverently when they saw him approach. Most of them had been children listening to Notre Dame games on the radio when he was in his glory. They acted as if they'd seen a holy man approach. One of them, a round-faced Irishman named Jim Cassidy, leaped to his feet and rushed over to help. Leahy acknowledged the gesture with a nod of his head. There was an awkward moment.

"How do the Irish look in spring practice this year?" Cassidy asked, almost as if this shadowy remnant was still the handsome, alert figure whose face was so often reproduced on the sports pages two decades earlier.

"Ooooh, excellent, James. Excellent! It would not surprise me if Our Lady had another national championship this fall," he said. "They have more team speed than I have ever seen before. Truly, a fine football team. I approve most heartily of their coach. As an alumnus I am quite proud of Mr. Parseghian's accomplishments. I believe he is the finest coach Notre Dame has had since . . well, since . . . hmmmm . . . well, I do not wish to seem immodest."

Then he moved slowly down the steps into the pool and, while the other residents watched with astonishment mixed with fear, he swam the length of the pool five times. He gripped the side and kicked exactly 100 times. With a flourish, because he knew people were watching, Leahy swam an extra half length to the steps and emerged. The white stubble on his chin stood out against the deepening yellow of his face. He nodded, in a most gracious manner, to the people who had watched him. Then he shuffled back to the apartment slowly and asked to be excused, so that he might lie down. The apartment grew silent. Clock ticks sounded like explosions.

"Frank is a strange man," said Floss, softly. "After all these years, I can't say I know him completely. The big trouble was when Frank needed me, he was too proud to tell me. When I needed him, he was never around and I was too stubborn to ask him to stay around more. I never really started drinking hard until after he left Notre Dame. I could stand the grief as long as I was the wife of the head coach of football at Notre Dame. But when he went into business, he never told me any details of what was happening. I only knew if something devastating was happening. I knew if we had lost money or that we were going to move again. He was troubled and he wouldn't say a thing. I was hurt. So I did what all cowards do . . . I ran and hid in a bottle.

"I guess we were a traditional Irish family. Frank went out and made the living, regardless of how much time it took and I was supposed to take care of the home and the family, with his strict supervision, of course. He couldn't understand my drinking. It was a sign of weakness to him. When I stopped and stopped cold about two year ago, he was so proud of me. I couldn't believe how proud he was. He c never shown that kind of admiration for me. These last two years we've been like a honeymoon couple, we've been just like the papers used to say we were when we weren't."

With native curiosity, the writer rose and opened the bedroom door just enough to permit a vision of the man on the coverlet. Frank Leahy looked like a man already in his casket. His hands were folded across his chest and his face was now a dull yellow. He responded weakly. The door closed.

"Better get an ambulance, Floss. This could be it. I'm afraid he's dying."

"Aw, don't worry about Frank, he's been close before. He always survives," she said. "But you're right. I'm worried. We'd better get him to St. Vincent's. He's probably having a blood sugar reaction. His diabetes doctor works out of St. Vincent's. Oh, she's a real sharp woman. Frank hates her because she won't let him have any ice cream."

There were no beds left at St. Vincent's and only four at Good Samaritan, an Episcopal hospital on Portland's northside. There was no choice. Slowly, Leahy pulled himself out of bed. There were deep, harsh pains in his chest and he tried to smile.

"I think it is best if we hurry, Floss," he said.

"The ambulance is coming, Frank. Don't worry. You'll be all right. You'll see."

This time he looked vaguely skeptical. He dressed himself in the small bathroom off the master bedroom, pulling on his pants in a clutter of medicine bottles. At last he emerged.

"Can I help you, Coach?" the writer asked.

"No," he said. "I'm afraid I can only help myself now. And, I think I will need a great deal of assistance from God and Our Lady."

The ambulance came and Frank Leahy who wanted to walk out had to be wheeled out. Young people who never heard of Johnny Lujack or Six Yard Sitko or Creighton Miller stood around on the front steps of the apartment building wondering who the weak old man was. On the way through the Portland expressway system, Jerry Leahy, driving home, saw the ambulance streak past. He was struck by an odd, ironic thought, one that was clearly a psychic vibration.

"I thought, 'That could be Dad going to the hospital to die and here we are going in opposite directions, as usual.' But I put the thought out of my mind because I didn't want it to be true," he said.

In the waiting room, Father William Rees, an Episcopal priest, joined Floss Leahy and began talking softly. Thincheeked and clerically pallid, he explained that he no longer had a parish, which hurt him deeply. But he had married a divorced woman against his bishop's orders. So they exiled him to a hospital chaplain's office. It was, he said, spiritually rewarding, but not personally satisfying. He sighed and began to talk about the Great Frank Leahy. The door opened and the doctor from the emergency room gave a short speech about the patient's condition, which was not good but in keeping with his medical record. When a man has cheated death as often as

Leahy had, even a physician can find himself growing too optimistic.

"Tell me, Mrs. Leahy, do you think his condition is serious enough to warrant being admitted to the hospital?" he asked.

For several seconds, Floss Leahy looked wildly around the small green-tinted room. The decision was obviously too much for her.

"Doctor, I don't think that is a fair question," said Father Rees. "You're asking a housewife to make a medical decision. Mrs. Leahy isn't qualified to give an opinion in this matter." Seemingly unhappy at the chaplain's uncooperative reaction, the doctor left the room and returned with the information that a bed would be made available.

"I wish I were still drinking," said Floss, laughing at the thought. "I'd have a double right now."

"Do you miss it?" asked the writer's wife.

"Naw!" she said. "Once you get over it, you wonder what you ever saw in booze in the first place. Funny thing is that there were whispers about me being an alcoholic while Frank was still at Notre Dame. But it wasn't true. Oh, I'd have a couple of cocktails at a party, but I was hardly a rooting-tooting drunk. It really started the year Fred Miller died. I think that was 1955. Well, Frank was just beside himself. Fred was so close to Frank. I'd try to console him and it didn't do any good. He wouldn't let me be a part of anything personal.

"I remember how it started. I'd go upstairs to do my bills and I'd think, 'Why do this? I'd rather have a highball.' Then I'd have another and another and another. Nobody really noticed it until 1958. I belonged to a bridge club. Pretty soon we stopped playing bridge.

"It became a straight drinking club. Those who had to get home to make dinner left at 5 P.M. The rest kept right on drinking. I bowled and played golf, but you'd always have a few drinks afterwards and then a few more when you got home. It comes on so gradually that you don't realize it until one morning you're only looking forward to your first drink. After what had happened at Notre Dame—oh, it was a terrible thing—Frank wasn't sure what he wanted. He went into Sports Enterprises with Billy Sullivan and then into an insurance business in Chicago. He was miserable. You know he never told me directly what happened. I knew that he and Father

Hesburgh did not get along well at all. He always pretended that everything was fine. He just shut himself off from me. When I'd get angry I'd bring up the stories that Father Hesburgh fired him and he would get furious. But I was trying to draw him out. He wouldn't confide a thing in me . . . nothing.

"I talked a lot and I think he didn't want me to know because his pride was hurt and he was afraid I'd tell too many people. We lost communication. He was drifting, really drifting. He is proud to a fault. That hurt our marriage when he was a head coach. He was beating himself, beating himself, beating himself to stay on top. He never realized that I was still young enough at the time to want some sort of social life. After they stopped going by train, I couldn't make the road trips anymore, so I'd invite friends from Long Beach and South Bend over to the house along with Father John and Father Frank and we'd have some drinks and some lunch and listen to the games on radio. That was about the extent of my social life. Frank never seemed to care about it. I guess I stored up a lot of resentment.

"I got suspicious about him resigning on his own because his health really wasn't that bad. He just needed to relax a little in the off-season and he would have been all right. It was pitiful to see him in 1954 at the home games. He'd sit in the box they gave him and he took a great deal of punishment. We just put on a face. That's all we ever did—put on faces.

"Frank was anxious to get out of there and he was gone all the time, looking for something to do with the rest of his life. It's funny the papers all said that he was quitting to spend more time with me and the kids and that we were going to take a six week vacation immediately. But we never did. If anything, he was gone more. So by 1955 and 1956, the booze had really caught up with me. He never yelled at me. But finally, Grammy, Leahy's mother, told him that it was hitting me pretty good, so they took me up to a sanitarium in Michigan. It really hurt him. He had me enter under my maiden name. When he came to see me, he was devastated.

"He didn't want to be recognized because he was so ashamed. That was wrong. It just made me rebel all the more. They gave me shock treatments and they were terrible. They didn't do any good. It was horrible. By 1959, when he went with the

Chargers, we were more or less separated. He was out on the West Coast and gone most of the time. We hardly communicated. He was drinking—the only time in his life he ever did that. I was at home drinking and I was escaping, too. He came home one weekend and put a huge padlock on the liquor cabinet. Before he left, I broke it open. It wasn't so much to get the booze as it was to show him I was a live human being, too. I said that everybody knew about my drinking and that everybody knew he had really been fired at Notre Dame. He went into an almost uncontrollable rage.

"Frank got in with that Hollywood crowd, which I never liked. Frank just became a sitting duck for everybody. The children were getting older and they needed a father and he was never there. He expected far too much from them and then was never around to do much with them. That scared me even more and so I drank more. That was the worst thing for the kids. I'm a mean drunk. They said when I was loaded I was the exact opposite of my regular self. I found out that Frank was going around telling everyone how horrible I'd been. I discovered that I was the scapegoat for all his frustrations. And I was taking all my frustrations out on the children when I was drunk.

"About 1962, after the disaster of the title insurance company, my drinking got really bad. Frank sent me up to a place in Seattle. It was supposed to be wonderful, but it was one of those places where they give you two weeks of treatment and then just throw you out with no follow-up. Well, it didn't work. Inside of a few months, I was right back at it. No, I wasn't cured until Frank and I decided I should go to Raleigh Hills here in Portland.

"They give you three weeks of concentrated treatment and then follow it up with a year's out-patient treatment. When you get through, you can't believe that you ever were a crude and vulgar drunk. You can't believe that was what you were like. Frank was sure I was going to fall off, but I didn't. Even the cab drivers who used to bring me bottles out from the town were rooting for me. It was wonderful. When Frank realized that I had licked it, something happened. For the first time, I really think he was proud of me. It was such a thrill. I'd never drink again. Not after I saw the effect my beating it had on Frank."

She leaned back against the wall and looked toward Father Rees. Her mouth was quivering.

"I met Frank some 38 years ago and I was so in love with him I would have done anything he said. It's funny . . . I've never really known whether he loved me or whether he was ready to get married and I just fitted his game plan. I was the right age and I was fairly pretty with a good figure. I came from a well-to-do Irish Catholic family. I was the perfect girl. But do you know . . . after all we've been through together . . . I still don't know whether he loves me. And he may be up there dying. Imagine that?"

EPISODE 4

The last bed available at Good Samaritan Hospital on June 20, 1973, was located in the corner of a four patient ward up on the sixth floor, a place where no air-conditioner had ever been seen. It had been six hours since Frank Leahy was admitted, a suspected heart patient, and no oxygen had been administered. His diabetic's lunch was four hours over-due, but the Master Coach had roused himself. He lay there, dank-skinned and skeletal, wearing only his shorts. He smiled graciously at his five visitors and reached out to clutch his wife's hand.

"Floss," he said, "ooooh, Floss, there is something I want to tell you."

"Aw, yes, Frank," she said, smiling. "What is it?"

"This is the worst hospital room I have ever had. See if you cannot switch me to a private room tomorrow."

Openly disturbed, Frank-Junior flashed past his model-thin wife Anne and charged down the corridor, looking for an oxygen tent and swearing to set one up himself if the hospital staff was unwilling.

"As long as you aren't feeling well, Coach, I think I'll head back to San Francisco and come back up here in early July when you're out of the hospital," said his biographer.

"I will be here in July," he said, speaking in parable as he did so often. "When Notre Dame had its long winning streak, my brother Jack, who was paralyzed, would come from California and join us as our guest at South Bend. He said he wouldn't die until Notre Dame was beaten. When it finally happened, he went home to California and died ten days later. When there is still a goal left that you wish to achieve, you do not quit until you achieve it. I still have something left to achieve."

The writer nodded and Leahy slumped backwards, smiling as if he was beginning to think he might survive even this crisis. After all, America was slipping down the corridor into a long, dark night. He would somehow prevent it.

"Oh, Floss," he said, as an orderly pulled the oxygen tent around him. "Take our guests from San Francisco to that Chinese restaurant we like so well. I had meant to take them there myself. We must be gracious to our friends."

Such are the last words a man speaks to his wife of 38 years. On the way to the elevator, Anne Leahy had a wistful thought. "You know these past two years were probably the happiest of his life. He and Floss were like two people who just fell in love and Pat O'Malley of Canteen had him out on the road letting him battle Communism, which gave him a sense of purpose for the first time since he left coaching. What's more, he played a lot with our three sons, playing football with them and coaching them and taking them down to get ice cream. He was trying to make up for all the time he should have spent with his own children by pampering his grandchildren. He's been tying up a lot of loose ends."

EPISODE 5

THURSDAY, JUNE 21, 1973

During the night there was a crisis. It was nothing new. It happened before. In six years of illness and disease, Frank Leahy had received the last rites five times. And there was that occasion in the locker room at the Georgia Tech game of 1953 when Father Joyce had anointed him. At his side on this final evening was Father Rees. At about 4 A.M., the doctors began to shake their heads. Fearful that he might die instantly, Father Rees ran to a telephone and called a close Catholic friend, Father James Larkin, and asked him to come immediately. He arrived just as Leahy's heart was stopping. Father Rees met him in the lobby and they hurried to intensive care. As the door opened, the heart started again.

"In that room," said Father Rees to his colleague afterwards, "I could feel that man's enormous will."

"So could I, Bill, so could I," said Father Larkin, who left to attend another dying patient at St. Vincent's. "However, I don't think he'll receive the last rites again."

It was just God and Frank Leahy now. Floss and the two youngest children, Mary and Christopher, who were merely babies when their father ceased to be the nation's best known football coach, were sitting in the waiting room. Shortly after 11 A.M., Dr. Kathleen Weaver, an antiseptic young blonde woman, explained the situation to the family. She did not fill her sentences with optimistic euphemisms, a failing among most doctors who don't honestly know how to tell relatives that someone is dying.

"He is an amazingly strong-willed man. Since four this morning, his heart has stopped beating five times. And still it starts again every time. He is still forcing himself to keep going. Anyone with his incredible medical history would have been dead years ago. He simply does not want to die. However, the chances for living are not good this time. You should know that."

It was nearly 12:30 P.M. when Floss Leahy went upstairs with the writer's wife to have a sandwich in the hospital lunch room. She sat down and picked at her food. How would he escape death this time, she asked the woman with her. Suddenly, she decided to return to the waiting room. She had not been seated more than a few minutes when Dr. Weaver came into the room.

At 12:51 P.M., on Thursday, June 21, 1973, the long struggle against death ended. Despite the vigorousness and self-discipline of the spirit, the body wore down and refused to respond to one last heroic effort. Frank Leahy's heart stopped a sixth time. There was no way to start it again. The impossible dream, the glorious quest, the years of incredible sacrifice had come to an end.

Roughly two minutes after it ended, Jerry Leahy came through the waiting room door, too late to be with his father at his last moment. He fell against the wall and sobbed openly.

"Oh, God! He died and I never had a chance to make it up to him," he said. "Why am I such a damned fool?"

None of the living seemed to notice the final irony. In a touch of unconscious ecumenicalism, Francis William Leahy, that most Catholic-acting of men, that head coach who so symbolized the spirit of the nation's best-known Catholic University, the hard-practicing Catholic layman who was the first football coach ever to be made a Knight of Malta by the Vatican, that towering figure who was so deeply loved by every Irish Catholic sports columnist in the country . . . died in an Episcopal hospital with an Episcopal priest, the only clergyman at his side. Outside in the hallway, telephoning his obituary to the nation was the only writer who covered the last act of Leahy's life. He was also an Episcopalian.

In such curious and unexpected ways do real men die and legends begin. Rockne died in a plane crash and Leahy expired in an Anglican hospital. It is, perhaps, the beginning of a whole new world and not as bad as it may have seemed to Francis William Leahy, who may have been America's last knight-errant.

EPISODE 6

Two small epitaphs for a dead football coach who knew all there was to know about paying the price and making sacrifices for excellence:

● *"Oh, my God, he's dead! He's dead! I barely had a chance to know him. You know I was 14 before he ever threw me a football. Oh, God, he's gone. I don't even know what he was really like."*—Fred Leahy, home on emergency leave from the Marine Corps reserve.

● *"I want him buried right here in Portland where I can go visit his grave on Sunday. He should be here with me. This is where we had the best two years of our marriage. They'll be angry at Notre Dame, but let them. They care more about their traditions than they do about the people who make them. They are all going to say that Floss is wrong again They'll*

want him buried back there where they can make some kind
of saint out of him, like they did with Rockne. Notre Dame
has had him long enough. He belongs to me now."—Florence
Reilly Leahy, making funeral arrangements with her eldest
son.

EPISODE 7

With all the recording tapes spun out like the
spools of life itself, the writer and his wife went off to the only
bar in Lake Oswego, to make some final notes and permit the
Leahy family to make plans for a wake and a funeral without
outside influences. The telephone rang behind the bar. A
waitress called the biographer's name. Lou Rymkus, starting
tackle on the 1943 team and a man who wandered much like
Leahy after being fired from a head coaching job with the
Houston Oilers, was calling from Texas. He was in mourning
because his tongue was thick with martinis.

"It's like losing your father," he said.

"I'll bet it is," Rymkus was told.

"The Coach taught me everything I knew. He taught me to
try to be a man. All my life, I've been able to call on things
he taught me," he said. "One time he had us practicing in
the snow. Oh, it was cold enough to freeze your ass off. Bob
McBride kept urging me to go over and ask The Coach if we
could finish the workout indoors.

"He looked at me with that cold stare of his and said, 'Louis,
I was reading a most interesting book last night. It was about
buffaloes. The book was so interesting that I couldn't put it
down.

"'It was about the great Northern Buffalo and the puny
Southern Buffalo. I read it chapter after chapter with no regard for the lateness of the hour. Let me tell you, Louis, a
little of what I learned about the Northern Buffalo. He stands
out there with his head into the wind and the rain and the
snow. He has a big strong neck and a big strong chest. The
weather doesn't bother this Northern Buffalo. Now you take
the buffalo of South America. He's in a warm climate. The
breeze is blowing off the ocean. The weather is nice so he has

313

a small neck, small legs, small body. Now, Louis, I want you to go over and tell those lads that we will continue to practice out here in the snow because we are Great Northern Buffaloes.' "

There was a pause on the other end of the line. Lou Rymkus, age 53, former Notre Dame player, former head coach, tough as hell, was crying.

"All my life, I've tried to be a Great Northern Buffalo, because that's what the old Coach wanted me to be," he said.

"That's nice, Lou," Rymkus was told. "That's very, very nice."

EPISODE 8

FRIDAY, JUNE 22, 1973

Now the old Christmas tree photo, with all the Leahy children grouped around their parents, was beginning to come to life, possibly for the last time. There were no more babies on the great coach's lap, no more clean faced teenagers leaning eagerly over the couch behind their mother—only mourners gathering for an Irish wake. There would be hard liquor and food and a thousand cheerful stories about the man just dead. It is an historical fact, little known, that Irishmen never cry at wakes.

The eight Leahy children are, by any standard, all adults now. They do not look alike, talk alike, think alike or live alike. They are eight individuals raised under the same roof by common parents. They fan out in opposite directions, like points on a compass. Frank-Junior works too long and too hard. His wife is displeased because she and the children never see him. Obsessed with success, he hides the depths of his character under a pitchman's bluster. Glib to a fault, he is startlingly sincere underneath. He has a habit of making friends out of people he originally turns off.

"Well," he says, "at least I'm not Frank-Junior anymore."

"Oh, but that's wrong," he is told, "ordinarily you can drop 'junior' at the time of your father's death. But not the son of a famous man."

314

"Somehow," he says, with a wistful laugh that comes from the seat of his origins, "I guess I always knew it would work out that way. Well, what the hell, there are a lot worse things."

"Did you enjoy being Frank Leahy's son?"

"A lot of the pleasure has worn thin. In business, he depended on me too much, I think. I'm glad he had confidence in me. But the time comes when you want to be your own man," he said. "With that Dad, that was pretty tough. Still, I wouldn't have changed him for anybody else. Life will be different from now on . . . much different. Who knows, maybe we were too much a part of each other."

Sue Leahy Moustakas and Florence Leahy Harter and Mary Leahy are all sisters, but no one would ever suspect they were even related. They are such radically different types that they hardly share any sort of common denominator. Sue is tall, soft-talking and suburban housewife-chic. She is the pretty wife of a handsome business executive. She runs a nursery school and, at one time, she has had as many as three of her younger brothers and sisters living with her. Florence is the carhop-thin wife of a Chicago truck driver. She is given to introducing herself as "coach Leahy's daughter." Her laugh is brittle and she spends most of her time in the kitchen, safely hidden from the people who keep returning from her father's past. Mary Leahy is short, solid and wholesome looking with an almost angelic politeness. She thinks largely in abstract terms. ("I could never conceive of my father in terms of fame. That was a different kind of reality. He was simply a warm and fascinating human being who happened to be my father. I can define him only in those terms.")

James (Jub) Leahy is large to the point of being overweight. He sits on chairs and they fall apart. He walks away laughing. He has the boisterous enthusiasm of an Irish bartender. Of the sons, his personality is the most overwhelming. Unlike Fred or Chris, who rarely saw their father and hardly got to know him, Jub Leahy did his best to figure out what it was the old man wanted. Then, partly out of stubborn determination and partly out of love, he did his best to live up to what Frank Leahy wanted his sons to be.

"I did it because that's what he wanted and because I wanted to prove to myself that I could do it," he said. "I wanted to come as close to my father's idea of success as

I could come. He was a great man and he had something to tell the world. So I listened. In my father's eyes, I was the No. 1 son, not because he loved me anymore than Chris or Jerry or Frank-Junior or Fred, but because I did all the things he expected. I was a success academically. I was on the football team at Notre Dame and I stuck with it even though I wasn't fast enough to play regularly. I married a really beautiful woman and I've got two little boys.

"My wife is from an excellent background and I've got a great job with every chance of moving up in business. I did these things for my father and I did them for myself. But I'll tell you, I resented *having* to do them. I would have done them anyway. One thing I do is make time for my family. I may have all kinds of business appointments, but I put it down on my calendar: 'Five-thirty, time with my wife and my kids.' I write it right down. I could have flown down from Pasco, Washington, to Dad's funeral, but I didn't. I drove, so the family could have time with me, so we could have the experience of going somewhere together. That way, we'd feel stronger and closer when we got here.

"I don't remember more than two family vacations that all of us took together when I was a kid. Both times they were some kind of free load that Dad was given. Togetherness? Well, the kids were together and we all loved Mom, even though when she was drinking Mary once got mad and poured a bottle of gin over her head. Who was the biggest influence in my life when I was growing up? You want to hear this? My mother was, drunk or sober. Dad was a great man. I wish he'd treated his sons the way he treated his football players. You know those Christmas pictures that Notre Dame arranged every year? As far as Mom-Dad-and-the-kids were concerned, that was about it. But . . . I admired him."

In a corner, away from the women who are preparing the food and liquor for the wake, sits Jerry Leahy, a thoughtful-minded, introspective drifter. He is red-headed like Jub, but infinitely younger-looking, even though in actuality he is three years older. It seems as if Jerry Leahy's clock stopped when he was 16 and nothing good has happened since.

Of him, his brother Frank-Junior has said: "When Dad told us kids to pay the price and make any sacrifice for success, some of us tried to do exactly what he said. Others didn't pay any attention, Jerry decided to do just the opposite. He's a soft, sensitive guy and very lovable in his own funny way, but ne's spent his whole life trying to get something for nothing. That's why he ended up in prison."

One of those Christmas picture children ended up in jail, for smuggling dope from Holland in cuckoo clocks, for God's sake. It happened while Francis William Leahy was out on the road, warning everybody about the evils that were threatening to destroy the Great American Ethic. When he returned, he discovered that those same parasites were chewing on the foundation of his own household. He was almost unable to comprehend what had happened or how it had happened. The Master Coach talked at length with his son, hoping to reach a resolution. When it became obvious that Jerry was going to jail, he did his best to keep it out of the Portland newspapers and he instructed everyone to say that his fourth child and second son would be studying in Europe.

EPISODE 9

They said the rosary with almost indecent haste and then moved the body out quickly, because there were two more services scheduled in the funeral chapel. Only a few of the old faces were present, Moose Krause, Billy Sullivan, Bob McBride, Joe McArdle and Johnny Lattner. Even though he played at Notre Dame ten years after Leahy left, John Huarte arrived. There hadn't been enough time since the death to gather and Portland was so far removed from South Bend. There would be a memorial service in Chicago's Holy Name Cathedral the Tuesday following and it would be easier for the players and alumni to go there than to fly halfway across the nation.

On the walkway outside the mortuary, Moose Krause showed somebody a copy of Dave Condon's column from the *Chicago Tribune*. It excused Floss Leahy for having her husband buried so distant from Notre Dame. He wrote at length about the beauty of the service they had on campus for Knute Rockne and finally concluded, "Yes, Portland is far from the happy haunts that Frank Leahy knew when he was making America love him. Portland is far from Leahy's spiritual home in South Bend. But Portland is where Floss Leahy and six of their children now make their homes and where Frank Leahy, one of the greatest coaches of them all, will rest eternally. And why not Portland as much as Notre Dame; why not Portland instead of the prairies of South Dakota? It's Portland because Frank Leahy always believed that home is where the family is and nothing was more important to Frank Leahy than his family. But Frank Leahy didn't just belong to South Dakota or his family or to Notre Dame.

"The Coach belonged to everyone, everywhere."

The unseasonable warmth forced the attendants at the wake out onto the patio. In the tall spires of the pine trees along the lake shore, water birds were honking eerily. Beyond the distant hills, heat lightning disturbed the darkness and shook thunder out of the clouds. They told all the Frank Leahy stories over and over again. In the corner, Billy Sullivan talked about Boston College and Father Joyce who would celebrate the funeral mass in the morning explained what an important contribution the departed had made to the glory that is Notre Dame. And Jack Leahy, Jr., who had cried for Uncle Coach all the way out on the plane from Chicago, was wandering around, hiding his sorrow behind a fine haze of Scotch whisky.

"He wanted to be a proper gentleman with all that elaborate language, that's what Uncle Coach wanted," he said. "Underneath, he was a proper Leahy. Could stay out 'til dawn if he wanted."

Bob McBride, curly-haired and earnest, stood off to one side watching the tableau. There never was an assistant coach that Leahy liked more. He tried to get McBride the head coaching job at Notre Dame, at Texas A&M and with the Los Angeles Chargers. He liked the younger man's honesty more than anything else. It never worked out and finally one day McBride began to realize that he would never be a head coach. So he forgot the whole project, but Leahy never did. McBride loved the man for his intense loyalty.

"There were things he'd do that people never heard about," he said, softly as the wind began to move quicker through the trees near the lake. "Years after I left Notre Dame one of the members of the faculty board of athletics told me the darndest story. It seems that the McBride family was growing rapidly. The Holy Cross fathers weren't well known for killing you with money. Coach Leahy used to say, 'They all took the vow of poverty and imposed it on others.' He requested a $1,000 increase for me and the word came back that there was no room in the budget. He thought he'd shame them a little bit so he sent them word to deduct $1,000 from his salary and give it to me. Well, he got a note from Father Hesburgh saying that if coach Leahy was serious to let Father Hesburgh know. So the Coach said: 'Certainly, I'm serious. I'm anxious that this man be rewarded.' It happened and I never knew until years later.

"When he told a kid that if he came to Notre Dame he would be taken care of the rest of his life, he meant it. Even after he was out of coaching, he would fulfill that promise. I remember when one of Coach Leahy's lads was a rookie with the Los Angeles Rams, somebody gave him a guest membership to an athletic club. One afternoon, for reasons the kid himself couldn't explain, he lifted some wallets in the locker room. They hauled him in and they gave him the chance to make one telephone call. He didn't ask for a lawyer, he wanted Frank Leahy. Just as soon as the Coach heard about it, he flew to Los Angeles. He got hold of a judge he knew. He called a lawyer he knew and he talked to members of the club that he knew. He got them together and charges were dropped. Then he sat down with the boy for several hours and talked to him about what he did. I don't think the fellow ever got into trouble again."

All evening long, Jerry Leahy had been sitting by himself in his father's bedroom. For nearly a year, they had been struggling to reach some sort of accommodation with each other. It had not been entirely successful. A man does not preach against encroaching evils, does not tilt with Communist windmills, does not fight against moral decay and then easily understand how his own son could deal in dope.

"They arrested me while Dad was away on one of his speaking engagements, can you imagine that?" he said, still twisting at the skin on his hands. "They held me overnight and when Dad got back they released me on bail. At first he was crushed. He said it was the worst thing that happened to him since he left Notre Dame. He said he was going to stop making speeches. It scared me. I knew I was in the wrong, but for him to take it that way made me realize what an ugly thing I'd done," he said.

"I'll never forget the date. It was December 29, 1970, and I'd brought my father to his knees, this great man I had worshipped since I was a child. What I did was mail 20 pounds of hashish from Amsterdam to my partner in Portland and ten pounds to myself and ten pounds to my brother Fred. It was hidden in cuckoo clocks, but a dog at Los Angeles airport sniffed it out. That's right, I got busted by a hound. They just followed the packages along. As soon as the mailman delivered the package, I realized something was wrong because it didn't have the cord on it I wrapped it with in Holland. There was a knock on the door and they had me.

"Dad kept saying he was going to resign because everything he stood for was in jeopardy with something like this hanging over his head. I begged him not to. For the first time in my life, we really had a gut level talk. I explained my philosophy to him and when it was over I think we breached a gulf. He understood that I had done an economically wise thing. I told him it was sort of semi-legal over there and I had a chance to make a fast $15,000. I explained that I had done a lot research and I knew the difference between a soft drug and a hard drug. I told him that this was no worse than smuggling cases of whisky during prohibition.

"He didn't even know what hashish was. Why, his first comment to me was, what is this 'hish-hish'? He knew nothing about it. Once I explained the difference between it and heroin and the fact that research has proved that it is less harmful than alcohol, he seemed to understand. I told him that you can buy it for one-sixth of what you have to pay over here and that it was simply a sound, if somewhat dangerous, business deal. I knew that would appeal to him. I wanted him to know that I wasn't a drug addict and I wasn't doing it to defy his authority. It's illegal to smuggle Levi's into South America, but yet a $6 pair will bring $24 and, frankly, what's the difference?

"Fortunately, Jub was here and he sort of softened the blow somewhat, but he used real sound logic on my father, convincing him that times and attitudes were changing.

"I didn't understand it would have any ramifications on Frank Leahy. I knew it was illegal, in a way. And I was going to use the money to pay Dad back. I owed him quite a bit. It was just going to be 'quick-in and quick-out' and I'd have the money to give Dad. I had borrowed the money at a time in my life when I was lost—really lost. I was a drifting weed and it really bothered me because I felt that if I could make money I would have some sense of self-value. That's why I went into this business deal. I was wrong and I was caught.

"I assured Dad that if I had to go to prison I'd make the time work for me and I'd come out stronger, mentally and physically from it. We were pretty sure I'd come out of it all right, with a suspended sentence or something. I had no arrests and I had served the community as a social worker. I had taught school and I'd always been employed except for when I was in college. While I spent that night in jail, I talked to people who were in for the third or fourth time and they were just being sent out to do three months planting trees. So I figured my chances were pretty good. Dad displayed real deep emotion that wasn't characteristic of him. Like once I put on a blue shirt. I made a sarcastic comment and he almost collapsed. I said something like, 'Well, this is what I'll be wearing soon.'

"He got so upset I thought it was theatrics at first, but it wasn't. Anyway, I went to court on the 29th of April and my lawyer seemed to antagonize the judge. It was such a funny thing. They were real rivals. At one point, the judge said something and the lawyer corrected him. When he began pleading my case, my lawyer started talked about marijuana and the judge broke in and said, 'This is hashish and that's different.' Then he blasted my lawyer all over the court. But hash is the same as marijuana, only more concentrated. Then he sentenced me to three years. I was in a haze and some big gorilla grabbed me and I couldn't even say goodbye to Dad. This guy was 6'4" and about 260 and I wanted to hit him so I could run back and tell Dad, 'Don't worry, I'll be okay.' Right away, he put the handcuffs on me and pushed and shoved me. He was really obnoxious. There was Dad standing down there at the end of the hall, looking so old and so lonely.

"I didn't see Dad until the first visiting day. He was there for two hours and he kept crying and asking how he'd failed me. I finally told him, 'Dad, maybe I just need something like this.' From then on, he wrote a lot. But he didn't come up often. He got very emotional every time. He said he couldn't even stand to hear the words 'McNeil Island.' I was there exactly a year and a day. Somehow, I think Dad and I grew closer. I think I tore up his pride badly.

"While I was in there, I made a point to tell him all the humorous things I could think of. He really enjoyed humor, you know. I came across two of his 'lads' at McNeil. One guy came up to me in the cell block and said, 'Your old man coach at Notre Dame? He coach at Boston College? Well, I was recruited by your Dad at BC. I was the starting center on the freshman team his first year and the second string center on the varsity his other year.' He was in on bank robbery.

"Toward the end of my term, I ran into a guy Dad had recruited who had played freshman football on scholarship at Notre Dame and hurt his knee and never played varsity ball. He was another lineman and he was in on bank robbery, too. He wouldn't tell me his name, but Dad knew who he was. Dad laughed and laughed and said: 'Well, I guess I didn't always build character, did I?' I was glad he could take it so well."

Outside in the hallway, Leahy's secretary, a buxom, blond ex-night club singer named Diane Tidwell was saying goodbye to Floss Leahy. She fumbled for the proper thing to say. After a long association, she was as deeply grieved as if she had been a relative.

"Mrs. Leahy, I'm going to miss the Coach so much," she said. "We had a very special relationship. He was just like a father to me."

"That's nice, Diane," she said, wearily. 'That's very nice. I just wish he had been just like a father to some of his children.'"

EPISODE 10

SATURDAY, JUNE 23, 1973

The hotel room located high above the expensive waters of suburban Lake Oswego was dark and shrouded with sleep when the telephone rang. All night long, Al Davis, the resident genius in the Oakland Raiders' executive office, had been struggling with a deep emotional problem. Years ago, when there was a recruiting scandal at the University of Southern California, several of the assistant coaches were fired, not necessarily because one was more guilty than another. Davis was just sort of shopping around for another position when Frank Leahy called him from the Los Angeles Chargers' office, said something that was both flattering and gracious and then asked him if he would like to join this new venture.

From that point in time, Al Davis' career began to move as if he had been anointed by a holy man. He became head coach of the Raiders and moved into the commissionership of the American Football League in its final desperate battle with the National League. When the league war was over and the merger a prosperous reality, Davis went home to Oakland as the largest single stockholder and as managing general partner. He never quite forgot what Leahy did for him. Once, when he was being rushed through to a first class by an airline representative, he saw Frank Leahy standing there in line, his degenerating legs barely able to hold him up. It struck him as inconceivable that a man of Leahy's stature should be treated so crassly. He informed the representative who that was in line and insisted that they board together. The older man was deeply pleased, as Davis knew he would be.

Now Davis had decided that it would not be right to let this man he so deeply idolized be buried without some representative of the old Football League present. Besides, he owed the man the courtesy, in life or in death, of showing how much he meant to him. Now he was at the Portland Airport with a limousine. He wanted to pick up the writer and his wife, so that he wouldn't have to go to the funeral alone.

"I hate funerals," he said as the limousine moved toward the University of Portland campus, "They don't do anything for me. They're morbid. If it was anybody else but Coach Leahy, I wouldn't have come. He was a giant, you know that? He was an absolute giant. He was a hell of a kind man, too. They spread a lot of nonsense around about him. But I understand that, shucks, they do that about me now. He was a damn good man, more worried about others than he was about himself. He knew what the word 'sacrifice' meant."

As the limousine moved up the drive at the University of

Portland and stopped in front of the chapel, Davis pulled a letter out of his wallet, one he had been carrying for more than a decade.

'This is really amazing," he said. "He only met my father once, but he sent me this really fine letter when my father died and apologized because he couldn't get back for the funeral. Isn't that something? Geez! What a guy."

The crowd of former players and alumni was surprisingly small. But Jim Cassidy, the neighbor from around the pool, had come and so had several Portland residents who never knew Leahy, but remembered what it was like when no college football team in the country had a chance to beat Notre Dame. Rain was beginning to fall in a quiet mist as the mourners moved down the path to the chapel. Television cameramen who had come to take pictures of hundreds of celebrities, settled for a few dozen. The University of Portland may be a part of the University of Notre Dame, but it is a remote, almost truncated part. Tradition cannot be transported across 1,800 miles of Western land. And Frank Leahy, was in a foreign land.

Father Edmund P. Joyce, who once gave Frank Leahy the last rites in a locker room, celebrated the requiem mass, but Father William Rees, the Episcopalian unwelcomed by his own bishop, read the gospel at the request of Frank-Junior. The ex-players who were present, many of them gone to fat and to gray hair, shuffled in the pews. At the pulpit was Patrick J. O'Malley, the shaven and shorn Irish businessman who made it possible for Francis William Leahy to jet across the skies of America on his last glorious quest.

"Frank Leahy's name was synonymous with perfection, with excellence. His trademark was integrity and compassion," he said. "Few men have enriched the lives of so many by motivation and inspiration and encouragement and strength. Today there is a tremendous void in mankind's ranks—a shattered star in our constellation. The adversity and pain with which he lived these past years would cripple the minds of all of us. Frank rose above these circumstances. He was a master at mind-over-matter. He ruled his dying body as if it were an inanimate object, like a carrot on a fork awaiting its fate. He stood a mountain among men.

"At the University of Notre Dame, he served with distinction as a student, coach, teacher. His football teams are legendary, and football greats throughout the world unanimously acclaim him as The Master. He loved his students with a passion generally reserved for the father of an only son. And they, in turn, worshipped him. He left his mark and part of himself with each of them.

"Anybody who dealt with him person-to-person realized he was a big man whose sense of values excluded pettiness. He was always in control of himself, focusing on the issue of the person at hand. Because he did not manipulate, he could not be manipulated. Because he was open, he had no taste for cunnning.

"Frank's interest in and his friendship with his lads did not end with graduation nor was it affected by material success. In every city of this country, there lives a colony of men who are endeared to this man with a devotion that rivals their love of family. Until a month ago, Frank Leahy traveled extensively; and if only he paused in a city, he was on the telephone renewing friendships with his lads, with Notre Dame alumni and with business associates. As a molder of men, he had no equal, not in his lifetime.

"Frank loved the University of Notre Dame as no man ever has. He loved his country, traveling the length and breadth of the land, presenting to thousands, with unmatched fervor and patriotic zeal, his game plan for preserving the greatness and beauty of America.

"Frank had planned the rest of his life. He wanted to devote it to helping youth. In this world of turmoil, drugs and distorted young minds, Frank Leahy never lost faith in the youth of America, because he remembered his own youth on the great Dakota frontier. He knew the children were great and hoped to make them greater. Many teenagers found new direction and inspiration, enabling them to live a new life through the words and wisdom of Frank Leahy. With some of them, he only spent a fraction of an hour. They have lost an honest idol and a true friend.

"I don't think Frank ever forgot the name of a person he met and I don't think he ever forgot an experience he had. To all, he imparted his conviction that a man could win any battle he set his mind to winnning. He was convinced he could win his battle against crippling illness; and only a few days ago, he promised he'd be back leading his own personal crusade again.

"I don't know too much about the way things are organized over there, beyond the curtain of death, but I've got news for that illustrious company Frank Leahy is joining—something new and beautiful has been added to the company of heaven; and if a few of our saints have grown a little stuffy or a trifle lazy through the ages, they had better shine up their halos and get with it because now that the Master Coach is there, it will never be stuffy in heaven again."

The words of the final blessing drifted through the air; and as a white puff of incense formed a question mark over the casket and hung there for a second, the notes from the chapel organ began to arrange themselves in a proper order. They seemed alien at first, as if somebody had written a special dirge. But it was the cadence that was all wrong. It was funeral time.

"Cheer, cheer for old Notre Dame . . . Wake up the echos cheering her name . . . send a volley cheer on high . . . shake down the thunder from the sky . . . what though the odds be great or small."

They played it over and over, without mercy.

The mourners filed by the open coffin, looking at a face gone youthful in death. Outside, rain drops were coming faster and faster. The pall bearers, all ex-players, moved slowly down the walk, as the campus bells picked up the Victory March, this time at a more joyous pace.

"This casket is heavy," whispered George Connors.

"You know the Coach," said Johnny Lattner, wistfully, "making us pay the price right to the end. Wouldn't you know it?"

The black doors of the hearse closed with a metallic abruptness and the funeral car pulled away from the curb. The bells were still playing the Victory March. Into mythology sped Francis William Leahy. That is what the University of Notre Dame prefers to do with its heroes, get them on stage quickly and off just as fast. Nothing is so embarrassing as a person who does not truly understand that the school lives off the freshness of new legends. Notre Dame quickly strips away the flesh and leaves the bare bones to be venerated. Leahy believed, until the moment when his heart stopped for the final time, that he had been touched by something sacred and that he could not rest until he repaid the debt. He did not know that he had committed two crucial sins against the very school that gave him life. He was too much a zealot, too firmly committed to an excellence that nobody honestly believed a mortal could deliver. And when he did, he became a threat to those same people who said they were the keepers of that most holy relic, the Notre Dame spirit. When he made the flame burn too brightly, they cast him out.

Oh, he had his chance to join Rockne, to have a feast day of his own. But he failed to die at halftime of the Georgia Tech–Notre Dame game of 1953. That was the second embarrassment. There could have been a large, mournful congregation present in Sacred Heart Church with students weeping on the lawn. Frank Leahy survived. He out-lived himself by 20 years, falling in and out of business and placing small droplets of blood on his most precious legend. Notre Dame was both his lure and his salvation. It was also a fixation, an obsession, a focal point for the strong streak of fanaticism in his soul. Unlike others, he truly believed. He honestly thought that the virtues taught him beneath the Golden Dome were attainable. There was not even the smallest touch of cynicism about him. It was easier for Rockne to die than it was for Leahy to live out his life.

He picked up the struggle for Our Lady the day he disassociated himself from that fine Catholic institution.

EPISODE 11

The storm was gathering strength now and the rented limousine was making waves on the expressway. Al Davis had decided not to go to the cemetery. Instead, he wanted to get on board an airplane and fly back to Oakland as quickly as possible. He was a strangely puzzled man, slumping back in the corner, hardly speaking. Finally, he overflowed.

"Where in the hell were all of his big name players?" Davis asked. "Where were all those hot shot writers who supposedly loved him so much? They were waiting to go to a memorial service in Chicago on Tuesday? That can't be. I'm glad I'm out of coaching. I could have ended up like that, all eaten up for nothing. I don't care how far it is to come or how short notice they all had. And where was Father Hesburgh? I'm not a Catholic, but even I know he should have been there. A great man shouldn't go out that way. And Frank Leahy was a great man—the poor bastard!"

The lightning was flashing in the distant clouds behind the Willamette River, up in the coolness of the mountains and the pines. Thunder was clattering down out of the skies and the landscape was turning cold. The family, some devoted players and a few friends were burying Frank Leahy on a hillside. The thunder grew louder and louder.

Farewell, Don Quixote! Farewell!